MERCHANTS AND REFORM IN LIVORNO
1814–1868

MERCHANTS AND REFORM IN LIVORNO 1814–1868

David G. LoRomer

UNIVERSITY OF CALIFORNIA PRESS
Berkeley   Los Angeles   London

University of California Press
Berkeley and Los Angeles, California

University of California Press, Ltd.
London, England

Copyright © 1987 by The Regents of the University of California

Library of Congress Cataloging in Publication Data

Lo Romer, David G.
Merchants and Reform in Livorno, 1814–1868.

Bibliography: p.
Includes index.
1. Merchants—Italy—Livorno—History—19th century.
2. Livorno (Italy)—Commercial policy—History—19th
century.   3. Livorno (Italy)—Economic conditions.
4. Livorno (Italy)—Social conditions.   5. Livorno
(Italy)—Politics and government.   6. Italy—History—
1815–1870. I. Title.
HF1550.19.L58L62   1986   381'.1'094556   85–24721
ISBN 0–520–05649–3 (alk. paper)

Printed in the United States of America

1 2 3 4 5 6 7 8 9

To Morgan and Lucy LoRomer

Contents

vii

Acknowledgments

        In a study that began as a doctoral dissertation and
that—in some real sense—has been living with me over the
past fifteen years, a full list of acknowledgments is impossible. The assistance of some individuals, though, has remained
impressive over the years, and to their names I must add
some of more recent vintage.

  First, I would like to thank the members of that original
doctoral committee—Professor Richard Herr, Gene Brucker,
and Neil Smelser—for their encouragement and critical suggestions. Earlier work at Berkeley with Professors Carl
Schorske, Hans Rosenberg, and Richard Webster also assisted
in my handling of this project. In Livorno I received the
consistent help of Paolo Castignoli at the Archivio di Stato;
of Bruna Palmati, Piero Brizzi, Luca Badaloni and the late
Francesco Tarchi at the Biblioteca Labronica; and of Aldo
Pratesi and his staff at the Livorno Chamber of Commerce.
They helped make my frequent stays in the port city enjoyable
and productive. My landlady, Margherita Nassi, with her
inexhaustible quest for that extra *mille* lire did much to
strengthen my language ability and to sharpen its polemical
vigor. I must also acknowledge the generous assistance in
Italy of Professors Carlo Corsini, Richard Goldthwaite, and
Antonio Molho, as well as the encouragement of another

student of Livorno's economic and social history, Jean-Pierre Filippini. On his frequent trips to Florence, R. Burr Litchfield gave me the benefit of both his friendly encouragement and his detailed knowledge of Tuscan social history.

Without the help of these people—and without the material support of an Italian-American Research Fellowship from the University of California, Berkeley, and Faculty Research Grants from Michigan State University—this study would have been impossible to bring to completion. Needless to say, any flaws that remain are to be attributed only to me.

In addition to the individuals I have named, I would like to acknowledge the assistance—both personal and professional—that I have received from colleagues in East Lansing. Particularly encouraging over the years have been Richard White, Peter Vinten-Johansen, David T. Bailey, Harry Reed, and Peter Levine. Harold Marcus assisted with his blue pencil, William McCagg with his fertile imagination, and Mary Wren Bivins with a good critical reading of the final product and assistance with the illustrations. Geoff Eley at the University of Michigan, Ann Arbor, gave me the benefit of his knowledge of Gramsci and of the political process in nineteenth-century Europe. Antonio Calabria and Marion Miller offered me years of friendship and a rich understanding of Italian history. Finally, to my daughters Morgan and Lucy who have been with me over the course of this project and have brought me much happiness along the way, I would like to dedicate this book.

Introduction

        This book examines the reform efforts of the mer-
chant community in Livorno—the major port city of Tuscany—in the period from the restoration of the grand ducal
government in 1814 to the abolition of the free-port status of
the city in 1868. By its very nature, a study of reform must
touch on many aspects of the city's economic and social life.
I begin with an examination of the city's economy, ascertain-
ing whether the port was in crisis or whether it had adjusted
its activity to a new set of commercial circumstances. I shall
examine the often one-sided views of contemporaries and
later commentators before passing to an analysis of the more
concrete data of commercial movements, changes in prices,
and demographic shifts. The first section seeks to analyze
some of the major elements that stimulated the reform movement and shaped its character.
        The second section examines the structure of the merchant
community, its economic and social values, and the institutions through which reforms were articulated and implemented. The third section concentrates on the economic reforms proposed by the merchant community to make Livorno
more competitive with its rivals, particularly Genoa. The
fourth section deals with the merchant community's efforts
to spread its norms and values to the expanding lower-class

1

population of the city, thus forestalling social unrest and establishing a stable basis for future economic and political progress.

My fundamental task will be to evaluate the success or failure of the merchant reforms within the context of Livorno's social, economic, and political setting. The revolution of 1848 will mark the climax of the presentation. My aim here is not simply to add to the mass of data already available on the urban political movements important in the struggle for Italian independence and unity but to assess specifically the impact of the revolutionary turmoil on the merchant community's reform program. Ultimately, as we shall see, the revolution would strike that program a fatal blow.

Although interesting in its own right, a study of the reform program of Livorno's merchant community can clarify many issues regarding the economic, social, and political life of nineteenth-century Italy and Europe and can illuminate more specifically the contribution of the business elite to the Risorgimento. In the initial stages of the Risorgimento, at the end of the eighteenth century, publicists in Italy emphasized the economic dimensions of the national question because they sought economic development and because they wished to mobilize the support of businessmen and professionals. Massimo D'Azeglio's *Programma per l'opinione nazionale italiana* (1847) provides perhaps the most striking example of this effort.[1] The Piedmontese publicist and statesman sought to show his audience that the patriotic movement was composed primarily of reasonable and responsible individuals working to achieve a nation state and along with it free trade, the abolition of internal customs barriers, the facilitation of communications, and the establishment of a unified system of weights and measures.

D'Azeglio's emphasis on economic considerations proved congenial to a group of historians writing in the early decades of the present century who wished to break with the prevailing tendency to stress personal, political, diplomatic, and military aspects of the Risorgimento. In *L'Origine del "Programma per l'opinione nazionale italiana," del 1847–1848* (1916), Raffaele Ciasca traced D'Azeglio's economic concerns to the second half of the eighteenth century and demonstrated that his recommendations enjoyed wide support, particularly in the north.[2] In 1920, Giuseppe Prato, the dean of Risorgimento economic historians, argued in *Fatti e dottrine economiche alla vigilia del 1848. L'Associazione Agraria Subalpina e Camillo Cavour* that the central place of Piedmont and its prime minister in the national movement was due less to personal qualities and political considerations than to the level of progress achieved by Piedmontese society over the previous century.[3] In the interpretations of both D'Azeglio and Prato—and in others of a similar vein which followed—emphasis was placed not on ideology but on fact, not on political conspiracy and individual heroics but on a long-term process of reform. Only persistence and effective conditions could pave the way for Italian unification at a time when established regimes in the peninsula were easily capable of blocking any overt challenge to their authority.

Within the context of an economic interpretation of the Risorgimento, Marxism has provided a more specific theoretical focus that, as we shall see, continues to command wide respect in Livornese studies today.[4] For Marxist historians generally, the Italian liberation movement represents a classic instance of the successful efforts of a rising bourgeoisie to transform society according to its progressive economic interests. The growth of the European economy in the late eighteenth century and the impact of the French Revolution produced an Italian middle class able to manipulate the factors of production in a free-market economy. With the defeat of Napoleon and the end of French dominion in Italy, however, the peninsula returned to what was essentially a "feudal" stage of development in which authoritarian regimes maintained watchful control over chiefly patriarchal economic and social relations. The consequent struggle between the forces of reaction and progress led to the revolution of 1848, the war of 1859, and the ultimate triumph of the bourgeoisie.

Over the past several decades this general interpretation has been subject to mounting criticism. In a short article that appeared in 1952, Gino Luzzatto, a leading Italian economic historian, summarized the anti-Marxist position on the role of economic factors in the Risorgimento.[5] First, he attacked the notion that the unification movement represented the product of a rising bourgeoisie looking to insure its progressive economic interests. Even on the eve of unification, Luzzatto argued, modern industrial sectors (steel and the metallurgical and mechanical industries) remained relatively undeveloped. Significant industrial production in foodstuffs and textiles was either geared largely to the export trade or was too modest to require a vast extension of the internal market. Ultimately, wrote Luzzatto, the economic argument for the Risorgimento was made not by businessmen, who possessed little felt need, but by publicists, who saw a tariff union and a national rail network as stimulants to future economic growth. It was they who perceived the giant strides being made elsewhere in Europe and who made urgent attempts to convince their more parochial compatriots to keep pace. Ironically, concluded Luzzatto, their arguments succeeded only too well, producing a pervasive pessimism in the late nineteenth century when the anticipated economic benefits of national unity failed to materialize.[6]

Luzzatto's views reflected the interpretation of one of the most significant monographs on the relationship of economic development and the Risorgimento, Kent Roberts Greenfield's *Economics and Liberalism in the Risorgimento: A Study of Nationalism in Lombardy, 1814–1848*. Luzzatto pseudonymously translated this work into Italian in 1940, when Fascist racial policies prevented his continuing to teach in the Italian university system.[7] In releasing his volume in 1934, Greenfield declared that his chief purpose was "to give an impulse to non-political studies of the Risorgimento,"[8] and he registered his dissatisfaction with the fact that the Risorgimento was too often described in the ringing tones of idealism and as a series of "insurrectionary episodes."[9] Greenfield highlighted the underlying economic and social forces;[10] and he sought to replace the historiography of patriotism and sentiment with one that emphasized the relationships among economics, social institutions and habits, and the evolution of ideas.[11] He concluded that in the case of Lombardy, the

Marxist view that the Risorgimento represented the culmination of bourgeois class interests did not conform to the facts.[12]

Greenfield believed that Lombard patriotic philosophy eventually came to turn on the view that the progress of the region and the nation were dependent on the force that free capitalistic enterprise could exert in modernizing the peninsula.[13] The impetus, however, came not from a class-conscious bourgeoisie with strong economic interests to serve but from landed proprietors and intellectuals, many of whom were aristocrats. In effect, these publicists were not following the articulated interests of the bourgeoisie but were themselves attempting to rouse a timid and lethargic bourgeoisie to a consciousness of its interests.[14] According to Greenfield, Italian public opinion after 1848 would never again be governed successfully by the methods of the Old Regime, not because the material interests of the Italian community had been revolutionized but because the public now had a new conception of those interests.

Within the context of this vibrant and often polemical historiographical tradition, a study of Livorno and its merchant community can make a significant contribution. First, it can clarify the role of the business elite in the Italian Risorgimento, indicating the degree to which this group represented a progressive force working for political union and for the eventual emergence of a modern industrial economy. In his writing, Greenfield concluded that the Lombard merchants were fundamentally conservative and that the call for reform came from sectors of society other than the business elite. Steeped in the traditions of a predominantly agrarian community, merchants resented any interference with their traditional practices and were reluctant to strike out along new lines. They did not seek new markets for their products even when spurred by the government, and they continued to distrust credit not secured by property in land. Despite the often sarcastic urging of progressive publicists, the merchants remained largely passive in a changing world.[15] Similar criticism was voiced by publicists against merchants in the very different economic environment of Genoa, especially for their reluctance to join together in modern forms of enterprise designed to improve the city's commercial situation and its tie to the hinterland.[16]

In an important study of the Venetian revolution of 1848, Paul Ginsborg has provided a more optimistic assessment of the reforming zeal of the Venetian middle class.[17] He has demonstrated the presence in both city and countryside of a group with considerable capital which was anxious to put an end to Venetian backwardness.[18] With the general revival of trade and commerce in the 1830s and early 1840s the activity of these landowners, businessmen, bankers, and members of Venice's Chamber of Commerce increased at a pace equal to that of the rise of their dissatisfaction with Austria's harsh fiscal policies, its excessive economic and political restrictions, and its lack of an effective social policy.[19]

Against Greenfield, Ginsborg has argued that despite the heterogeneous social character of this progressive group, it lay at the cutting edge of a bourgeois revolution. In the countryside the real distinction was not between noble and bourgeois landowners but between those who were trying to introduce more efficient and clearly capitalist methods and those who were not:[20]

> The leaders of a revolutionary movement do not necessarily belong by origin to the class in whose interests the revolution is being made. Nor can or does the whole of that class reach the same level of consciousness and aspiration at the same time. All classes are uneven in composition and ideology, containing both backward and advanced elements. The northern Italian bourgeoisie of the 1830s and 1840s . . . was a class still very much in the process of formation. But within its ranks there existed highly ambitious sections and individuals . . . whose intentions were quite clear: to seek support for a movement that amounted essentially to "an attempt by the bourgeois to gain control of society." The history of Venetia in the 1840s is the history of just such a group, composed primarily of a small number of businessmen and lawyers of the city of Venice. They appealed, with increasing clarity as the decade passed and conditions changed, to the commercial and landed interests in Venetian society, in the name of first economic and then political alternatives to the status quo.[21]

Nevertheless, Ginsborg suggests that the efforts of this group were fundamentally flawed. The failure of the urban bourgeoisie and its political supporters to make timely alliances with the peasantry was one of the major causes for the failure of the revolution.[22] Even on the national issue a number of merchants and businessmen remained averse to fusion with the other states of northern Italy—"They feared that with Milan the capital and Genoa the principal port of the new kingdom, Venice would be reduced 'to less than Chioggia.'"[23]

Clearly, traditional municipal sentiments were inhibiting attachment to the national ideal. Not surprisingly, therefore, the period after the failed revolution of 1848 witnessed a growing rapprochement between the Austrians and the wealthy elements of the Venetian bourgeoisie who had supported the revolution. When Venice finally became part of the Italian state in 1866, it was not the result of an armed insurrection but of the might of the Prussian army and the good offices of Napoleon III.[24] Bourgeois revolution or not, therefore, the efforts of the progressive elements of Venetian society were short-lived and ultimately ineffective.

This book will explore the degree to which such an assessment can also be applied to the merchant community in Livorno. More specifically, it will provide an analysis of the programs and underlying attitudes of the merchants in Livorno, the ways in which their efforts were shaped by the economic and social character of the free port, and the degree to which they contributed to more modern forms of economic and political life. As such, this work can also deepen our understanding and test the insights of the most influential interpretation of the Risorgimento to appear in postwar Italy, that of Antonio Gramsci.

In studies prepared during his active political career and while he was confined to a Fascist prison, Gramsci reflected on the political, moral, and intellectual foundations of Italian history. Two concepts in particular, *hegemony* and *passive revolution*, were fundamental to his interpretation of the Risorgimento.[25] *Hegemony* reflected the role of influence, leadership, and consent in the political process. Like many of

Gramsci's concepts, it is best considered in relation to its dialectical opposite, in this case *domination*. Whereas to Gramsci domination implied force and constraint, hegemony reflected the way in which one social group influenced other groups and responded to their needs so as to gain their consent for its leadership role in society at large.

While domination was exercised through the state (*stato politico*), hegemony was as a rule transmitted through more decentralized agencies, which Gramsci associated with civil society (*stato civile*). These agencies included labor unions, educational institutions, newspapers, charitable organizations, and representative assemblies, which were designed to foster a consensus on common, prevailing norms.[26] The relative strength of state and civil society, said Gramsci, varied from place to place, reflecting a society's level of development and—from Gramsci's perspective as a practical revolutionary—determining its vulnerability to challenge.[27] In Russia, for example, where "the State was everything" and "civil society was primordial and gelatinous," a frontal attack (in Gramsci's terminology, "a war of manoeuvre") could bring the whole edifice crashing to the ground; not so in the West, however, where "a proper relation between State and civil society" made for a "sturdy structure." In this case, "the State was only an outer ditch behind which there stood a powerful system of fortresses and earthworks," which constituted civil society.[28] To bring down such states, argued Gramsci, a "war of position" was more appropriate. Here one needed to systematically construct a series of counterditches and counterfortifications—that is, to weaken the dominant hegemonic consensus by building a counterconsensus designed to erode society from within while preparing the way for a new social order.[29]

To Gramsci, *passive revolution* reflected a society's inability to achieve a full hegemonic relationship. He derived this concept from Vincenzo Cuoco, whose *Saggio storico sulla rivoluzione napoletana del 1799* (originally published in 1801) had argued that the collapse of the Neapolitan Republic was the result of a mistaken effort to impose the principles of the French Revolution on a very different social environment.

The ideas of the Neapolitan revolution could have been popular had they been drawn from the depths of the nation. Drawn from a foreign constitution, they were far from ours; founded on maxims too abstract . . . they sought to legislate all the customs, caprices and at times all the defects of another people, who were far from our defects, caprices, and customs.[30]

In his essay Cuoco noted the enormous gap between the elite and the masses in the Neapolitan kingdom, and he suggested that the former had drawn its programs from foreign models that "offered nothing to the entire nation, which in turn scorned a culture which was not useful and which it did not understand."[31]

Like Cuoco, Gramsci saw passive revolution as revolution without mass participation. Unlike Cuoco, however, he condemned the elite not for endeavoring to implement the reforms of the French but rather for its failure to implement them effectively enough to win the support of the masses and to stem the tide of reaction. Indeed, Gramsci deeply admired the French Jacobins both for their incredible energy under pressure and for their successful efforts in forging a firm alliance between city and countryside.

Without the agrarian policy of the Jacobins, Paris would have had the Vendée at its very doors. . . . Rural France accepted the hegemony of Paris; in other words, it understood that in order definitively to destroy the old régime it had to make a bloc with the most advanced elements of the Third Estate, and not with the Girondin moderates. If it is true that the Jacobins "forced" its hand, it is also true that this always occurred in the direction of real historical development. For not only did they organise a bourgeois government—i.e., make the bourgeoisie the dominant class—they did more. They created the bourgeois State, made the bourgeoisie into the leading, hegemonic class of the nation, [and] in other words gave the new State a permanent basis and created the compact modern French nation.[32]

Gramsci also used the term *passive revolution* in a second way, with the meaning of a molecular social transformation that takes place beneath the surface of society in situations in which the progressive class cannot operate openly.[33] He derived this perspective from the view of Karl Marx, as expressed in the preface to *A Contribution to the Critique of Political Economy*:

> No social order ever disappears before all the productive forces, for which there is room in it, have been developed; and new higher relations of production never appear before the material conditions of their existence have matured in the womb of the old society. Therefore, mankind always takes up only such problems as it can solve.[34]

Gramsci saw in the survival of traditional economic and social institutions a basic characteristic of Italian history. In the late medieval and Renaissance periods, Gramsci noted, the urban corporate bourgeoisie failed to challenge the entrenched position of the feudal elites. Concentrating on its narrow corporate interests and operating in a cosmopolitan economic and political world, the bourgeoisie succeeded in amassing wealth and power but, notwithstanding the exhortations of Machiavelli, failed to forge the links with the countryside necessary for the achievement of a truly national society.[35] Similarly, in 1848 the radical Action Party, under the influence of Giuseppe Mazzini, failed to organize the urban and rural masses into a concerted attack on the forces of the old regime. In the immediate aftermath of the 1848 revolution, Camillo Cavour, the Piedmontese prime minister, absorbed disaffected members of the Catholic neo-Guelf movement into his own party and in molecular fashion incorporated the Action Party, so that in effect the masses were decapitated and not absorbed into the ambit of the new state.[36]

The history of Italy after formal unification continued this process. "Transformism" in the political life of the nation enabled the ruling class to coopt individuals but left the masses systematically excluded from effective political life.[37] The democratic reforms on the eve of World War I and the impact of the war and its aftermath shook the traditional political system. However, the rise of fascism and the erection of a totalitarian state reimposed restraints on this process.[38] Nevertheless, Gramsci suggested, throughout Italian history changes had been occurring which progressively modified the preexisting composition of forces. In the nineteenth century, elements of the bourgeoisie had succeeded in creating an Italian state and achieving a level of capitalist development without revolutionary upheaval. Even under fascism, Gramsci noted, economic development continued, and there existed political forces that were working to erode the existing authoritarian order.[39]

Despite these gradual changes, however, Gramsci refused to abandon a revolutionary perspective. Passive revolution existed only dialectically; it was to be taken not as a call to defeatism but as a stimulus to a vigorous antithesis. One should not remain passive, Gramsci wrote, but should work to overcome the shortcomings of the Italian bourgeoisie, to incorporate the masses fully into the political system, and to create a truly national community. At the same time, one needed to take full account of the preexisting social and political forces so as to avoid a frontal attack when this could lead only to certain defeat.[40]

The study that follows is designed to explore Gramsci's interpretation of the Risorgimento in a particular regional context. Gramsci's concept of hegemony reflects the Livornese merchant community's reform impetus and its efforts to inculcate its norms and values in the masses. While Gramsci concentrated on the latter half of the nineteenth century, however, this study focuses on the first, indicating that hegemony had deep roots. It suggests that in Livorno the drive for hegemony was initially as vital but perhaps ultimately less successful than Gramsci supposed.

The process of political change in the city seems to conform to Gramsci's concept of *passive revolution*. The Livornese elite clearly worked to transform society in a bourgeois direction without provoking mass insurrection. The 1848 revolution, however, shattered this effort. And although a radical-democratic alternative also failed, as we shall see, the previous deferential patterns linking the city's elite and the masses would never be reconstituted. Ironically, during the ensuing "decade of preparation" the Livornese moderates would find themselves on the margin of the political struggle. Shaken by the revolution, they would lose the desire for leadership and would allow effective political power to pass first to the central government in Florence and then, with the collapse of the grand ducal regime, to Piedmont.

The failure of the moderates in Livorno appears to support Gramsci's view of the inability of the elements of a potential ruling class throughout the peninsula to unite and contribute actively to the formation of the new Italian nation.

> These nuclei existed indubitably, but their tendency to unite was extremely problematic; also, more importantly, they—each in its own sphere—were not "leading." The "leader" presupposes the "led," and who was "led" by these nuclei? These nuclei did not wish to "lead" anybody, i.e., they did not wish to concord their interests and aspirations with the interests and aspirations of other groups. They wished to "dominate" and not to "lead." Furthermore, they wanted their interests to dominate rather than their persons; in other words, they wanted a new force, independent of every compromise and condition, to become the arbiter of the Nation: this force was Piedmont and hence the function of the monarchy.[41]

Regrettably, Gramsci's view of the role of Piedmont (and his concept of *Piedmontization*) has been generally ignored by commentators, which has hampered a full appreciation of his view of a failed bourgeois revolution in the peninsula.[42] To Gramsci the initiative of the Piedmontese state replaced that of the local elites and in effect extended the concept of passive revolution from the masses to a broad section of the elite.

> This fact is of the greatest importance for the concept of "passive revolution"—the fact, that is, that what was involved was not a social group which "led" other groups, but a State which, even though it had limitations as a power, "led" the group which should have been "leading" and was able to put at the latter's disposal an army and a politico-diplomatic strength. . . . The important thing is to analyze more profoundly the significance of a "Piedmont" type function in passive revolutions—i.e., the fact

that a State replaces the local social groups in leading a struggle of renewal. It is one of the cases in which these groups have the function of "domination" without that of "leadership"; dictatorship without hegemony. The hegemony will be exercised by a part of the social group over the entire group, and not by the latter over other forces in order to give power to the movement, radicalise it, etc. on the "Jacobin" model.[43]

The failure of a truly organic solution to Italian unification represented a fatal flaw to Gramsci. True hegemony was never established, since state and civil society were not integrated. Italy's social elite failed to provide leadership and to respond to the needs and aspirations of the masses. Piedmont in the end exercised effective hegemony only over the elite, while over the rest of the country its position was largely one of dominance. Political ties were bureaucratic rather than democratic.

The morbid manifestations of bureaucratic centralism are the product of a deficiency of initiative and responsibility from below, that is of a political primitiveness of the forces on the periphery, even when they are homogenous with the hegemonic territorial group (phenomenon of Piedmontism in the first decades of Italian unity).[44]

The product of bureaucracy was "no unity but a stagnant swamp, on the surface calm and 'mute,' and no federation but a 'sack of potatoes,' i.e., a mechanical juxtaposition of single 'units' without any connection between them."[45]

[The authorities] said that they were aiming at the creation of a modern State in Italy, and they in fact produced a bastard. They aimed at stimulating the formation of an extensive and energetic ruling class, and they did not succeed; at integrating the people into the framework of the new State, and they did not succeed. The paltry political life from 1870 to 1900, the fundamental and endemic rebelliousness of the Italian popular classes, the narrow and stunted existence of a sceptical [sic] and cowardly ruling stratum, these are all the consequences of that failure.[46]

Although characteristic of Gramsci's general ideas about the failure of the Italian unitary solution, Livorno's response was shaped by its particular situation, as we shall see. The city's free-port mentality, the shock of the 1848 revolution, the relative backwardness of central Italy, and the comparative indifference of the new Italian state to the city's problems would all hamper Livorno's full integration into the economic and political life of the nation. An examination of Livorno's history and its institutions, therefore, can help clarify the place of regional diversity and particular economic and social structures in the Italian Risorgimento. At the same time, it can reinforce a deeper understanding of those general patterns of strength and weakness which Gramsci saw as characterizing the process of Italian historical development right up to the time of his imprisonment and untimely death.

The issues to be addressed here do not pertain only to the Italian peninsula, for questions on the nature of the middle class—its economic activities, social composition, political relationships, and culture—represent significant concerns in the historiography of early nineteenth-century Europe as a whole. This concern was underscored several years ago by the French economic historian Ernest Labrousse at the meeting of the Tenth International Congress of Historical Sciences in Florence.[47] In his report, Labrousse opposed abstract, generic definitions of the bourgeoisie and called for an investigation of its character, activities, and attitudes in specific settings. His charge echoed the work of historians which was already under way and helped to stimulate further research. This study is intended to make a modest contribution to that continued effort.

Before beginning, I will address a consideration that is fundamental to the interpretation to be set forth here. From the second half of the sixteenth century, when Livorno became a free port, the city's prosperity was based primarily on its ability to attract enterprising foreign merchants. The attraction was not expected to be permanent. Upon the merchants' retirements or whenever there was a worsening of the economic situation, the government anticipated that the merchants would return to their native states or would settle in other, more comfortable locales. This tenuous relationship between the merchant community and the Tuscan state was reinforced by the city's privileges. As a free port, Livorno owed its prosperity to its extraterritorial status—that is, its position outside the normal schema of state taxes and regulations. Ironically, though, these very privileges reinforced the merchant community's detachment from the long-range concerns of the hinterland.

By the second half of the eighteenth century, I will suggest, this situation was changing, and Livorno's merchant community was becoming more involved in working for the long-term stability of the urban economy and in strengthening the relationship of the city and the hinterland. These efforts represent the initiation of a systematic reform program. In arguing for them, however, I wish to distance myself from a facile determinism that would link this growing involvement to the declining economic fortunes of the city and, more specifically, to the ending of its position as an international entrepôt. The economic changes in this period were far more complex. In addition, reform currents in the merchant community reflected a complex interplay of ideological considerations and institutional arrangements of a progressive and conservative bent: progressive, because the advocates of reform were interested in improving the economic and social life of the city to ameliorate the living situation of the city's masses, and conservative, because at the root of their efforts was the belief that only in this way could they counter the threat of social turbulence generated by the demographic pressure, economic uncertainties, and ideological ferment of the age. This situation and the response of the city's commercial elite were not unique to Livorno. For this reason, a clearer understanding of the reform movement in Livorno will allow us to better appreciate the anxieties and aspirations of European elites in that turbulent period that ushered in more modern forms of economic and political life.

PART ONE

The Economic Background

CHAPTER ONE

Patterns in Livorno's Commerce

Continuity, Change, Crisis

Both contemporary observers and recent studies agree that Livorno's commercial situation changed radically in the period following the wars of the French Revolution and the restoration of the grand ducal government in Tuscany. Previously, the city's prosperity had been based on its unchallenged ability to function as a free port of deposit open to the goods, ships, and merchants of all states. Commercial conditions of the seventeenth and eighteenth centuries had favored the development of these ports. The difficulty of communication, the insecurity of the seas, and the modest carrying capacity of ships encouraged the establishment of free ports in convenient locations on the major trade routes, where commercial transactions could be handled easily and securely.

Livorno had been well endowed to prosper in this commercial situation. From the time of its absorption into the Florentine state in 1421—and especially during the two centuries of Medici rule—the city benefited from a series of provisions designed to encourage the settlement of foreign merchants and tradesmen in the area, to develop the city's commercial facilities, to establish the port as a privileged tariff zone, and to affirm its neutrality in disputes involving the major powers.

19

The basic provisions encouraging settlement in the area were promulgated by Ferdinand I in the 1590s.[1] In an attempt to foster the economic development of a region that was underpopulated and insalubrious, the state promised to provide houses, shops, and warehouses for those settling in the city, to prevent the imposition of guild restrictions, and, for a certain period, to waive tax assessments. In addition, for those willing to reside in the area, the state annulled all personal debts under 500 scudi and suspended previous penal condemnations, making exceptions only for the crimes of heresy, lese majesty, murder, and counterfeiting.[2] In the famous *Livornina* provision (10 June 1595) these fiscal and penal immunities were extended to religious minorities, especially Jews, who were in addition granted certain civic rights and freedom of residence and religion.[3]

Even though this provision was severely criticized during the nineteenth century for attracting undesirable elements to the city and for blackening its reputation, at the time of its enactment it did encourage population growth and the settling of a number of enterprising merchants in the area.

Due largely to the efforts of Cosimo I, Ferdinand I, and Cosimo II, Livorno acquired a port and storage and quarantine facilities, which made it among the best-equipped ports in the Mediterranean. Cosimo I completed work on a navigation canal linking Livorno and Pisa. Ferdinand I contributed the lazaretto of San Rocco for the purgation of ships arriving from areas that were sanitarily suspect and the pits (*buche*) constructed throughout the city for the storage of grain. In 1611, Cosimo II ordered the construction of the wharf that bears his name. With its completion, the port of Livorno acquired the shape it would retain for more than two centuries.

The foundation of Livorno's prosperity as a free port, however, lay in its fiscal privileges. A series of piecemeal customs' reforms which began in 1451 culminated in a decree by Cosimo III (11 March 1675) abolishing the gabelles on most goods entering Livorno by sea and instituting in their place a small, fixed duty called the *stallaggio*.[4] Having paid this charge, a merchant could introduce his goods into the city and sell, store, or refine them, then reexport them by sea without undergoing any further fiscal obligation. This provision provided the juridical basis for Livorno's existence as a free port.

The city's neutrality assured that its commercial activity would remain unharmed by the disputes of the great powers and that, if anything, it would benefit from them. First declared by Ferdinand II in a treaty with the French in 1646, Livorno's neutral status was confirmed by the great powers in 1691 and officially recognized in the treaty of 3 October 1735, which sanctioned the succession of the House of Lorraine to the Grand Duchy of Tuscany. As the only port in the Tyrrhenian Sea which for most of the period could declare itself securely neutral, Livorno prospered particularly well during the times when war upset the commercial patterns of its rivals. In addition to taking over their commercial functions, Livorno was able to act as a marketplace for booty and to provision ships on both sides of a given conflict.[5]

Livorno's privileges enabled it to achieve a level of prosperity unknown to most other cities of the Italian peninsula. The centuries of its most rapid expansion paradoxically coincided with a period of economic and demographic stagnation in the rest of Tuscany. The city's commercial prosperity was clearly not predicated on the economic growth of the hinterland nor on the resourcefulness of an indigenous commercial elite.[6] The predominant activity of the port—the deposit and transshipment of merchandise—was handled primarily by foreign merchant companies or Jews, because only these two groups possessed the necessary capital resources and business contacts to succeed in commercial activity of this type. These merchants showed little interest in the marketing of Tuscan products or in the economic development of the Tuscan state.[7]

The fiscal privileges that Livorno enjoyed served to reinforce the city's detachment from the rest of Tuscany. Merchandise deposited in Livorno and transshipped out by sea was subject only to minimal stallage and port charges. However, merchandise that moved from Livorno into the internal market or, conversely, from the Tuscan hinterland into the port city was subject to the full duties of the Tuscan state.

While some commercial exchange did of course take place between Livorno and the Tuscan hinterland, in 1765 this direct, two-way commerce formed only a minimal part of the port's activity.[8]

Livorno's position in the seventeenth and eighteenth centuries, then, was exceptional. Both fiscally and economically the city remained detached from the Tuscan state, and the most important sector of its commerce was primarily in the hands of foreigners or Jews. Indeed, Livorno's facilities and privileges enabled it to prosper especially during those periods of dislocation when the Mediterranean world was beset by one or more of the principal scourges of the age—that is, plague, famine, and war. It was precisely at such times that the city's superb lazaretto facilities could guarantee the secure purgation of merchandise shipped from suspected areas, that its storage depots could ensure ample supplies of grain at a relatively stable price, and that its neutrality could guarantee that the port would remain open to the ships and goods of all states.[9]

After 1814, however, Livorno's traditional role as a free, neutral port seemed destined to provide a more tenuous foundation for its commercial prosperity. The period of relative peace following the wars of the revolution ended the special advantages that Livorno had derived from its neutral status.[10] The growing security of Mediterranean commerce coupled with the development of larger and faster ships and improved communications seemed to render free, deposit ports superfluous; the necessity to perceive the maximum profit on every commercial transaction made the expenses of transshipment undesirable.[11] Commercial transactions tended to become simpler everywhere as producers sought to establish direct links with consumers. In such a situation, the economic position of a given port would be increasingly forced to reflect the productive capacity of the state of which it formed a part. Because of the low productive capacity of the Tuscan economy during this period, the situation therefore did not offer bright prospects for Livorno's future prosperity.

The most succinct presentation of Livorno's position in the new commercial age was made in an article that appeared in

1837 in the prestigious Milanese journal *Annali universali di statistica. . . .*[12] It was understandable, the author noted, that those who predicted a brilliant commercial revival for Livorno should see it in terms of the reflorescence of a commerce of deposit, for the facilities that the city possessed for a commerce of this sort were such to make it preferred to all other ports in the Mediterranean. Unfortunately, he wrote, this type of commercial activity was by its very nature becoming less important every day. In an age of stiff competition and low profit margins, every effort was being made to rationalize business practices and eliminate unnecessary expenses. Commerce was tending toward its simplest expression, that is, to the direct exchange of merchandise between producer and consumer. All other parties were considered to be drones living at the expense of either one or the other of these and were eliminated from the commercial process whenever possible.

Livorno, the article's author noted, had already begun to suffer from these commercial changes. At one time the port had received colonial products from America and Holland and manufactured goods from England. In exchange for this merchandise the Levant would send its cottons, silks, and dyed cloths. Now, however, the English were going directly to Smyrna, Constantinople, and Alexandria to make their exchanges. They were carrying their sugar and salt products [*salumi*] to Civitavecchia, "and they would go to the mouth of the Arno if they believed that they could sell a cargo there."[13]

It was highly unlikely, the author felt, that Livorno could develop its commercial ties with northern and central Italy to compensate for the loss of this commerce. In the eighteenth century, Lombardy, the Marches, Modena, and the Papal States had turned to Livorno for their colonial products and their dyed and manufactured goods. With the reopening of the free port in Trieste, however, the city had lost its markets in northern Italy and in much of the Papal States, for these regions could supply themselves more conveniently and cheaply there than in Livorno. Indeed, the author stressed, because the Apennines served to divide Livorno from the plains of Lombardy the port could not hope to reassert its position in the transit trade. Geographic configurations would increasingly restrict Livorno's commercial range to Tuscany, Lucca, Massa, and Carrara. The few commissions still arriving from Modena, Bologna, and the Papal States were decreasing daily and would soon disappear altogether.[14]

Although the appearance of this article caused considerable stir, many of its points had been noted by members of Livorno's political and commercial elite long before the French Revolution, indicating that what appeared to be an incipient commercial crisis had deep roots. As early as 1758, in response to an inquest set up by the government, various spokesmen for the "nations" into which the merchant community of the city was then divided had stressed the decline of Livorno's commerce of deposit and transshipment and the growing tendency of producers to establish direct contacts with consumers.[15] The Jewish community reported that since 1748 the government of Naples had attempted to enter into direct commercial relations with Great Britain and the West by granting concessions to merchants willing to settle in that region. The policy had proved successful, with the result that much of the silk, grain, oil, fruit, and wine of Naples and Sicily were now passing directly to the West instead of going through Livorno. The French emphasized the growing spirit of enterprise and competition which was impelling states to handle their own commerce when possible instead of relying on foreigners. The auditor of the governor (Pierallini), in his *Osservazioni sulla pace cogli Ottomani*, stressed that the real decline in Livorno's role as intermediary occurred in 1748. In that year, in response to the peace treaty between Tuscany and the Ottomans, Livorno was placed under a stringent interdict by rival ports and had its traditional commercial patterns severely disrupted.[16]

Gloomy reports on the decline of Livorno's traditional commerce continued into the first half of the nineteenth century. A long, anonymous report in French sent to the Tuscan government in 1820 stressed again the decline of Livorno's commercial ties with Great Britain.[17] Traditionally, it said, Livorno had been the center of English commerce in Italy. With the establishment of a general European peace, however, "this commercial protectorate, which had carried the prosperity of Livorno to the farthest limits, underwent several modifications." Feelings of rivalry toward the Continent encouraged Britain to use its maritime superiority to consolidate a firm commercial monopoly—"Its merchants wished to exploit directly, and by themselves, all branches of Mediterranean commerce which previously they had turned over to their factors." Other reports on the commerce of Livorno did not bother to discuss the reasons for the city's decline as a port of deposit, but simply took it as a given.[18]

Commentators corroborated another point made in the *Annali di statistica*, that the development of rival ports in the Italian peninsula was seriously weakening Livorno's hold over its traditional markets. In the inquest of 1758, Giuliano Ricci, a Tuscan merchant, noted that the mercantilist principles of the age were encouraging governments to channel commerce through their own ports. The Papal States were utilizing Civitavecchia or the recently established free port of Ancona, and Lombardy was establishing closer commercial ties with Venice.

In response to the same inquest, the Jewish community laid particular stress on the danger of Ancona, which, it said, derived its strength not so much from the facilities and privileges of its port as from its location. From Ancona one could ship goods to the major centers of northern and central Italy without having to repack them in smaller bundles, as was necessary in Livorno. The result was a considerable savings in time and money. In the first half of the nineteenth century, as we shall see, efforts were made to strengthen Livorno's ties with northern Italy. Evidence will suggest, however, that despite these attempts Livorno's transit commerce remained largely within the boundaries outlined in the Milanese journal.[19]

Although commentators agreed that Livorno could not hope to revive its commerce of deposit or even to preserve the majority of its markets in the Italian peninsula, many were unwilling to accept the commercial decline of the city as inevitable and believed that an expanding commerce in

Tuscan products could compensate the port for the loss of its traditional trade. In its report of 1758, the Italian nation (composed of merchants from the states of the Italian peninsula) had emphasized that with the growing competition from other ports it would be increasingly necessary to exploit the commercial possibilities of Tuscan agricultural and manufactured goods.[20] By 1830 this appeared to be taking place, for the *gonfaloniere,* the head of the municipal administration, proclaimed in his annual report that the marketing of Tuscan products had strengthened Livorno's commercial ties with other states and that it had "compensated us for the loss of traffic which previously was nourished by those foreign products of which the deposit has been lost."[21] The *Giornale di commercio* (Florence) noted in 1829 that although in a previous epoch Livorno's every resource had been based on its existence as a port of deposit, "it has become today the permanent and necessary vehicle for the export [*sfogo*] of many indigenous products [*produzioni territoriali*]."[22]

This belief in the fundamental shift in Livorno's commercial activity during the late eighteenth and early nineteenth centuries has continued to the present and forms a basic tenet of recent studies on Livorno's commerce.[23] This is particularly evident in the work of Giorgio Mori, a historian who has had great influence in defining Livorno's social and economic position in this period. In an important article published in 1956,[24] Mori attempted to present a more concrete picture of Livorno's commerce in the early nineteenth century. To do so he restudied the statistics presented in 1837 by John Bowring to a parliamentary committee of the British House of Commons (see table 1).[25] On the basis of these statistics Mori concluded that of a total of 84,524,770 Tuscan lire (14,873,960 pezze) worth of merchandise imported into Livorno in 1835, only 19,346,000 lire (3,400,500 pezze)—or little more than 23 percent—was destined for deposit and successive reexport. The rest, he argued, was consumed in Livorno and the hinterland. To Mori these findings were of fundamental importance, for they indicated that "the nature of the port of Livorno and of its commercial emporium was radically changing in this period. Up until then it had been

TABLE 1

VALUE BREAKDOWN OF LIVORNO'S IMPORTS-EXPORTS, 1834*

Imports		Value
A. Colonial products	Pezze	1,435,000
B. *Salumi* (England, Northern Europe, Spain)	Pezze	626,500
C. *Salumi* (Mediterranean)	Pezze	187,010
D. Products of the North	Pezze	497,500
E. Metals, etc.	Pezze	248,950
F. Manufactured goods— England and Switzerland	Pezze	4,423,000
G. Grain and merchandise from the LeVant	Pezze	3,191,500
H. Products from Tuscany and Italy	Pezze	864,000
I. Merchandise in deposit for export (Mercanzie in deposito per l'esportazione)	Pezze	3,400,500
	Total	14,873,960
	Equal to Tuscan Lire	84,524,770

Exports		Value
England and America	Pezze	1,550,000
Northern Europe, France and Italy	Pezze	1,860,000
Greece	Pezze	520,000
Tunisia, Algeria, Tripoli	Pezze	1,415,000
Alexandria	Pezze	1,300,000
Soria	Pezze	625,000
Corsica, Sardinia, Sicilia, Spain, etc.	Pezze	830,000
	Total	8,100,000

Summary

Imports	Pezze	14,873,960
Deduction as in Item I of the imports for goods in deposit for reexportation (Deduzione come nella Tavola I per la riesportazione)	Pezze	3,400,500
Total value of imports (from abroad)		11,473,460

*(From Giovanni Bowring, *Statistica della Toscana* . . . [1838], pp. 21, 24)

substantially extraneous [*estraneo*] to Tuscany. . . . From now on its wealth and its life would depend ever more on the wealth, life, and economy of the state at its back."[26]

Not considering for the moment whether an excess of imports is in itself evidence of the wealth and vitality of a state, it should be noted that Mori based his conclusions on a total misreading of Bowring's statistics. What Mori considered as merchandise imported into the city and deposited there for later reexportation was clearly not meant to be that at all. True, for reasons that will be explained shortly, Bowring used the term *riesportazione* to describe this merchandise in his final summary.[27] In the tables themselves, however, he called it *varie manifatture e articoli d'esportazione*.[28] That the latter is the more precise description appears evident in looking at the specific items, for nowhere to be found are the spices, cereals, or foreign manufactured goods that had traditionally been imported into Livorno for successive reexport. Instead, one finds olive oil, coral, tanned hides, pit carbon, boric acid, potash, marble, and so on—articles traditionally produced in Tuscany.

That Bowring resorted to the confusing use of the term *riesportazione* probably resulted from his desire to distinguish Tuscan products imported into Livorno (which, in terms of the tariff structure, stood outside the Tuscan state) for simple consumption from those imported into Livorno and held there for successive reexport. Such a distinction would be crucial in attempting to work out Livorno's balance of trade. Thus, in working out his final summary, Bowring subtracted this item from the import side of the ledger and considered it solely as an export.

The complexity of this analysis reflects Livorno's nebulous relationship to the Tuscan state. Nevertheless, when due allowance is made for this, the major categories in Bowring's statistics and what they tell us about the structure of Livorno's commerce in the mid-1830s become, I think, fairly clear. Read accurately, they show that of the imports the value of merchandise from abroad deposited in Livorno for successive reexport (4,699,500 pezze) totaled not 23 percent, as Mori supposed, but 41 percent. Of the exports, Tuscan products (valued at 3,400,500 pezze) equaled 42 percent of the total, while the value of goods imported into Livorno and deposited there for successive reexport reached 4,699,500 pezze, or 58 percent of the total exports. Clearly, apart from indicating a real imbalance in Tuscan trade, these figures show that while direct, two-way commerce between Tuscany and other states was important, Livorno's traditional commerce of deposit and transshipment retained a dominant share of the city's commercial activity.

Another report helps to confirm this view. In 1838, Edoardo Mayer, director of Livorno's discount bank, prepared a long memorandum for Emanuele Repetti.[29] In his memorandum, Mayer indicated the final destination of many of the city's major imports. Of goods from the Levant (given an average annual value of 6,500,000 Tuscan lire), Egyptian raw cotton was reshipped in its entirety to manufacturing centers in Switzerland, England, France, and Belgium; two-thirds of the wool passed into France, England, and Piedmont; the silk not consumed in Tuscany was sent primarily to Genoa; wax and linens were consumed largely in Tuscany, though much of the former was marketed also in Sicily; gall nuts, saffron, and so on were reexported to England, Belgium, Holland, and Germany; and opium was reexported to England, France, and America. Of goods from the West and the North, salt fish (*salumi*), metal, wood, pitch, tar, linens, and cowhides (valued at 6,750,000 lire) were consumed largely in Tuscany. Colonial products (valued at 9,500,000 lire) were consumed in Tuscany or shipped to other areas of the Italian peninsula. The most important single item that Mayer listed was manufactured goods from England, France, and Switzerland, to which he gave an average annual value of 23,000,000 lire. Only one-fourth of the manufactured goods imported into Livorno were consumed in Tuscany or in other parts of Italy; the remainder were reexported, primarily to the Levant.[30] Mayer concluded that "Livorno is a central point where, with a bustle of activity [*con somma attività*], products arriving by sea from opposite points are exchanged." Clearly, then, the city had not lost its character as an international emporium.

Regrettably, Mayer made no attempt in his report to assess

the final destination of cereals imported into the port (valued at 15,000,000 lire). Nevertheless, the report does possess the real merit of documenting the importance of a deposit trade in manufactured goods well into the nineteenth century. Table 2 shows that the volume of this trade remained important in the late 1840s. At the same time, however, this table illustrates the overwhelming predominance of another item in the city's commerce: cereals. Indeed, by the late 1840s (if

TABLE 2

LARGE SQUARE-RIGGED SAILING SHIPS ARRIVING WITH
CARGO AT THE PORT OF LIVORNO IN 1815 AND 1847
(By Port of Origin and Nature of Cargo)

Port of origin	1815	1847
America	48	16
Barbary Coast (Barberia)	34	40
Egypt	73	168
France and the Mediterranean	102	612
Greece and the Levant	119	322
West Indies	1	—
England	114	162
Black Sea	65	871
Holland	20	22
Sicily/Malta	124	224
Spain and Portugal	28	38
Sweden and the North	43	9
Trieste and the Adriatic	13	17
Totals	784	2,501

Nature of the cargo	1815	1847
Grain	238	1,429
Salt products (*salumi*)	78	56
Colonial products	61	78
Manufactured items	32	159
Diverse merchandise	375	779
Totals	784	2,501

Source: ASF, *Fin. C.R.,* f. 20. Livorno, 4 July 1848: Uffizio doganale della Bocca del Porto.

not earlier), cereals from the Black Sea seem to have become the single most important item in Livorno's commerce. This question merits further consideration.

Because of the destruction of the city's annual customs records and the lack of a complete statistical series on the port's commercial movement, tracing the growing importance of cereals in Livorno's commerce is hazardous, at best. One important indicator of this trend, certainly, can be seen in the repeated pleas of the merchant community for an expansion of the city's grain-storage facilities. The capacity of these facilities—both public and private—at the end of the eighteenth century was estimated at approximately 522,000 sacks.[31] In 1817, at the high point of the post-Napoleonic famine, the first requests were made to expand this capacity. In a letter to the secretary of finance, the governor of Livorno reported that comestibles were almost the sole staple of the city's commerce: grain and corn (*biade*) were arriving daily; 400,000 to 500,000 sacks were already in deposit; and additional arrivals were imminent. The governor opposed the request of the chamber of commerce for the utilization of the lazarettos as grain-storage warehouses. However, he frantically searched the city for other possible storage depots.[32] During the 1820s the grain trade leveled off, and requests for additional facilities declined,[33] but the impetus picked up again in the late 1830s. The destruction of the old wall of the city in 1834 had eliminated many of the old ditches (*fossi*) and pits (*buche*) that had been located in or near it, and officials in charge of the government grain-storage warehouses and members of the chamber of commerce argued that new facilities would have to be constructed to replace them.[34]

Pressure on the government to this end increased in 1843 because of a growing fear of competition from rival ports. In his third quarterly report in that year, A. G. Mochi, the government commissioner appointed to oversee Livorno's discount bank, indicated that the grain trade was deserting Livorno for Marseilles. According to some, he said, this was because of the opinion that good storage facilities had been lost with the enlargement of the city and no new ones had been constructed to replace them. Giovanni Chelli, president of the chamber of commerce, made a similar point and stressed that "it is absolutely necessary to demonstrate that we do not lack the necessary means . . . [and that] if some storage facilities have been destroyed, they have been replaced with new and better ones."[35]

Underlying these demands, it seems, lay the sense that the grain trade now formed the foundation of Livorno's commercial prosperity. In 1844, Carlo Bargagli, the captain of the port, stated succinctly that "the deposit of grain is today the principal branch of commerce in this city."[36] In 1845 the governor reechoed this sentiment in a report to the secretary of finance.[37] And in 1850 the chamber of commerce remarked more broadly that "experience had demonstrated that the city of Livorno is considered the principal cereal deposit of the Mediterranean."[38]

While they are revealing, reports of this sort are nevertheless fundamentally impressionistic. A more concrete sense of the relative importance of the grain trade in Livorno's commerce was provided by Mochi in several of his reports, in which he presented annual summaries of the value of goods (expressed in Tuscan lire and broken down into two categories, cereals and other merchandise) sold on the wholesale market (*vendite di primo mano*) in Livorno. This material is summarized as shown in table 3.[39] Mochi admitted that his figures, drawn from Livorno's *Giornale di commercio*, were at best approximate.[40] However, at no point did he question their fundamental indication of the predominant value of grain sales. Indeed, his only comment on this point was to note that the disadvantageous position of other merchandise vis-à-vis grain appeared less than many had supposed.[41]

The most concrete and dramatic evidence of the growing importance of grain in Livorno's commerce, though, can be found in some general summaries of the port's commercial movement. These summaries are reproduced in tables 2 through 9. They include the number of sailing ships arriving in the port as a raw annual aggregate and broken down according to their port of origin and the nature of their cargoes. The data are regrettably sparse. The summary of large

TABLE 3

Year	Cereals	Other merchandise
1838	31.916.420	11.271.010
1839 (first half)	12.812.160	5.356.500
1840	18.292.370	18.143.220
1841	15.875.300	12.286.600
1842	13.905.100	10.894.900
1843	16.699.900	10.704.300
1844	27.546.900	8.314.700

sailing ships arriving in the port is reasonably complete but provides no information on cargo or port of origin. This latter information is available in a complete annual series only from 1815 to 1826. Information for three years in the 1830s has been discovered and for only one—but an exceptional one—in the 1840s. None of these summaries by itself furnishes a complete picture of the grain trade in Livorno from 1815 to 1850. Taken together, however, they can provide a sense of the general profile of this trade and of its relative importance to other merchandise.

All these summaries document the massive movement of ships into Livorno during the two brief periods of famine (1815–1817 and 1847) which struck Europe during the first half of the nineteenth century. In both these periods the failure of the domestic harvest and the resulting increase in demand and soaring prices led the Tuscan government to temporarily suspend all charges on grain imports, which stimulated commercial activity in the port. Thus, in 1811, at the culmination of the French occupation of Tuscany, the number of large sailing ships entering Livorno had fallen to a low of 81 (table 4). By 1814—when Tuscany regained its independence—the number climbed to 422. In 1815 it jumped to 943, and in 1816 the number of arrivals peaked at 1,124.

A similar sharp increase is evident in the movement of

TABLE 4

SUMMARY OF LARGE (*vela quadra*) AND
SMALL (*vela latina*) SAILING SHIPS
ARRIVING AT THE PORT OF LIVORNO, 1766–1837

Year	Large	Small	Year	Large	Small
1766	173	472	1802	1,017	1,945
1767	462	1,686	1803	637	1,734
1768	—	—	1804	914	2,021
1769	—	—	1805	712	1,578
1770	378	1,694	1806	590	1,896
1771	380	1,795	1807	454	2,065
1772	403	1,717	1808	134	1,699
1773	383	1,761	1809	118	1,440
1774	529	1,587	1810	139	1,411
1775	384	1,659	1811	81	1,144
1776	371	1,755	1812	89	1,242
1777	375	1,685	1813	95	2,902
1778	347	1,591	1814	422	4,552
1779	373	1,430	1815	943	4,396
1780	345	1,567	1816	1,124	4,088
1781	341	1,508	1817	1,078	3,004
1782	435	1,702	1818	1,047	3,984
1783	480	1,519	1819	947	3,909
1784	434	1,299	1820	847	4,397
1785	404	1,495	1821	945	3,674
1786	553	1,527	1822	869	4,308
1787	485	1,749	1823	780	4,450
1788	477	1,958	1824	940	4,631
1789	461	1,852	1825	907	4,969
1790	484	1,746	1826	903	5,141
1791	530	1,728	1827	1,060	4,847
1792	661	1,951	1828	986	4,598
1793	546	1,925	1829	964	4,465
1794	1,211	1,879	1830	1,101	4,619
1795	1,091	1,260	1831	1,033	4,232
1796	535	915	1832	1,266	4,390
1797	719	1,773	1833	1,150	4,488
1798	608	1,664	1834	1,211	4,442
1799	417	1,224	1835	1,234	3,986
1800	1,003	905	1836	831	4,500
1801	320	1,276	1837	1,075	4,356

Source: E. Repetti, *Dizionario,* vol. 2, p. 768.

ships from the Black Sea, which almost exclusively carried grain from the ports of southern Russia (see table 5). Here the number increased from 65 in 1815 to a peak of 195 in 1817. Finally, the arrival of ships in the port carrying grain climbed from 238 in 1815 to 398 in 1817 (see table 6). This last summary illustrates the relative importance of the grain trade at the climax of the post-Napoleonic famine. Of a total of 891 ships arriving in the port with merchandise in 1817, 398 (45%) were carrying grain.

A similar sharp increase in the movement of the port occurred in the famine year of 1847 (table 7). From 1846 to 1847 the arrival of large sailing ships jumped from 1,712 to 2,201. In 1848, as the result of a good harvest and the uncertainty of the political situation, arrivals dropped to 1,587, and in 1849 they fell still further, to 1,307. From figures provided by the customhouse one can obtain a sense of the relative importance of the grain trade in 1847 (table 2). Of the 2,501 arrivals noted in the customs records, the largest number by far (871 or 35% of the total) came from the Black Sea; 1,429 (57%) arrived with grain. From sixth place (8% of the total) in 1815, the Black Sea in 1847 had become Livorno's chief source of supplies. Grain cargoes arriving in the port in 1847 surpassed all other cargoes (including the large catchall category of "diverse merchandise") combined.

Between these two brief periods of famine the grain trade in Livorno was relatively less important. From 1818 well into the 1820s the commercial movement of the port slackened (table 5). In part, as commentators have pointed out, the decline was a result of disturbances in Levantine commerce caused by the revolution in Greece. It also reflected, however, a series of good harvests in Europe and, as we shall see shortly, the rigid tariff policies instituted by many European states to protect their agricultural producers. Thus, the number of large sailing ships arriving in Livorno with cargo dropped from a peak of 891 in 1817 to 682 in 1818 and reached a low of 501 in 1826 (table 7). An even sharper downturn is evident in the arrival of large sailing ships from ports in the Black Sea (table 5). The number of ships arriving with grain showed a similar drop, although with a much more erratic profile (table 6).

TABLE 5

LARGE SAILING SHIPS (*Bastimenti di vela-quadra*)
ARRIVING AT LIVORNO WITH CARGO, BY COUNTRY OF ORIGIN

	1815	1816	1817	1818	1819	1820	1821	1822
America	48	81	72	43	68	46	78	58
Barberia	34	23	37	35	57	51	44	44
Egypt	73	124	169	138	53	74	71	68
France and the Mediterranean	102	98	77	42	96	91	107	69
Greece and the Levant	119	117	76	73	89	64	35	42
West Indies	1	3	2	2	7	8	6	11
England	114	141	88	103	105	105	166	101
Black Sea	65	139	195	105	72	76	47	43
Holland	20	20	5	11	16	9	21	13
Sicily/Malta	124	83	105	64	68	95	56	62
Spain and Portugal	28	18	23	26	29	14	28	14
Sweden and the North	43	23	19	20	28	21	66	43
Trieste and the Adriatic	13	7	23	20	25	26	13	47
Totals	784	877	891	682	713	680	738	615

TABLE 5—Continued

	1823	1824	1825	1826	1830	1831	1839	1847
America	42	66	53	42	43	43	34	16
Barberia	47	42	47	55	54	50	33	40
Egypt	46	103	50	39	30	78	17	168
France and the Mediterranean	75	51	21	38	128	110	438	612
Greece and the Levant	57	54	38	38	42	55	81	322
West Indies	8	2	2	2	2	1	2	—
England	92	93	95	89	137	106	108	162
Black Sea	39	28	75	58	260	121	601	871
Holland	11	9	5	7	7	4	15	22
Sicily/Malta	52	40	34	41	88	89	154	224
Spain and Portugal	13	8	10	11	16	22	41	38
Sweden and the North	24	35	40	47	37	30	36	9
Trieste and the Adriatic	32	39	32	34	19	23	50	17
Totals	538	570	502	501	863	732	1,610	2,501

Source: 1815 and 1847, ASF, *Fin. C.R.*, f. 20; 1816–1825, ibid., *Misc. di Fin. A. II*, f. 541; 1826, ibid., *Seg. di Gab.*, f. 391; 1830–1831, ibid., *Misc. di Fin. I*, f. 13; 1839, ibid., *Seg. Gab. Append.*, f. 54.

TABLE 6
LARGE SAILING SHIPS (*vela-quadra*) ARRIVING AT LIVORNO, BY NATURE OF CARGO

	1815	1816	1817	1818	1819	1820	1821	1822	1823	1824	1825
Grain	238	362	398	261	140	355	325	156	86	96	102
Salt products (*salumi*)	78	71	62	45	65	80	40	42	47	61	55
Colonial products	61	77	79	70	96	60	94	67	52	63	30
Manufactured products	32	45	61	58	64	33	75	60	33	27	32
Diverse merchandise	375	322	291	248	348	152	204	290	320	323	283
Totals	784	877	891	682	713	680	738	615	538	570	502

	1826	1829	1830	1831	1832	1833	1834	1835	1836	1839	1847
Grain	93	164	318	216	311	269	204	226	269	670	1,429
Salt products (*salumi*)	43			47						51	56
Colonial products	28			23						99	78
Manufactured products	34[a]			47						193	159
Diverse merchandise	303[b]	600[c]	545	399	537	531	559	544	766	597	779
Totals	501	764	863	732	848	800	763	770	1,035	1,610	2,501

Source: 1815 and 1847, ASF, Fin. C.R., f. 20; 1816–1825, ibid., Misc. di Fin. A II, f. 541; 1826, ibid., Seg. Gab., f. 391; 1829–1830 and 1832–1836, ibid., Misc. Fin. A II, f. 530, b. 59; 1831, ibid., Misc. Fin. I, f. 13; 1839, ibid., Seg. Gab. Append., f. 54.
[a] Called in this source *manifatti in tessuti*. [b] Called in this source *merci non nominate*. [c] Source does not break down other merchandise.

TABLE 7
NUMBER OF LARGE SQUARE-RIGGED SAILING SHIPS
(*Bastimenti di vela quadra*)
ARRIVING AT THE PORT OF LIVORNO, 1815–1852[a]

1815	784[b]	1828	959	1841	1,619
1816	877	1829	948	1842	1,534
1817	891	1830	1,059	1843	1,826
1818	682	1831	993	1844	1,951
1819	713	1832	1,204	1845	1,723
1820	680	1833	1,118	1846	1,712
1821	738	1834	1,186	1847	2,201[d]
1822	615	1835	1,187	1848	1,587
1823	538	1836	1,264	1849	1,307
1824	570	1837	1,465	1850	1,536
1825	502	1838	1,517	1851	1,326
1826	501	1839	1,634	1852	1,561[e]
1827	1,044[c]	1840	1,627		

[a] This category includes the following types of sailing vessels: *navi, brigantini, pollacche,* and *bombarde.*

[b] The series from 1815 to 1826 is drawn from the following: ASF, *Fin. C.R.,* f. 20 (for 1815); ibid., *Misc. di Fin. A. II.* f. 541 (for 1816–1825); ibid., *Seg. di Gab.,* f. 391 (for 1817–1826). This series is based on the records of the customhouse and enumerates large sailing ships arriving at the port with cargo.

[c] The series from 1827–1846 is drawn from ASL, *Gov.,* f. 266, n. 281. The figures were supplied by the captain of the port and include all large merchant ships (*vela quadra*) that paid the anchorage fees of the port (figures drawn from the *Registri campioni di ancoraggi*). As merchant ships arriving without cargo would also have been required to pay the port fees, this would probably explain why the curve in this source is higher than those cited in the previous note.

[d] The series from 1847–1852 is drawn from ASF, *Fin. C.R.,* f. 101.

[e] Note that the statistics in this table are lower than those provided by E. Repetti in Table 1. This is probably due to Repetti's inclusion of warships in his general summary.

By the end of the 1820s, however, with the Greek question settled and more flexible tariff policies being instituted by European governments, the grain trade in Livorno had become stable and prosperous. This is evident from the following list, which indicates the number of large sailing ships arriving in the port with grain from 1829 to 1836.[42]

1829	164	1833	269
1830	318	1834	204
1831	216	1835	226
1832	311	1836	269

Finally, summaries covering two periods from 1780 to 1789 and from 1816 to 1825 provide useful comparisons, since both cover periods of relative peace and security in the Mediterranean and include years of active trading and relative stagnation. Together, these summaries (presented in tables 8 and 9) graphically illustrate the fundamental expansion of Livorno's commerce with the Black Sea and testify to the growing predominance of the grain trade in the port.

The first summary, broken down by country of origin, not only testifies to the drop in commercial relations with Sicily and Malta (a fact that, as we have seen, was emphasized by many commentators) but also illustrates in detail the expansion of the city's contacts with the Black Sea. From 1780 to 1789 an average of only four ships a year (0.93% of the total arrivals) came from ports in the Black Sea, while in the decade from 1816 to 1825 the yearly average had jumped to 82 (12%). This was still below the average of 109 ships a year arriving from England and of 90 arriving from Egypt, many of which undoubtedly also carried grain. However, in rate of growth the Black Sea outclassed all other areas (1,950% versus 41%).

The second summary, broken down by cargo, shows that in the period from 1816 to 1825 the average number of ships arriving with cereals per year was superior to the number of ships carrying any other single product, and it also shows that the rate of growth for cereals from the first to the second decade was one and a half times greater than that of all other products combined.

The difficulties involved in using commercial statistics drawn from different sources and measuring different things are obvious. Not only do these statistics often confuse ships arriving in the port with and without cargo and occasionally

TABLE 8
DECADE SUMMARIES OF LARGE SQUARE-RIGGED
SAILING SHIPS ARRIVING WITH CARGO AT
LIVORNO, BY PLACE OF ORIGIN

Place	Annual average 1780–1789	Annual average 1816–1825
America	20	61
Barbary Coast (Barberia)	29	43
Egypt	21	90
France and the Mediterranean	31	73
Greece and the Levant	63	64
West Indies	—	5
England	59	109
Black Sea	4	82
Holland	19	12
Sicily/Malta	104	66
Spain and Portugal	14	18
Sweden and the North	39	32
Trieste and the Adriatic	25	26
Totals	429	681

Source: ASF, *Misc. di Fin. A. II*, f. 541, b. 59.

fail to clearly distinguish war and merchant ships but they also do not take into account that ships of the same type can differ greatly in tonnage. Value, moreover, does not at all necessarily follow from volume: a small cargo of spices is worth much more than a large cargo of grain or salt. Finally, as we shall see, a more active commerce does not necessarily indicate a more prosperous one. Crude as they are, however, these statistics do provide at least a rough indication of relative growth. Some reasons for this growth will be examined shortly. At present, it is sufficient to reaffirm that in the first half of the nineteenth century cereals had become a

TABLE 9
DECADE SUMMARIES OF LARGE SQUARE-RIGGED
SAILING SHIPS ARRIVING AT LIVORNO,
BY NATURE OF CARGO

Cargo	Annual average 1780–1789	Annual average 1816–1825
Grain	77	228
Salt products (*salumi*)	53	57
Colonial products	30	69
Manufactured products	18	49
Diverse merchandise	251	278
Totals	429	681

Source: ASF, *Misc. di Fin. A. II,* f. 541, b. 59.

predominant, if not *the* predominant, branch of Livorno's commerce.

What factors enabled a deposit trade in cereals to flourish at a time when, as we have seen, commentators were predicting the end of Livorno's traditional role as a port of deposit? Probably the most important single factor was the basic inability of the states of Western Europe to provide their expanding populations with domestic grain at moderate, stable prices. This inability, coupled with the availability of relatively cheap, high-quality Russian cereals, led European governments to eventually adopt more flexible policies toward the admission of foreign grain into their internal markets. These policies, as we shall see, would prove especially advantageous for a deposit trade in cereals.

Government policy toward the admission of foreign grain, however, had not always been flexible. The famine years of 1815–1817 had witnessed a tremendous influx of foreign— particularly Russian—grain into the markets of Western Europe, and once the crisis had ended governments had moved to erect controls to protect their domestic producers from competition with this cheap, high-quality product. England set the trend with its Corn Law of 1815, under the provisions of which the importation of foreign cereals was prohibited when the price of grain on the domestic market fell below 80 shillings a quarter and was entirely free and unrestricted when the price exceeded that figure.[43] France imposed similar controls in 1819, permitting entry of foreign grain only if domestic prices rose, according to region, above 20, 18, or 16 francs per hectoliter. Prussia, Switzerland, Holland, Spain, and Portugal followed suit, setting up virtually prohibitive tariffs on cereal imports and waiving them only during periods of famine. These protectionist policies held sway in the 1820s, a period when the grain trade in Livorno was for the most part stagnant or in decline.

By the late 1820s, however, under pressure from consumers to stabilize the price of grain in their domestic markets, governments began to take a more flexible approach to the introduction of foreign cereals. In 1828, England provided the model once again by introducing a sliding-scale tariff for grain imports. Under its provisions a tariff of 23 shillings per quarter was levied on foreign grain when domestic prices reached 64 shillings; 16 shillings, 8 pence when the price reached 69 shillings; and 1 shilling when the price rose above 73 shillings.[44] Similar graded tariff systems were later adopted by Sweden (1830), France (1832), Belgium (1834), Holland (1835), and Portugal (1837).

It was no accident that the introduction of sliding scales coincided with the resurgence of the grain trade in Livorno, for these tariffs especially favored a deposit trade in cereals. For the maximum profit to be made under the new system, large amounts of grain had to be stored in ports near the great markets so as to be available promptly for taking advantage of passing opportunities. Thus, in 1833, after the introduction of the sliding scale in France, the price of wheat on the domestic market rose sufficiently to permit the importation of foreign grain. The effect on Livorno was immediate. Massive shipments to France over a two-month period depleted Livorno's grain deposits. Ships from the Black Sea that would normally have deposited their grain in Livorno were hurrying on to Marseilles to unload their cargoes under the low tariffs. As a result of these massive imports, however, the price of grain was falling. Speculators in Livorno were predicting that the French market for foreign grain would soon close and that cereals would again reenter Livorno for storage until a new opportunity for their profitable sale presented itself.[45]

However, cereals deposited in Livorno not only supplied the demands of foreign states but also responded to the needs of the Grand Duchy itself. These needs were especially great in years of famine. Of the 702,565 sacks extracted from Livorno in 1815, for example, 507,059 passed into the Tuscan hinterland.[46] Of the 2,382,784 extracted in 1847, 1,914,028 passed into the hinterland.[47] Even normal years witnessed massive shipments from Livorno into Tuscany. O. Forni, a high-ranking member of the Tuscan customs administration, estimated that an average of 1,049,000 sacks of cereals were unloaded each year in Livorno and that of this total, 800,000 (roughly 80%) passed into the hinterland.[48] Luigi Serristori estimated that imports equaled about 13.3 percent of Tuscany's annual consumption of six million sacks, enough to feed its population for seven weeks and three days.[49] According to the administrator of the Royal Revenues, these imports were on the increase, reaching an annual average of 1,157,793 sacks in the five-year period from 1835 to 1839.[50]

Tuscany clearly was unable to feed itself. This had not always been the case. In the eighteenth century Tuscany had imported wheat only in times of famine, and in good years it had been able to export some of it.[51] The situation changed after the Napoleonic Wars. The disruption caused by war and the protracted fall in wheat prices in the 1820s coupled with the general unsuitability of the Tuscan terrain for intensive grain cultivation forced the state to rely increasingly on foreign grain to feed its expanding population.[52]

In this situation Russian cereals possessed distinct advantages on the free Tuscan market. As we shall see in more detail later, Russian grains were far less expensive than comparable products grown in Tuscany or the rest of Italy. Only Egypt could provide cheaper grain, but Egyptian wheat, subject to weevils and deterioration if exposed to dampness, traveled poorly and was more difficult to maintain in storage than its Russian counterpart. In addition, Egyptian wheat was lighter in character (i.e., weight per volume) and was subject to sporadic export restrictions by the Egyptian government.[53]

Russian grain, moreover, was rich in gluten. This was especially important for hard wheat and indispensable for the manufacture of pasta, an important item in the Tuscan diet. Hard wheat could not be grown in Tuscany, and millers previously had imported it from Sicily. But Sicily could not supply the demand, and its commerce was periodically subject to vexing restrictions on grain exports. For these reasons, pasta makers in Tuscany increasingly came to rely on imported Russian grain, much of which was ground into flour at mills near Livorno.

Russian soft wheat also found great favor on the Tuscan market. Although some Tuscan soft wheat was better than the Russian, it was in short supply, was more expensive than Russian wheat, and was much demanded abroad—especially in England—for seed. Unknown to the Tuscan consumer, perhaps, Russian soft wheat was employed in the manufacture of even the finest bread. In December 1845 the British consul in Livorno reported to the Foreign Office that contrary to the reports of bakers, Tuscan soft wheat was probably not being used in the manufacture of prime-quality bread. "At the present prices," the consul said, "it could never suit the bakers to use it, as they profess to do, and the consumption in Livorno is known to be very limited." More likely, he felt, Russian and Polish were the types chiefly used, "the former because it is a wheat which yields an excellent result and the latter to impart whiteness."[54] Price, availability, and quality, then, served to give Russian grains a distinct advantage in the Tuscan market.

Periodically, tension was generated between the Tuscan government—which was concerned with maintaining its tax base and with protecting producers and consumers in the hinterland—and grain merchants in Livorno who were speculating on the Tuscan market. Grain speculators in Livorno, the secretary of finance remarked sarcastically in 1818, were quick to celebrate the outbreak of famine in the interior of Tuscany and correspondingly quick to lament the prosperity of the local harvest and a drop in the price of grain, demanding in compensation that the government sacrifice the income it gained from its modest charge on the import of this product.[55] Save in periods of famine, the Tuscan government refused to modify its charges on grain imports and resolutely opposed attempts by the merchant community to transfer fiscal burdens from itself to consumers in the hinterland.[56]

But tension on this issue tended to be lessened by the basic adherence of the Tuscan government to the principle of free trade, which had provided the foundation of the state's political economy since the reign of Peter Leopold (1765–1790). Grain tariffs existed, but their aim was fiscal and they had in no sense been conceived to protect the Tuscan producer. Government officials and most of Tuscany's landowning elite realized that Tuscany could no longer produce sufficient grain to feed its population, and they believed that one of the best defenses against famine lay in the maintenance of Livorno's facilities and privileges so as to encourage grain merchants to settle there and make the port their base of operations.

In the 1820s and 1830s some proprietors did urge the Tuscan government to adopt the practice of other European states and impose protective tariffs on cereals.[57] But these efforts won little support from either the government or from the vast majority of the members of Tuscany's most important economic circle, the Academy of the Georgofili. For the leading members of this circle—men such as Gino Capponi, Cosimo Ridolfi, and Raffaello Lambruschini—the granting of special protection to Tuscan grain producers would serve merely to encourage inefficient and marginal production, force up the price of grain, and ruin commerce. Wise policy, they argued, dicated that Tuscan agriculture be allowed to adjust freely to the new economic situation and that it be encouraged to transfer its major effort from cereal production to other products such as wine, silk, oil, wool, and minerals, which promised Tuscany a more secure place in a free, competitive market. Within this context, acceptable government support of agriculture would consist of the following actions: adjusting the tax burden of agricultural producers to reflect more accurately their place in the Tuscan economy, and initiating reclamation and road construction projects to increase the area of profitable cultivation and to facilitate the movement of products from farm to market. These projects would possess the additional attraction of providing employment for Tuscany's surplus population, enabling it to purchase its bread in a free, unregulated market.[58]

Perhaps, then, the comments made in the first half of the nineteenth century on the changing character of Livorno's commerce did have some foundation. Both the structure of the Tuscan economy in this period and the economic attitudes of its political and social elite seemed to encourage the development of a two-way commerce of consumption and export: while government officials and important members of the Academy of the Georgofili stressed the commercial value of Tuscan raw materials, at the same time they recognized Tuscany's growing dependence on foreign cereals.

It would be a mistake, however, to see in these developments the definitive eclipse of Livorno's traditional commerce of deposit. As indicated in the statistics provided by Bowring, Tuscan raw materials still formed a small percentage of the port's exports. Although grain shipments to the Tuscan hinterland were increasingly important to the commerce of the state, they did not conflict with Livorno's traditional role as a port of deposit and a center of speculation. For the grain merchant in Livorno, Tuscany was simply one of several potential customers. In pushing for tariff reductions or for extensions of the port's privileges, the merchant community in Livorno still wanted to keep all of its options open, as we shall see shortly. To understand the economic impetus for the reform proposals of the merchant community, then, we must pass beyond the notion of a radical shift in the port's commercial activity and examine other factors that can better explain the timing and the specific character of the reform proposals.

Commercial, Demographic, and Pricing Movements

To describe Livorno's commerce is only the first task, for by itself such a description cannot entirely define the economic condition of the city nor respond adequately to the general question raised at the beginning of this book—that is, whether Livorno's commercial situation was improving or deteriorating in the period that followed the French Revolution and the restoration of peace in Europe. In an attempt to answer this question we must examine other factors, such as the general level of commercial activity in the port city, the nature and movement of its population, and the prices of the most important items of its commerce. With this information we shall be in a better position to understand not only Livorno's economic situation but also the response of the merchant community to the changing economic and social environment in which it lived and operated.

What, then, was Livorno's economic situation in the period after 1815? On the surface it looked promising. Commercial statistics indicate that the number of sailing ships entering the port from 1815 to the 1850s increased steadily and that their number was augmented considerably by the arrival of an increasing number of steamships (see table 10).[59] The population of the city expanded from 57,446 in 1815 to 83,537 in 1850.[60] In describing Livorno, contemporaries stressed the dynamic character of the city, its bustling population, and the signs everywhere of an expanding opulence.[61]

Commentators stressed that the conjunction of these aspects was a sure sign of Livorno's continuing prosperity. To Guido Sonnino the figures on Livorno's commercial and demographic expansion "more and better than any digression demonstrated the falsity of the myth of Livorno's decline and showed on the contrary an ever-increasing activity."[62] They led Emanuele Repetti to conclude in his *Dizionario* that under Leopold II (1826–1859), Livorno had arrived at the most brilliant and fortunate period of its history.[63] This sentiment was warmly supported by Giovanni Baldasseroni, a minister of finance under Leopold II and a noted apologist for the regime.[64]

Historians who have tried to present a more pessimistic picture of Livorno's economic situation during this period appear clearly daunted by the commercial and demographic statistics. In his study of the city, Giorgio Mori remarked that

TABLE 10

NUMBER OF STEAMSHIPS ARRIVING AT THE
PORT OF LIVORNO, 1827–1852

1827	4	1840	450
1828	8	1841	503
1829	17	1842	478
1830	26	1843	551
1831	92	1844	527
1832	149	1845	456
1833	194	1846	562
1834	225	1847	669
1835	174	1848	483
1836	330	1849	463
1837	334	1850	571
1838	398	1851	581
1839	374	1852	595

Source: ASL, *Gov.*, f. 266; ASF, *Fin. C.R.*, f. 101; ASL, *Gov.*, f. 195. These
sources are in agreement for the years in which they overlap.

all students of Livorno's commercial history were in agreement that the maritime traffic of the port grew "with a certain
rhythm" during the period, and he concluded reluctantly that
while the early years of the restoration may have been difficult
for the Tuscan economy as a whole, Livorno, "at least from
this point of view," did not seem to have been much affected.[65] Mori also noted that the population of the city from
1814 to 1856 had almost doubled, though he hastened to
caution, somewhat lamely, that it would be too simplistic and
not always correct to link population expansion with the improvement of the economic condition of a given area.[66]

Mario Baruchello, anxious to depict the early nineteenth
century as the beginning of a long period of economic decline
for the port city, attacked more directly the "problem" raised
by Livorno's demographic statistics. He argued that the population of Livorno continued to expand at a rapid rate even as
the economic crisis of the city became grave and definitive.

This, he argued, though without evidence, was because people continued to come to reside in Livorno even though the prosperity of the city was now based more on past reputation than present fact. In addition, he argued, the population of Livorno, now more stable, was expanding from its own natural increase.[67]

In fact, however, the causes of Livorno's demographic expansion in the period after 1815 are far from clear, and commentators have seemed wont to attribute it to natural increase or immigration as much from a desire to reinforce their own points of view as from a careful consideration of the statistics. In his 1855 study of the population of Livorno, Cesare Caporali, strongly Malthusian and anxious to demonstrate the prosperity of the city, argued that the population increase in Livorno was due primarily to immigration. "The prodigious development of the population, inseparable from the principle of subsistence, is evidence of the prosperity of the city, prosperity constant and continuous and demonstrated not, of course, by an excess of births but by the annual immigration."[68] Giuliano Ricci, on the other hand, concerned with demonstrating the stable, indigenous character of the population of his native city, argued that the increment of Livorno's population was due almost entirely to natural increase.

> The constant growth of its population did not fail to demonstrate the prosperity of Livorno. . . . It was consoling to see that this population growth sprang from the intrinsic life of the city and was not due to accidental circumstances. . . . Almost the entire population resident in Livorno is *livornese* as much by birth, custom, and affection as by simple residence. In this respect the population of Livorno is like that of any other commercial city . . . it would have a truly indigenous population of more than 60,000 inhabitants, about nine-tenths of the total, calculated at 78,000.

> These few figures demonstrate the falsity of the opinion which wishes to consider Livorno as a temporary place of residence for foreigners rather than [as] a truly Italian city populated by a population which is politically and civilly its own.[69]

Analysis of the population statistics provided by P. Bandettini has enabled us to obtain a clearer picture of the character and growth of Livorno's population during this period than that advanced by the advocates of prosperity or doom (see table 11).[70] From an examination of the yearly population changes between 1815 and 1850, it becomes apparent that, save for the plague year of 1835, the natural rate of population growth after 1814 was relatively steady. In contrast, the movement of population in and out of the city was far more erratic—an extraordinarily large movement of people into the city in one year would be followed by a more moderate exodus in the succeeding year or years. When the totals are considered, one sees that in the period from 1814 to 1850 the population of Livorno grew by 33,482. Of this figure, 19,989 resulted from natural increase and 13,493 from immigration. Clearly, then, natural increase was the more important factor behind Livorno's population growth in this period, although the contribution of immigration was not as insignificant as some would have liked to believe.

Further examination of these annual population figures indicates that Livorno's demographic expansion during this period was not constant. From 1814–1819, Livorno's population increased by 12,182 (24.3%); from 1820–1829, by 9,515 (15.1%); from 1830–1839, by 6,083 (8.3%); and from 1840–1849, by 1,670 (2.1%; 4.5% if we use the more normal year of 1850). Clearly, then, the phenomenon of Livorno's population growth contains internal variations that vitiate somewhat the optimistic picture of its general, long-term growth.

Moreover, if the growth of Livorno's population was not constant, neither did it seem excessive in comparison with that of other Tuscan cities or with the growth of Tuscany as a whole. True, the rate of Livorno's population growth from 1818 to 1848 was greater than that of Florence 38.2% as opposed to 33.5%), but it was far below that of Pisa (50.05%) as well as that of Tuscany as a whole (48.06%).[71] In summary, then, Livorno's population growth does not represent the unmistakable sign of the city's prosperity, as the optimists had hoped and the pessimists had feared.

The same can be said for the commercial statistics. Indeed, at the very time that such optimists as Repetti were stressing the expansion of Livorno's commerce, the local chamber of commerce was bombarding the central government in Flor-

TABLE 11
Population Characteristics City of Livorno, 1814–1850

Year	Population	Marriages	Births	Deaths	Population change	Births over deaths	Immigration over emigration
1814	50,055	478	1,546	1,929	− 264	− 383	+ 119
1815	57,446	472	1,830	1,498	+ 7,391	+ 332	+ 7,059
1816	54,309	497	1,945	1,741	− 3,137	+ 204	− 3,341
1817	56,995	435	2,013	2,668	+ 2,686	− 655	+ 3,341
1818	59,914	586	2,478	1,814	+ 2,919	+ 664	+ 2,255
1819	62,237	532	2,551	1,677	+ 2,323	+ 874	+ 1,449
1820	62,827	602	2,623	1,999	+ 590	+ 624	− 34
1821	64,015	527	2,630	1,775	+ 1,188	+ 855	+ 333
1822	64,950	545	2,603	1,576	+ 935	+ 1,027	− 92
1823	65,560	487	2,583	1,624	+ 610	+ 959	− 349
1824	66,594	536	2,590	1,733	+ 1,034	+ 857	+ 177
1825	67,698	538	2,634	2,316	+ 1,104	+ 318	+ 786
1826	68,631	532	2,703	1,904	+ 933	+ 799	+ 134
1827	69,348	586	2,675	1,933	+ 717	+ 742	− 25
1828	70,489	553	2,724	1,758	+ 1,141	+ 966	+ 175
1829	72,342	534	2,670	2,580	+ 1,853	+ 90	+ 1,763
1830	73,066	543	2,752	2,151	+ 724	+ 601	+ 123

TABLE 11—Continued

1831	73,775	531	2,163	+ 709	+ 578	+ 131
1832	74,522	525	2,228	+ 747	+ 468	+ 279
1833	75,421	558	2,248	+ 899	+ 464	+ 435
1834	74,291	591	2,070	− 1,130	+ 803	− 1,933
1835	76,412	511	3,440	+ 2,121	− 816	+ 2,937
1836	76,552	680	2,078	+ 140	+ 617	− 477
1837	76,346	584	2,862	− 206	− 158	− 48
1838	78,099	550	1,950	+ 1,753	+ 714	+ 1,039
1839	79,149	526	1,860	+ 1,050	+ 799	+ 251
1840	79,912	566	1,979	+ 763	+ 725	+ 38
1841	78,601	550	2,195	− 1,311	+ 418	− 1,729
1842	78,463	541	2,039	− 138	+ 554	− 692
1843	79,677	610	2,090	+ 1,214	+ 674	+ 540
1844	80,056	668	2,089	+ 379	+ 606	− 227
1845	80,365	648	1,843	+ 309	+ 906	− 597
1846	82,009	647	1,825	+ 1,644	+ 1,158	+ 486
1847	82,788	736	2,634	+ 779	+ 9	+ 770
1848	82,827	727	2,473	+ 39	+ 601	− 562
1849	81,582	741	2,218	− 1,245	+ 792	− 2,037
1850	83,537	608	2,218	+ 1,955	+ 820	+ 1,135

Source: P. Bandettini, *La Popolazione della Toscana dal 1810 al 1959*, p. 181.

ence with memorials stressing the competition that Livorno was facing from other ports—particularly Genoa—and warning the government that if all existing charges on goods were not abolished and the port made truly free, Livorno would increasingly lose place to its rivals.[72]

In part the position of the merchants in the chamber of commerce was a prudent one, and their dire predictions should not be taken too literally. Regardless of the economic situation of Livorno, it would never have been a wise policy for the merchants to emphasize their prosperity, thus alerting the secretary of finance in Florence to new sources of tax revenue.[73] Rather, sound counsel advised that the chamber consistently place in evidence the poverty of the merchant community, bring pressure to bear for the elimination of as many charges as possible, and urge the government to maintain and develop the physical facilities of the port.

Underlying the demands of the chamber of commerce, however, was the basically unfavorable economic situation in which commerce operated in this period. A drop in prices and profit margins in all ports was caused by the tremendous increase in production—in both agriculture and manufactured goods—and the greater facility in moving goods from producer to consumer, combined with the increase in the general volume of commerce.

Manufactured goods set the trend.[74] The fall of Napoleon and the sudden cessation of hostilities created an explosion of speculative enthusiasm in British business circles. With the opening of continental ports after eight years of blockade, both large and middling business interests felt that fortunes could be made by responding to the pent-up demand for British manufactured goods. The productive capacity of the metallurgical and textile industries had been absorbed during the war years with producing arms and uniforms for Great Britain and her allies, and they were now turned once again to the production of consumer goods. Manufactured items that had accumulated in warehouses during the blockade years were suddenly thrown onto the consumer market. In 1815 the value of British exports rose to an unprecedented 51.6 million pounds sterling, and speculators felt that the rise would continue.

But the capacity of European and American markets to absorb this flood of exports was soon revealed as inferior to prediction. After the most immediate needs of foreign consumers were met, much of the exported merchandise remained unsold. By 1816, the total value of exports had already fallen to 41.6 million pounds sterling. The famine that struck Western Europe in this period because of the rise in the price of foodstuffs made the sale of British manufactured products still more difficult.

Pessimistic reports flooded the Board of Trade in London from consuls stationed throughout Britain's commercial empire. Typical of these reports were the dispatches of John Falconar, the British consul in Livorno. In his dispatch summarizing British commercial activity in the port in 1816, Falconar remarked that cargoes imported from Great Britain and Ireland in the year totaled 124, while cargoes moving in the opposite direction amounted to only 16. Of the imports, the vast majority consisted of British manufactured goods (chiefly from Manchester and Glasgow), about which the consul sadly remarked, "I am sorry to state [these] have been sold at such prices as, in many instances, to produce a loss instead of a profit to the shipper."[75] In 1817 imports fell to 79 cargoes, and exports rose to 55. But the market, Falconar reported, remained glutted with British manufactured goods, a situation made more difficult by the closing of the old escape valve for these products into Austria.[76]

After 1821 the situation would improve, and production of manufactured goods would better reflect the capacity of the market to absorb its products. But the very anarchistic organization of production and commerce in Britain would prevent any satisfactory, permanent solution to the problem. Throughout the period the situation facing British manufactured products would be one of low prices and profit margins and periodic crises of overproduction, resulting in fresh price declines, business failures, and mass unemployment.

A similar situation existed in the grain trade. In the period after 1815 the volume of cereals in the European market increased considerably. Technical improvements in agriculture, good weather, and the pull of an expanding consumer market were undoubtedly all factors in increasing the quantity of grain arriving in the markets of Western Europe. The most important single factor, though, was the opening of the Black Sea and the rich cereal-producing areas of Southern Russia to European commerce. The first step had been taken with the Treaty of Kutchuk Kainaidji (1774), which had opened the Black Sea and the Straits of Bosphorus to Russian shipping, a concession that ten years later was also extended to the Austrians.[77] Only with the establishment of peace in Europe, though, was Russian grain sent to European markets in massive, regular quantities.

With the growth of production and availability came a decline in price. From 1818 to 1847, even in years of mediocre harvest or momentary political or economic uncertainty, grain prices never returned to the level reached in the period before the French Revolution or during the famine years of 1814–1817.[78] Unfortunately, it is difficult to measure in detail this decline in grain prices on the wholesale market of Livorno, as no official government price figures exist for Livorno and the price series that I have constructed is based on incomplete and not entirely reliable figures extracted from the local *Giornale di commercio* (see table 12).[79]

Drawing on figures from other sources, however, enables me to provide a series that is more rounded and reliable, at least in its general configuration. The state archive in Florence contains some early miscellaneous copies of Livorno's commercial journal which indicate that the price of soft wheat in the early weeks of 1815 had risen to 30 lire per sack.[80] Antonio Zobi reported that at the peak of the famine the price of grain reached 63 lire per sack.[81] Needless to say, the averages that we have constructed from prices in the *Giornale di commercio* never approach these levels. At the beginning of our series, in the mid-1820s, grain prices reached rock bottom. They recovered briefly during the period of political and social unrest at the end of the decade and then went into a new slump in the 1830s. The period 1839–40 marked a new period of recovery, but the years from 1841–1847 witnessed another drop in the price level.

Incomplete and untrustworthy as they are, the figures drawn from the *Giornale di commercio* are roughly equivalent to the more solidly grounded Florentine price series constructed by Bandettini.[82] Here, too, the year 1816 provides the major peak, with minor price recovery taking place briefly at the end of the twenties and thirties and during the period of general famine in the late 1840s (see table 13).

The decline in grain prices was reflected in the deflation of other important items in Livorno's commerce. Two of them, coffee from Santo Domingo and English cotton thread (*cottoni fillati inglesi*), are analyzed by year in the following list:

| | Price[83] | |
Year	Coffee (Santo Domingo)	Cotton thread (England)
1822–23	21.9	24.5
1824–25	12.3	20.7
1825–26	11.7	21.5
1827–28	9.0	16.7
1829–30	7.4	17.0
1831–32	13.5	15.5
1833–34	12.0	18.0
1834–35	10.6	18.0
1837–38	47.5	125.6
1838–39	51.5	127.2
1840–41	49.0	103.6
1842–43	38.7	92.3
1847–48	41.0	92.3
1848–49	34.5	92.0

The general decline in price levels would prove more important than any shift in the port's commercial activity in determining Livorno's economic and social relationships in the period following the restoration of the grand ducal regime. It would fix in large part the relationship of the mer-

TABLE 12

Sample Grain Prices Drawn from the Current Price Listings of the *Giornale di Commercio* (Livorno)[a]

SOFT WHEAT (*Grani Teneri*)

| Year | Number of listings | Tuscan | | Odessa | Egypt |
		White	Red (second quality)	(first quality)	(white and red)
1823–24	12	16.16	12.83	11.66	7.33
1826–27	16	18.71	14.31	13.67	8.40
1828–29	17	23.54	19.67	20.25	14.50
1830–31	8	20.31	18.56	16.68	NL*
1832–33	8	20.31	18.00	13.31	NL
1834–35	8	17.75	15.12	13.06	NL
1837–38	9	19.00	16.50	13.00	9.00
1839–40	9	20.22	18.61	15.77	12.00
1841–42	7	17.25	15.39	14.78	9.57
1842–43	9	16.00	15.00	12.00	7.38
1847–48	9	18.61	17.38	15.61	11.50

TABLE 12—continued

HARD WHEAT (*Grani Duri*)

| Year | Number of Listings | Tanarok | | Odessa |
		First quality	Second quality	
1823–24	12	13.66	12.66	12.66
1826–27	16	15.82	12.81	12.87
1828–29	17	25.50	23.50	22.50
1830–31	8	17.21	15.84	14.93
1832–33	8	14.46	13.62	13.71
1834–35	8	16.87	NL	14.50
1837–38	9	13.00	12.50	12.50
1839–40	9	16.77	14.88	15.33
1841–42	7	15.50	NL	13.25
1842–43	9	13.50	NL	11.75
1847–48	9	16.94	15.94	15.44

* [No Listing]

a Prices are in Tuscan lire per sack (73.0986 liters) and represent the average of the listings in December and January of the years cited.

TABLE 13

AVERAGE ANNUAL WHOLESALE PRICES OF
FIRST-QUALITY GRAIN ON THE FLORENTINE MARKET[a]

Year	Price	Year	Price	Year	Price
1815	40.89	1827	23.11	1839	23.07
1816	44.36	1828	22.83	1840	20.12
1817	42.10	1829	23.98	1841	17.93
1818	29.93	1830	19.82	1842	19.38
1819	27.15	1831	21.78	1843	19.20
1820	25.48	1832	21.90	1844	18.71
1821	25.97	1833	19.03	1845	19.16
1822	23.10	1834	18.61	1846	21.84
1823	21.07	1835	17.08	1847	25.15
1824	17.60	1836	16.46	1848	20.74
1825	15.94	1837	19.85	1849	20.50
1826	18.35	1838	20.51	1850	18.39

[a] Prices are expressed in new Italian lire per hectoliter. Twenty-five lire
fiorentine are equivalent to twenty-one lire nuove. P. Bandettini, *I Prezzi sul
mercato di Firenze dal 1800 al 1890*, p. 9.

chants with the central government and with bankers, commercial agents (*mezzani*), and port workers (*facchini*) with
whom they had regular contacts. At a time of falling prices,
traditional economic and social relationships could no longer
be automatically maintained. Merchants could be expected to
challenge vigorously residual charges on goods moving into
the port, to demand the establishment of institutions providing easier access to credit, and to contest the normal charges
paid to their commercial agents and to dockworker companies
in the city. An increase in the commercial movement of the
port per se, then, was not an unmistakable sign of prosperity
at times of falling prices. Indeed, it might serve merely to

mask an underlying reality of shrinking profits, dried-up sources of credit, lack of currency, and a resultant uneasiness in the merchant community. Having sketched the patterns of Livorno's commerce and its commercial, demographic, and pricing movements, therefore, it is time to turn to the response of the merchant community to the economic and social environment in which it operated.

PART TWO

The Merchant Community

CHAPTER TWO

The Merchant Community: Social Structure, Economic Values, Institutions

Having traced the complex patterns of Livorno's commerce and the movement of the city's population in the early nineteenth century, we must now broaden the scope of the investigation. An intelligible presentation of the response of the merchant community to the economic and social situation of the city can come only after an examination of the community itself: What was its structure, and what aspects served to divide it or to give it a sense of cohesion and unity? To what degree did the values of the merchant community stimulate efforts for social and economic reform in the city? And finally, what key institutions provided the leverage that would make it possible to change the environment in which the merchants lived and carried on their business?

Social Structure and Community

With regard to Livorno's social structure, innumerable observers have commented on the city's vibrant economic and social character and its atypical position in a predominantly agrarian and aristocratic state. By the early seventeenth century, immigrants were already being drawn to the city by the evident signs of its potential for prosperity

65

and, perhaps, by stories of men who reputedly had arrived in the city dirt poor, begun operating as peddlers or worse, and ultimately succeeded in opening a small business, buying a house and ship, and eventually passing for members of the city's commercial elite.[1] The examples of Giovanni Bertolli and Domenico Scotto were not representative (the former was probably even apocryphal), but both served to reinforce the impression of the city as bestowing the possibility of wealth and rapid social mobility.[2] Bertolli, the story ran, had begun in 1774, wandering through the streets of Livorno in rags selling fish. A cache of jewels is said to have been deposited with him by two itinerant Jesuits from Spain and never reclaimed, making Bertolli one of the richest men in Tuscany. Scotto's rise was less fortuitous: as the owner of a small tavern, he had won the concession of supplying wine to the Russian fleet at enormous profit.

Linked to a belief in the possibility of unhampered social mobility was a sense of Livorno's unique character within the Tuscan state. James Fenimore Cooper contrasted the capital of the state with its principal commercial city, noting in particular the special spirit of enterprise that gripped everyone entering the port.[3] The noise, rush, and stench, the governor argued in responding to the complaint of a foreign consul, were common to any vibrant commercial center and afflicted even persons universally acclaimed as privileged.[4] Henry James noted that although Livorno was in Tuscany, it was not very Tuscan.[5] Giuseppe Mery called Livorno a place where one could go to breathe freely—where one's self-esteem could have full play and one need no longer feel mortified before the monuments of the great nor belittled by family names crowned with five centuries of admiration.[6]

Mobility and atypicality did not mean the absence of social hierarchy and division. In this respect Livorno possessed status gradations common to many commercial centers.[7] At the peak of the social scale were a small number of nobles and men of citizenship rank (*cittadinanza*), whose social position gave them tax privileges and the right to staff municipal offices. Next in rank came the large bankers and wholesale merchants. Though generally more wealthy than the nobles and citizens, they were—with the exception of those who were Jews—almost entirely of foreign extraction. In the seventeenth and eighteenth centuries, this made them ineligible for municipal office. This group had traditionally provided the capital and enterprise for Livorno's predominant commerce of deposit and transshipment. At the pinnacle of this group were the foreign consuls, who facilitated the commercial affairs of their respective nations as well as engaging in commerce themselves. As we shall see, a clear division separated this group from the so-called merchants of second order. This latter group included many local merchants engaged in regional trade or in dealing with merchandise purchased from the principal wholesalers, and it also included those local shipowners who, in addition to their principal activity, engaged in modest commercial activity.

A clear line of demarcation separated wholesale merchants and bankers from merchants involved in retail trade. Undoubtedly, many large retail firms might be involved in wholesale operations. However, a legal stigma attached to retail commerce prevented such firms from enjoying credit status with the dogana (the customhouse), hence making them ineligible to serve in the city's chamber of commerce.[8] The stigma appears to have had a social dimension as well[9]— few, if any, shopkeepers can be found in the membership lists of the city's philanthropic associations.

A group somewhat apart were the *mezzani*, or commercial agents. According to regulations laid down in the second half of the eighteenth century, this group controlled important mediating services in the port, drawing up contracts for the sale and shipment of merchandise as well as facilitating currency transactions. *Mezzani* were therefore subject to strict government supervision.[10] The status of the individual *mezzano* depended in part on what operations he was authorized to perform (currency transactions were the most lucrative field, and the number of *mezzani* allowed to engage in this activity was strictly limited), on the volume of his affairs, and on his degree of independence from any specific commercial firm (many *mezzani* were virtually subordinate employees of a single firm). The occupation was considered an important point of entry into the merchant community, as it enabled one to gain experience in the commercial operations of the city without a large investment of capital.[11] Be this as it may, I have discovered no instance in which a *mezzano* moved up into the rank of the bankers and large wholesale merchants.[12] As a *mezzano*, an individual was strictly forbidden to engage in commercial affairs on his own behalf because it was feared that this would jeopardize his role as an impersonal mediator—though given the number of complaints, this regulation appears to have been continually abused.[13]

The place of manufacturers in Livorno's social hierarchy has generally been misinterpreted. Most historians of the city consider the position of merchant and manufacturer to have been in fundamental opposition.[14] Increasingly, they argue, capital tended to shift out of a commercial sector in full crisis into the development of industries serving the Tuscan market. All of this served to exacerbate conflicts over economic policy. Merchant capitalists remained firmly attached to the free-trade policy of the past, while manufacturers pressed for tariff protection and for free access to the markets of the hinterland (in effect, for the abolition of Livorno's free-port status and the absorption of the city into the Tuscan state).[15]

While perhaps compelling from the point of theory, this interpretation fails to take into account the particular relationship of commerce and manufacturing in the free port. Far from being in conflict, the two sectors tended to complement each other. Livorno's major manufacturing concerns—coral, clothing, liquor, candy, and furniture—prospered precisely because of their ability to introduce the necessary raw materials, rework them, and export the finished products without having to pay the tariffs of the Tuscan state.[16] The fastest-growing industry in Livorno in the first half of the nineteenth century, shipbuilding, as well as the subsidiary concerns of ropemaking and sailmaking, were also dependent on the privileges of the free port for the importation of their raw materials (pitch, timber, cotton, and hemp) and for the sale of their finished products at competitive prices. Evidence of direct investments in the manufacturing concerns in the city by the commercial elite is relatively rare and is limited primarily to shipbuilding and several manufacturing concerns connected with the grain trade (milling and the preparation of hardtack).[17] However, this evidence suggests not a flight of capital from commerce to industry but an attempt to develop sectors that would complement the predominant commercial activity of the port and place it on a more secure base. Far from there being an antithetical division between merchants and manufacturers, then, these groups tended to complement each other. In the course of this essay we shall see that this general harmony of interests went beyond the economic sphere to include a common concern for the social stability of the city.

Two other groups, professional men and semiskilled porters, must enter into any discussion of the merchant community in Livorno. With regard to the professions, one should note at the outset the relative absence of intellectuals and clergy, who tended to reside in the older, aristocratic centers of the state. Doctors and lawyers, however, played an important role in the social life of the city in the early nineteenth century. Several aristocratic and many high commercial families sent members into the professions. As a group these people not only served the needs of the city's commerce but also actively participated in the effort for economic and social reform, especially in attempts to improve the health and education of the lower classes. While the semiskilled porters represented the lowest rung of the merchant community, they were not at the bottom of society. Below them were the unemployed, vagrants, and criminals, toward whom the merchants demonstrated only dim perception and much fear. In effect, the porters represented a labor aristocracy, with a disciplined trade and definite job security. To the merchants, the porters represented the lowest stratum of society with which they could feel a definite community of interest (since both were dependent on the commercial activity of the port) and among whom they could hope to receive understanding and support. It was by this group that the merchants hoped to see the virtues of labor and thrift demonstrated, and it was not by chance that the merchants turned to the porters in attempting to quell revolutionary agitation in the city in 1848.

What emerges from this brief discussion of Livorno's social structure is, predictably, the picture of a variety of social groups existing in a rough hierarchy and attached in different ways to the predominant commercial activity of the port. I have presented merely a rough outline, ignoring a host of other occupations (artisans and tradesmen) active in the economy of Livorno. I have also not examined systematically the issue of social mobility, because given the haphazard way in which vital statistics in the period were taken and also the chaotic state of their current preservation, this would have produced few concrete results.

Certainly, even a general overview of the social history of Livorno during the early nineteenth century would show that the dramatic cases of social mobility cited earlier were exceptional: even in that relatively open society, it must have been difficult to move very far up the social ladder. Nevertheless, despite the relative fixity of the social divisions, it is important to stress the community of interests which served to link together members of different social ranks. In the course of this study I will demonstrate the consciousness of this sense of community and show how the commercial elite of Livorno attempted to strengthen its bonds through conscious efforts at economic and social reform.

The Process of Assimilation

It must be remembered that we are dealing with a commercial elite that was traditionally foreign in character and allegiance. For this reason, a sense of community could only follow a process of assimilation whereby foreigners were somehow integrated into the economic and social life of the zone.

Many have attempted to sidestep the whole problem of assimilation by arguing simply that with the weakening of Livorno's predominant commercial position, the foreign merchant elite tended to leave the city. These people say that this elite gave place to a more modest stratum of Tuscan merchants, who somehow were more sympathetic to the economic and social needs of the city and its hinterland. Certainly, the concerns voiced by the so-called Italian nation and by Tuscan merchant Giuliano Ricci in memorials advanced to the central government in 1757, arguing that Livorno's future would depend principally on the economic development of the Tuscan hinterland, have lent some support to the view that the place of foreign merchant firms greatly diminished in the first half of the nineteenth century.[18]

However, even Mario Baruchello, one of the principal advocates of the existence of a commercial crisis in the period, admits that while some nations had almost totally abandoned the city, others still considered it an important commercial base in the Mediterranean.[19] In 1858, Luigi Torelli noted that of the commercial firms in Livorno with a capitalization of 1 million francs, six were Tuscan, eight were Greek, and ten were from other states.[20] Certainly, the composition of the chamber of commerce in the period after 1814 continued to reflect the cosmopolitan character of the commercial elite. A regulation drafted in 1815 called for the continued distribution of seats in the chamber by nation—four Tuscans, six from "the nations most representative of the commerce of the city"; (including two English, one Greek, and one northerner [*Oltremontagni*]), and two were Jews.[21]

The issue, however, was more than one of formal nationality. With the continued importance of a commerce of deposit and transshipment in the city's economy, even the success of a Tuscan firm would be defined largely by the degree to which it comported itself as a foreigner—that is, possessed the requisite business contacts and sources of capital outside the state which alone could make this commerce viable.[22] Commissions from foreign firms remained an important component of Livorno's commercial operations throughout the first half of the nineteenth century, a fact closely related to the growing importance of the grain trade.

This fact is strikingly evident in the business history of the important local firm of Michelangelo Bastogi and his son, Pietro. Founded in 1840, the firm immediately inspired the confidence of foreign firms because of Bastogi's reputation, and as a result it received many commissions. During this period the firm's profit was based largely on these commissions, which paid only 3 percent on the value of the transaction but required no direct investment of the firm's capital and therefore virtually no risk. In its first year of operation, Michelangelo Bastogi and Son returned 6 percent on its actual investment (the usual rate was 4%) in addition to a sizable net profit. In the famine year of 1847, the firm received on commission the freight of 117 ships carrying grain and other comestibles. Its return on these commissions alone (at 3%) totaled 440,000 francs.[23]

An exploration of investments in real estate and of the procurement of noble or citizenship rank will be particularly useful in demonstrating the assimilation of the commercial elite into the economy and society of the zone. A close study of both areas will serve not only to demonstrate the nature of this assimilation but also to correct certain distortions concerning its character and motivation and its relationship to the economic situation of the port.

Those who see the early nineteenth century as a period of decline for Livorno's traditional commerce of deposit and transshipment generally interpret merchant investments in real estate, as well as in other areas, as an almost automatic response to commercial crisis.[24] With the decline of the port's traditional activity, the argument runs, merchants sought to secure their capital by investing it in other sectors of the economy. Real estate investments appeared especially attractive. The demographic expansion of the city and the extension of the free-port zone placed property at a premium and stimulated the active participation of merchant capital.

The view of a shift of capital from commerce to real estate is not without foundation, though the motives cited for that shift must be questioned at the outset. In 1834 a committee that had been empowered to study the commercial situation of the city concluded in a cryptic note that merchants had indeed drawn a large portion (*una gran massa*) of their capital from commerce to invest it in real estate and other areas. Strangely, the committee saw this phenomenon as a manifestation of commercial crisis but at the same time argued that commercial operations still proved a more useful form of investment (one assumes both to the individual investor and to society as a whole) than other areas, which the committee called "of little use" (*di poca utilità*).[25]

The replacement of the old port charges with a direct tax levied on the merchant community of the city—the principal result of the committee's efforts—did not appear to improve the situation. The records of the chamber of commerce in the ensuing period contain the protests of several people defining themselves as property owners and arguing that as they are no longer primarily engaged in commerce, they should be exempted from the commercial tax.[26] In 1841, when the whole tax system in the port city once again came under study, the governor remarked that the heavy levies imposed on the principal firms in the city (8,800 lire for those placed in the first class) were forcing some of them either to move elsewhere or to transfer their capital to real estate, solely to avoid paying this tax.[27] In all of this it is important to note that the fundamental cause of the shift in capital from commerce to real estate was not considered the result of a commercial crisis per se but rather of a specific system of taxation which, as we shall see, was capable of modification and reform.

But a clarification of the motives behind the transfer of capital from commerce to real estate requires consideration of more fundamental structural issues. For example, in what areas of real estate did merchants tend to invest? To what degree did this investment reflect the urbanizing process of the port city, the city's relationship with the surrounding countryside, and shifts in the pattern of development within the city itself?

At first glance the economic links between Livorno and the surrounding countryside appear extremely tenuous. Agriculture in the plain and hills adjacent to the city suffered under several liabilities. Sandy soil and a dry summer climate hampered the spread of vegetation and made it unfeasible to cultivate important subsidiary crops such as corn and beans. While grain and fodder (*biade*) plantings produced a respectable yield in certain areas of the zone, the nature of the soil and climate restricted the total yield. This factor combined with the general decline in grain prices made the agricultural area of production an increasingly unattractive investment. In the fifteen years after 1810, local production had met on the average only one-sixth of the needs of the inhabitants of the zone, far below the average for Tuscany as a whole.[28]

With regard to oil and wine—together, increasingly the mainstay of Tuscan commercial agriculture—the situation appeared little better. Olive groves dotted the hills of Montenero to the south of Livorno and provided a product of good quality. These groves, however, were not extensive and produced a yield far below the needs of the local population. As for wine, the salt air of the coastal zone tended to produce grapes of low resistance, suitable primarily for making a young table wine for ordinary consumption.

The one major bright spot in agricultural production in the area was fruit, for while the salt air proved harmful for wine it proved excellent for fruit, producing a product of distinct flavor. The expanding population of the zone, coupled with the consistent needs of the mercantile population, insured a continuous demand for this product and provided a secure profit to the cultivator. For this reason, fruits (along with vegetables) "were by preference cultivated in the environs of the city and provided a revenue which was continuous and secure."[29] It is small wonder that the descriptions of farms and villas outside the city walls noted that important parts of the property were given over to the cultivation of fruits and vegetables.[30]

What was the specific relationship of the merchant community to the agricultural activity of the surrounding countryside? Property assessment records of the community covering the thirteen-year period from 1821 to 1833 provide a valuable—though admittedly limited—source for examining merchant real-estate holdings in the area outside the city walls.[31] An analysis of these records indicates that for many merchant families an integral part of the family holdings was a villa (or, as the document often states, "a house used as a villa [*casa ad uso di villa*]" and adjacent land that was given over to gardens, fruit trees, and vines. From the detailed descriptions in the assessment records, many of these so-called villa properties appear to have been extremely modest, with a restricted area of land available for cultivation and a house that often appears to have been little more comfortable than the residence of a cultivator. Occasionally, as we shall see, the property could become more pretentious, a clear sign of aspirations for noble status.[32] For the most part, however, the attraction was probably more simple and immediate: cool, fresh air in the hills surrounding the city must have had the same appeal in the early nineteenth century as it does today, and the cultivation of vines, fruit, and vegetables undoubtedly served both to supply the family table and to provide a modest and secure income for the cultivator.

From the assessment records it appears that the villa property was a merchant family's most significant piece of real estate outside the city walls. Only occasionally do the records note that a merchant possessed a detached parcel of land in the countryside or a house in the older suburbs that had developed to the north of the city, on the road to Pisa. Really extensive tracts of land in the area surrounding Livorno tended to belong to noble families, to the church, or to the state, a result of custom and social pretension on the one hand and of the traditional fortress character of the city on the other.

Regrettably, because of the short time span of the extant assessment records it is not possible to concretely document the changing patterns of rural tenure in the merchant community. It remains difficult to assess, therefore, whether the purchase of villa properties was related to changes in the commercial situation of the city or whether it reflected a more constant aspect of taste in the merchant elite. I tend to support the latter view, and I see several indications of permanence even in the short series at our disposal. For example, only one of the many villas described in the assessment records was a new construction.[33] Most of the villas noted were contained either in listings of family property at the time of the death of the head of the household, or else (less often) they represented changes of title within the family itself. Finally, with one exception, in those few cases in which title to a villa passed from one family to another both buyer and seller were merchants.[34] Thus, even in the short series available to us, the signs of permanence outweigh the signs of change, and villa properties appear to have had an important place in the holdings of many merchant families long before the onset of the so-called commercial crisis of the early nineteenth century.

Several factors appear to date these properties from the second half of the eighteenth century and to pinpoint as the motive for their development not the commercial situation of the city but specific dispositions of the government. According to Lando Bortolotti, maps drawn in the latter part of the eighteenth century indicate numerous villas under construction.[35] The process was undoubtedly stimulated by a government regulation in March 1780 which decreed that property in the area adjacent to the city walls was to be assessed no more than one-thirtieth of the total tax due from the community. As a result, property values being equal, the rural proprietor had to pay only from one-fifth to one-sixth as much property tax as did his urban counterpart.[36]

A second important disposition during the same period made it possible for Jews to acquire real property. This concession would prove extremely significant for the proprietorship of villa holdings, for in the early nineteenth century the Jewish community was the best-represented single group in the city, with eight of the sixteen villas noted in the assessment records clearly in the hands of its constituents.[37]

The merchant community, then, appeared to be a stable fixture in Livorno's rural landscape. Merchant investments in this area, however, were at best peripheral, for the bulk of the real property of this group was to be found not in the countryside or even in the enticing speculative area to the immediate south of the city but in the older quarters of the urban center.

Property transfers registered in the municipal tax records provide compelling evidence that the primary area of merchant investment lay in the houses and warehouses of the center city. As one might expect, the leasing and purchase of shops and warehouses occupy a predominant place in these records.[38] Qualitatively more impressive, however, are the frequent merchant acquisitions of large urban palaces. These palaces were generally four stories high each, with a cellar, attic, and spacious quarters for businesses, shops, warehouses, and several residences.[39]

More revealing of the extent of urban real-estate holdings in the hands of merchant families are the lists of real property drawn up at the time of the death of the head of the household and the transfer of title (and tax liability) to the legitimate heirs. The most striking example is that of the Abudarham family, which possessed no fewer than six large buildings in the old city and received an annual property tax bill of over 247 scudi, with all but approximately 10 scudi of this amount for property within the city walls.[40] The Bacri family reported title to three large buildings and many scattered urban holdings (warehouses and parts of buildings) and was taxed over 165 scudi, 148 of it for property within the walls.[41] To present a case-by-case listing of merchant real-estate holdings would be more tedious than informative. From consultation of the cadastral records, however, two principal facts emerge: first, that the predominant merchant investment in real property lay within the city walls, and second, that the major participants in real-estate investment both within and outside the walls were members of the Jewish community, a clear indication of the greater affinity of this group to the traditional patterns of real-estate investment in Livorno and the surrounding zone.[42]

This situation appeared to have already stabilized by the early nineteenth century, and it ultimately served to link merchant investments in real estate closely to the traditional activity of the free port. The principal holdings of the merchant community were concentrated in the following three areas of the old city: the southern zone around the synagogue (probably encouraged by government attempts in the second half of the eighteenth century to restrict Jewish residence to a single quarter), the central east-west axis running from the port to the Pisan gate, and the quarter known as Venezia Nuova. The latter area in particular provides convincing reasons for such a heavy investment of merchant capital in urban properties.

The quarter was designed at the end of the seventeenth

century on the site of the leveled central section of a gigantic fortress in the northern zone of the city, and it was called "Venice" because the terrain had to be consolidated with pilings and because the quarter's design included the three canals that had formed part of the old fortress. All was done to make Venezia Nuova comfortable and convenient for the city's commercial elite. The zone itself was constructed on two levels, street and canal. The canals facilitated the movement of goods from ships in the port to warehouses in the inner city. Small boats and barges brought the merchandise up the canals and deposited it in vast warehouses under the streets. When necessary, this merchandise could be brought up to street level on gigantic ramps (*scalandroni*) and worked or stored on the ground floor of the quarter's palaces. Given the rational character of the design, it is not surprising that the quarter quickly became the residence of the elite of the merchant community and the site of virtually all the foreign consulates.[43]

This traditional pattern of merchant settlement and investment, however, underwent some important changes in the first half of the nineteenth century. One reason for these changes was the gradual relaxation of government restrictions on construction in the adjacent suburbs, and another was the government's 1828 decision to relieve population pressure in the city's central area by opening a new gate (the future Porto Leopoldo) in the southern section of the wall and by leveling the adjacent bastion, called the Casone. These government actions helped to soften the fortress character of the old city and provided a fertile new area for development.[44] The new gate was opened in 1832, but new construction in the suburbs was already prodigious. The desire for increased personal comfort (e.g., more spacious and better-lighted abodes) was an obvious factor in stimulating development. With the leveling of most of the remaining fortifications in the mid-1830s and the utilization of the old moat (the Fosso Reale) for a navigation channel, the factor of commercial convenience also began to play an important role.

The response of the merchant community to the speculative

possibilities in this area newly opened to development is worthy of serious consideration. A comparison of the location of those who were assessed the highest amounts of family tax in 1830 and 1851 appears especially revealing. In 1830, 95 percent of these people lived in the old city. By 1851 more than 49 percent had moved outside the old limits of the city and had settled in the new quarters, with a clear preference for the zone of the leveled Casone and for the Via Leopolda, the street running from the Casone to the south.[45]

One should not, however, exaggerate the shift. The family tax included a range of social categories broader than the merchant community. As a corrective, a guide to the city in 1844 indicated that with the exception of the warehouses constructed along the old moat, members of the merchant community demonstrated a strong tendency to remain in the traditional commercial sections of the city.[46]

The assessment records provide a few clues about the nature of merchant settlement in the area of the Casone. Such settlement appears not to have been massive, at least in the early years following the opening of the new gate. Modest amounts of land (i.e., 1,000 to 4,000 *braccia quadrata*) in the area were purchased by members of several important merchant families—Mayer, Tedeschi, Castelli, Pate, Uzielli, and Alhaique.[47] A member of one of these families, Cristiano Mayer, soon constructed a new building on the site. If this example is any indication of the trend, however, the whole operation must have been modest, for the house consisted of only three floors, with simple living quarters on the second level and much of the rest of the space devoted to the manufacture of beer.[48]

Far more significant was the participation of two men on the fringes of the merchant community: Carlo Sansoni, an attorney in the city, and Giovanni Brandi, described as an impresario and work contractor.[49] In May 1830, Sansoni and Brandi together bought a total of eleven pieces of land in the area of the Casone from the government for over 112,000 lire.[50] In the ensuing years both men were actively engaged in buying more land and selling small parcels of it to those of more modest pretensions.[51] Noble families, such as the Malenchinis and the Michons, also made large profits by selling portions of their extensive holdings in the area.[52]

Because merchant real-estate investment was primarily located in the central city, the development of the suburbs in the 1830s must have appeared less an opportunity than a threat. The sudden appearance on the market of a vast number of new constructions, superior even to the needs of the city's growing population and at an attractive price, could not help but depress the value of the older dwellings. In June 1838 the civic magistrates were forced to discuss a rectification of values assigned to property in the central city in the cadastral survey, under the threat that if something were not done to bring the estimated revenue in line with actual income, "it would be better for them [the proprietors] to carry the keys to the commune and cede to it their unfortunate possessions."[53]

In summary, then, the real-estate investments of the merchant community were extensive but did not undergo dramatic changes in the first half of the nineteenth century. Certainly, changes were not commensurate with the onset of any so-called commercial crisis. These investments remained largely traditional—modest villa properties in the area to the south of the city and important holdings in the urban center. The newer speculative possibilities in the suburbs do not seem to have attracted large amounts of commercial capital.

Scattered evidence suggests that the merchant community in this period did make some important landed investments over a wider zone. Giovanni Baldasseroni, a minister of finance under Leopold II, remarked that large amounts of Livornese capital had been invested in land-reclamation projects in Cecina and Vada, on the Maremma plain.[54] Additional capital was invested in societies established for the development of the Tuscan subsoil.[55] Closer to home, in 1840 five members of the merchant community organized a limited-liability company for the purpose of purchasing ten hectares from Carlo Michon and constructing a large resort south of the city.[56] If anything, it was these investments rather than speculation on individual properties per se that seem to have caught the fancy of the merchant community in this period. The long-term, uncertain nature of the returns on these investments, however, made them more likely a complement to rather than a substitute for commercial activity.[57] They did indicate, nevertheless, that the community was giving consideration to the economic possibilities of the hinterland.

As investments in real estate tended to root the merchant community more firmly to the economy of the zone, the process of assimilation was strengthened from another direction: the merchant elite tended to adopt noble and citizenship rank in the city and thus added honorific status and important functions within the municipal government to its predominant economic position in the port.

On the whole, aristocratic traditions were not deeply rooted in Livornese society. In the nineteenth century the city still possessed the character of a new commercial emporium, more suited to entrepreneurial activity than to the refined pleasures of the post-Renaissance aristocracy. Villas dotted the hills outside the city, but few possessed the grandeur of their counterparts in Pisa or Florence, cities where an important section of the local nobility preferred to spend its time. A reflection of Livorno's character is that it obtained an indigenous nobility relatively late. The first noble patent in the city was granted in 1768. Only 41 families were elevated to noble rank there during the eighteenth century, with 126 more so elevated during the period from 1800 to the fall of the Lorenese dynasty in 1859.[58] The city achieved patrician status only in 1816, finally joining the seven other major cities in Tuscany which possessed the right to elevate the more long-standing and worthy members of the nobility to a special rank.[59]

Noble status, however, was not merely honorific. Many municipal offices, including those of the *gonfaloniere* (head of the municipal administration) and of two *priori* (councillors), had required officeholders to possess noble patents. In this respect, the waiving of municipal land taxes for officeholders was considered less a status distinction than a form of payment for services rendered. Indeed, the necessity of staffing municipal offices in a city that had become the second most populous in Tuscany served to increase the tempo of noble patents and to stimulate the gradual assimilation of the commercial elite into the noble ranks.

This process, however, did not occur suddenly. In 1818 municipal officials had complained about the restricted number of noble families remaining in the city. Some former nobles had transferred their residence (and part of their property) to more aristocratic centers; others had died without direct heirs or had lost their possessions in the turbulent period of foreign occupation and were thus incapable of holding office in the municipal magistracy. The restricted number of nobles in the city appeared especially serious because, by law, noble priors could not serve more than two consecutive terms. Beyond practical considerations, though, the magistrates argued that the whole situation reflected badly on the honor (*lustro e decenza*) of a city that was the second largest in the kingdom and was the one most frequented by the residents of foreign nations.[60]

To remedy the situation, the magistrates proposed the elevation to noble rank of six families (the Bartolomei, Cipriani, Coppi, Danti, Papanti, and Rodriguez families). In making their recommendations, the magistrates repeatedly stressed the wealth of a given candidate and emphasized that this wealth had its primary source in real property. Occasionally, they also noted the intelligence of the family head and the family's links—generally through marriage—to a more elevated status.[61] On the whole, the primary justification for a nomination came less from a candidate's expected ability to fill a municipal office than from his purported affinity, through the nature of his wealth and his social bonds, to the kingdom's traditional aristocracy.

The magistrates, however, went even further and demonstrated a clear reluctance to permit the elevation to noble rank of anyone currently engaged in commerce. Of the candidates formally proposed, the most significant case was that of Pietro Cesare Papanti. The justification for Papanti's nomination was extremely elaborate: Papanti was married to a member of a noble family, possessed large landholdings, was a citizen of the city, and had already demonstrated great talent in filling numerous municipal offices.[62] However, Papanti exercised the profession of a commercial agent (*mezzano*), which both the magistrates and the governor considered "incompatible with the dignity [*onorificenza*] that one wished to impart [to noble rank]."[63] Only Papanti's distinguished qualities and his agreement to renounce his profession enabled him to win the nomination.

Although the governor and the magistrates could agree on the unsuitability of a mezzano for noble rank, they differed on the appropriateness of the more elevated sections of the merchant community. To the list of men nominated by the magistracy, the governor attempted to add three names (Dupony, Janer, and Giera). However, all three men were still engaged in commercial activity, and the governor was told by the magistrates that they were therefore unsuited to the honor. In the face of such stiff opposition, the governor remarked, he was forced to drop the whole issue and to content himself solely with concurring in the nominations already proposed.[64] Despite the necessity for intelligent personnel to staff municipal offices, then, it appeared clear that the magistrates were resolutely determined to prevent access to their rank from the commercial elite.

The situation had changed significantly by the mid-1830s, when it became evident that not only the more aristocratic members of the community were being admitted into the ranks of the nobility but merchants and professional people were being admitted as well. The major break occurred in 1836. In that year candidates who were approved for inscription into the aristocratic Golden Books included the merchant families Ghantur-Cubbe, Regini, Prat, Grant, Panajotti-Palli, Senn, Ulrich, Ott-Traxler, and Chelli, and the professional families Mochi and Sansoni.[65] In 1838 the government approved the elevation of several additional merchant families—the Bastogi, Castelli, Giera, Manteri, and Stub.[66] Some explanation and justification for a broadening of the social basis of recruitment to noble ranks is provided in a letter that accompanied the nominations of the local magistracy in 1838.[67] In a stylistically contorted passage, the *gonfaloniere* stressed the need to honor and preserve in the city important local families by awarding primary offices to those engaged in commerce or in other liberal professions. Such awards would be made only to families that were amassing significant possessions, distinguishing themselves by their wisdom and talent, and living in such a way as to be worthy of being received in the best society and of winning the recognition of the community.[68] Among the magistrates, it appears, there now existed at once a desire to root the existing talent and fortune of the commercial elite to the city and a recognition that both these groups were capable of living nobly and, through their elevation, of enhancing both the honor and dignity of the city.

That grants of nobility and citizenship (a lower dignity but one that provided access to certain municipal offices, with tax exemptions) were used consciously to root commercial wealth to the city appears evident in the favorable reception given to Graziano Cubbe's request for Tuscan naturalization in March 1833. On the surface, Cubbe's qualifications were not spectacular. He was unmarried and had settled in Livorno to handle the affairs of the family firm in Aleppo (in northern Syria). Cubbe had never opened a commercial establishment in Livorno but had used the facilities of a firm operated by a brother. He enjoyed a reputation for honesty but possessed no patrimony in the state. In recommending a favorable response to his request for naturalization, however, the governor stressed that it would be a way of insuring that Cubbe and, more importantly, the firm would remain in the city, for the brother too was unmarried and without heirs.[69]

If the desire to root commercial wealth to the city appears conscious, so too, it seems, were the aspirations of many merchants to adopt the accoutrements of nobility. Information provided by the auditor to support the request of Emmanuele Rodocanacchi for a noble patent noted not only that he possessed a personal patrimony of over 150,000 scudi but also that he was the proprietor of a "large, richly furnished house" and had recently acquired Giovanni Grant's palatial villa at Monterotondo, where he already possessed some land. Rodocanacchi also possessed a carriage and lived, the auditor stated, "under every other aspect in the manner of a noble or seigneur."[70]

The qualifications of another aspirant to noble status, Domenico Castelli, were perhaps less solid but were equally aristocratic. The first firm that Castelli opened in Livorno failed. After a period of absence he returned to the city around 1814 and opened another firm, which succeeded splendidly. The means of his success remained a mystery—many suspected that they were dishonorable—but from his wife he derived stature (*illustrazione*). In addition, Castelli had acquired a house and garden near the city and a farm farther out, and he had taken great pains in the education of his sole male offspring, applying for his admission to the College of the Tolomei in Siena, attended by many of the sons of the Tuscan nobility.[71] The combination of wealth (without consideration of its origins) and a decorous manner of life made the Castelli family equally worthy to receive a noble patent.

In the first half of the nineteenth century, then, the commercial elite of the port city gave clear signs of assimilation into the economy and society of the zone. Neither the real-estate investments of the merchants nor their aspirations for noble status, however, should be taken as evidence of their turning away from the dominant commercial activity of the port. Investments in rural property went back to the eighteenth century, to a period when Livorno's commercial position had not yet undergone serious challenge, and they absorbed only a minimal part of the merchant community's investment capital. Investments in urban real estate, while more important, served ultimately to complement the commercial activity of the free port. Similarly, the achievement of a noble patent did not represent a break with commercial activity but rather a desire on the part of the community to provide a social inducement that would tie merchant capital and talent more securely to the city's future. With regard to the relationship of social status and economic activity, it was significant that the tendency toward social assimilation was accompanied by a fundamental change in economic attitudes—that is, by a desire to break with the old pattern of monopoly and privilege in the Livornese economy (which, in any event, had been made no longer practicable by commercial changes in the post-Napoleonic period), to confront the situation of the port clearly, and to devise new solutions for the city's economic and social problems. Needless to say, an examination of this change in attitude and of the institutions that could translate it into concrete programs is fundamental for understanding and evaluating the reform activity of the merchant community in the first half of the nineteenth century.

Economic Values

In 1838, in compiling his *Dizionario geografico fisico della Toscana,*[72] Emanuele Repetti turned to Edoardo Mayer, director of Livorno's discount bank, for information on the commercial situation of the city. Mayer's response, interestingly, went beyond the usual cataloging of the port's commercial statistics to deal with an area that he considered far more significant—the change in economic attitudes in a community in which Mayer, as director of the city's most important financial institution, was an important observer and participant.[73] Mayer asserted that Livorno's commercial position had improved, but he based his view on changes in the mode of economic activity rather than on a demonstrated increase in the volume of commerce. Traditionally, said Mayer, most commercial activity in the city had remained in the hands of a few large merchant houses. In this situation commercial operations ran like clockwork. At a certain period each year, orders arrived from northern Europe for products from the Levant. The goods were then sent from the eastern Mediterranean to Livorno, distributed to the respective merchant houses, and shipped to the buyer—"Selling, buying, shipping, all was handled in the holy peace of monopoly."

However as Mayer noted, times had changed. While the wars of the French Revolution had brought excessive prosperity to a select group of merchant houses in the colonial trade for a brief period, they had ultimately plunged the entire city into depression. With the Restoration, however, commercial operations passed into a new phase. Commerce no longer possessed its former security and regularity, and the city not only suffered from the general decline of a commerce of deposit but also faced serious competition from a host of rival ports. Commercial operations could no longer be relied upon to run automatically, and both the government and the merchants would have to remain vigilant lest Livorno's commerce deteriorate further. One must struggle with rival ports, said Mayer, and win over the greatest amount of commerce possible by granting concessions and facilitating communication and exchange.

In the disappearance of the traditional situation of security and privilege, however, Mayer found not a source of despair but of challenge and hope. He expressed the fundamental change in merchant economic attitudes and the desire for a situation in which free, rational activity would have full sway, for, he concluded, "if man is called upon to show his worth through his activity, isn't this better than the . . . apathy of the past?"

Indications of this change in economic attitudes are present in a host of other sources. They form the basis, for example, of two articles on the commerce of Livorno written by Luigi Serristori and Giuliano Ricci[74] at approximately the same time as the Mayer-Repetti correspondence. For both Serristori and Ricci, the commerce of the port city had traditionally been the monopoly of a few large foreign houses. The mass of smaller merchants (*trafficanti di secondo ordine*) lacked the intelligence and initiative to correspond directly with foreign ports, and as a result these merchants were forced to do business through the principal local firms. Both authors agreed, however, that over the past twenty years the situation had changed dramatically. Serristori noted that not only were many of the approximately 280 wholesale merchant and banking firms in the city in direct contact with foreign firms but that some had also opened branch offices in other cities. This distribution of business activity to more hands had produced a vital, competitive situation in which the individual merchant had become more active, more intelligent, and endowed with a keener spirit of enterprise than in the past.[75]

To Ricci the signs of prosperous economic activity were present in many sectors—in the expansion of the city's population, in the vast number of new constructions, in the increase in the amount of operating capital, and in the minimal number of business failures. Also, to Ricci prosperity was the result not of the preservation of Livorno's traditional commercial position but of changes in the economic habits of the city's commercial elite. Cautious speculation and a growing propensity to save had enabled merchants to survive and even to prosper in more straitened economic circumstances.[76]

The interest in the moralistic writings of Benjamin Franklin provides another illustration of the change in economic attitudes among the city's commercial elite. Franklin was introduced to the Livornese public in 1829 through an extensive review of a French version of his autobiography and an edited Italian translation of *The Way To Wealth*.[77] The writings were featured prominently under the rubric "Morality" in several issues of the journal *Indicatore livornese*.[78]

The *Indicatore livornese* provided a natural forum for the series of articles on Franklin. In January 1829 it had been transformed from a single commercial sheet into an organ of conscious reform and had elicited the collaboration of a host of contributors, from younger, more progressive members of the city's commercial and professional elite to many prominent liberals in Tuscany and throughout the Italian peninsula. Much of the effort of the journal was directed toward literature and jurisprudence and toward keeping its readers informed of events that might have a bearing on the city's commercial activity. Several of the contributions, however, of which the Franklin articles are a prime example, sought to reinforce the change in economic attitudes in the community from a nostalgic longing for Livorno's privileged commercial position to the more progressive effort to introduce modern forms of business enterprise and to instill in the businessman an active and rational dedication to the pursuit of profit.[79]

The author of the articles was Sansone Uzielli, an important Jewish merchant banker and a prominent participant in the reform movement in the city.[80] The memoirs of Franklin, he began, could be summed up as "the manual of a man of good sense," for it was Franklin's moral character and not the force of a supreme intellect that had raised him to a level of wealth and fame which was especially notable given his humble origins. Consequently, the principal value of Franklin's work resided not in its extraordinary character but in its very commonplaceness, which insured that the reflections that it inspired arose naturally and were of clear, practical application. Uzielli held up several aspects of the autobiography for special praise. For example, he felt that Franklin's forthright assumption of responsibility for his misadventures was an important illustration of the principle that each man is his own providence and that success or failure depends not on the actions of others but on one's own moral behavior. Franklin's stress on the love of work as one of the most necessary qualities of social man served to correct a tendency in Italian education which saw work as a necessity only for the poor or the greedy. Uzielli particularly praised Franklin's scheme for arriving at moral perfection and urged every young man keen enough to distrust himself to have recourse to it as a system capable of producing good habits. Franklin's great contribution, he argued, was to consider morality as an applied science for the improvement of mankind. His most important accomplishment was to study the passions and to counter the normal weaknesses of human nature with a daily practice of private virtues and social duties.

Being an eminently imitable product of his own doctrines, said Uzielli, enhanced Franklin's effectiveness as a moralist. His biography was thus able to inspire in the common man not only admiration but emulation. Since every man considered himself capable of perceiving his true advantage, it did not appear difficult to achieve the merit of a man whose norms of moral conduct clearly served that end and were accessible to any understanding. Franklin's clear and simple explanation of his principles never failed to arouse sympathetic echoes, especially as the reader was preserved from a morass of abstruse argument and impossible ideals. All was calculated to provide a compelling, rational, and sure means for inculcating civic and economic virtues. Significantly, perhaps, for the appeal of the doctrine, the first local convert was Temistocle Pergola, a young apprentice in the firm of Vignozzi, which published the *Indicatore livornese*. Reading the biography of Franklin in the columns of the newspaper, Pergola said, produced in him intense excitement and inspired the years of hard work and the careful husbanding of resources which enabled him to pass from the ranks of a simple worker to that of an independent entrepreneur.[81]

The change in economic attitudes and the employment of new forms of business enterprise found reinforcement from another outside cultural force, the doctrines of Saint-Simon. Here the impact came less from the writings of the master himself than from those of his disciples, Enfantin, Bazard, and Rodrigues. The contact was made primarily through the diffusion of the books and journals of the school in the peninsula: the *Nouveau Christianisme* (Saint-Simon's last major work); *Doctrine de Saint-Simon, Exposition* (from a series of public conferences held in 1828–29); numbers of the *Producteur* and the *Organisateur*; and, especially, *Le Globe*, which was the most widely diffused Saint-Simonian periodical in the peninsula.[82] Tuscany was the major center of distribution. The writings arrived clandestinely by sea at Livorno and were shipped to the Corresponding Society of Gian Pietro Vieusseux in Florence, and they were then distributed along the coast of Liguria (toward Genoa) and into central Italy.[83] The line of distribution insured that the writings of the group could be most easily procured in Tuscany, and this coupled with the general tolerance of the Tuscan police made the state the greatest center of Saint-Simonism in Italy.[84] Still, the impact was primarily limited to the progressive upper classes (for reasons that will be discussed further on) and to specific points of cultural contact. In Tuscany the doctrines were disseminated by two principal centers, the Corresponding Society in Florence and the house of Professor Giuseppe Montanelli in Pisa.[85] The Corresponding Society provided a place where the writings were collected and could be read and discussed.[86] In Pisa, Montanelli had succeeded in opening a clandestine church of the new sect in 1832. Through his position at the university he was able to propagate the doctrine among the more progressive sectors of the student body, which included several young men from Livorno.[87]

Several aspects of Saint-Simonism were especially appealing to reformers in Livorno and Tuscany. First there were the economic aspects of the doctrine. The Saint-Simonians stressed the importance of economic organization. At the base of their doctrine lay the conviction that only through sound economic planning and the association of capital in large concerns could one achieve economic development and social stability. It was this emphasis that led the Tuscan moderate reformer Cosimo Ridolfi to term the spirit of association a healing ointment for all the economic and social disgraces of the state.[88] More specifically, Giuliano Ricci—a key figure in the reform movement in Livorno—criticized the fragmentary character of Tuscan economic production and the emphasis given to the small independent producer, which, he said, hampered the formation of large associations of capital and enterprise and made it difficult for Tuscan products to compete in a free, competitive market.[89]

The desire to achieve more modern forms of economic organization also tended to strengthen the critical posture of the younger generation toward the economic methods of its predecessors. A notable example was the letter written by a young Livornese Carlo Bini to his father Giulio in July 1836.[90]

One must confess [Carlo Bini noted in opening] that till now we have worked in a chance manner rather than according to a constant, uniform method . . . based on a clear sense of probabilities. We have seen the effects of this in the grave and frequent losses that we have suffered and in a certain languor which seems to me to have begun to infect our commercial operations. Given the nature of our affairs, it is essential to keep an eye on the goals, because the risk is great and the profit slight.

Following this rather general opening, Bini's remarks to his father became more personal:

Strange phenomenon of your character! On one side an extremely tenacious greed, a remorse for every loss, a remorse, I would say, almost for making the necessary expenses; on the other side lethargy, inertia, a postponement of things from one year to another, as if the things, and you and the men of this world were eternal.

Bini closed his letter with a recommendation of how one's affairs should be conducted, a recommendation that reflected the more progressive ideals of rationality and association.

> Here there is need for activity, for continual attention, for cooperation, since your efforts alone for one reason or another today no longer are sufficient. Your inertia, your postponing from one year to the next, your lethargic attitude toward things which require a heavy investment of energy ultimately can not produce but extremely grave effects.

A similar, though more impressionistic, sentiment was contained in Francesco Domenico Guerrazzi's criticism of the excessive isolation and greed of the merchant of the old style—"the bill-of-exchange-man, arid as a number, abhorring nothing that can be multiplied, a calculator of famine, plague and blood."[91]

The social implications of the Saint-Simonian doctrine were appealing as well. The Saint-Simonians laid great stress on the creation of a new order based on international peace and internal social harmony. The energy previously devoted to war would be channeled into peaceful efforts for the technological development of the world. Internally, the social order would be guided by the producers, principally the bankers, who would supply the sources of credit and would thus assume the function of economic planning. Internal social relationships would be both orderly and harmonious as the individualism and anarchy of the previous century gave way to a new era of cooperation and social progress. Society would be hierarchical and paternalistic: those with the requisite ability would be responsible for promoting the well-being of the class that was the most numerous and the most poor. This paternalism and the sense that both capitalist and worker belonged to the same social category (*les industriels*) would insure for both a set of common interests and common goals which would not only be favorable to the economic development of the society but would also be opposed to the continued power of the older privileged classes (*les oisifs*), which continued to consume without producing. To reinforce the stability of the new social organization, the leaders of society would reinforce a common set of values and provide the basis for harmonious social action. In addition, they would foster policies designed to give the proletariat the strongest interest in maintaining public order.

Such a program could not help but appeal to the Livornese elite, whether or not its members chose individually to adhere formally to the sect. Peace and unhampered control over one's affairs were, after all, two of the cardinal principles of the free port. The promotion of internal social harmony was obviously good for business. The Livornese elite, as we shall see, made every effort to develop educational and philanthropic programs designed to unite capitalist and worker, rich and poor, in a common cause through the development of common values and aspirations. In championing the development of commerce and manufacturing in the city, the merchants sought not only to increase their own profits but also to give the city's expanding population a way of integrating itself into the productive life of the city and of obtaining a stake in the maintenance of public order.

All this is not to say, however, that formal adherence to the sect was overwhelming. For all of its obvious appeal, certain aspects of the doctrine prevented it from becoming widely accepted, even among members of the business community who had aspirations for economic and social reform. The general hostility of the school to questions of political liberty and its rejection of laissez-faire (which led the Saint-Simonians to admire Great Britain's industrial preeminence but to scorn its political institutions) could not appeal to a group that saw its economic well-being bound up with a traditional conception of economic freedom (and that would push for the association of capital only on a voluntary basis) and that ideologically was already preparing the ground for the constitutional struggles of the late 1840s. Similarly, the Livornese moderates, like their counterparts elsewhere in the peninsula, could not accept the more radical formulations of the Saint-Simonian doctrine—for example, the abolition of inheritance and the establishment of highly centralized bureaucratic controls to insure that the capital resources of the society would be allocated to those who would best be able to employ them in the general interest. Finally, the religious aspects of the doctrine (propounded by Saint-Simon himself in his last work, *Nouveau Christianisme,* and carried to the absurd by his principal heir, Enfantin) could never appeal to a group that, for all of its liberalism, tended to retain its ties to traditional religion. Indeed, the appearance of a pope (Pius IX) who seemed at once orthodox and liberal would serve to destroy any residual appeal of Saint-Simonianism *qua sect.* Even Giuseppe Montanelli would move to the new camp and frantically endeavor to convince his former followers of the error of their ways. Nevertheless, as we shall see, despite all absurdities and limitations the Saint-Simonian principle of association as a way of insuring economic and social well-being would prove to be an important tool for stimulating and articulating the reform efforts of Livorno's merchant community.

Institutions

Two institutions in particular in the city would serve to reflect the new concerns of the merchant community and to aid in their articulation and implementation: the local academy, the Labronica, and the chamber of commerce.

The Labronica Academy was officially constituted in 1816 as a literary society dedicated to encouraging the cultural interests of its members.[92] Internal disputes over the activity and scope of the new organization, it seems, forced it to suspend its activity in 1829. In 1837, with the encouragement of the governor the academy was opened under new auspices.[93] In his opening address the academy's new president, Pietro Cercignani, indicated that the academy was adopting a more practical focus in line with the needs of society and the interests of its younger and more progressive membership, which included several leaders of the reform movement in the city. Under the old system, he remarked, members had presented papers on subjects more suited to enhancing the vanity of the speaker than to producing the utility that should result from individuals' joining together in a collective enterprise. Under its new program the academy pledged to promote commerce, industry, and any other public or private branch of the economy. Its ultimate goal was to contribute to the moral improvement and happiness of mankind.[94]

With this reformulation of its activities and goals, remarked the secretary of the academy, F. S. Orlandini, the Labronica had arrived at the highest stage in the development of academic culture in Europe, passing from the sterile and impractical arcadian phase to one that not only expressed a concern with practical affairs but also endeavored to systematically implement this concern.[95] The new, progressive aspect of the academy was clearly evident in the reports delivered at its first major session the following month: Giuliano Ricci's presentation of the actual state of industry in Italy, Pietro Bastogi's report on begging, and Zanobi Lattini's work on the economic and social utility of refining borax in Tuscany rather than shipping the raw material abroad.[96]

This is not to say that the new academy totally escaped the problems of its youth. Orlandini described sessions that made him want to bang his head on the wall and that led him in desperation to call the academy irretrievably juvenile.[97] Nevertheless, Orlandini's frustration was tempered by an understanding of the force of inertia that plagued municipal association, which made it necessary, he said, to expend ten times the effort to accomplish in provincial cities what one could accomplish with comparative ease in the capital.[98]

Despite its dramatic transformation, then, the Labronica Academy would serve largely as a symbol of the new practical orientation of the merchant community rather than as an agency for the implementation of specific programs and goals. For this one would have to turn to the chamber of commerce, the principal institution in the city charged with formulating the concerns of the merchant community and articulating them to the government.

The long and turbulent history of representative bodies of merchants in Livorno is not without interest, but to trace it in detail here would only prolong our discussion unnecessarily.[99] Suffice it to say that the various experiments attempted in this sector during the eighteenth century—specifically, the first Consiglio di Commercio, established by order of Cosimo III in 1717 and abolished in 1730, and the second Consiglio di Commercio, decreed by Francis I of Lorraine in 1746 and abolished in 1769—demonstrated the seemingly insurmountable barriers to establishing a viable representative body of merchants in the city. On the one hand, the merchants themselves proved extremely reluctant to delegate judicial power to a body composed in part of their competitors.[100] On the other hand, the central government—especially in an age of growing bureaucratic centralization—proved increasingly reluctant to delegate power to a group that represented specific local interests.[101] Only the initiative shown by the merchant community during the turbulent period of the first French occupation of the city in 1796 in organizing itself and in asserting its role as representative and protector of the city's commerce convinced the Tuscan government of the feasibility of establishing a chamber of commerce to represent the interests of the merchant community and to regulate specific activities related to the smooth functioning of its commercial operations.[102]

The government defined the structure and functions of the chamber of commerce in the period under study in a series of provisions promulgated in September 1815.[103] These provisions charged the chamber with advising the government of all questions relating to commerce, of suggesting improvements in existing regulations, and of proposing new laws or organizations to foster the commercial prosperity of the city and the state.[104] In addition, the chamber received some specific administrative functions: regulation of the Stanze dei Pubblici Pagamenti (the organization handling monetary exchanges between commercial firms in the city), participation in the supervision and appointment of the mezzani, and the advising of judges in cases involving commercial law and practice.[105]

In general, the specific powers granted to the chamber under the provisions of November 1815 appear circumscribed and bland. Its more general role as defender of the commercial interests of the city, however, would insure for the chamber an increasingly important function as a clearing-house for the sentiments and complaints of the merchant community and would make it a powerful agent for molding these opinions and bringing them to the attention of the policy-making bodies of the state. Indeed, as we shall see, the very skill with which it performed these functions would make the chamber of commerce the focus of much suspicion and ire on the part of government officials in Florence. At times of particular tension certain officials would ask whether the establishment of a representative body of merchants had been politic.[106] In general, though, the government sought merely to blunt the power of the chamber by restricting its ability to marshal public opinion in the community and to concentrate pressure on the central government.[107]

In addition to the unofficial attempts to extend its authority, the chamber succeeded in extending its official regulatory powers in two important new areas. In 1834 the chamber was given the responsibility of supervising the assessment and collection of the new *tassa di commercio* levied on the merchant community, becoming in effect the legal representative of that body.[108] In 1847 it was granted absolute regulatory power over the newly formed local companies of dockworkers, the *facchini di manovella* and the *facchini saccajoli*.[109] In both cases, the chamber would ultimately regret the authority and responsibility that it exercised over these sensitive areas.[110] That these additional grants of authority, however, enhanced its position as representative of the interests and attitudes of the merchant community was without question.

What was the internal structure of the chamber of commerce during this period, and how well can it be said to have represented the attitudes and interests of the merchant community? As in previous representative bodies of merchants in Livorno, deputies were selected in a way that would provide at least nominal representation to the dominant sectors of the city's commerce: the provisions of 1815 stipulated that four seats would be given to Tuscans, six to the "nations" most involved in the commerce of the city, and two to Jews.[111] In addition, to give a greater sense that the chamber represented general commercial rather than specific individual interests, the regulation emphasized that the chamber should be conceived as composed of twelve merchant houses rather than of twelve individuals. To reinforce this sense, deputies who were unable to be present at meetings could be represented by a partner or an assistant, provided only that the substitute was empowered to sign for the firm.[112]

Eligibility requirements insured that representation in the chamber of commerce would be limited to the more reputable wholesale merchants in the city. Needless to say, merchants involved in criminal or bankruptcy proceedings were not eligible.[113] In addition, the regulation stipulated that prospective deputies had to have been resident in Livorno for five years with a commercial firm and had to enjoy good credit with the customhouse.[114]

Within the limitations set by the eligibility requirements, how wide was the representation of the chamber? The government, it seems, hoped that the movement of deputies into and out of the chamber would be relatively steady. In a January 1819 dispatch, the government moved to eliminate the possibility of a deputy's perpetuating his stay in office by substituting fixed two-year terms for the previous procedure of determining the end of a deputy's term by lot.[115] To encourage the circulation of offices, ex-deputies would have to wait two years before again being eligible for office.[116]

A regulation, however, is no quantitative test of the degree of representation. In theory, given the number of posts and the term of office, a maximum of 216 members of the merchant community could have been selected to participate in the chamber of commerce between 1815 and 1850. In fact, from a careful calculation of the deputies present at the meetings of the body, it appears that 154 merchants were chosen to serve in this period. Considering that the number of merchants enjoying credit status with the customhouse was 144 in 1814 and 91 in 1847, the level of representation appears to have been quite high.[117] This impression is strengthened when one considers that 102 deputies—the vast majority—served for only one or two years and that the average length of service for all deputies in this period was 2.8 years. True, 24 deputies would remain in office from five to eleven years and, often serving as president or vice president of the body, would provide a sense of continuity in the deliberations. But at the same time the remaining 130 deputies, each serving from one to four years, would insure that the views of a wide spectrum of the commercial elite would find direct representation in the chamber.

That this was the desire of the deputies themselves appears evident from an examination of the selection process. The administrative edict setting up the chamber stipulated that one month before the end of each year the deputies currently in office would unite and vote on a slate of two candidates for every seat due to be vacated. This list, drawn up in order of the number of votes each candidate had received, was then transmitted to the secretary of state in Florence (via the governor), where half the candidates would be selected to hold office for the following two-year term.[118] When these lists are examined closely, however, it becomes evident that in fact candidates were selected strictly according to the priorities expressed in the votes of the chamber.[119] Under an elaborate selection procedure, then, the chamber of commerce was virtually a cooptive body. That membership in this body was open to a large segment of the merchant elite, albeit within the confines of a rigid set of eligibility requirements, can only serve to reinforce the sense of community which would provide the essential core for all aspirations of economic and social reform. How successfully the sense of community among the merchant elite was broadened to include the interests of other segments of the city's population will be examined in the following chapters.

PART THREE

Toward Reform—
The Economic Response
of the Merchant Community

CHAPTER THREE

Tariffs and Port Charges

From the early years of the Restoration, the merchant community in Livorno pressured the central government through the chamber of commerce to abolish those fiscal provisions that it felt were impeding the return of Livorno's commercial prosperity. Its areas of particular concern were tariff provisions restricting Tuscan imports and exports, and the various charges levied on goods entering the free port. The efforts of the chamber would serve to illustrate at once the cohesiveness and discipline of merchant opinion in Livorno and, ultimately, the responsiveness of the central government to the needs of the city's commerce. At the same time, however, these efforts would reveal important sources of tension and division within the merchant community itself, which have too often been either misinterpreted or simply ignored.

In pressing its case, the chamber found the government much more amenable to reforming existing commercial restrictions than to sanctioning a fundamental modification of the port charges. The revival of restrictions on imports and exports, after all, was relatively recent and was in conflict with a belief in the virtues of free trade which was held by the dominant sector of the state's intellectual and social elite. The Tuscan tariff of 1781 had enshrined this ideology by explicitly abolishing absolute prohibitions on the import, export, and transit of any merchandise.[1] Only under pressure of popular agitation had a new tariff in 1791 retreated from this position, particularly in the area of foodstuffs. That many of these restrictions were maintained after the restoration of the grand ducal government in 1814 was largely the result of an impulse on the part of the government to return to the situation that had prevailed on the eve of the French occupation and also of a desire by the government to preserve existing sources of revenue.[2] Nevertheless, given the continued strength of a free-trade ideology among the social elite, the relative weakness of interests in Tuscany demanding protection, and the fundamental willingness of the government to do all in its power to facilitate commerce, the efforts of the chamber in the area of tariff reform would ultimately prove successful.[3]

The abolition of restrictions on the import of foreign iron (originally designed to protect Tuscan iron production on the island of Elba) marks a case in point. An edict published in July 1816, which added teeth to an earlier restriction, prohibited the introduction of foreign iron into Tuscany and laid down strict regulations for disposing of foreign iron already on deposit in the city or soon to arrive. This measure evoked an energetic response from the chamber of commerce, which argued that the provision would "gravely damage that liberty which provides the basis of our commercial prosperity."[4] The appeal was not without effect, for the regulations on the export of foreign iron were considerably liberalized.[5] Finally, in January 1832, the import prohibition itself was replaced with a high but provisional tariff. Meanwhile, import restrictions were being eased on other items. In 1825 the government reduced the excise tax on salt,[6] and in 1831 it reduced the taxes on raw and spun cotton.[7] In 1833 the government facilitated the introduction of foreign wool cloth into the state, notwithstanding the protests of manufacturers in Florence and Prato.[8] Only Tuscan wine, it seems, could count on firm protection from the Tuscan government.[9]

The chamber of commerce also pressured for the liberalization of exports. In April 1814 the chamber refused to support the petition of a number of paper manufacturers to prohibit the extraction of rags,[10] and a month later it sought to limit the effects of an edict that implicitly prohibited the reexport of foreign machine oil.[11] The government gradually fell into line. In 1818 it suppressed export charges on agricultural products and livestock, and in 1822 these charges were abolished on oil, lard, and other foodstuffs.[12] This policy of liberalization also extended to raw materials. In 1817 an important notification permitted the export of raw Tuscan wool,[13] and in 1819 this provision was extended to silk.[14] In 1825, under steady pressure from the merchant community, the government agreed to exempt raw and finished foreign silk in transit from the payment of all duties.[15] Finally, laws providing tariff exemptions for the extraction of wood and carbon,[16] reductions of tariffs on copper,[17] and the abolishing of prohibitions on the export of Tuscan rags and hides[18] reinforce the picture of a government moving haltingly in the direction of its traditional ideology and endeavoring to reconcile the demands of agriculture and commerce with its hard-pressed finances.

If demands for the liberalization of restrictions on Tuscan imports and exports had met a sluggish, though ultimately positive, response from the central government, pressure exerted by the chamber of commerce for the elimination of charges levied on goods entering the free port—representing as they did more important sources of state revenue—evoked greater hesitation (and, on occasion, open rancor) on the part of government officials in Florence. Nevertheless, spurred by a sense of the competitive position of rival ports and by the general decline in prices and profit margins, the chamber continued to push its demands until, with the edicts of July 1834, its position was completely vindicated. The successful completion of this campaign represented at the time a clear, dramatic victory for the reform movement in Livorno. However, this victory would soon produce as many problems as it had temporarily resolved. An examination of the campaign for the elimination of port charges, the victory, and the ensuing disintegration will tell us much about the merchant community and its initial articulation of a program of reform.

It was perhaps only natural that the first fiscal exaction singled out for attack by the chamber of commerce would be the tax of 1 percent levied on merchandise entering the free port, for, unlike the stallage duties—a charge woven into Livorno's traditional privileges—it had been imposed relatively recently. This tax had originally been levied in 1800 as a 2 percent charge on goods entering or leaving the port. Its express purpose was to pay the French occupation forces to discontinue their practice of sequestering merchandise declared to belong to the enemies of France.[19] The charge—later lowered to one percent, as noted—continued to be levied throughout the period of French occupation. In 1816 the government of Ferdinand III confirmed its status as a regular levy on the commerce of the city. Thereafter, until its suppression in 1834, the tax provided a major source of revenue for the customhouse in Livorno.[20]

The chamber of commerce responded forcefully to the reconfirmation of this tax.[21] Merchants in the city, the chamber argued, had expected the government to suppress the tax of 1 percent which had been imposed as a temporary levy since its inception. Instead, they found the tax not only confirmed but exacted according to a tariff schedule that made it more onerous than in the past and far superior to the current value of merchandise entering the port. These financial exactions placed Livorno in a difficult competitive position. A government declaration that it would feel free to change tariffs at will—while expressly motivated by a desire to keep charges in line with the current value of merchandise—would pose another problem. Before sending their goods to the port, foreign merchants demanded to know precisely which charges they would be subjected to. Government flexibility in revising these charges, coupled with its refusal to publish current tariffs, would make this information difficult, if not impossible, to supply.

The actions of the government, the chamber concluded, showed a total disregard for the true basis of Livorno's commercial prosperity. Unlike other Italian ports, Livorno controlled access only to a restricted hinterland. As a result, the city did not possess a vital, indigenous commerce, and the bulk of its activity sprang from a commerce of commission and pure speculation. Based largely on the goodwill of foreign merchant capitalists, this commerce would continue to thrive only if facilities and charges in Livorno remained competitive with those of other ports. The enterprise and capital of the merchant community could effect nothing if these efforts were not sustained by a government that would do all in its power to facilitate the movement of merchandise and to maintain charges at as moderate a level as possible. Failure to follow such a policy would not only serve to injure the commerce of the city and the well-being of its population but would also—because of the resultant loss of tax revenue— prove prejudicial to the royal treasury.

The memorial of the chamber of commerce appears to have evoked no direct response from the central government,[22] which clearly considered the tax of 1 percent both equitable and just.[23] This same indifference, however, was not evident nearly two years later when the chamber presented a memorial far more sweeping in its demand for reform.[24]

In part, the extension of the grievances reflected a deterioration of the economic situation. The years 1816 and 1817 had been prosperous ones for the commerce of Livorno, especially in grain. Perhaps, as the secretary of finance noted sarcastically, the happy anticipation of profit from the famine in the interior had served to temporarily silence the perpetual laments of the merchant community.[25] In any event, while the reconfirmation of the tax of 1 percent on a permanent basis had aggravated the community, criticism by the chamber had been based primarily on a desire to defend the port's traditional privileges and on a fear of possible future consequences. The charge itself, however, could be borne with relative ease, and after the initial protest the furor had subsided. By comparison, the year 1818 was a bad one for Livorno. Speculation, especially in cereals, was not propitious, and, while contemporaries were naturally not aware of the extent of the problem, prices had begun their long descent.[26]

In its memorial of 1816, the chamber criticized only the tax of 1 percent. In 1818 it attacked a whole series of charges and practices as detrimental to the city's future commercial prosperity. With regard to the charges on commerce, the chamber cited not only the tax of 1 percent—as the most recent and therefore least legitimate charge—but also the stallage duties, which had been set at the time of the official declaration of the privileges of the port in 1675. The chamber also criticized quarantine and credit regulations. Sanitary practices were unnecessarily harsh. Even though they might be in possession of the requisite patents, ships were often forced to pass quarantines lasting several weeks. In ports such as Genoa, certain merchandise could be purged directly aboard ship, but in Livorno such merchandise had to be transported to a lazaretto, resulting in considerable trouble and expense.[27] Harsh quarantine practices required a revision of the customhouse credit regulations, as merchants were often forced to pay the charges on goods that were not yet available for sale.

The issues, then, were interrelated, and their successful resolution (and, with it, the future prosperity of the port), the chamber concluded, lay entirely in the hands of the sovereign. Previously, especially during periods of political crisis, Livorno's geographic position and its declared state of neutrality had enabled the port to prosper and even to exercise a dominant position in Mediterranean commerce, notwithstanding the existence of exactions and practices not entirely consonant with its traditional privileges. Such a situation, however, was no longer possible. Competition and the decline of prices and profits had made every small saving an important item of speculation. To survive, Livorno would have to become competitive.

Although requesting the benevolent intervention of the sovereign, the memorial of the chamber of commerce received from the ministry a response that was anything but kindly. The officials most closely involved in the issue—Leonardo Frullani, the secretary of finance, and Isidoro Pistolesi, the director of the customhouse in Livorno—lined up in staunch defense of Tuscany's fiscal exactions, opposed the requests of the merchant community, and severely attacked the governor of the city, Francesco Spannocchi, for giving the merchants the support of his office.[28]

Livorno, the secretary of finance argued, was not in crisis. In 1814 the grand ducal government had restored the free-port privileges of the city, and Livorno had soon regained its character as a populous and thriving commercial center. True, 1818 had not been a brilliant year for the city, but neither had it been prosperous for other Mediterranean ports. Temporary lulls in commercial activity, however, were a natural occurrence and should not be imputed to the charges levied on merchandise entering the port, which were no more onerous in Livorno than elsewhere. In any event, Frullani argued, any comparison between Livorno and other free ports had to take into consideration not only charges but also facilities and the extent of the free tariff zone, factors that weighed decidedly in Livorno's favor. In 1816 the 1 percent tax had indeed been made a permanent charge on the city's commerce. However, Frullani argued, this was simply a way of augmenting revenue without tampering with the decorum of the traditional stallage duties, thus providing adequate compensation to the state for its increased expenditures on the city's behalf (which were still far superior to the sums extracted from it in taxes). With regard to sanitary practices, Frullani agreed that some discussion was possible. However, he strongly opposed extending the grace period for customs payments, which, he argued, would make it difficult for the state to meet its current fiscal obligations.[29]

Frullani also openly gave vent to his hostility for the chamber of commerce, which, he felt, tended now as in the past to consider only its particular interests and to ignore those of the society as a whole. He even suggested that it might be wise, given the "insidious maneuvers" of the chamber, to suppress this troublesome institution once and for all.[30] The brunt of Frullani's ire, however, was directed against the governor of Livorno.[31] The task of a good minister, Frullani repeatedly warned Spannocchi, was to inform himself on the principles and motives that guided the public administration so as to shape accordingly the opinion of those under his charge. Instead, Spannocchi had aligned himself with the chamber of commerce and had become the protector and promoter of its incessant laments. Small wonder, then, that when the governor held such opinions and propagated them so openly they were radiated throughout the entire society, not only among the merchants but among the porters (*facchini*) as well. Could such a minister, Frullani concluded, be expected to perform adequately the duties entrusted to his care?[32]

The line of the controversy, then, was clearly drawn. The chamber of commerce, indicating the critical economic situation, stressed the necessity for a fundamental revision of charges and practices in the port. The secretary of finance and the director of the customhouse, however, based their position on a narrow defense of the immediate fiscal concerns of the state and stressed the temporary nature of any commercial downturn. It was perhaps natural, therefore, given the general pricing movements set out in the first part of this work, that the more accurate assessment of the chamber of commerce would gradually win the field. This trend was evident in the partial concessions won in the 1820s. The most important of these were contained in a notification dated 12 March 1822 which exempted cereals in transit (that is, transferred directly from one ship to another without being contracted) from the payment of the entire 1 percent charge, from one-half of the stallage duties, and from the small fee owed to the Royal Grain Office.[33] Other stipulations called for the publication of the current tariff of 1 percent, for its reevaluation and adjustment to current values every six months, and for the extension of the grace period for the payment of customs charges from two to three months.[34] In transmitting this notification to the governor, Frullani also agreed to study the lazaretto charges, which were finally liberalized in July 1826.[35]

In spite of these piecemeal reforms, however, the basic problem remained. This seems particularly clear from a series of petitions advanced in April 1830 by the English merchant house of Bell, De Young and Company, long established in Livorno and perhaps the largest dealer in colonial products in the city.[36] In March of that year, a petition states, the company had received a shipment of 2,800 sacks of coffee from Santo Domingo, and in accordance with sanitary regulations it had deposited this merchandise in a lazaretto for routine purgation. A dispute arose over the charges. The statutes declared that lazaretto charges should equal 1 percent of the value of the merchandise purged. While the value of Santo Domingo coffee in the official tariff was fixed at 80 lire per 100 pounds, however, its current market price was only 36 lire per 100 pounds—less than half of the fixed value. As a result, instead of paying the stipulated one percent the company was forced to pay 2.25 percent. The same injustice extended to stallage duties, which, because of the official valuation (4 lire for each 500-pound bale) equaled another 2.25 percent instead of the statutory 0.5 percent. Thus, for these two charges alone the company was assessed 4.5 percent of the value of its merchandise.

It was true, the petition noted, that the injustice of the charges had been caused by the current depreciated value of the merchandise on the market and that if this situation were only temporary one might pass over the whole issue in silence. However, it was now clear that the depreciation of coffee, like that of many other items, was not simply fortuitous but was natural and permanent, with the result being that "there is little possibility that the price will rise and every probability that it will continue to fall in proportion as human industry and activity increase."[37]

The petition of Bell, De Young and Company won approval, and the official value of the product in question was revised.[38] However, it was becoming increasingly clear not only to individual merchants and the chamber of commerce but to the central government as well that the problem was becoming too great to be solved by creating piecemeal reforms or by simply juggling the values of specific merchandise.[39] Rather, the whole tariff structure of the free port required a close, critical examination.

This final step was taken only after additional prodding from the merchant community. In January 1834 about a hundred of the principal merchant firms in Livorno presented a memorandum to the chamber of commerce in which they outlined the inevitable decadence of the city's commerce and the illusory character of its privileges.[40] Displeased that in the past the government had seized on a division of opinion in the merchant community as a pretext for not taking its requests for reform under serious consideration, the chamber voted to meet with these merchants to work out a common proposal to present to the government. The president was instructed to obtain the necessary permission.[41]

The request, however, was denied. The secretary of finance, R. Cempini, reported that the government found it neither necessary nor expedient under the circumstances to authorize a reunion of merchants with the deputies of the chamber of commerce or the dispatching of a deputation to the capital. Furthermore, Cempini stated, in line with current regulation the government would continue to ignore any petition advanced by an unauthorized, collective delegation.[42]

This reply served only to increase discontent in Livorno. The governor of the city reported to the president of the Buon Governo (the state police) that the local commissioner, perhaps fearing criticism, was playing down the level of agitation in the city.[43] In fact, the governor noted, discontent was rampant among all sections of the population, not only among the "lower and more dangerous classes" but also among those that as a rule were sympathetic to the royal government. He remarked that the latter were especially upset that the central government was adamantly refusing to consider proposals that had been repeatedly advanced to it and by the sense that policy in this area was being set by someone whose interests were clearly hostile to the city's commerce.[44] The only way of effectively handling the discontent in the merchant community, the governor concluded, would be to subject its grievances to a careful, impartial examination.[45]

On the basis of these recommendations the government dispatched to Livorno Alexander Humbourg, head of the administrative office of the Royal Revenues, and Orazio Forni, director of the customhouse of Siena. They were instructed to unite with Antonio Filicchi, a respected local mer-

chant, to listen to the observations of merchants and other
interested members of the community. The particular task
of the committee would be to come up with recommendations for strengthening the city's commerce without damaging the royal treasury.[46] In the meantime, the chamber
of commerce selected three of its members (C. Grabau,
L. Pillans, and L. Tedeschi) to draw up a report on the city's
commerce, presumably to help the government commission
to prepare its recommendations.[47]

The extant papers of this commission contain only sketchy
forms of its conclusions.[48] Far more revealing is the report of
the Tuscan Administrative Council.[49] Based primarily on data
supplied by the commission and the customhouse, the council report stressed the decline of Livorno's traditional commerce of deposit and the harmful effects of this decline on
the Tuscan economy. It was readily apparent, the council
argued, that the level of commercial activity in Livorno was
dropping and that this was due primarily to the excessive
charges on the city's commerce. Many respectable merchants
had presented letters from their correspondents attesting that
because of these charges it was now more advantageous to
send merchandise elsewhere. While direct imports into the
Tuscan hinterland were more important than they had been
in the past, they could not compensate the city for its loss.

Deposits in Livorno were low. Goods from Sicily and the
North were in short supply, and sugar and coffee for the
consumption of the local population had to be provided sec-
ondhand (in Genoa and Marseilles). The drop in colonial
imports made it especially difficult to find carriers to export
Tuscan silk, rags, linen, oil, and marble, which previously
had provided profitable return cargoes, especially for the
Americans. With the decline in commercial opportunities,
capital was being drawn out of commerce and invested elsewhere, to the distress of the local population. Most critical,
the council felt, was the constant drop in Livorno's customs
revenues. In the last three months of 1833, this income was
lower by 122,000 lire than it had been during the same period
in the previous year. In the first three months of 1834, the
decline (from the first three months of 1833) was 163,000 lire.

Since the early years of the Restoration, customs revenues had dropped by about 22.5 percent, and the decline showed every sign of continuing. The only hope of reversing this trend, the council felt, lay in radically reforming charges and practices in the port in order to reattract its traditional commerce.

The recommendations of the Tuscan Administrative Council went far beyond any previous proposal and marked a sharp reversal of the council's attitude in 1818. The recommendations called for the total abolition of stallage duties and the tax of 1 percent, for elimination of the business tax on commercial agents (*mezzani*) and on wine and coffee vendors, and for an ending of the costly requirement that merchants weigh their grain only at public scales. The council also recommended the reform of sanitary charges and practices. These recommendations were embodied in a dramatic decree of 23 July 1834, which, in effect, granted "entire freedom to foreign merchandise introduced into Livorno by way of sea."

The most difficult task of the council had been to devise a means of compensating the Royal Treasury for its loss of revenue from the old charges. Based on the value of imports in 1826, Emanuele Repetti estimated the annual loss at 1,200,000 lire.[50] After taking into account the decline of customs revenues, the council lowered its estimate of the annual sacrifice from 1,330,927.13.2 to 1,008,216.12.3 lire.[51]

Compensation would come from three principal sources. A tariff wall constructed at government expense would serve to integrate the suburbs of Livorno within the area of the free port, increasing its size by roughly ten times and more than doubling its population. Upon completion the suburbs would be subject to a consumer tax that had previously been assessed only on goods sold in the old city. The council estimated the annual return from this tax alone at 6,000,000 lire.[52]

In addition, members of Livorno's merchant community (comprising, the law stated, merchants [*mercanti*], traders [*negozianti*], bankers, insurance brokers, discounters of commercial bills [*scontisti di effetti negoziabili*], commercial agents, and wholesale dealers [*trafficanti di non minuto taglio*]) would be subject to an annual personal levy. The individual amounts would be set by a board of assessment (*repartitori*) composed of twelve members chosen by the chamber of commerce from various sectors of the city's economy. Appeals would be reviewed by seven of the most distinguished representatives of the city's commerce. The total assessment was fixed at 330,000 lire, which included a 10 percent margin. The assessments were to be the responsibility of the entire body of contributors, so that the failure of any member of the community to meet his obligation would simply result in an increase in the burden on his fellow taxpayers.[53] Since the new tariff wall necessary for the wider exaction of the consumer tax would require time to complete, the chamber of commerce agreed to an assessment of 500,000 lire for the first year only.[54]

The third source of compensation would come from a charge on cereals shipped from Livorno (or from the mouth of the Arno) into Tuscany.[55] This measure was a positive response to the request of the chamber of commerce that part of the burden of compensation be transferred from the merchant community to consumers in the hinterland, who would be forced to absorb the charge in the higher cost of cereals. The charge itself was higher even than that suggested by the chamber,[56] and if it were levied primarily on grain shipped from Livorno, it would theoretically put the city in a poor position to compete with inland transit points. The absence of protest from the merchant community is indicative of the relative unimportance of these transit points for grain shipments during this period (certainly, these points were in any case handicapped by the export restrictions of Tuscany's neighbors) and of Livorno's dominant position as a source of supply for the internal market.

Needless to say, merchants in Livorno responded enthusiastically to the edict of 23 July. The chamber of commerce showed up in a body at the governor's office to express its satisfaction and requested permission to send a delegation to Florence to thank the grand duke in person, a request that this time was granted.[57] As another sign of its gratification, the chamber collected money for distribution to the community's monitorial schools and to indigent commercial families.[58] From Livorno's point of view, the response in Genoa could not have been better. Genoa's *Corriere mercantile* reported that the Genovese merchant community was up in arms against the fiscal exactions of its own government in Turin. It also reported that after publication of the edict of 23 July, an American ship unloading coffee in Genoa had been ordered to immediately weigh anchor and carry the remainder of its cargo to Livorno.[59]

The law of 1834 seemed the definitive solution to the major problems troubling Livorno's merchant community. The results, however, soon proved to be otherwise, revealing serious tensions between large and middling merchants in the city and friction between commercial interests in the free port and manufacturing interests in the surrounding suburbs.

From the beginning, the new system of taxing the merchant community in Livorno ran into serious difficulties. The first board of assessment had trouble in deciding who was actually subject to the tax, and it requested additional clarification from the government and a postponement of the deadline for the completion of its work.[60] The government acceded to the latter request but failed to provide any additional clarification of liability beyond the general guidelines set out in its original notification.[61] In addition, the board had difficulty in fixing the assessment of individual contributors. Theoretically, the tax was to be in proportion to the importance of one's affairs. But profits could be hidden, and capital, being mobile, could easily be transferred elsewhere.[62]

The announcement of the first assessment gave rise to many complaints. Typical of these was the position of an anonymous correspondent in a letter to the secretary of finance.[63] To the writer, the intent of the sovereign disposition of July 1834 had been to tax only those who had directly benefited from the abolition of the ancient charges—that is, merchants whose commercial activity had been subject to the stallage and 1 percent duties. Instead, he argued, under the new system those merchants were taxed relatively lightly, while a disproportionately heavy burden had been placed on small merchants and traders, who were not engaged directly in foreign commerce and therefore received no benefit from abolition of the old charges. Indeed, the tentacles of the new tax had extended even to those exercising a simple trade, with the result that almost no class of the citizenry had succeeded in escaping assessment. Small wonder, then, the writer concluded, that the tax had produced an infinite number of laments and protests and a sense of smoldering discontent in the merchant community.

The argument that only those who had benefited from the abolition of the stallage and 1 percent duties should be subject to the new tax would have been difficult to sustain, since article 7 of the notification of 24 July explicitly stated that bankers and insurance brokers would be liable to the tax, and neither of these categories had profited directly from the abolition of the ancient charges. More difficult was the problem of retail tradesmen. Here, the issue was not primarily one of corresponding benefits, because many tradesmen had profited from the abolition of the business tax on wine and coffeehouses. Rather, the problem lay in deciding whether the sovereign injunction to tax only large merchant houses (*trafficanti di non minuto taglio*) meant that all retail traders or only small ones were to be excluded.[64] The board of appeal sustained the latter interpretation, affirming the general liability of retail merchants to the tax but, notwithstanding the opposition of the chamber, eliminating from the rolls all those assessed under thirty lire.[65]

The most difficult problem raised in connection with the assessment lay in deciding the relative weight to give to each category of taxpayer. No provision on this matter had been made in the law itself. As a result, whether the burden fell more on one category or another was left entirely up to each board of assessment, a situation certainly not designed to mollify criticism of the tax's arbitrary nature. In its report to the chamber of commerce in 1840, the board of assessment declared that it had endeavored to pursue the policy that seemed least arbitrary and most just and, insofar as it had been able to obtain the necessary information, that it had taxed merchants strictly in proportion to the level of their business activity.[66] But notwithstanding the desire for equity and justice (or the more immediate aim of avoiding widespread, popular discontent), efforts were continually made by the assessment board to keep demands on Livorno's large merchant speculators moderate so as not to alienate a group considered crucial to the city's commercial prosperity.[67]

The communal nature of the tax, however, made such a policy difficult. As noted earlier, the annual levy of 330,000 lire had been charged as a debt to the whole body of taxpayers. If for any reason an individual had his assessment reduced or canceled, the burden would automatically revert to his fellow contributors. Had the number of taxpayers increased, all would have profited, but instead the number fell: by July 1838 it had fallen to 1,600 from the original 1,900. In response the maximum individual assessment was raised from 2,800 to 6,000 lire.[68] The extent of the increase seemed arbitrary to many, but there could be no denying that a year earlier the board had for the first time returned a deficit assessment and that the chamber of commerce—which was ultimately responsible for the payment of the tax—had had to work long and hard to repair the breach.[69]

As the obligation became more difficult to meet, the tax itself fell increasingly into discredit. The unfortunate person who found himself appointed to the board of assessment complained that he received little more for his time and effort than the hatred of his peers.[70] Some refused to serve, preferring to pay the penalty of a double assessment.[71] Others were said to have accepted the post with the intention of lowering their own assessments and raising those of merchants who in the past had exercised the hated office. Supposedly, the ultimate aim was to discredit the system to the point of forcing the government to make some necessary reforms.[72]

By 1838 even the chamber of commerce was beginning to agree that the tax was unworkable.[73] The time had clearly come to once again begin the difficult negotiations for a complete revision of the system. This time the government showed no unwillingness to negotiate. It stipulated only that memorials not simply lament the current system of taxation but that they also propose concrete alternative methods that, while providing for a fairer and more efficient operation, would continue to guarantee the government an annual income of 300,000 lire.[74]

Following the suggestions of a Mr. Rodocanacchi,[75] the chamber of commerce proposed in March 1839 that the direct tax levied on the merchant community be reduced to 150,000 lire and calculated by means of a graded system of patents, and that the balance come from the exaction of a small charge on merchandise moving from Livorno into the Tuscan hinterland.[76] The estimated return from the new system was carefully calculated. Patents would run from 30 to 800 lire for merchants, from 24 to 300 lire for commercial agents, and be equal to the last assessment under the old system for shopkeepers. This section of the tax would provide an annual income of approximately 171,428 lire. A levy of two soldi a sack on cereals and .75 percent on the value of other merchandise introduced into the Tuscan hinterland would provide approximately 177,500 lire. The total would be well over the 300,000 lire demanded by the government.

For the chamber of commerce, the plan possessed several distinct advantages. The patent system would fix an individual's contribution once and for all, thus ending the conflict and bitterness of the annual assessments. The ceiling of 800 lire would decidedly lighten the burden on large merchant speculators and would encourage their continued participation in the city's commerce. The indirect charges in the proposal would not undermine the privileges of the port, since these would affect only goods moving from Livorno into the hinterland. In this way approximately half the burden of the current tax would be lifted from the shoulders of merchants in Livorno and placed on merchants and consumers in the hinterland—justly, the chamber felt, for had not the latter group also benefited from the abolition of the ancient charges?[77]

The first, and perhaps most damaging, criticism of the patent proposal advanced by the chamber of commerce came from within the merchant community itself.[78] In November 1838—even before the official proposal of the chamber had been formulated—twelve obscure members of the merchant community sent a memorandum to the chamber opposing, they said, a plan recently formulated by several leading merchants to reduce the commercial tax to 200,000 lire and the maximum amount levied on any individual to 1,000 lire. Such a plan, they argued, would serve only to benefit the first class of merchants at the expense of those who were less able to meet the annual exactions. They wrote that had the proposal been in effect that year, the fifty-four merchants assigned to the first class would have contributed only 54,000 lire instead of the actual 126,000 lire—a savings of 72,000 lire for this class alone. The great mass of poorer taxpayers would have been left to divide the paltry 28,000 lire saving remaining. Moreover, should the number of contributors continue to drop as in the past, only the members of the poorer group, who had no ceiling on their contributions, would be liable for the increasing burden. All classes of the merchant community, the twelve concluded, were opposed to the existing tax, and a plan should be formulated to benefit all of them. As the impartial representative of the merchant community, the chamber of commerce had the obligation of insuring that if the plan of the large merchant speculators came to the attention of the government, their memorandum should be presented as well.

The same points were later amplified in two memorandums of the administrative office of the Royal Revenues criticizing the proposal of the chamber of commerce.[79] Following a careful consideration of the hypothetical effect of the chamber's patent system on the assessments of 1838–1839 and 1839–1840, the office concluded that the result would be far from salutary. The seventy or so merchants who stood to benefit most from the proposal would probably consider it an act of tardy justice. The remaining 1,130, who would benefit little, would likely add envy to their general sense of discontent, feeling that their interests had been sacrificed to the merchants who had gained most from the suppression of the current charges. Figures aside, the administrative office argued, direct taxes levied by merchants on merchants would always appear onerous and arbitrary. To avoid an air of injustice, it concluded, the existing commercial tax should not simply be transformed into patents but should instead be suppressed in its entirety.

The problem lay in finding an alternative source that would provide suitable compensation to the royal treasury. The administrative office strongly opposed increasing the tax on goods moving from Livorno into the hinterland (proposed both by the group of twelve merchants and by the chamber of commerce), for such a tax would draw a large portion of its revenue from imports on grain and would thus weigh disproportionately on the poor, who were already burdened by the additional charge levied on this commodity in 1834. Rather, both social justice and sound finance required that the compensatory tax rest on as broad a range of contributors as possible. To this end, the administrator proposed the establishment of a declaration tax to be levied on all merchandise arriving in the free port. True, such a charge would represent a retreat from the principles and privileges of 1834, but it would possess the distinct advantages of being relatively light (about one-half of the old stallage duties), easy to collect, and shared by merchants and consumers.

A long memorial drawn up in August 1840 by the governor of Livorno, Neri Corsini, sought to gain acceptance for the proposals of the chamber of commerce, if only in a modified form.[80] By then, however, the government seemed definitely opposed to any suggestion of levying a charge on goods moving from Livorno into the hinterland. As early as July 1838, the secretary of finance had declared that no substitute charge would be accepted which attacked either the free status of the port or increased the burden on consumers in the hinterland.[81] This position was reaffirmed even more forcefully in June 1841: while consumers in the interior may have benefited from the abolition of the stallage and 1 percent duties in 1834, the minister noted, the law had not been drafted for them, and they should not be expected to bear the burden of its revision.[82]

Of course, the declaration tax proposed by the administrative office—and finally adopted in 1842—weighed on the free port and the consumer alike. However, the specific advantages of the tax lay in its being moderate and in the universality of its application. Certainly, if permanence in this turbulent commercial situation was the mark of success, then the new tax—lasting as it did until the final abolition of Livorno's free-port status in 1868—would have to be judged as eminently successful.

Far from resolving problems, the commercial tax of 1834 served ultimately only to exacerbate tension within Livorno's merchant community. The happy results that had been expected to follow the abolition of the stallage and 1 percent duties failed to materialize. Livorno failed to regain the prosperity of its golden age. The disappointment of the city's merchant community, however, should not be taken as *prima facie* evidence of Livorno's commercial decline. The general fall in prices and the competition of rival ports would, in any event, have made a return to the past impossible. At the same time, as we saw in chapter one, grain speculation during this period could furnish inordinate profits to the skillful merchant, thus providing the city with compensation for the loss of its traditional commerce.

Indeed, merchants in Livorno seem to have resented the tax of 1834 as much for its character as for its weight. After the relative anonymity of the ancient charges, the merchants found themselves suddenly subject to a direct tax that was assessed by their peers and that could not be passed on to the supplier or consumer. Moreover, they were resentful that merchants in the hinterland, who also benefited from the abolition of the ancient charges, avoided much of the burden of the compensation. The declaration tax imposed in 1842 represented a retreat to the older method of commercial exaction. Still, while this tax was levied on all merchandise entering the free port, it was far lighter than the old stallage and 1 percent duties had been, and it was not linked to the host of other charges and practices which had plagued the old system. In short, the declaration tax represented a relatively successful resolution of one of the merchant community's principal complaints.

The commercial tax, however, was not the only controversial aspect of the law of 1834. The incorporation of Livorno's suburbs into the free port provoked serious complaint from residents and manufacturers in the densely populated areas that had sprung up outside the walls of the old city. Why, then, was the decision made to expand the free port, and what were the consequences of this decision?

Moderate reformers of a strong paternalistic cast tended to justify the extension of the free port on moral grounds. By tearing down the walls of the city (which, in any event, were no longer necessary for its defense) and constructing a tariff barrier around the city and its suburbs, they argued, it became possible to place the entire urban population under a single fiscal system. In this way one could totally suppress the practice of contraband, which these reformers felt was dangerously sapping the moral fiber of the local population (*basso popolo livornese*).[83]

A closer examination of this issue, however, reveals that the practice of contraband perhaps owed more to fiscal inequality than to moral depravity. For example, retail tradesmen—in particular, butchers and bakers—operating in the free port labored under a severe handicap.[84] The materials that formed the principal expenses of their operations (for butchers and bakers, these were animals and flour) had to be extracted from the hinterland and hence were subject to the standard levies on goods leaving the Tuscan state. In addition, tradesmen in Livorno were required to pay business taxes to the community and to maintain their shops at an acceptable level of sanitation, all of which increased their costs of operation and hence the price of their products. Tradesmen in the suburbs, however, escaped these burdens. Resident in areas that were technically outside the city, they were neither required to pay excise and business taxes nor forced to meet the sanitation levels imposed by the community. As a result, they could sell their wares at prices lower than those demanded in the free port.

The natural outcome of this situation was the practice of contraband. Occasionally, large quantities of supplies were smuggled into the free port and clandestinely sold at prices prevailing in the suburbs. More generally, though, people in the city would go to the suburbs, buy what they needed, and smuggle it back home. The operation was safe and easy. By now the suburbs pressed up against the walls of the city, and the government had long since abolished the requirement prohibiting the sale of meat and bread within one mile of the bastions. The mass of people continually moving back and forth between city and suburbs and the petty nature of the contraband made detection virtually impossible.[85] A simple consideration of the number of butchers and bakers exercising their trade in the city and suburbs provides a graphic sense of the phenomenon: although the population of the two areas was roughly equal, seven butchers and ten bakers had shops in the city, while thirty-six butchers and forty-two bakers operated in the suburbs.[86]

Several possible solutions were advanced for the problem. The prohibition on doing business within a certain distance of the city gates could be reimposed, thus making it inconvenient for consumers in the free port to purchase their supplies in the suburbs.[87] Animal carcasses could be required to be stamped at the time of their slaughter, which would prevent the butchering of meat in the countryside and its introduction into the city for clandestine sale.[88] The director of the customhouse, however, considered both of these suggestions to be unworkable.[89] The governor suggested that the most effective solution—and, certainly, the one that would provide the greatest increase in tax revenue—would be to wall in the suburbs and to subject them to the same excise taxes being paid in the city.[90] In the event that this proposal might seem too radical, the governor—in agreement with the director of the customhouse—suggested as an alternative the lowering of charges on consumer goods entering the free port, thus establishing a compatible situation between city and suburbs and eliminating any incentive for fraud. This measure, the customhouse estimated, would cost the treasury approximately 25,000 lire a year.[91]

Ultimately, however, the government chose the more ambitious solution and ordered the construction of a new wall, a project that would eventually cost more than 4 million lire and would impose a severe strain on the Tuscan treasury.[92] While considerations of public morality and the complaints of tradesmen may have played a role in the government's decision, the measure was particularly geared to serve the needs of the merchant community, especially those merchants whose fortunes were linked to the city's traditional commercial activity. For them, the expansion of the free port provided the possibility of new, more comfortable, and more economical business locations.[93] More important, the construction of the new wall enabled the government to extend consumer taxes to the suburbs, thus obtaining the compensatory revenue necessary for the suppression of the old port duties. In this respect, the victory of the merchants was gained at the expense of the consumers in the suburbs (and—by ending the possibility of contraband—at the expense of many consumers in the city as well). Given this situation, even the administrative council recognized that any discussion of the advantages accruing to the general population from the suppression of the ancient charges would appear to be a cruel joke.[94]

The disenchantment of consumers over the provisions of the law of 1834 was echoed in the complaints of manufacturers. Many of the latter had located their establishments in the suburbs with a careful eye to gaining the maximum advantages of doing business in a well-populated area with free access to the raw materials and markets of the Tuscan hinterland.[95] The inclusion of the suburbs within the free port threatened to change the situation of these manufacturers completely, cutting them off from their supply of raw materials—or at least making the materials more costly to obtain—and making it more difficult for them to market their finished products.

In studying the provisions of the law of 1834, the administrative council gave the situation of manufacturers in the suburbs special consideration.[96] Already, rumors of the plan to expand the free port were beginning to trouble several of these manufacturers.[97] Their apprehension, the council declared, could best be stilled by informing them immediately that when the suburbs of Livorno were separated from the Tuscan hinterland, "consideration would be given to the establishments currently operating there and provisions adopted to preserve them in their present condition." A formal government notification of 24 July 1834 contained that assurance.[98]

On 25 February 1837, with construction of the new tariff wall finally completed, the government promulgated the provisions designed to protect existing manufacturers in the suburbs. The provisions must have disappointed many. Only twenty-two firms in five categories, it was felt, would be sufficiently handicapped by being incorporated into the free port to merit special consideration. These included three manufacturers of soap, three of wax candles, four of lead munitions, six of tallow candles, and six of hides.

Special controls imposed to insure that these firms would not profit from the customs exemptions to better their position vis-à-vis competitors in the hinterland vitiated the beneficent intent of the provisions. Myriad checks and counterchecks hampered the operations of the specially named firms. The customs exemptions enabled these firms to survive, but the restrictions and controls shackled their development. With exemptions applied nominatively rather than by category, the establishment of new firms in the privileged sectors became impossible.[99] The act, in short, had an ad hoc quality. Firms covered under it were maintained in the status quo-ante, while many of the firms not covered under it could choose either to die quickly or to move elsewhere.[100]

The law of 1834, then, represented a sweeping attempt by the government to strengthen the foundations of Livorno's traditional commerce. For this reason the law tended to favor the interests of large merchant speculators (whose views predominated in the chamber of commerce) at the expense of more middling merchants and retailers in the city and of consumers and manufacturers in the suburbs. Government officials, however, were sensitive to the clash of interests generated by provisions of the new law. They endeavored— with varying degrees of success—to work out a solution that would be fair to all groups, including consumers in the hinterland, while not losing sight of the solution's primary aim of fostering the commercial development of Livorno and strengthening the fiscal resources of the state. Several critics would later stress what they considered to be the class nature of the law, arguing that nascent manufacturing interests in the suburbs of the city were being sacrificed in a vain attempt to strengthen the position of Livorno's traditional, commercial elite.[101]

In chapter two, I cast some doubt on the notion of a fundamental clash of interests between merchants and manufacturers in the free port. In chapter five I shall broaden the investigation of this matter to assess the place of manufacturing in the general reform program of the merchant community. In chapter six I shall attack the question from a different perspective, showing that the merchant community sought to improve Livorno's commercial position not only by pressuring the government to strengthen the traditional privileges of the port but also—and more importantly—by itself endeavoring to eliminate abuses that were impairing the city's commercial reputation abroad and to develop institutions that would facilitate commercial operations in the port city. The success of these measures can be ascertained only after careful evaluation. That they were undertaken, however, is indicative of a definite spirit of reform. The scope, strengths, and limitations of this spirit will be the next subject of examination.

CHAPTER FOUR

Elimination of Abuses:
Formation of New Institutions

Although the law of July 1834 was subject to severe criticism, it nevertheless marked an important transition in the merchant community's response to the commercial situation of the city. Theretofore, merchants (and the chamber of commerce) had concentrated their efforts on pushing the government to revise or abolish the traditional charges on merchandise entering the free port. Following the promulgation of the law, however, the merchant community considered that the government had done all that it could be expected to do directly to improve Livorno's commercial position. In future, the prosperity of the port would depend on the general economic situation and on the ability of the merchant community to undertake its own reforms to strengthen the city's commerce.[1]

The impetus for internal reform, however, did receive an initial boost from the central government. A notification in August 1836 announced the suppression of what for many was the most "embarrassing" provision of the city's fundamental charter, the *Livornina*, the section that had conceded personal and proprietary immunity to debtors who elected to settle in Livorno.[2] The desire for instant respectability was so great that it appeared to blind commentators to the value of the *Livornina* in promoting the initial economic development of the city. Typical was the attitude of Giuliano Ricci, who remarked that "the *Livornina* had done nothing but draw to Livorno men despicable in their habits and morals and without capital resources." "Such men," he added, "live at the expense of the society like small fish on the vast members of a cetacean, who remains unaware of their presence. Rarely, if ever, do they render any effective succour to the society that they are disfiguring." The conclusion was predictable: "The abolition of the *Livornina* served to save one of the great Italian cities from the blight of being an asylum for the bankrupt of Europe."[3]

A more sweeping measure to improve the city's reputation and facilitate its commerce was effected the same year. The prevailing system of weights and measures in Livorno had long been considered a scandal. The heterogeneous nature of the merchant community seemed to be reflected in the wide variety of moneys—both real and hypothetical—and measures used to express the value and weight of merchandise bought and sold in the free port. Transactions might be made with pezzi, ducati, scudi, franchi, lire, zecchini, or a host of other currencies. A merchant could take advantage of fluctuations in the exchange rates by buying his goods with one currency and selling them for another. Transactions could be expressed in pounds, sacks, bundles, or barrels, each with varying unit measures. If this were not complicated enough, every commercial operation was encrusted with a variety of tares and supertares, discounts, and "courtesies" granted in the most capricious and arbitrary fashion possible.

The whole system—if indeed it could be dignified with that title—made it virtually impossible for anyone without long experience in the city's commercial operations to calculate the price of a given cargo much less the probable net profit on a given transaction. The foreigner who hazarded to send his goods to Livorno was forced to rely totally on the judgment of his local correspondent, a situation that often generated resentment and recrimination.[4]

The chamber of commerce had endeavored for years to simplify and rationalize this system, which it considered to be one of the principal causes of Livorno's commercial decline.[5] In 1822 the chamber proposed that in future all prices be expressed in lire fiorentine, that the weight of bulky items be represented solely in multiples of 100 Tuscan pounds, and that tares reflect only an honest computation of the weight of the container. In addition, it proposed the abolition of discounts and courtesies of every sort.[6]

The impetus for reform at that time, however, was blunted by the inertia of the government and the opposition of a large section of the merchant community. The old system of weights and measures, after all, had been in operation for centuries, and many merchants found it comfortable and— more to the point—profitable. This was particularly true in the case of small retail merchants. To them, Livorno's reputation in foreign commercial centers was of little concern. Far more preoccupying was the fear that a rationalization of the current system of weights and measures and the ending of discounts and other courtesies would hamper their freedom of manipulation, thus cutting them off from important sources of profit.[7] Their response to the feared reforms consisted of playing down the abuses of the current system, stressing the magnitude and uncertainty of the proposed changes, and calling for the necessity of further study, thus stalling for time.[8]

A similar strategy, it seems, was being followed by the government. In 1823 the governor of the city remarked that since the proposed reforms were so sweeping and had sparked such opposition, they should be subjected to the most serious examination before any decision on the matter could be made.[9] Two years later the issue was just as unsettled. Opinion in the merchant community, the governor remarked, was still so divided that it was impossible to foresee which decision would win the general approval of the community or would prove more advantageous to the city.[10] The governor was clearly beginning to find the whole issue most embarrassing, and in hopes of burying it once and for all he cynically suggested that before proceeding further those advocating reform should be asked to ascertain the sentiment of the entire merchant community. Only if the reforms were supported by an overwhelming majority, he said, should the government take steps to implement them.[11]

The cynicism of his proposal stemmed from the government's repeated opposition to any attempt by the chamber of commerce to poll the merchant community or to work out a common proposal with it to submit to the central government. In fact, when the chamber did attempt to solicit the views of the community on the proposed reform of weights and measures, the secretary of finance refused to permit the appeal.[12]

In the mid-1830s, as the government appeared more amenable to proposals for reform, the chamber of commerce renewed its campaign. In June 1835 the chamber drew up a carefully worded appeal defending the proposed new system.[13] The request for a simplified system of weights and measures, it argued, did not spring from a blind desire to destroy practices that had the sanction of centuries but simply from the need to adjust Livorno's commercial operations to the requirements of the present. Commerce was now far more diffused and competitive: more goods were in circulation in smaller lots, and profits on any given transaction were lower. Given this situation, merchants demanded that their business be expedited in the quickest, most rational and economic manner possible. No longer were they willing to tolerate the ten or twelve currencies and the tares, supertares, and discounts that plagued commercial operations in Livorno and made doing business there cumbersome and expensive. Rather, they would ship their goods to ports that had one or (at most) two official currencies and that expedited their affairs in a clear, rational fashion. Contrary to fear, the chamber argued, there was no evidence that in these ports small, retail speculation had suffered; nor was there evidence that with the proposed reforms it would suffer in Livorno. The times, the chamber concluded, demanded a sacrifice, one not of material gain but of the set of practices which was hampering efforts to maintain, much less to strengthen, Livorno's competitive position.

Although the chamber of commerce was prohibited from formulating a common proposal for the entire merchant community, it forwarded to the governor the individual petitions of many important merchant firms in the city in support of the proposed reforms.[14] They seemed to produce a positive effect on official opinion. In October 1836 the auditor (the chief police official in the city) remarked that "it was not only useful but necessary [to establish] in this city one single weight, one single measure, one single money, not ideal, not abusive, but genuine and real."[15] Even the governor now placed himself solidly behind the request of "the rich and enlightened section of the merchant community, which was principally concerned with large, foreign commercial transactions."[16] The section concerned with small, retail commerce, he remarked, would fall into line after the reforms were promulgated.[17] Shortly thereafter the central government announced the complete vindication of the position of the chamber of commerce: from the first day of 1837, the proposals that it had long advocated would have the force of law.[18]

While efforts to institute a more simplified and rational system of weights and measures had resulted in total victory for the position of reform, attempts to regulate more strictly the activities of the city's *mezzani* met with far less success.

Complaints about the *mezzani* were a standard feature in discussions about Livorno's tarnished commercial reputation.[19] Abuses cited varied from outright fraud—in which *mezzani* were said to have intentionally misrepresented the value of a given cargo or to have engineered the sale and consignment of merchandise to a nonexistent merchant (an ingenious form of theft)—to unauthorized (and unethical) dealing in the buying and selling of merchandise on their own behalf. Many criticized the low level of preparation, intelligence, and moral character of those exercising the profession.[20]

The government had endeavored to eliminate these abuses and to supervise more closely the activities of those exercising the profession.[21] In 1815 the chamber of commerce was given an important supervisory role in this area.[22] All petitions for authorization to enter the trade were transmitted first to the chamber for an opinion, and once each year the chamber met with the governor, the auditor, and the director of the customhouse to scrutinize the contracts recorded in the books of each *mezzano*.

These provisions, however, did little to ameliorate the situation. Application and annual review tended to become merely formal procedures, the latter more useful perhaps in eliminating from the rolls those no longer exercising the profession than in detecting the abuses of those who were. Indeed, from the government's standpoint, the most serious abuse was that many were acting as *mezzani* without any authorization whatsoever, a situation that rendered formal controls virtually meaningless.

Demographic expansion and the decline in prices and profit margins exacerbated the problem. The position of *mezzano* had long been exercised by those who desired to make their fortune in commerce but who lacked capital or experience.[23] After 1815 the profession was engulfed by many recent immigrants, especially those from the Levant (*Greci* and *Levantini*). To this group must be added the even larger number of clerks (*giovani di banco*) in commercial firms who exercised the functions of *mezzani* without official authorization. The whole situation obviously would not have been possible without the connivance of many merchants. Pressed by more competitive business conditions, many of them, it seems, were employing the services of adventitious *mezzani* at fees far below the legal tariff. It was estimated that these *mezzani* handled at least a third of the port's commercial transactions.[24]

In reading the correspondence that passed between the chamber of commerce, the governor, and the central government on this question, one cannot help but conclude that one of the major reasons—if not *the* major reason—for the persistence of abuses among the *mezzani* was that no party felt sufficiently motivated either to push resolutely for the elimination of the abuses or to work for a radical reform of the profession. It was not, certainly, that the chamber of commerce countenanced fraud or unethical behavior or did not want to see the profession in the hands of men who were intelligent and upright, but the chamber made no secret of its belief that it considered the profession already burdened with too many restrictions. Repeatedly, it opposed the policy of the government to limit the number of *mezzani* authorized to practice in the port and to define precisely their area of competence.[25] It considered the tariffs set by the government too high and felt (though here the opinion was not unanimous) that supervision could best be handled not by the government or the chamber of commerce but by a disciplinary body set up by the *mezzani* themselves.[26]

A group of merchants and bankers in the city empowered to study the whole problem remarked in 1850 that what was clearly needed was not a stricter set of regulations but the opening up of the profession to the beneficial effects of free competition. The law would be observed only if it were in harmony with the needs and practices of the city's commerce. Should a conflict exist between law (the *principio tecnico*) and practice (the *principio popolare*), the latter would invariably prevail.[27]

The concerns of the government were different but perhaps tended to the same end. The government's interest in the *mezzani* was linked to its perception of a 5 percent tax on the declared earnings of those authorized to practice the profession. The progressive decline of this tax (from approximately 71,000 lire in 1816 to 24,000 lire in 1822) stimulated an investigation by the customhouse in 1823, which sought to isolate the causes of the decline and to make proposals for its reparation.[28] It was perhaps only natural that the interest of government officials in a radical reform of the profession would wane after the tax on *mezzani* was incorporated into the new *tassa di commercio* in 1834 (and perception of it passed from the customhouse to the chamber of commerce). Discussion of proposed new regulations for the *mezzani* were protracted into the 1850s. The issue, however, had clearly lost the sense of urgency that, as we shall see, was so necessary for bringing any proposed reform to fruition.[29]

In another area, however, the stimulus for reform was greater, for many members of the merchant community seriously believed that Livorno needed a discount bank to insure a ready source of capital for the city's commerce at a modest rate of interest. The scarcity of currency in the city appeared serious and served to hamper commercial operations and to generate tensions within the merchant community. In 1815, on learning that a large quantity of gold francesconi had been sent to Genoa, the governor expressed his displeasure to the chamber of commerce along with his fear that such operations could have grave effects on the city's commerce.[30] In 1818 he informed the secretary of finance that the supply of liquid capital in the city was virtually exhausted. As a result, merchants were unable to pay freight and other charges on cargoes arriving in the port, and captains were forced to carry their goods elsewhere.[31]

The lack of currency in Livorno also reinforced a situation of imbalance in the Tuscan economy. In general, payments made in gold in Tuscany received a maximum discount of from 4 to 5 percent. However, due to the pressure on available supplies of currency, the discount in Livorno climbed to 7 percent. This, the governor complained, tended to encourage currency speculation and often harmed those who brought their goods from the hinterland for sale in the port city (who, with the inequality of the discount, would in effect receive less for their merchandise).[32] The scarcity of liquid capital tended to reinforce the prudence of the city's moneylenders. Generally, only modest sums of money were advanced, and as a rule goods in storage were not considered as possible sources of collateral but as liabilities.[33] The latter situation was particularly damaging in a city such as Livorno, whose prosperity was based primarily on a commerce of deposit. If a merchant needed cash, he was often forced to look for it elsewhere (in Genoa, Milan, or Rome, if not further afield), where he often found himself at the mercy of local speculators and liable to heavy transportation and insurance charges to get the specie back to Livorno.[34]

Perhaps the most serious drawback connected to the shortage of currency in the city was that it made the commerce of Livorno excessively liable to the whims of the individual—particularly foreign—capitalists. This became especially apparent in 1829, when two of the largest firms in Livorno, S. C. Bacri and Isaih Arbib, suspended their payments. The event, given ample coverage in the *Gazzetta di Firenze*[35] and in foreign journals, threatened to unleash a wave of panic in the merchant community. An article in a local newspaper, the *Indicatore livornese,*[36] attempted to reassure the public and to prevent capitalists from suspending their operations. But the task, the writer noted, was exceedingly difficult, because at the first sign of trouble moneylenders tended to close their safes and to refuse credit even to the most worthy. The whole problem lay in the individualistic character of commercial speculation.

> An individual who is determined to make a profit on his capital by lending it to commercial speculators tends with the first rumour or minimal clouding of the atmosphere (which he sees or thinks he sees) without taking the trouble to examine or verify the situation to place himself brusquely on his guard and refuses to listen to anybody. . . . The prosperity of commerce, of the city, of an entire nation are nothing to him. He is not and cannot be other than portfolio and strongbox.[37]

The situation was quite different, the writer argued, in places where the development of a "spirit of association" had favored the establishment of such institutions as discount banks. Here, capital resources were not under the control of single individuals but were spread out among a large number of small and middling investors. As a result, a continuous supply of capital could be channeled into commercial operations, for the risk and responsibility were collective, and administrators could thus take a longer perspective and avoid being overwhelmed with panic at the first sign of difficulty. "Everyone knows," the writer concluded, "that agencies with a moral purpose [*i corpi morali*] are much less subject to whims than are men."[38]

The establishment of a discount bank promised also to resolve a related problem, the high rates of interest charged by moneylenders in the city. While the rates of interest were not higher than in the past, the general decline in prices and profit margins made the traditional rates of 5 or 6 percent (not to mention the 1.5 percent monthly rates charged by some moneylenders) no longer practical.

No longer does one realize from 10 to 15 percent profit on every single sale. Now the profit on the exchange of merchandise is very moderate, and therefore the subvention of the capitalist must be paid at a lower rate. . . . All is relative.[39]

Responding realistically to the needs of the city's commerce, a discount bank would grant credit at lower rates of interest, thus enabling merchants to extend their operations into areas that promised only slender profits and permitting them to increase the volume of their transactions to compensate in part for the lower margin of profit. The bank would also help to insure that a maximum amount of capital would be employed directly in commercial operations—that is, in the production and exchange of goods and services—and would not be drained off by parasitic interest rates. Existing money-lenders would be compelled either to lower their interest rates or to employ their capital directly in commercial enterprises, both obviously advantageous for the city's economy.[40]

While proposals for the establishment of a discount bank in Livorno had been advanced in the eighteenth century,[41] the first serious appeal to the merchant community of the city to support the project appears to have been made in 1815. The merchant-banking firm of Senn, Guebhard and Company requested the chamber of commerce to support a proposal for the establishment of a corporation with a capitalization of 500,000 pezze di otto reali—200,000 in cash advanced by the shareholders, and 300,000 in paper notes emitted by the bank and having the force of legal tender.[42]

A formal reading of the project met with the general approval of the chamber. However, since the provision in the project calling for the issuing of paper money had aroused heated discussion, the president of the chamber, Panajotti Palli, decided to postpone final resolution of the issue and to invite a group of leading merchants in the city to present their opinions and to participate in the vote.[43] After prolonged discussion, these men decided to modify the resolution: the notes emitted by the bank would not have the force of legal tender, and everyone would have the option of accepting or rejecting them as he saw fit. Even with the modification of this controversial aspect, however, the proposal was narrowly defeated, eleven votes to ten.[44]

Given the summary nature of the records, it is not possible to discern which merchants opposed the proposal and for what reasons. Commentators close to the discussion later emphasized the egoism of a few large capitalists, who pushed their private interests at the expense of the interests of the community as a whole, and the shortsightedness of others, who were inert and suspicious of innovation.[45] From the general summary of the discussion, it appears that many were shaken by the specter of paper money. Others no doubt felt that given the current commercial situation—resulting from the prosperity that had followed the return of peace in Europe—such a radical innovation in Livorno's business practices was not warranted and that existing facilities were more than adequate to meet the demand for liquid capital in the city.

In any event, the setback in 1815 did not check the pressure for the establishment of the bank for long. In 1818, with the reversal of the economic situation now apparent, Governor Spannocchi urged government support for the proposal as a way of remedying the scarcity of currency in the city and combating usurious interest rates.[46] The secretary of finance, Frullani, supported the request (though not the idea of issuing notes) as a way of helping merchants pay their customs charges without giving in to pressure for an extension of the terms of credit.[47]

Only in 1829, however, did the proposal once again take the form of a concrete project. Three leading merchant-bankers in the city, Pietro Senn (whose father had made the proposal for a bank in 1815), Giovanni Olderigo Walser, and Moise Cohen Bacry, advanced a project calling for the formation of a corporation with 1,000 shares, each bearing a face value of 6,000 lire. The capital of the society would consist of two million lire in cash and four million in circulating notes (*obbligazioni girabili*). The maximum interest rate on discounted bills would be set either at 5 percent or at the rate deemed by the government to be most suitable. The sponsors cautioned that every effort should be made to keep the rate as low as possible so that the commerce of the city would obtain the greatest possible advantage from the new institution. The statutes governing the bank would be geared to render the bank secure and profitable both to those who utilized it and to those who advanced the capital for its establishment.[48]

By 1831 the project appeared to have won not only the support of the government and of important merchant-bankers in the city but that of the chamber of commerce as well. In its meeting of 15 March 1831, the chamber unanimously agreed to press for the establishment of a discount bank in the city, arguing that the advantage of such an institution was no longer in doubt and that Livorno, especially at present, was feeling the sad effects of being deprived of it.[49] It was not much use to the commerce of the city, the chamber argued, that in tranquil periods money was offered at modest discount rates of 4.5 or 5 percent if at the first sign of trouble this money was no longer available to the middling merchant (*alla classe secondaria*) and lent to principal merchant houses only on onerous terms.

> Commerce in general [the chamber concluded] requires a solid foundation on which, regardless of the circumstances, every accredited merchant can count. Where such facility is wanting, commercial operations decline and die. Such a danger, however, is not met where there exists a public discount bank that can assure the negotiability of all solid paper.[50]

Over the years the establishment of a discount bank had clearly assumed an important place in the efforts of the chamber of commerce to strengthen Livorno's commercial operations.

Despite the chamber's enthusiastic recommendation, final government approval for the project was not obtained until five years later, in a decree of 29 September 1836. In all probability, this delay is not attributable to residual opposition to the reform. The period after 1831, as we have seen, witnessed intense efforts at reform in various areas of the city's economy. Within this context, the abolition of commercial duties and the expansion of the free port would naturally take precedence over the establishment of a discount bank. Also, I do not think that the overwhelming sentiment of approval for the projected bank expressed in the chamber of commerce in 1836 can be attributed, as Mario Baruchello seems to suggest, to an almost complete change in the makeup of Livorno's merchant community.[51] True, of the twenty-one merchants who voted on the project in 1815, only three—Panajotti Palli, Giovanni Ulrich, and Michele Rodocanacchi, all of whom were favorable to the bank—were still active in the chamber at the time of the bank's final approval. But the twenty-five merchants who expressed support for the project in 1836 were not, as Baruchello implies, new arrivals in the merchant community. Seventeen of them had been active in the chamber on other occasions—six in the period from 1814 to 1819 and four others in the years from 1820 to 1829. Five had served as deputies on other occasions in the 1830s, and two held the office after 1840.

The reforms, then, were not sudden, reflecting a sharp change in the composition of the merchant community, but instead resulted from pressure exerted over a period of roughly twenty years. As such, they reflected a gradual maturation of opinion in the merchant community consonant with the increasing clarity of its perception of the city's true economic condition.

Once established, how successfully did the bank live up to the expectations of its backers? The ability of the discount bank in Livorno to facilitate the port's commercial operations was, it seems, severely limited from the beginning. In his early reports, Antonio Mochi, appointed by the government to supervise the bank, noted the disappointing level of activity of the new institution and attempted to explain it. Cholera epidemics in the Mediterranean and the collapse of large commercial firms in England and America had paralyzed economic activity, he said, leaving large supplies of capital dormant in the business houses of the city. As a result, few merchants were discounting notes, and their business was severely contested. When necessary, private bankers would lower their rates to 3 percent to undercut the position of the new bank. Many merchants felt that there was a stigma attached to discounting notes, and they preferred to do business with the private firms, where they considered the confidentiality of their affairs to be more assured. In addition, *mezzani* tended to channel their business to private discounters, who paid high commissions. Finally, Livorno's growing role as a supplier of grain for the Tuscan hinterland did not encourage discount activity in the city but impeded such activity. Virtually all grain sales in Tuscany were made on a cash basis, and during the three or four months of the year when this trade was especially active, more than 1 million lire a month in cash would flood into Livorno, augmenting the supply of specie in the city's coffers.[52]

In spite of the initial difficulties, by 1840, the discount bank seemed to be winning a degree of public acceptance. The market value of the bank's shares had risen from a base of 100 to 112, and the activity of *controbaratto* (the exchange of specie for bills issued by the bank) had grown enormously, indicating increasing confidence in the institution and in its notes. In addition, merchants from all classes had begun to present their bills to the bank for discount, surpassing even the bankers, who previously had been the institution's chief customers.[53]

The general economic situation, however, appeared unfavorable to the bank's expansion. Commerce remained sluggish, capital abundant, and competition with private discounters intense. Commissioner Mochi reported that in May 1842 the administrators of the bank met to discuss the difficult economic situation. More than 2.5 million lire were lying dormant in the bank and almost no notes were being presented for discount. The situation, he said, was worse than that experienced during the cholera epidemic in the 1830s. The only recourse of the bank's administrators was to lower the discount rate first to 4.5 and then to 4 percent in a feeble attempt to attract business.[54]

The problem of an overabundance of idle capital, Mochi indicated, was not peculiar to Livorno. A similar situation prevailed throughout Europe. In 1842, for example, more than nine million sterling were lying dormant in the Bank of London, and notes were being discounted on the London market at 2 percent.[55] The prevalence of the situation perhaps provoked Mochi's restrained appraisal of the discount bank's utility a year later:

> It is in times of restricted currency—which occur every so often in the course of commercial affairs—that the public utility of the establishment of the bank in Livorno will be evident. In prosperous times it is useful only to regulate the discount rate and perhaps to check abuses and the activity of monopolists. In the ordinary movement of commerce, and as long as the city possesses large capitalists, the individuals with shares in the bank cannot hope (*lusingarsi*) for a large return.[56]

Ironically, the most prosperous period of the bank's history occurred during the years of political and social disorder in the city in the late 1840s. Needless to say, the success of the bank in this period did not spring from the vitality of the commercial situation. On the contrary, it was the decline in commercial activity and the large supply of capital lying dormant in the bank that spurred the administrators of the institution in 1848 to consider other sources of investment. To avoid a radical change in the bank's activity, which would have required the unanimous consent of the shareholders, the administrators decided simply to admit for discount the notes of the six principal cities of Tuscany. The cities that were granted the facility of discounting their notes were Florence and Livorno (for a total of 200,000 lire each), Pisa, Lucca, and Siena (for 100,000 each), and Arezzo (for 80,000). The move was justified as a way of working in the public interest without altering the bank's statutes. At the same time, however, the administration stressed that the bank's primary function remained that of supporting commercial operations—"The assembled agree that it will be up to the executive council to refuse in whole or in part the notes emitted [*recapiti emessi*] by the aforesaid communities whenever it is necessary to hold in reserve the resources of the bank for [its] current needs or for those of the commerce of Livorno."[57]

Other factors of an extraordinary nature contributed to the bank's success in this period. The uncertain political situation tended to force liquid capital off the market, stimulating the discount activity of the bank. The government's agreement to suspend the *baratto* (the exchange of bank notes for specie) on notes having a face value superior to 200 lire was received without panic in the city and enabled the bank to cut its cash reserve and to employ more of its resources in revenue-producing operations.[58] Finally, the decision of the government early in 1849 to issue interest-bearing treasury notes having the force of legal tender, while opposed by the majority of the merchant community, did permit the bank to earn interest on a portion of its cash reserve.[59] This happy combination of circumstances enabled the bank in 1849 to pay its highest annual dividend—7⅜ percent. The situation, however, was exceptional and was little predicated on the bank's primary function in support of commerce.[60]

In the long run the success of the bank as a source of investment reflected closely both its ability to attract customers and the discount rate that it was required to pay. Only rarely, it seems, did bankruptcies or suspensions of payments cut significantly into the bank's net profits.[61] The administrators of the bank hoped to provide the shareholders a net annual return of 7 percent on their investment.[62] However, given the general commercial situation, the abundance of specie in the city, and the competition of private capitalists (all of which compelled the bank repeatedly to reduce its discount rate from 5 percent to 4 or even 3.5 percent), however, this aim proved impossible to realize. Indeed, in 1842 the return dropped to about 3.3 percent, and although it climbed to 6.5 percent in 1844, it soon dropped back to little over 4.5 percent.[63]

In 1847, Commissioner Mochi was forced to conclude that notwithstanding its invaluable contribution to the stability of commercial operations in the city over the past decade, the discount bank had not proved to have been an exceptionally lucrative investment.[64] As if to corroborate Mochi's opinion, the dividend for 1847 fell to 2.22 percent, the lowest in the bank's history. This was the first time that it had fallen below the level set by the bank's statutes to indicate sufficient public interest in the institution.[65]

Despite the bank's modest economic condition, however, its very establishment testified to the progressive character of the Livornese merchant community. True, a discount bank had been operating in Florence since 1816. However, the institution in the capital was under the close control and supervision of the central government: the government itself was the largest shareholder and provided an absolute guarantee for the convertibility of its bills. The bank in Livorno enjoyed no such guarantee, obtained its support solely from private capitalists, and yet showed far more willingness to run the risks necessary to serve the needs of the city's commerce.[66] In Milan—long reputed to be the most prosperous and progressive center of business activity in the peninsula—attempts by merchant firms to repair the inelasticity of short-term credit through the institution of a discount bank met the repeated opposition of the chamber of commerce of that city. The inveterate conservatism of the business community and its distrust of credit not secured by property in land, it seems, made reforms of the type being instituted in Livorno impossible.[67]

In an age of periodic and often colossal bank failures, the discount bank in Livorno appeared surprisingly stable and well administered. For twenty years it provided a secure source of credit and exercised a stabilizing influence on interest charges for the merchant community. A prearranged credit system helped to insure the reliability of merchants presenting their notes to the bank for discount and guaranteed a source of credit even to retail businesses and tradesmen.[68] Great care was taken to maintain an adequate cash reserve for the circulating notes of the bank. As an investment the returns may have been modest, but they were considered secure.[69] The cash value of the bank's shares remained high, although those held in Livorno were rarely sold.[70]

Most important, the discount bank represented a common endeavor for the city's merchant community. When the shares of the bank had originally been distributed, care was taken to insure maximum personal participation in the institution. The number of shares granted to each individual was limited, and preference was given to local residents who could participate actively in the bank's governance.[71] Prominent merchants in the city (such as C. A. Dalgas, Carlo Grabau, Agostino Kotzian, and Emanuele Rodocanacchi) regularly held important offices in the bank's administration. A close tie existed between the bank and the chamber of commerce. After some initial hesitation, it was the chamber of commerce that organized pressure for government approval of the bank project, and it was to the chamber to whom the administrators of the bank turned when they wanted some concession from the central government. In short, the discount bank represented another successful example of the widely extolled principle of the "spirit of association," of individuals pooling their capital and talent in an enterprise designed to further the public good.[72]

The reform efforts of the merchant community, however, were not limited to currency and banking but also extended into the area of transportation. They led to serious efforts to foster the growth of the Tuscan merchant marine, to improve the physical facilities of Livorno's port, and to provide the state with a rail network.

Traditionally, the Tuscan government had not expected merchants in Livorno to support the development of an indigenous merchant marine. The decision to establish the marine and to build a navy to protect it was made in 1748 without even consulting the merchant community, and the government vowed at the time that it in no way expected the community to help defray the expenses of the project. All agreed that merchants in Livorno stood to gain little from the development of an indigenous marine. It would certainly not facilitate ties with the more developed commercial nations, for the mercantilist policies of these states discouraged the employment of foreign shipping. The marine could not even enjoy a similar privileged position in the commerce of the Tuscan state, because the traditional freedoms of the port of Livorno guaranteed that ships of any flag would receive equal treatment in port charges and tariff duties. This freedom had permitted merchants in the city to utilize the flag that at any given moment, depending on the business at hand, offered them the greatest benefit. Since it had enabled the city to flourish at a time when an indigenous marine did not even exist, merchants could not now be expected to willingly support the trouble and expense necessary to maintain it.[73]

Scattered evidence indicates that the situation changed after 1815 and that the merchant community was now favorably disposed to the development of the Tuscan merchant marine. This is strikingly evident in the pressure exerted by merchants and the chamber of commerce to secure the right of passage for Tuscan ships into the Black Sea. In July 1823 a small group of Tuscan merchant-shipowners petitioned the governor to attempt to remedy the situation, which was working "to the great prejudice of their commerce."[74] The governor agreed and forwarded the petition to Florence, along with a personal letter emphasizing the steady growth of the marine and its contribution to the commerce of the city and the well-being of its population.[75]

Resolution of the affair, however, proved long and difficult. In November 1823, the secretary of state apologized for his delay in responding to the original petition of the merchant-shipowners, remarking that only recently, with the conclusion of negotiations between the Ottoman government and several of the great powers, had there existed the possibility of a resolution of the existing difficulties.[76] But by March 1825, still no progress had been made. Moise Fernandez, one of the signers of the original petition, was forced to request permission to withdraw his ship from the Tuscan marine, "remonstrating that with large stocks of cereals of his property in the ports of the Black Sea—where Tuscan ships could not navigate—it would be extremely damaging to him not to be able to reach them with his own ship."[77]

In view of the circumstances, the governor supported the request but urged the central government to continue efforts toward working out an agreement with the Turks, "of supreme interest to the Tuscan merchant marine and to the commerce of this city."[78] The chamber of commerce also actively supported a favorable resolution of the issue. In January 1828 the president of the chamber, Francesco Janer, on the urging of the deputies, emphasized once again the great stimulus that an agreement with the Turks for right of passage into the Black Sea would give to the development of the merchant marine and consequently to "its utility to the state, to commerce, and to all our maritime population."[79]

Despite pressure from all sides, five more years of uncertainty were to pass before the issue was finally resolved in a direct treaty between the grand duke of Tuscany and the emperor of the Ottomans, signed in Constantinople on 12 February 1833.[80]

The interest of the merchant community in the development of the Tuscan merchant marine was also reflected in the support given by the chamber of commerce to more indirect measures thought to favor its welfare. In October 1833 the chamber, "in accordance with the requests repeatedly advanced to it by many merchants and by the proprietors and captains of Tuscan ships," urged the appointment of Tuscan consuls in various ports of the Mediterranean and the Black Sea, "and especially in Odessa, Cyprus, Gibraltar, and Marseilles, with which we have extensive commercial contacts." At that time the Tuscan interests in these ports were being handled by the resident Austrian consul, and "this [the chamber argued] was certainly not very favorable for Tuscan commerce and the Tuscan marine, which could not possibly hope to obtain all the efficacious assistance and protection needed, which certainly would be given them by their own consul."[81] At the same time the chamber urged the preparation and publication of a naval code to inform the public at home and abroad of the regulations governing the merchant marine and so to enhance its reputation.[82]

Evidence scattered through the papers of the governor indicates that the favorable attitude of the merchant community to the development of the Tuscan merchant marine was based, in part, on personal economic considerations. Important merchants in the city owned ships flying the Tuscan flag. In 1823, Janer, a seven-year member of the chamber of commerce and a staunch defender of the interests of the merchant marine, had requested a Tuscan passport for his 136-ton *brigantino, Il Veloce*.[83] In the same year Domenico Castelli obtained a passport for his *brigantino, L'Aristide,* and was granted the renewal of a passport for another of his ships, the *brigantino L'Irene.*[84] In May 1824, Pietro Senn requested a Tuscan flag for a 91-ton *brigantino, Il Pacchetto di Livorno,*[85] and in June of the same year he requested Tuscan status for a ship that he had recently purchased, the 83-ton *goletta Santa Maria.*[86] The papers of the Tuscan consul in Algiers indicate that in 1838, Senn and another important merchant in Livorno, Niccola Manteri, were proprietors of two ships arriving in the port that year with grain.[87]

The motives that induced merchants in Livorno to become shipowners and to endow their ships with the Tuscan flag are a matter of speculation. The absence of a series of freight charges makes it difficult to ascertain the appeal of this activity as an investment.[88] Convenience and the desire to insure the availability of a carrier when needed might have been just as important as freight income in inducing merchants to own their own ships, with the relative moderation of Tuscan maritime exactions perhaps providing a further inducement to adopt the local flag.[89]

Besides private economic motives, one should also consider the social justification for the development of the merchant marine, which was repeatedly expressed by members of the merchant community. Niccolo Pezzer, vice president of the chamber of commerce, perhaps summarized this concern best when he remarked in 1833 that "the growth of our merchant marine has become today an object of supreme importance for this city, since for its ever-growing population it is necessary to extend as much as one can the means of subsistence [i.e., employment]."[90] In 1748 economic and social considerations had underlain state sponsorship of the maritime project. Roughly a century later, these same concerns were the property of the merchant community as a whole.

Under pressure from Livorno, the central government in Florence endeavored to strengthen the merchant marine. The physical aggrandizement of the Tuscan state in the post-Napoleonic period served to reinforce this concern. The port of Piombino was ceded to Tuscany at the time of the restoration of the grand ducal government, the Island of Elba after the Hundred Days (when Napoleon attempted to recapture power in France), and the state of Lucca (with its port of Viareggio) in 1847. The 900 ships and roughly 8,000 inhabitants who lived off the sea in these territories could not help but induce the Tuscan government to take a more active concern in its marine.[91] Neither could the government remain insensitive to the concern shown by neighboring states in the development of their marines and the contribution that these were making to the commercial prosperity of their states.[92]

The Tuscan government endeavored to favor the development of its merchant marine by negotiating with other states to obtain "most favored nation" status for its ships. The treaty signed by Tuscany with the Ottoman government in 1833 is a case in point.[93] In 1836, in response to a request made by the governor of Livorno through the Tuscan consul in New York, the U.S. government agreed to abolish all special duties and tonnage charges levied on Tuscan ships and their cargoes in U.S. ports.[94]

But Tuscany's position in these negotiations was fundamentally weak. Almost all states in this period attempted to favor the growth of their merchant marines by imposing high differential tariffs and port charges on foreign shipping. Thus, for example, anchorage duties for a ship of 200 tons in Genoa in 1833 were set at the equivalent of 285.14.2 lire if the ship were Tuscan and only 71.8.8 lire if it were Sard.[95] Tuscan shippers operating in the kingdom of the Two Sicilies in 1849 found themselves forced to pay a supplementary charge of 10 percent on the value of goods introduced and extracted from that kingdom, a charge that in the important case of oil reached one-third the value.[96] These duties, of course, could be negotiated, and a state was often willing to modify its own charges in return for a similar concession from the other party. Tuscany, however, whose principal port was already one of the most free in Europe, had little to offer. As Giovanni Baldasseroni, the future secretary of finance, later remarked, "Foreign states took advantage of Tuscan liberality without giving anything in return, and not esteeming something which was conceded to everyone, claimed that Tuscany had nothing to grant in order to obtain a favor."[97]

The desire to win reciprocal treatment for the Tuscan merchant marine gradually overcame the reluctance of government officials to establish some form of differential charges. The publication in 1846 of a new scale of navigation, sanitary, and port charges provided a fitting occasion for the government not only to standardize these charges in all ports of the Grand Duchy but also to obtain a lever for winning concessions from other states. The increases were modest but were pointedly levied against those states that had not yet worked out reciprocal agreements with the Tuscan government.[98]

Shortly before the new charges were to take effect (1 March 1847), the government announced that agreements had been concluded with the United States, the kingdoms of Sweden and Norway, and the Russian Empire. The agreements would grant to the ships of these states full parity of treatment with ships flying the Tuscan flag, and vice versa. On the basis of continuing negotiations, Tuscany granted England and the Papal States provisional parity.[99] Negotiations continued with other states. Finally, in 1853, Tuscany signed agreements with the two outstanding holdouts, France and the kingdom of the Two Sicilies.[100]

The government provided concrete support for the development of the Tuscan merchant marine. The potential strength of the local shipbuilding industry made the prospects of success in this sector ever more sure. Indeed, Livorno's natural position, coupled with the privileges of its free port, made the area especially propitious for the development of this activity. Raw materials were relatively cheap, of high quality, and available. The hills behind Livorno abounded in timber,[101] and iron was easily available from the royal mines in Elba. Hemp of high quality (for the manufacture of rope) was brought from Bologna, and pitch, tar, and fir poles (for masts) were imported in quantity from Sweden and Russia.[102]

Although employing methods that even by contemporary standards were considered archaic, manufacturers producing for the shipbuilding industry in Livorno turned out goods of unrivaled excellence. Indeed, the very "handicraft" nature of these trades, combined with the quality of raw materials employed, seemed to provide the key to the excellence of the finished products. Rope manufacturers in Livorno used the superior hemp of Bologna.[103] Even after the development of mechanical apparatuses they continued to spin their rope by hand, thus insuring a more uniform distribution of the fiber along the entire cord and giving the finished product greater strength and durability. So excellent was the product that the majority of it was shipped to Genoa, Ancona, Trieste, and even Greece.[104] Livorno was also noted for the quality of its canvas sails. Made of linen or hemp and stitched by hand, this product too proved especially favored by foreign buyers, in particular the English.[105]

Unfortunately, little information exists on the shipbuilding industry in Livorno in the late eighteenth and early nineteenth centuries. Facilities were undoubtedly always available for caulking and repairing ships in the port, and several workshops existed then (as they do today) for the construction of barges and small ships particularly suited to the coastal trade and for fishing. Evidence suggests, however, that in the early nineteenth century a shipbuilding industry oriented toward the construction of larger vessels was still in its infancy: commissions tended to be extraordinary occurrences, and shipbuilding clearly played a role that was subordinate to the port's primary commercial activity. Such, it seems, was also the case with the individual shipbuilders, as is evident from Governor Spannocchi's description of Giovanni Bastiani in 1820.[106]

Bastiani had originally acquired favor with the Algerian Regency for repairing one of its corvettes. As a result, in 1820 the Algerian government authorized him to construct a merchant ship and to send it to Algiers with a stipulated cargo. That the vessel during construction suspiciously took on the aspect of a warship and prompted a demand for clarification from the Tuscan government, ever vigilant to preserve its reputation for neutrality, need not concern us here. More important is the governor's description of Bastiani as being in close, regular contact with the regency from which he had received numerous commissions. Indeed, said the governor, on several occasions Bastiani had been requested to send wood, iron, pitch, cables, and even grain to Algiers, "which, it seems to me, must have facilitated the negotiations for construction of the ship."[107]

The best-known shipbuilder in Livorno in this period was Luigi Mancini. Although he had undoubtedly been operating earlier, Mancini became generally recognized for his talents only in the 1820s, when he was commissioned to build two warships for the viceroy of Egypt. Mancini's role in the commission was restricted to the actual design and construction of the vessels. The delicate negotiations that had resulted in the awarding of the contract to Livorno—severely contested by shipbuilders in other ports—were handled by Dionisio Fernandez, who was in charge of the whole operation.[108] The job was an important one and had a definite impact on the economy of the city: the *gonfaloniere* estimated that the construction of the two ships had put more than 700,000 pezze into circulation in Livorno, "to the great advantage of the general population."[109]

Descriptions of the launching of the larger of the two vessels on 9 November 1826 provide a further sense of the importance of the commission and of the still extraordinary character of the shipbuilding industry in Livorno. The ceremony was attended by the court and by 40,000 spectators. From the grand duke, Mancini received the Royal Cross of Merit and a commission in the royal navy, and Fernandez presented him with a gift of 200 gold zecchini. That evening Mancini was present in Fernandez's box at the theater and received a standing ovation from the assembled company.[110]

The impact of special commissions on the economy of the city, then, was strikingly apparent. By 1830, however, officials such as the *gonfaloniere* had decided that it was time to pass from extraordinary commissions to regular production, which could best be assured by developing the Tuscan merchant marine. The moment seemed especially propitious. The recent French conquest of Algeria had virtually eliminated the threat of the Barbary pirates, a major hindrance to the free movement of ships in the Mediterranean. The treaty between the Russians and the Turks at roughly the same time generated hopes for the imminent granting of Black Sea access to Tuscan ships.[111]

Notwithstanding the efforts of government officials and members of the merchant community, the growth of the Tuscan merchant marine in this period was not spectacular. A prospectus in the state archive in Florence covering the thirty-year period from 1820 to 1850 indicates that after 1829 the number of large sailing ships (*bastimenti quadri*) based in Livorno leveled off and remained relatively stationary through midcentury.[112] The year 1830 marked the first occasion since the restoration in which the total tonnage of the Tuscan merchant marine actually declined.[113]

Several factors, it seems, served to restrict the growth of Tuscan shipping. One important cause, the policy of differential tariffs and port charges, has already been noted. The Tuscan government, as we have seen, succeeded in negotiating reciprocal agreements with many states. Failure to reach a lasting accord with France and the kingdom of the Two Sicilies before 1853, however, made it virtually impossible for Tuscany to develop its potential for steam navigation, as steamship lines in the Tyrrhenian Sea were expected to touch the ports of Marseilles and Naples. As a result the steamships *Leopoldo II, Maria Antonetta, Dante,* and *Lombardo*—all built in Livorno and universally admired for the solidity of their construction—were forced to renounce the Tuscan flag for that of France or Sardinia, states that possessed the requisite agreements for a viable itinerary.[114] Another holdout was Spain. As a result of the prejudicial duties levied in the ports of that state, the Tuscan merchant marine in 1830 lost nine ships placed on the run between America and Barcelona.[115]

More fundamental causes served to hamper the growth of the merchant marine in Livorno. State regulations required that the captains and two-thirds of the crew of ships flying the Tuscan flag be Tuscan subjects or at least residents in the Grand Duchy. This requirement often proved difficult to meet. Notwithstanding the existence of a school of navigation in Livorno, competent captains were in short supply.[116] The recruitment of honest crewmen was just as difficult.[117] The population of much of the Tuscan littoral was sparse, and young men in the zone were reluctant to take on the fatigue and peril of a life at sea when a city like Livorno offered them a more enticing source of work and gain.[118] The problem was simple, remarked Luigi Serristori, with the fatalistic tone natural to one who was a principal practitioner of the prevailing liberal ideology. "The existence of a national marine could not be but the child of necessity. It would make itself felt only when there existed an excess population in Livorno itself or on the Tuscan littoral, a population that could no longer earn its livelihood save through maritime navigation."[119]

As with other sources of tension in Livorno's economic and social structure, the problem of the merchant marine came to a head during the period of political turbulence in the late 1840s. In 1847 and 1848, fourteen large merchant ships renounced the Tuscan flag for that of Jerusalem, a paper government that was under the protection of France and that sold navigation patents for the benefit of the holy places.[120] From February 1849 to January 1850, twelve more ships—totaling 1,773.68 tons—did likewise.[121] The government in Florence received a barrage of memorials discussing the exodus and attempting to pinpoint its causes.[122] Several causes have already been discussed. Others, such as the weight of the navigation taxes and other charges levied on shipowners by the Tuscan government, were of more recent vintage and perhaps reflected the pressure of new competition. In addition, several cited as a principal cause of the defection the popular disturbances in the city.[123] The demands advanced by Tuscan sailors in this period calling for work and wage guarantees[124] may have had an important effect in scaring shipowners away from the Tuscan flag, as the government had feared.

In any event, notwithstanding the outcry, defection to the flag of Jerusalem did not drastically alter the number of large Tuscan merchant ships based in Livorno.[125] From a broader perspective the situation might even be considered to have improved. While the number of Tuscan merchant ships based in Livorno, Elba, and Orbetello in the period of 1846–1855 dropped by eleven, the total tonnage of the Tuscan ships in these ports rose from 24,147.86 to 46,695.45, and the number of their crewmen rose from 5,142 to 5,598.[126] These figures illustrate a general diminishment of interest in the coastal trade and a growing involvement in the hauling of bulky cargoes—especially grain—over long distances, which we have already examined in another context.[127] Ultimately, then, the impact of the revolutionary turbulence of 1848 may have been positive. Perhaps it served to force government officials to temper their optimism and to aspire not so much for a massive merchant marine as for one that would be well regulated and would be served by competent captains and honest crews.[128]

The interest of the merchant community in developing the marine led almost naturally to a concern for improving the facilities of the port. The efforts of merchants in this sector are interesting to look at not only because they reinforce the picture of the merchant community as being vitally interested in improving the commercial situation of the city but also because—along with the railway projects, which we shall examine next—these efforts throw into greater relief the capitalistic impulses that provided an important ingredient of the merchants' reform movement.

Laments on the poor state of the port were a recurrent theme in the memorials of the merchant community in this period. This was perhaps natural, because the government had made no major effort to enlarge the port or to better insure the safety of ships awaiting admission to the docks since its construction of a new dock (the *Molo Cosimo*) in 1620. In 1821 the governor sent a long dispatch to Florence outlining various projects designed to make the port more secure. In it, he stressed that the adoption of these projects was essential to block the growing defection of ships to Genoa and Marseilles.[129] The government, however, short of funds and already pledged to a massive project for the reclamation of the city of Livorno itself, was unable at that time to assume responsibility for the port project.

In the 1830s the project was picked up by a small group of local merchant bankers. The origins of their initiative are uncertain. In a letter to the captain of the port, in 1840 a certain A. Mighi (not further identified) remarked that in October 1838 he was requested by a foreign banking firm (Valaken and Company) to suggest a project in Livorno in which one could profitably employ a large sum of capital. Mighi proposed the construction of a new pier, "which would render the port of this city more spacious and secure and facilitate access to it and would end the necessity of forcing ships arriving in Livorno to spend part of their period of quarantine at the shore [outside the port] where they were always insecure and often lost with their cargoes."[130] After drawing up a firm project, Mighi argued, he was requested to lend it to Giovanni Ulrich, who instead of returning it submitted the project to the government under other auspices.[131]

Regardless of the veracity of Mighi's claim (certainly not unusual at the time with projects of this sort, though impossible to substantiate given the lack of documentation), the first official recognition of the port project is contained in a letter from the secretary of finance to the governor of Livorno authorizing three commercial firms in Livorno—Santi Borgheri, Son and Company, Simiani E. Borgheri, and Fortunato Regini—to draw up at their own risk and expense plans for the construction of a new wharf for ships in quarantine (*molo di quarantina*). The request of these firms to set up a limited-liability company and to sell shares to the public was not approved pending completion of the preliminary studies.[132]

The major source of information on the port project is Giuseppe Vivoli, sanitary commissioner and part-time chronicler of Livorno's history.[133] Vivoli, it seems, acted as secretary for the project and served as a liaison between its backers and the central government. A map in his manuscript "L'Accrescimento progressivo di Livorno" provides a sense of the magnitude of the project and its potential profit.[134] It involved both an enlargement of the dock area and the construction of a new port. The two sections of wharf nearest the shore would be filled with the debris from the leveled bastions of the Murata and Cappuccini gates and with earth from the hill of the Fortezza Nuova. The area reclaimed by this operation would be ceded to the company, and on it would be constructed a plaza and eleven large blocks of housing. The three major streets of the city would be extended to the new port area, thus facilitating the circulation of fresh air. The leveled

terrain of the Murata gate would be utilized as a deposit area
for bulky materials and as a shipyard. The present port would
become the new wharf area and would be far larger and
deeper than the old. Beyond it would be constructed the new
dock, which would in effect enclose a second port equal in
size to the first. With the completion of this project, said
Vivoli, Livorno could by right call itself the "Emporium of the
Two Ports."[135]

Vivoli worked diligently to win government approval for
the project. In May 1840 he wrote to the private secretary of
the grand duke, outlining a project being drawn up in Genoa
for the construction of a large free-warehouse zone. Completion of the project, he argued, would threaten Livorno's pri-
macy as a port of deposit for grain from the Black Sea. Only
the construction of a new port for ships in quarantine—where
grain could be unloaded swiftly and inexpensively under all
weather conditions—would enable Livorno to keep pace with
its rivals.[136]

Despite Vivoli's efforts, however, the project remained
stillborn. Contrary to an injunction on publicity, an article
containing detailed information about the project appeared
in the Milanese financial newspaper *Eco della borsa*. The reaction of government officials was especially bitter because the
article not only represented a breach of faith but also contained a strain of satire, suggesting that the project was not
an original creation but was simply following the traces laid
down by previous sovereigns. In a situation in which the
royal prerogative still had meaning, the episode, as Vivoli
feared, could not help but undermine the whole project.[137] In
any event no further mention was made of it, and efforts to
enlarge the port only recommenced with the explosion of
commercial activity in the late 1840s.

The famines that began to affect Europe in the fall of 1846
provided the stimulus for this renewed commercial activity.
In 1847, 1,043 large ships (*di grossa portata*) carrying grain and
other comestibles from Russian ports in the Black Sea alone
dropped anchor in Livorno.[138] Toward the end of June so
many ships were arriving simultaneously that they could not
all be admitted into the port.[139] In the spring of the following

year the situation appeared even more critical. The dock areas were solidly packed, no free space in which ships could maneuver remained in the port, and the entrance was cluttered with ships directly transferring their cargoes. The captain of the port argued that the government must reconsider enlarging the port, for with the increasing commercial movement and the greater size and carrying capacity of the ships involved, its inadequacy had become glaringly apparent.[140]

Once again pressure for a definitive resolution of the issue began to mount in the merchant community.[141] C. A. Dalgas, an important merchant in the city, suggested a plan for dredging the port and building a deposit for bulky merchandise. His proposal won the support of many individual merchants as well as of the chamber of commerce, which invited him to go to Florence with a delegation to present the project to the central government in person.[142] Dalgas's proposal ultimately proved too modest to provide an adequate response to the city's needs, and a concerted, successful effort to solve the port problem would have to wait until after the hiatus provided by the revolution of 1848.[143] The proposal itself, however, is important to an understanding of the reform movement in Livorno, for it included a strong plea against entrusting large public works to private corporations.

> Too often in recent times [Dalgas remarked], limited-liability societies have fallen into discredit, and not unjustly, considering the paralysis that they injected into the veins of even our merchant community [*corpo commerciale*], the abuses of their administration, and the incredible lethargy with which they carried on their work. Today, even a company promoted by upright merchants aiming for the public good and perceiving only an honest gain would have difficulty finding capital, and having raised it would run the risk of seeing the whole enterprise fall . . . into the hands of avid speculators, who would renew the usual scandals and abuses. Far better for the dignity of the government and the public good that such an enterprise be carried out at the order and expense of the state.[144]

Dalgas's plea provides clear evidence of a reaction against that spirit of association, which had provided the ideological underpinnings for the association of private capital in large public or semipublic enterprises. Whether this disenchantment was general and would serve ultimately to weaken the efforts toward economic and social reform in the city remains to be seen. At present our task will simply be to indicate possible sources of this disenchantment and to pinpoint it in time. Perhaps the best way of initiating this task is to examine railroad construction projects in the state. It is this sector of the Tuscan economy in which public utility and private gain came together in the most volatile manner.

The distinction between public and private interests in Tuscan railway projects was made explicit early, thanks to the decision of the secretary of finance in February 1836 to obtain the opinion of important merchants in Livorno on whether a projected rail line linking Livorno and Florence would stimulate Tuscany's transit commerce.[145] The overall response was not encouraging. The merchants who were questioned recognized in theory the importance of the railroad both as a stimulus to entrepreneurial activity and as a relatively inexpensive way to transport raw materials to the producer and finished products to the market. Several commented specifically on the importance of the rail network in Belgium and on the line linking Liverpool and Manchester in Great Britain. Turning their attention to Tuscany, however, they universally agreed that the proposed project offered little commercial promise and, moreover, posed a definite threat to those currently transporting merchandise between the two cities.

None of the merchants questioned considered that the proposed line linking Livorno and Florence would extend transit commerce beyond the narrow sphere to which it was currently restricted. To Antonio Filicchi, the volume of goods in transit between the two cities would remain the same regardless of the means of transportation.[146] In any case, asserted Ignazio Torricelli, an associate of Ulrich, Florence was not a manufacturing center like Manchester, which required large daily injections of raw materials from its coastal emporium. It made little difference whether goods made the journey in three hours or in twelve. If necessary, a producer could ship merchandise to Livorno in a few hours at a slight

additional expense. Generally, however, speed was unnecessary, as the departure time of a ship was known well in
advance.[147] All merchants questioned took a similar position.
Dalgas, who considered this aspect of the question from several perspectives, argued that although the project might
stimulate the spirit of entrepreneurship in Tuscany and the
movement of passengers between the two principal cities of
the state, only if the line were extended beyond Florence to
the rich centers of northern and central Italy would commercial considerations justify the trouble and expense.[148]

Along with doubts about the commercial advantages of the
project went fears about its impact on those currently engaged
in the transport trades. At present, remarked Torricelli, the
gains that this trade brought to a portion of the Tuscan population were enormous and were readily apparent in the bustle
of activity and the signs of prosperity along the route, which
gave the line between Livorno and Florence the aspect of a
continuous suburb.[149]

The social effects of disturbing this activity were well
known. During the drought of 1833–34, when the Arno River
was closed to traffic, hundreds of individuals of all ages wan-
dered through the countryside and clustered on the public
thoroughfares begging for some succor to meet their most
urgent needs. How much greater the misery would be if not
just one but *all* existing means of transport between the two
cities were to be suddenly and permanently crippled by a
powerful new competitor![150]

The proposed rail line, then, appeared impossible to justify
on either economic or social grounds. It would not stimulate
transit commerce, and it threatened to reduce to the most
abject misery the hundreds of families who were engaged in
transporting merchandise and passengers between Livorno
and the capital. Given these factors and the generally negative
assessment of both the merchants and the director of the
customhouse, it might appear strange that many merchants
and bankers (including some of those questioned) would later
rush to invest in the project and that the line itself would
ultimately win the approval of the central government.

The reason is not difficult to discover. As merchants, the

future backers of the rail project appeared lukewarm; as investors, however, they were extremely anxious to take advantage of the project's speculative possibilities both for themselves and for their correspondents outside the state. Indeed, the early history of the project witnessed a struggle for control between several contending groups of capitalists. On 24 March 1838, Pietro Senn (head of an important banking firm in Livorno) informed the grand ducal government that he had received more than 7 million lire in pledges from his correspondents, and sent his associate, Agostino Kotzian, to Florence to press the government for concession of the line.

In a personal petition to the grand duke, Kotzian asserted his reliability and loyalty to the Tuscan state (points that were necessary to affirm when a petition was advanced from a merchant in Livorno) and urged that the government approve the project while the enthusiasm of the investors was still high.[151] The Florentine banking firm of Emmanuele Fenzi had in the meantime advanced a similar request. A protracted struggle between the chief contenders for the project was averted when Fenzi and Senn announced that they had decided to unite "to effect the things previously requested separately."[152] The union appeared to be a sensible one. Both men had previously been the principal financial intermediaries of an earlier rail project sponsored by Dini-Castelli and Luigi Serristori (and therefore both had some sense of the difficulties of raising the capital),[153] and they possessed different, though complementary, talents for winning the concession and carrying the project to fruition. Senn contributed the bulk of the capital, while Fenzi provided solid contacts at court, especially with the secretary of finance.[154]

Ironically, Senn and Fenzi's main competition for the concession came from a group of capitalists in Livorno, several of whom had previously condemned the project.[155] Like most issues affecting the commerce of the city, the proposal of the local capitalists went first to the chamber of commerce, where it won overwhelming support. In making its recommendation the chamber reversed many of the reservations that had been expressed by the merchants and the director of the customhouse in 1836. The movement of goods between Livorno and Florence was now described as "vast and continuous," and reservations about the social impact of the line were replaced by fear that if Tuscany did not act quickly its commerce would be harmed by lines projected in other states.[156]

But the backers of the project approved by the chamber of commerce proved unable to overcome the strong position of Senn and Fenzi at court,[157] and on 24 April 1838 the two bankers announced that they had received government permission to begin amassing capital and preparing studies for the projected line.[158] In making the announcement, the promoters immediately began trying to sell the project to potential backers by stressing the suitability of the line and its potential for facilitating communications between Livorno and the Adriatic.[159] The sales talk was not needed to drum up the enthusiasm of local capitalists—three-quarters of the 50,000 shares reserved by the act of incorporation for Tuscans or foreign residents in the state were subscribed four hours after being placed on the market, and those remaining were sold within only a few days, despite the decision to limit individual purchases to 50 shares.[160]

Foreign investors, however, appeared reluctant to snatch up the approximately 24,000 shares remaining. Many, the promoters reported, found the 10 percent down payment that had to be made at the time of purchase too high for a project that still lacked the secure approval of the government, and they feared—correctly—that the interest paid on this sum would be at the expense of the general society. In addition, the inauguration of a host of similar projects in Europe (especially in France), even though these were less solid and less potentially profitable, tended to dampen the general speculative enthusiasm and to make investors more cautious. Never ones to end on a pessimistic note, Fenzi and Senn stressed that despite these adverse circumstances, three-fourths of the capital had already been collected by June 1839 and that the rest would be immediately forthcoming when the project received the definite approval of the government.[161]

The estimate on the state of capitalization was probably high, for in December, Kotzian announced that the projected company had secured only 11 million lire.[162] Understandably, the promoters became more pessimistic. Government approval of the project would now not simply facilitate the raising of the necessary capital but was absolutely crucial to the effort.

> As long as it remains doubtful whether the government will or will not grant the concession, one cannot hope to discover any new shareholder.[163]

In addition, to assure a sufficiently high rate of return and to attract additional investors, the promoters requested the right to set rates for passenger and freight service without government interference, subject only to the stipulation that they would not exceed current charges on the service between the terminal cities. This was certainly a far cry from the notion that the railroad would produce a significant reduction in transportation costs, a prominent argument in earlier petitions. Most indicative of the growing sense of caution, however, was the demand that the company be permitted to construct the first section of the line (from Livorno to Pisa) and to assess its profitability before continuing the line to Florence.[164] Finally, the promoters criticized a provision that gave the Tuscan government the right to take over the line at any time simply by reimbursing the society for the expenses of construction. So important did the promoters consider this stipulation in discouraging investment (particularly foreign investment) that they criticized it forcefully even as they announced the successful completion of their campaign to raise the necessary 30 million lire.[165]

Although cautious, the central government generally supported the efforts of the promoters. Baldasseroni, secretary of finance when the line was completed, noted that two fundamental considerations determined government policy in the area of railroad construction: first, that it was neither proper nor opportune for the state to take on the expense necessary to endow Tuscany with a suitable rail network, and second, that private companies in Tuscany with foreign contacts could best supply the capital lacking within the state.

Such a policy, Baldasseroni argued, was not only financially expedient but was also in harmony with a favorable attitude toward free trade. In these circumstances, the best way to encourage railroad construction would be for the government to leave the largest scope to private enterprise, intervening only when necessary to support and coordinate the effort and to protect the public interest.[166]

Thus, the government took an active role in examining the details of the line—in approving the route, in supervising the amount of compensation paid to proprietors along the way, and in regulating rates and schedules. To provide the greatest incentive to private enterprise, however, the government's final approval of the project included a 100-year guarantee to the promoters over the profits of the line.[167]

Although public opinion in Tuscany had been only mildly stirred by the railroad project, the mood soon changed. The first section of the line from Livorno to Pisa proved remarkably successful. From March 1844 to January 1845, approximately half a million people were conveyed between the two cities. The returns were twice the amount estimated and gave rise to expectations of a 6 percent dividend.[168] A distinct ardor for speculative ventures replaced the previous attitude of suspicion and reserve.[169] More than twenty projects for rail lines in the state were drafted and presented to the government for approval.[170] The backers of a proposed line linking Siena and Empoli (the Centrale) were reported to have raised nearly all the capital required for construction in Livorno within twenty-four hours after shares were placed on the market.[171]

The impetus behind this speculative activity, however, appears to have been less that of a desire to foster the public interest than of a desire for private gain. Indeed, it often appeared more important to project a line than to actually build it, for by glorifying the commercial advantages of a proposal and exaggerating its probable return one could obtain a premium on the sale of shares (or even of share pledges [*promesse d'azioni*]) without undergoing the work and risk of actual construction.[172]

Perhaps the most notable—or notorious—example of railroad speculation in Tuscany was the so-called Maremmana project, which proposed the linking of Livorno with the Papal States by way of the Tuscan city of Grosetto. In April 1845 the government awarded the preliminary concession for the line to a group of capitalists from Livorno.[173] What followed, however, was a great deal of propaganda for the project but little effort at initiating the preliminary studies. Newspaper advertisements reported that the line would pass through fertile plains and, with the line linking Livorno and Florence, would serve to tie the Tuscan capital to Rome and Naples: "It was destined to become the most natural avenue of communications between these three capitals and one of the most useful and beautiful lines of the peninsula."[174] The words were mellow, but the facts should have aroused the suspicion of the informed reader. Only in a flight of fancy could one characterize the plague-ridden Maremma as "a fertile plain," and the small, miserable population that stayed in the area year-round could scarcely be expected to provide an adequate social and economic base for the line's support.[175] In addition, the papal government's general attitude of disfavor toward railroads raised some doubt as to whether it would be possible to push the line to Rome, much less to extend it to Naples.[176]

The promoters not only exaggerated the beauty of the terrain and the probable usefulness of the line but also underestimated its cost and misrepresented the demand for shares. Thus, as one critic noted, a simple consideration of the length of the projected line and the probable cost per kilometer would set the estimated cost of construction at 47,228,300 rather than the 32 million lire indicated by the promoters.[177] In addition, the *Annali universali di statistica* (Milan) revealed that the promoters were reporting requests for 140,000 shares, even though only 32,000 were available for sale. All of this, it appears, was done in the interest of stimulating enthusiasm for the project and enhancing the value of its shares.[178]

Efforts to construct a railroad network in Tuscany, then, gave rise to the full range of speculative practices. As a result, government policy in this area came under increasing criticism. As noted, the primary considerations of the government were to spare the public treasury and encourage the utiliza-

tion of foreign capital.[179] The grand duke, at least in the beginning, seems not to have entertained high hopes for the future
of the railroad in Tuscany or for its beneficent impact on the
economy of the state. In line with the dominant economic
principles of Tuscan society, the government refused to hin-
der the efforts of private enterprise, considering simply that
those projects that had true and recognized utility would
succeed and that those that did not would fail. Only in April
1845 did the government attempt to impose firmer guidelines
for the approval of future projects,[180] and these guidelines
appear to have had little effect in improving the situation or
checking the abuses.[181]

Despite the censure, even one of the harshest critics, Corrado De Biase, admitted that notwithstanding the abuses Tuscany had been endowed with one of the best rail networks
in the peninsula. He also noted that the state would not have
been able to construct this network solely with its own
resources.[182] Nevertheless, the abuses did leave their mark
on the spirit of reform in Livorno. They clearly underlay
C. A. Dalgas's attempt to block efforts to institute a private
corporation to repair the physical inadequacy of Livorno's
port.[183] The same scandals and abuses cited by Dalgas were
present in Francesco Domenico Guerrazzi's response to the
address from the throne in June 1848.[184] In reply to the government's assertion of the commercial advantages of railroad
construction in Tuscany, Guerrazzi stressed the lack of coor-
dination among the various projects and the pure, speculative
intentions of the backers. An opportune moment had been
clearly lost and a sincere desire for public utility had been
allowed to give way to a thirst for private gain. Coming from
Guerrazzi—who was one of the principal members of the
reform movement in Livorno (though certainly not the least
critical), and who had guided the efforts of the progressive
Indicatore livornese during its brief existence[185]—the criticism
is significant. No longer, it seems, could one present the
idea of "association" in the same idealistic hues employed
in the 1830s. Despite recognized achievements in the economic sphere, the communal spirit of reform had been tar-

nished by blind speculation and the selfish pursuit of profit. Whether this experience would also occur in the evolution of social attitudes and programs will be our next subject of investigation.

PART FOUR

Reform Continued—
The Social Response
of the Merchant Community

CHAPTER FIVE

Social Attitudes and
Voluntary Associations

Up until now we have concentrated on the economic concerns of Livorno's merchant community. We have examined the economic attitudes of the community and its reform proposals in light of the actual commercial situation of the port city. Demands for tariff reform, for a rationalization of business practices, and for improved transportation and port facilities were all seen as part of an effort to improve Livorno's economic situation at a time of declining prices and profit margins and increased competition from rival ports. To concentrate solely on the economic concerns of the merchant community, however, would serve only to distort the nature of its reform activity, for in virtually every instance the desire for economic improvement was tempered by an equal if not more pressing concern to reinforce the stability of the social order.

The tension that could result from a desire for both social order and economic progress is readily apparent in two articles on the state of the Tuscan economy written in 1838 by Giuliano Ricci.[1] In both articles, Ricci (a Livornese notable) criticized the fragmentary character of the Tuscan economy and the emphasis placed on the small, independent producer. Large associations of capital and enterprise, Ricci noted, were virtually nonexistent in the state, and as a result Tuscan products were in a poor position to compete with those of more highly developed economies in the free market. The state of the Tuscan economy could be summarized in the following fashion: "Highest importance given to agriculture. Infinite subdivision of the land. Few or no large industrial associations. Few large manufacturers. An almost infinite number of small [manufacturers]. Scarcity of most industrial products. In a word, individuality in all forms of industry."[2]

The degree of Tuscan economic backwardness, Ricci recognized, was difficult to measure. Rudimentary statistics on the volume of exports and internal sales indicated that Tuscany remained extremely poor. However, statistics measured only goods sold in the market; they did not include the value of goods consumed directly by their producers or exchanged through simple barter. This limitation, Ricci argued, was of crucial importance in a country like Tuscany, where the peasantry formed the predominant sector of the total population and consumed a large portion of the goods that it produced. Moreover, the Tuscan peasant was not simply a farmer—he, along with members of his family, also performed the tasks of woodsman, spinner, weaver, and shoemaker. Small wonder, then, that with so large a portion of the Tuscan population more or less economically self-sufficient, commercial statistics provided a poor indication of the true state of the Tuscan economy.[3]

Ultimately, though, to Ricci the real worth of the Tuscan economy could not be assessed on the basis of mere quantitative factors but only from the perspective of the qualitative benefits that it offered to the producer and, through the producer, to the society as a whole. In this regard, Ricci considered the Tuscan economic system clearly superior to those of more highly developed countries. Small business and small, independent landholdings in Tuscany may have hampered economic specialization and the accumulation of large amounts of capital. But at the same time, these factors served to encourage the development of an independent and prosperous working-class population that felt a personal stake in the existing economic order. As a result, workers in Tuscany were firm supporters of the law, insuring that the society would remain virtually immune from any threat of serious social disturbance.[4]

Certainly, one could argue that Ricci's view of the Tuscan economy was too optimistic: a simple consideration of the number of presentations at the Florentine Academy of the Georgofili devoted to the themes of technical backwardness and social pauperization should be sufficient to divest anyone of the notion that the Tuscan economy was in a healthy state.[5] Nevertheless, Ricci's cautious approach to the problem was characteristic of the general attitude of Tuscan reformers. Thus, Cosimo Ridolfi, Rafaello Lambruschini, and Lapo de' Ricci (to cite only three of the most notable reformers) all moved from the premise that Tuscany had to develop its economic potential, if only to retain its competitive position in an evolving world and to supply the needs of its expanding population.

While advocating progress, however, none wished to dissolve the bonds of the traditional social order. Their principal efforts were directed toward strengthening the most important—and conservative—sector of the Tuscan economy, agriculture. Their interest in manufacturing extended only to the refining of Tuscan agricultural and mineral products, which currently were being exported as raw materials. Proposals for reform in other areas—for example, in facilitating internal communications, encouraging the voluntary association of capital, and improving the state of primary education—also had a conservative thrust. Progress was desired, provided that it would not erode Tuscany's traditional forms of economic organization, dissolve the paternalistic tie between capital and labor, undermine the principles of free trade and competition, or require governmental intervention in sectors that had long been the preserve of private enterprise.[6]

Ricci's conservative emphasis, however, was not invariable. In discussing the economy and society of his native city, Livorno, he seemed far more amenable to the forces of modernity. He was proud that historically the landed aristocracy of the province, high ecclesiastical offices, and the institutions of classical culture were based not in Livorno but in Pisa. As a result, the port city was able to retain its character as a vibrant, open society in which individual status in the community was defined not by the position of one's family in a fixed social order but by personal achievement. Given this situation, opportunity appeared virtually unlimited, and in choosing a profession each individual could follow his own inclinations and select education and training appropriate to his chosen goals.[7]

But even here an underlying note of caution soon emerged, for while praising Livorno's open social character Ricci expressed the fear that in the future that character might prove to be a source of social turbulence. He therefore urged the adoption of measures designed to provide the city with more stable forms of social organization. Ricci's primary concern was with artisan groups (to him, these groups were key sources of either social stability or disorder, depending on the circumstances) and with institutional arrangements designed to encourage these groups—along with other sectors of the working-class population of the city—to exercise a stabilizing influence on the society.[8]

Ricci's caution was reflected in his view of popular education. Here, he quickly moved from praise of free educational choice to advocating the tailoring of the education of a student closely to the social situation of his parents. With regard to the artisans, for example, he argued that it was crucial that members of this group receive an education that would instill in them both a love for their profession and the skills necessary to exercise it well. To extend education beyond this point, though, would serve only to cause the student to lose time from gainful employment and, more seriously, to develop aspirations and appetites that he would not have the means to satisfy. It was this disproportion between aspiration and means, Ricci argued, that would provide the source of personal frustration and social turbulence. Given this danger, it would be far preferable for the sons of artisans to concentrate on becoming proficient in the professions of their fathers. In this way society would benefit from the presence of a large group of prosperous and independent tradesmen who were content in the successful exercise of their profession and immune to the fatal temptations of misery and frustration.[9]

This desire on the part of Giuliano Ricci and, as we shall see, of an important segment of the community to strengthen the social fabric of the port city (countering the more threatening aspects of its open social character) led to the establishment of a series of private educational associations designed to instill the attitudes necessary for the "healthy" functioning of the society along with instruction to meet the specific needs of its component population. Four institutions in particular—the Istituto dei Padri di Famiglia, the Scuola Michon, the schools of reciprocal instruction, and the kindergartens—manifested these new, active, philanthropic concerns of the Livornese elite.

The Istituto dei Padri di Famiglia,[10] organized by Professor Giuseppe Doveri in the 1820s and utilizing for many years the talents of Ricci as its director of studies, aimed at improving the quality of elite education in Livorno, specifically the education provided to the sons of the city's commercial elite. The innovative character of the school was apparent in several of its features. First, instruction concentrated not on the elements of a classical education but on subjects more appropriate for students planning a career in business. Modern languages, geography, geometry, arithmetic, and natural history—"subjects of direct interest to merchant and manufacturer"—formed the core of the school's curriculum.[11] Second, important stress was laid on the active participation of the students' fathers (or their surrogates) both in the governance of the school and in the educational process. Despite its innovative character, then, the school possessed certain fundamentally conservative aims. Instruction, as Ricci had hoped, was tailored to the needs of a specific social group (merchants and manufacturers) and sought to reinforce traditional forms of social organization and deference (the tie between father and son).

The Scuola Michon possessed a similar blend of progressive and conservative goals. Established in 1825 through the personal effort and financial backing of Carlo Michon, an important member of the local nobility, the school aimed specifically to provide artisans in the city with an education appropriate to their social position and vocation. Mechanical drawing formed the core of the instruction and was considered important both for training draftsmen and masons and for improving the general quality of artisan trades in the city as a whole. Given Ricci's expressed interest in this group, the school understandably won his warm praise.[12] In the first ten years of its operation, Ricci noted happily, more than 100 young men had completed the school's instructional program and had brought into the workshops of the city a whole store of practical knowledge, enabling them to become better artisans without growing to despise their humble occupation.[13]

From the standpoint of the reformers, however, the most important educational institutions in Livorno were the schools of reciprocal instruction (scuole di reciproco insegnamento) and the kindergartens (asili infantili). In these organizations, merchants and professional men in the city formally expressed their affiliation with the general effort to moderate reform in Tuscany and throughout Europe and committed themselves to a coordinated program for the socialization of the city's lower orders.

Schools of reciprocal instruction had been first instituted in England in 1798 by William Lancaster as a practical and effective means of educating the lower classes. After the Napoleonic Wars, they spread rapidly on the Continent: by 1820 schools employing the new method were functioning in France, Belgium, and parts of Italy, and in 1829 they were introduced into Austria and Russia. Within these schools instruction was given "reciprocally"—that is, one teacher would handle the general supervision of the school and the instruction of a select group of older children, and these children (called "monitors") would in turn teach their younger classmates.

The method had great appeal, because one teacher working through several monitors could reach far more students than had been possible under the old magisterial system. This was especially important at a time when little money and few qualified teachers were available for mass primary education. The method had other advantages as well: the large number of class sections in a monitorial school made it possible for the student to find a level of instruction closely related to his ability, and the small number of students assigned to each section insured that each received a good deal of personal attention and drill. The intensity of the instruction, it was hoped, would enable students to complete their education quickly, for parents could generally not afford to keep their children from gainful employment for very long.[14]

In May 1819, Cosimo Ridolfi (backed by 116 subscribers) initiated in Florence the first school employing the new method. As the first of its kind, the new institution soon took on the character of a normal school. The Society for the Diffusion of Reciprocal Instruction was formed to facilitate the exchange of ideas on the new method and to encourage its employment in popular education projects throughout the state. Three years later, thirty-two schools in Tuscany were using the new method.[15]

The rapid diffusion of the schools of reciprocal instruction throughout Tuscany can be attributed primarily to their close affinity to the attitudes and interests of Tuscan moderate liberals. First of all, such an institution reinforced the strain of social conservatism that formed the basis of moderate attitudes toward the lower classes. Needless to say, this quality was continually reiterated at the periodic meetings of the societies. In 1826, Lapo de'Ricci remarked to the Society for the Diffusion of Reciprocal Instruction in Florence that it would be fortunate when the children of the poor were educated and could compare their happy state with that of their fathers.

> Moral and submissive, they will soon learn how useful it is to respect the superior authorities, how necessary it is for the maintenance of order to stand united to that social chain which binds all who belong to the same community . . . [and] who obey the same laws—respect that neither blind ignorance, nor servile fear, but only a well-regulated and drilled education can impress upon their tender minds.[16]

In 1823, Carlo Pucci had remarked in a similar strain to the society that while poorly conceived instruction could do more harm than good, the society had avoided the danger by limiting instruction to reading, writing, arithmetic, and linear design. The intention, he said, was "to give students the tools [*soccorsi*] with which they could maintain themselves with greater advantage in the station of their fathers." One must avoid at all costs, he said, educating the worker to despise his situation and awakening in him a desire to change it; rather, one must give him an education that would make him and other members of his class "devoted, industrious, and moral [in] their work." That the society was succeeding in its aim, Pucci argued, was clear, for students graduating from the schools were "running into the workshops to assure themselves an honest living." "Their happiness," said Pucci, "was assured."[17] The social attitudes of Ricci, which we discussed earlier, clearly possessed a general resonance in the Tuscan elite.

The impulse behind the establishment of schools of reciprocal instruction, however, was not simply conservative. More progressive aspects of the moderate ideology also favored the diffusion of the new method. Chief among these aspects was a stress on the necessity of like-minded individuals uniting to further the work of liberal reform. Reading the annual reports of the local school societies, one is struck by the constant references to the "spirit of association."

When the local school was prospering, as in Florence in 1829, the invocation of the spirit had an optimistic ring: "Behold what the zeal of private citizens can accomplish when the spirit of association unites them and unselfish courage [*un coraggio disinteressato*] urges them on."[18] And when the local school was not prospering, as in Livorno in 1831, when it had been temporarily beset by a rash of absenteeism, mention of the spirit of association often served to boost the spirits of the dejected membership. Thus, Professor Doveri closed his report to the society in Livorno by remarking that "if we have in part suffered because of unforeseen obstacles, let us nevertheless console ourselves with the thought that nothing can resist the spirit of association, the overwhelming [*prepotente*] moral force of the century."[19] To the men assembled to hear the annual report of the local society, the "spirit of

association" was not a meaningless phrase but served to for-
tify them for the difficult task to which they were committed,
a task that Professor Doveri described as no less than "the
moral perfection of the population."[20]

Perhaps the most important reason for the member's attachment to the method of reciprocal instruction *qua* method,
however, was that it, unlike the old magisterial system of
education, symbolized a liberal society, which for them was
the highest form of social organization. Under the magisterial
system absolute authority lay in the hands of the teacher, and
students obeyed more from fear than from a sense of justice.
The principle that governed the schools was too often simply
the law of the strongest. Now, said the supporters of the new
system, make an experiment: take the teacher away from his
pupils, proclaim in the school a law that is simple, just, and
beneficent to all, and have the students themselves insure
that their schoolfellows observe it. In this way there will be
formed a small state in which the law is everything and force
is nothing. From here will proceed a spirit of order and
submission to the law that will be influential and fertile in its
consequences. "It is beautiful," said Enrico Mayer, the
younger brother of Edoardo Mayer (president of Livorno's
discount bank), "to see the older children follow precisely
and willingly the command of a boy very much smaller, all
of whose force consists in the words, 'You must!' or 'You
mustn't!' The gain in morality derived from this environment
is too clear to need mentioning."[21] Mayer's judgment was
seconded by that of the noted Tuscan reformer Rafaello
Lambruschini, who felt that the new kind of society (i.e.,
well-ordered, just, and benevolent) provided by the school
of reciprocal instruction would serve as a model to tender
hearts, happily as yet ignorant of the bitterness and discord
of domestic life and the turbulence and iniquity of civil society. This consoling and moralistic spectacle was, by itself, he
said, a powerful education.[22]

While ideological considerations encouraged the utilization
of the method of reciprocal instruction throughout Tuscany,
its appeal in Livorno remained fundamentally practical.
Livorno, most observers agreed, was especially suited to the

spread of popular instruction made possible by the new method. The underemployed, volatile population of the port city necessitated the establishment of a well-organized system of primary education to improve the moral character of the lower classes and to safeguard property. Certainly, Governor Corsini noted, one could not hope for the commercial prosperity of a city where one's goods and one's person were not absolutely secure.[23] Public immorality was more widespread in Livorno than in any other locality of Tuscany, the superintendent of public instruction remarked, and no more effective remedy existed for it than mass primary education.[24] To Giovanni Pera, a local chronicler, the situation was not so bleak: the common people were basically kind, sincere, and capable of praiseworthy actions, and efforts at popular education in the city had already reaped important results. Still, he said, one must avoid self-delusion: "We are still distant from the culture of the most civilized areas of Italy, and we have need to cancel the old reputation with new deeds."[25]

In August 1828 a newly formed Society of Reciprocal Instruction in Livorno announced its intention to open a free elementary school for indigent Catholic males from seven to ten years of age.[26] Reading, writing, arithmetic, and design would be the principal subjects taught. The number of students admitted would be limited only by the capacity of the school and by the society's financial resources. At the time of its formation, the society's income came primarily from the dues of its sixty sustaining members. To join the society one was required to pay a twenty-lire initiation fee and a continuing fee of five lire a month. This latter fee, it was estimated, was sufficient to maintain two children in the school.[27]

The early years of the school were in general a period of optimism and expansion. In the second annual report of the society, Carlo Sansoni, the secretary, noted that classes had been inaugurated in June 1829 with 145 pupils and that during the course of the year the number had increased to 150. Further expansion of the student body, he remarked, had been checked only by limitations of space. Sansoni praised the quality of instruction and discipline. He marveled at the serious manner with which the young monitors carried out their tasks and their dignified bearing. Especially noted were the gentleness (*mansuetudine*) and harmonious interaction of the students and the improvements in their general physical condition.[28]

With the active encouragement of the society, the method of reciprocal instruction was adopted by other schools in the city.[29] In March 1832, a Jewish Society for Reciprocal Instruction was formed and opened a school serving fifty students. At the time, two Jewish charity schools, a communal primary school, and a private school were already utilizing the new method. Thus, approximately 515 children in Livorno were benefiting from the reciprocal method of instruction.

Membership in the original society grew rapidly, from 60 in 1828 to 115 in 1831. By February 1835, membership in the society stood at 120, and the number of children in its school had expanded to 243 (an increase of 13% over the previous year). At the time, however, the secretary estimated that approximately 2,000 school-age children in Livorno were still not receiving the benefits of formal education.[30] Partially to rectify this defect, Giuseppe Doveri announced in the society's sixth annual report the imminent opening of a new school—the largest in Tuscany—capable of handling about 400 students. Before the eyes of the assembled membership danced the vision of 200 graduates a year snatched from a life of vice and crime and furnished with an education and sufficient instruction to enable them to become productive members of society.[31]

Small wonder that with this prospect the Society of Reciprocal Instruction won the support of the leading members of Livorno's commercial elite. In 1828, seven of the ten non-Jewish deputies in the chamber of commerce became charter members of the society.[32] In 1837, when membership in the society totaled 138, all eligible deputies in the chamber were members. Of the twenty non-Jewish deputies who served in the chamber for five or more years in the period from 1815 to 1850, all but four were members of the society in 1838. By 1837 only one (Francesco Rodocanacchi) was not included, perhaps because his family was already represented by two other members (Michele and Giorgio).

The chamber of commerce officially recognized the importance of the school and its method of instruction in 1834 when, as a sign of its gratification for the extension of the privileges of the port, it voted to distribute a sum of money to both the Christian and Jewish societies.[33] Members of the merchant community, moreover, not only paid dues to the society but also held offices in it. Among others, Carlo Grabau and Domenico Monticelli served as school inspectors, G. G. Ulrich and Niccola Manteri as auditors, and Pietro Senn and C. A. Dalgas as part of a delegation to recruit new members. Understandably, though, the duties of the more demanding offices, such as those of president and secretary of the society, as well as the bulk of other duties were performed by members of the city's professional elite of lawyers, doctors, and educators (men such as Enrico Mayer, Giuseppe Doveri, and Augusto Dussauge), who had the talent to formulate the society's ideological appeals and more time to devote to its day-to-day operations.

Similar in character to the schools of reciprocal instruction were the kindergartens. Both sought to channel private philanthropic energy into popular education and both assumed a key role in liberal reform programs not only in Italy but also throughout Europe. While the schools of reciprocal instruction in the city, however, concentrated on the education of boys, the kindergartens dealt exclusively with girls. Heretofore, its sponsors argued, female education had been shortsightedly neglected: not only were women often required to work outside the home to support themselves and their families but they also played a crucial role in the domestic economy and in the raising of children. To neglect the education of females, then, would serve only to weaken the family—the very foundation of the social order—and to insure the ignorance and low moral character of the future generations, thus perpetuating a cycle of debasement. Rather than being neglected as in the past, therefore, the education of females should be made the cornerstone of popular education: "The generous concern to improve the lot of the poorer classes of society cannot begin to be achieved except through women."[34]

The first project for a kindergarten in Livorno was drafted by Enrico Mayer—a leader in the incipient philanthropic movement in Tuscany. When Mayer left the city temporarily in the early 1830s, control over the school that he had succeeded in founding passed first to a provisional committee composed of his brother Edoardo, Giuseppe Doveri, and Carlo Grabau and ultimately (in July 1833) to a group of women who had provided financial support for the original project. Upon taking control, the women decided to abandon the existing school and to open a new one in a more suitable location and with a better set of regulations.[35] The popularity of the enterprise increased rapidly. By January 1836, 97 girls from two to seven years of age were attending the school, and 121 more had requested admission.[36] In response to the demand, the society opened a second school in June 1836.[37] Ten years later, enrollment in the two schools had reached 417, a clear indication of the organization's popularity, even though both schools were serving the needs of only a fraction of the potential demand.[38]

Attempts to establish a secondary school to provide more advanced, specialized training for girls leaving the kindergartens—a plan enthusiastically endorsed by Enrico Mayer[39]—proved unsuccessful.[40] Nevertheless, even at the primary level much effort was directed to teaching the students practical skills (e.g., cooking and needlework) to prepare them for their domestic functions or for assuming employment outside the home as housekeepers or seamstresses, common occupations for the unmarried women of the city.[41] As in the schools of reciprocal instruction, care was taken to assure that students were not being trained above their social station but were simply being enabled to better discharge the duties inherent in that station and to perform with greater facility their more universal roles, in this case those of wife and mother.[42]

While the Society of Reciprocal Instruction remained under the control of the leading merchants and professional men in the city, responsibility for the kindergartens after the reorganization of the society in 1833 passed largely to the female members of the same families. In its official regulation the organization was termed a "Società di signore" (i.e., a society run by wives or respectable women), and at its inception it included many of the city's important families.[43] As with the schools of reciprocal instruction, support for the kindergartens was given on a voluntary basis, and, as one might expect in an organization run by women in this period, a relatively large proportion of this income came from extraordinary donations. Bazaars, lotteries, and theatrical benefits served at once to enrich the city's social life and to provide the kindergartens with a major portion of their operating revenue.[44] As with other philanthropic organizations of this type, great pride was taken in the achievements wrought by the spirit of association.

> And to what is this spirit not capable? While it educates, it civilizes and creates extraordinary people. From your small institution to the greatest enterprises of public and private beneficence on which the capitals of Europe take pride: all is owed to the law of association.[45]

Concurrent with the school societies there appeared another institution that seemed geared to performing an important role in socializing the lower orders—the savings banks. In September 1829 the *Indicatore livornese* reported the opening of the first Tuscan savings bank in Florence and predicted the imminent establishment of a similar institution in Livorno.[46] Not only, it was argued, would the elite of the city not wish to appear inert spectators in the general effort of social reform, but Livorno itself seemed especially suited to benefit from the new institution. The city's commercial activity, which directly or indirectly gave sustenance to a large portion of its working-class population, was by nature sporadic. In periods of prosperity, returns to the worker were high and tended to encourage dissipation and destroy a healthy concern for the future. With subsequent shifts in the port's commercial activity, however, this lack of foresight often produced the most abject indigence, a fertile breeding ground for every form of social disorder.[47] A well-run savings bank could help to relieve this problem. In it the worker would find a place for his surplus earnings and could secure protection against the misery of sickness, unemployment, and old age. As a result, the bank would encourage industry and improve the general level of public morality, thus helping to guard society from the attacks of the dishonorable and the desperate.[48]

Small wonder, then, that a project for the establishment of a savings bank in Livorno won warm support from the city's social elite. The prospectus itself began circulating in Livorno early in 1835 and rapidly received 121 signatures, with each signatory pledging to purchase a share of stock in the bank at 100 lire. The total projected capitalization (10,000 florins) would serve as the bank's initial cash reserve, and, if necessary, could be employed to meet the expenses of its administration. As in other organizations of this type, no interest would be paid to the shareholders, whose contributions were considered purely philanthropic.[49]

With the establishment of the bank in 1839 it became apparent that the principal difficulty would not be convincing the elite of the value of the new institution but of demonstrating to the poorer classes of the city that, in fact, the bank was not designed for the benefit of its shareholders, as a typical financial speculation, but solely for the advantage of its more modest depositors. The secretary of the bank, Guglielmo Pachò, remarked six years after the circulation of the original prospectus that "our lower classes either do not sufficiently know or sufficiently appreciate the benefits that our institution provides. They have need of a stimulus, of a strong stimulus to be induced to profit from it."[50]

A primary stimulus, Pachò hoped, would come from two traditional sources, the priest and the employer. The former—understanding the relationship between frugality, temperance, and the exercise of many virtues—would preach the advantages of thrift. The latter could by design withhold part of his workers' pay and place it in an account at the bank. Through the use of this "moral coercion" Pachò hoped to teach the worker the advantages of saving so that he would thereafter pursue the practice on his own. In order to succeed, however, all those who were convinced of the value of the new institution would have to make a concerted effort to reach the lower classes. To this end, one had "to approach [*avvicinare*] the people, mix with the crowd, whisper in its ear a word of advice, inviting it to work and to parsimony." To do this effectively it was necessary "to know the individuals who composed this stratum of society, their character, their habits, their vices, and their virtues." Inexperienced and hesitant members of the elite were quickly assured that "all this is less difficult than one might think."[51]

Given the social function of the savings bank, the administration took special care to make it a convenient and secure place for savers of modest means. It obtained from the bishop of the city permission to keep the bank open on Sundays so as not to distract people from their work.[52] It drafted the institution's regulations with the precise intent to reinforce security and to discourage the participation of speculators: the maximum single deposit was fixed at 20 florins, and interest was paid only on the first 1,000 florins of each account (plus accumulated interest) and on funds held for a full year.[53] The bank placed the majority of its deposits in a secure, interest-bearing account in the central bank in Florence. Provided that the rate of return were higher, the administration could loan the remainder of the deposits to stipulated classes of borrowers—municipal governments, semipublic organizations such as the discount bank, or private institutions of recognized stability working in the public interest (*corpi morali*).[54]

In the interest of guaranteeing the security and liquidity of its assets, the bank's regulations strictly defined its lending policy. Efforts were made, however, to increase the social value of the institution by liberalizing it. Artisans and small manufacturers obtained the right to discount notes at the bank to avoid the necessity of paying usurious interest rates elsewhere.[55] Private philanthropic associations could maintain larger interest-bearing accounts than those of private individuals.[56] Pachò suggested increasing the support to educational and philanthropic organizations[57] and even, should circumstances merit, eliminating the prohibition against granting loans to private individuals.[58] In this manner, he

argued, the value of the institution to those that it was set up
to serve would be doubled.

> The savings of the poor, of the industrious artisan, of the small
> property owner are deposited in our bank. We act as the guaran-
> tors of them and in the meantime lend to other small proprietors
> the accumulated savings. In this way the advantage achieved is
> doubled.[59]

At the same time, however, the poorer classes were not
alone in finding the savings bank an attractive place to deposit
their surplus earnings. This is not surprising. The interest
rate of 3.6 percent paid on deposits was superior to that
provided by many public funds, the flexibility of the regulations governing deposits and withdrawals was great, and the
security of the bank would have reassured even the most
cautious. In November 1838 the central bank in Florence
passed a resolution that seemed designed to encourage the
more prosperous depositor. It raised the maximum single
deposit that could be made to any of the member banks from
20 florins to 100. As a result the bank in Livorno reported that
in 1839 (the first year under the new system) the number of
individual deposits fell from 8,906 to 8,491, while at the same
time their total value jumped from 98,328.78 to 169,260.57
lire.[60] Clearly, people with more money to deposit were
finding the bank more convenient; no longer would they be
forced to build their accounts through the tedious accumulation of small deposits.

As the bank became more attractive to the larger depositor,
however, its sponsors began to fear a blunting of its original
social and philanthropic goals. Too often, projects of high
social purpose appeared ruined by the mania for profit, the
idealism present at their origin giving way to a brutal cynicism. In an effort to counter this tendency, Pachò—breaking
down the bank's deposits in 1839—deliberately chose to emphasize the positive. The minimal deposits that, he reported
(which clearly had to be attributed to the lowest orders of the
population) had increased since the previous year and represented more than a third of the total. If one added to this
category the medium deposits of up to eight florins, "a sum

that could occasionally be set aside by the artisan, the domestic servant, or the head of a not wealthy family," one arrived at more than half the deposits made in 1839. Only the 2,200 deposits of sums above twenty florins (a quarter of the total), he said, could clearly be attributed to the well-to-do.[61] One can easily fault the impressionistic character of the secretary's analysis. The important thing to note here, however, is his ultimate aim in attempting to assure the sponsors of the institution that their original goal had not been lost and that, "if the rich abuse, the poor and the artisan still benefit from our bank."[62]

Still, one could not be too certain. Curiously, the central bank in Florence, which had raised the whole problem in the first place by increasing the maximum permissible deposit, began a study to ascertain whether the bank was proving more useful to the wealthy individual than to the man of mediocre fortune and whether or not it would be in the interest of the administration and the public to devise measures to discourage the first type of depositor and to encourage the second.[63] Pachò suggested a more practical solution to the problem and certainly one more in harmony with the paternalistic aspirations of the bank's sponsors. A personal interview with each person opening an account, he argued, would not only be a useful way to obtain information on the social composition of the depositors, thus helping to discourage the participation of speculators, but it would also offer a unique occasion to strengthen the resolve of the poor while reinforcing the bond of charity between rich and poor and insuring the public peace.

> The poor would meet their benefactors without being ashamed of their poverty. This coming together, stimulating the sense of charity in the one and reawakening a sense of gratitude in the other, would slowly retie the bonds of humanity broken by the disparity of fortune. On the basis of this solid bond of reciprocal affection the poor and the rich would return one day to form a single family.[64]

Few passages summarize better the aspirations and tone of the moderate liberal program of social reform.

CHAPTER SIX

Merchants and Porters

The social concern of the merchant community was not limited to the spheres of education and thrift. Attention was paid also to the economic condition of the city's working-class population. The aim, as we have seen, was to foster the development of a large stratum of prosperous, independent, and conservative workers and small producers. In terms of the specific implementation of this policy, most revealing was the relationship of the merchant community to the largest and potentially best-organized groups of workers in the city, the porters and dockworkers. Attempts by the merchants to strengthen the economic position of these workers and to weld them more closely to a defense of civic order would be a dominant theme in the social history of Livorno in the first half of the nineteenth century. During the turbulent period of the late 1840s the desire to achieve this aim would even induce the merchant community to suspend, albeit temporarily, its most cherished principles of free trade and competition. Before discussing merchant attitudes and their application, however, it is important to identify the workers.

A formal organization of dockworkers existed in Livorno almost from the founding of the city. The first local company was established in 1602 as the result of a public contract between city officials, merchants, and a group of thirty workers from the area around Bergamo, in northern Italy. Previously, the movement of merchandise in the port had been entrusted to workers sent from the company in Pisa. With the increasing movement in the port and the general shift of commercial activity from Pisa to Livorno, it seemed desirable to establish a new company dedicated solely to handling the work in Livorno.

Why the government chose to grant a concession to port workers from outside the state is not clear. Mario Baruchello suggested that at the time Livorno did not have an adequate population from which to draw the needed workers.[1] As the newly founded company numbered only thirty, however, and as few skills were required and the pay was high, this explanation is not persuasive. More likely, the concession was granted to the thirty because they were already formally organized when they advanced their request, were prepared to deposit a large sum of money to guarantee merchants against the breakage or theft of their goods, and were able and willing to pay a substantial yearly compensation to the Tuscan government for their privileges.

In any event the practice of entrusting the principal porter duties in the city to a company drawn from outside the state persisted until 1847 (with one noticeable interruption during the French occupation of Tuscany from 1808 to 1814). Under this system the dominant share of porter charges on goods arriving in the port city by land and sea passed into the hands of a small, privileged group of foreigners. Members of the company rotated on a two-year basis, lived in dormitories in the customhouse and were forbidden by law from bringing their families with them to the city. Peculiarities of dress and language served to strengthen the isolation of the group and to provide the basis of a growing resentment on the part of the local working-class population.[2] Nevertheless, throughout much of the period port workers from Livorno were able to exercise a secondary but important role in handling goods within the city. They hauled merchandise not specifically included in the concession granted to the company from Bergamo and, as the volume of goods moving through the port increased and the number of members of the privileged company was now legally fixed at fifty, assisted the company in moving goods covered by the monopoly. This auxiliary function was formalized in 1799. An indigenous company of dockworkers was established under the control and supervision of the privileged company to primarily handle the more manual tasks of the service. For their efforts they were paid one-half the set tariff for transferring merchandise directly from one ship to another and two-thirds the tariff for depositing it in a warehouse. The remainder of the tariff went to the treasury of the privileged company.[3]

Predictably, this arrangement failed to satisfy the local dockworkers, who eventually began demanding more work, a greater share of the profits, and increased job security.[4] The issue came to a head in the early 1830s. The expansion of the free port and a severe cholera epidemic disrupted established patterns of work in the city. At the same time, the continued drop in commercial profits, coupled with the growth of the working-class population and the rising cost of living (due principally to the extension of the consumer taxes of the free port to the suburbs), insured that the control of porter operations in the city by a foreign, privileged company would prove increasingly unacceptable to an important segment of the city's residents.[5]

The most important assault on the position of the privileged company in this period came not from the dockworkers, however, but from the chamber of commerce, which in a forceful petition in 1831 called for a revision of porter charges in the city to favor the local workers. As one might expect, a combination of philanthropic and more practical considerations motivated the chamber's appeal. The petition stated that the chamber was not only anxious to improve the living conditions of an important section of the city's population but was also interested in securing the property of its constituents. The two questions were obviously related. Should the crowd of casual, semi-indigent laborers in the city be given the means to support itself with its own resources, it would not be be tempted to touch those of others. The quantity of merchandise moving through the port, the petition noted, was certainly sufficient for the task; only the existence of a privileged company of foreigners in control of the trade prevented these resources from reaching the local population.[6]

Although the chamber appeared extremely critical of the existing situation, its specific proposals were relatively modest. The petition did not call for the abolition of the privileged company, only for the ending of its jurisdiction over merchandise exported from the port city. From the merchants' standpoint, the proposal of the chamber made sense both tactically and materially. In theory the government would be far more willing to relax controls on exports rather than imports, for it received the bulk of its duties on the latter. Moreover, although the privileged company controlled this activity and thus had a right to at least a portion of the tariff, the work itself was traditionally in the hands of porters chosen by the individual merchant firms (the *facchini di banco*). Thus, despite the demogogic tone of the appeal,[7] the proposal of the chamber was less likely to benefit the local population (which already controlled the jobs in this sector) than to increase the profits of the merchants, who would not only be freed from the constraints of the established tariff but would also no longer have to pay compensation to the privileged company for work done by their own employees.[8]

The government, and in particular its chief police official, the president of the Buon Governo, made rapid countermoves in an attempt to reaffirm the authority of the privileged company—so necessary, the government felt, to the orderly functioning of the customhouse. First, the president of the Buon Governo endeavored to counter a rumor reportedly spread by local dockworkers that under the provisions of the laws of July 1834 the privileged company was being abolished along with the traditional port charges. He declared that the recent laws made no mention of the dockworkers and ordered the governor to insure that the company was maintained in the tranquil exercise of its privileges.[9]

Concessions and special pleas were made to facilitate the operation. First, the company adjusted pay scales to win over the local dockworkers, guaranteeing assistants a blanket two-thirds tariff on all jobs (previously, in transferring merchandise directly from the prow of one ship to another they had received only half the scheduled compensation).[10] The remaining third, however, would continue to be received by the privileged company.

The government provided an elaborate argument to justify continuing this practice. Given the responsibilities of the privileged company, it said, the charge was not excessive. From it the members of the company not only had to provide for their own sustenance but also had to assume all the expenses and risks of the trade: they had to assure, without compensation, porter service within the customhouse itself and at the public scales, and they had to maintain all the equipment used in the handling of merchandise, assume liability for goods lost or damaged, and, for their privileges, turn over to the royal treasury an annual sum of 9,000 lire. To win over the merchants the company agreed to reduce its charges on certain operations. To help insure the acceptance of the concessions by all concerned, the president of the Buon Governo instructed the governor to observe and discreetly warn those stirring up trouble on the issue that it was not in their interest to continue to do so.[11]

Despite concessions and threats, however, the issue could in no sense be considered resolved. From the merchants, protest would spread to the working-class population of the city, providing a foretaste of that confusion of principles and aims which, as we shall see, would characterize the revolutionary situation of the late 1840s. The immediate opposition to a settlement with the privileged company came from the merchants. Arguing that the government had not solicited their opinion on the new tariff schedule, merchants refused to pay the customary one-third compensation due to the company on jobs handled by their own porters (the *facchini di banco*).[12] The boycott continued for approximately four years. Only in 1837 did the combination of a stern government provision and several court actions enable the privileged company to regain its rights in this area.[13]

Nevertheless, by the early 1840s the position of the privileged company appeared to be under definite assault. Even the governor of the city agreed that the moment seemed opportune for replacing the company with a group of local dockworkers. The prevailing economic philosophy, he argued, had changed radically since the privileged company had been established, and over the years the local dockworkers had proven that they enjoyed the confidence of the merchant community.[14] How the substitution of one company (admittedly local) for another could be reconciled with the principles of free trade and competition was not explained, and this inconsistency would remain to plague the resolution of the whole affair in the late 1840s and beyond.

In the meantime there emerged another source of potential conflict. A group of local dockworkers assisting the privileged company in moving grain (the *facchini saccajoli*) attempted at once to free itself from the obligation of turning over a third of its earnings to the company and to assert an exclusive right over all jobs involving the direct transfer of any cereal from one ship to another.[15] The first demand—challenging the privileged company—evoked little response. The second, however, in threatening to close off a potential source of employment to other sectors of the local working-class population, met the united opposition of the customhouse, the grain office, and the chamber of commerce.[16] In the face of this energetic response the dockworkers were forced to back down. The attempt, however, would soon be repeated. At roughly the same time another group of porters in the city (the *facchini baulai*), provoked by its failure to "control" goods moving between the San Marco Gate and the new railway station, attempted to assert an exclusive right to handle the baggage of all travelers arriving in the city and pressed its claim, the president of the chamber of commerce reported, with insolence and even violence.[17] No one was fooled by the pretense. However, the governor began to wonder whether in the interest of public order the claim might not receive a favorable response.[18] The suggestion was ominous. The principle of free trade and competition appeared to be winning with one hand, only to be losing with the other. The impression would be reinforced as the decade progressed.

The pressure of local dockworkers to abolish the authority of the privileged company intensified in 1847 during the general ferment of liberal constitutionalism which initiated the revolution of 1848. The weakening of traditional political authority in the state—begun with the demands for a constitutional regime and accelerated with the subsequent flight of the grand duke (February 1849) and the establishment of a radical regime under Francesco Domenico Guerrazzi—served to make moderates even more anxious to solidify ties with the working-class population of the city and hence gave its demands greater possibility of success. In June 1847 the chamber of commerce supported a resolution that the privileged company be abolished and that the local dock-workers who were assisting it be formed into a disciplined and well-regulated company to take its place.[19] Many deputies in the chamber—perhaps skeptical of the honesty and decorum of the local dockworkers—were reluctant to abolish the company. However, they feared earning the resentment of the local workers, who were men of determination (*da imporre*) and were obviously anxious to learn the outcome of the chamber's every meeting.[20]

Indeed, the campaign of the local dockworkers to abolish the privileged company was disciplined and effective. On the one hand they forcefully dismissed members of the company dispatched to supervise their work[21] and criticized merchants who hesitated to sign petitions for the company's speedy liquidation.[22] On the other hand, as the tide began to turn in their favor,[23] the local dockworkers publicly thanked their supporters[24] and, more important, assured them that they would not prove unworthy of the anticipated benefit. In the future, they declared rhetorically, they would point out to their children the men who had worked for the "new pact" and would say to them: "Those men recognized our rights: we must protect them by exercising our duties, upholding honest faith and civic concord."[25] Nothing could have been better geared to reassuring the chamber of commerce of the wisdom of its support.

In the final stages, the government's fear that civic order might be jeopardized if the local dockworkers did not come rapidly into possession of their anticipated rights facilitated agreement on the issue. It was also helped by the willingness of the dockworkers themselves to come to a quick understanding on the matters of compensation (both to the government and to the privileged company) and service.[26]

The new government regulation sanctioned two important innovations in the organization of porter service in the city. It certified the transmittal of the rights of the privileged company to the two local companies—the Manovella and the Sacco—that had previously assisted it. The Manovella—the larger of the two companies—was empowered under the new system to handle most of the functions of the dissolved company. Exceptions were made only for the unloading of dried fish, which was entrusted to a company from the popular Venezia quarter of the city; for the loading of merchandise, which was handled by porters employed by the individual merchant firms (the *facchini di banco*); and for the movement of cereals, which was under the jurisdiction of the Sacco. The second important innovation was the responsibility enjoyed under the new system by the chamber of commerce, which had previously had no direct role in supervising porter services in the city. The regulation granted the chamber primary authority in selecting the officers of the two companies, in expelling members guilty of criminal acts or of simple insubordination, and in administering pensions. An important summary article gave the chamber of commerce an ill-defined blanket authority over all matters affecting either company.[27]

The new system seemed to fulfill the fondest expectations of the merchant community for a close, paternalistic relationship with the working-class population of the city. The relationship, however, was not simply one-sided. The revolutions of 1848 disrupted the regular commercial activity of the port. Economic dislocation coupled with a heightening of the political tension in the city increased the danger of popular unrest. As a result, the merchant community found itself relying increasingly on the newly formed dockworker companies—as well as on other privileged sectors of the working class—to help maintain public order.

In August 1847 moderates in the city were already suggesting the possibility of organizing a squad of local dockworkers to protect commerce and discourage popular unrest.[28] During the first serious popular uprising the following January, the suggestion took concrete form. The agitation itself reflected the spirit and aims of the opening, liberal phase of the revolution of 1848. On the evening of January 6 the populace, angered by the hesitancy of the government in arming the newly constituted civil guard and in granting full freedom of the press, staged a massive demonstration that forced the governor to abandon his post and appeared to place the city on the brink of chaos.[29] The municipality quickly formed a deputation to reassure the demonstrators that their demands would be transmitted to the central government. However, a liberal ministry in Florence—recently constituted under the presidency of Cosimo Ridolfi—refused to appear to give way to mob pressure and hastily mobilized an armed force to march on the city. Emboldened by the resolution of the central government and anxious to avert a direct clash between the army and the local population, moderates in Livorno hastened to repress agitation in the city before the arrival of the troops. To do so they relied on a force of about 2,000 civic guards, supplemented by a host of volunteers drawn from the privileged sectors of the working-class population. Particularly noteworthy were the large deputation from the Venezia quarter and the dockworkers from other quarters of the city who had recently been awarded the rights of the old privileged company. With an important section of the popular element in the city clearly supporting the restoration of order, commentators noted that the possibility of resistance quickly vanished and that by the time the troops arrived from Florence the city had returned to a state of perfect calm.

Given the impact of the French Revolution (particularly its Jacobin phase) on moderate opinion throughout Europe, one might suppose that the merchant community in Livorno would have been hesitant to rely on an armed populace for the maintenance of public order. Although understandable, however, this supposition fails to take into account the long-standing policy of moderates in the city to build effective alliances with the "responsible popular elements" (*plebe non povera*) of the community. Certainly, the uprising of January 1848 could not but prove the wisdom of this policy. A letter written by Giuliano Ricci captures well the optimism bubbling in moderate circles in the immediate aftermath of the uprising: "Order has been restored. The people, conscious that it had provided the essential contribution to the return of order, has obtained greater confidence in its own ability and a heightened sense of its place in the community. Guided by leaders 'worthy of history,' this group had showed itself willing to defer to the counsel and to back the efforts of the men of a superior class who have merited their esteem."[30]

The moderates could not have been more pleased, and they were especially gratified by an incident that occurred after the arrival of Ridolfi from Florence. In a public ceremony on January 9, the president of the council of ministers thanked Pietro Pedani, representing the Venezia quarter, for the efforts that he and his companions had made in the restoration of public order in the city and indicated that the government would gladly seize the occasion to present to those "valorous citizens" a sign of its deep satisfaction. Pedani's reply, which follows, could not have satisfied the moderates more or provided a clearer affirmation of the value of their efforts on behalf of the people.

> We are people who live on our daily wages. Our farms [*poderi*] are our arms. We love our country and are ready to make any sacrifice for the public good, but our quarter, which is very populated, contains many poor. Many are not able, as they would wish, to have their children educated so that they might grow up to be good and honest citizens. Excellency, the most beautiful reward, the thing that the entire population would welcome as the greatest benefit, would be a school.[31]

Ridolfi, who had devoted considerable effort to improving popular education, was ecstatic: "Honor to the people that requests instruction!"—these and similar expressions were offered by Ridolfi with evident emotion.[32]

This incident created a certain resonance in the community. On the plaza that evening a man of the people (*popolano*) shouted "Long live order!" and another asked that other poor and populous quarters be given a school.[33] At the time, the government was unwilling to assume responsibility for mass instruction. However, to fulfill the pledge made to Pedani, the secretary of finance announced that the government would provide funds for the establishment of a primary school in the Venezia quarter and suggested that a local commission be formed to draw up a project and implement it.[34] To eliminate any cause for jealousy or bitterness among the dockworkers outside the Venezia quarter and to affirm their efforts to preserve public order in the city, the governor suggested that the sovereign convey officially through the chamber of commerce his immense satisfaction at their conduct during the recent turmoil and that, as a token of its approval, the government pay for the metal nameplates that dockworkers in the company were required to wear by law.[35]

The events of January provided the first and perhaps the most dramatic expression of the efforts of the dockworkers to maintain public order. This was not, however, the only occasion. A month later, in response to another popular tumult, both companies of dockworkers—along with the *Veneziani*—expressed their determination to defend the public tranquillity that was indispensable, they said, for the prosperity of the city.[36] Fosi, the head of the dockworkers, criticized repeatedly the stupidity [*imbecillità*] and weakness of the government and concluded that to maintain calm in the city "we will have to rely solely on ourselves."[37] For the moderates, the dockworkers had clearly become "the most valid defenders of the city's internal order."[38]

In May 1848 the dockworkers gave a more concrete expression of their support. Acting on a report that drivers (*vetturini*) from Pisa, Empoli, and other points in the hinterland were converging on the city to stage a public demonstration (probably in protest against the damage suffered by their profession from the construction of the railroad), the dockworkers warned the prospective troublemakers that even though they were unarmed they would assist the militia in maintaining order in the city. When the crowd menaced several members of the civil guard during the demonstration, the dockworkers ran to the guards' aid and helped to disperse the assembly. That same evening, 200 dockworkers went voluntarily to the barracks to spend the night so as to be ready to assist the militia in case of trouble.[39] Throughout May and June the dockworkers (along with the *Veneziani*) patrolled the city,[40] aided the police in making arrests,[41] protected the lives of moderates,[42] and persuaded noted troublemakers to leave the city.[43] In June, Giuliano Ricci remarked that to the shame of the government the public peace was due solely to the bayonets of the militia and the knives of the dockworkers. "Troublemakers," he said, "scare the individual citizen; the people scare the troublemakers; the government scares nobody."[44]

The motives for the dockworkers' vigorous defense of law and order were readily apparent. Guaranteed an important share of the port's hauling duties by the regulation of October 1847, they had a definite stake in the prosperity of Livorno's commerce, which could only be insured if the city remained tranquil. Merchants and government officials repeatedly emphasized the links between internal order, commercial prosperity, and work. In April 1848 the merchants suggested to the people that if internal peace continued, Livorno would that year become the largest and most active port of deposit in the western Mediterranean.[45] The governor repeatedly advised that popular disturbances would serve only to ruin commerce, the source of income for the working population of the city.[46] Enrico Mayer stated the issue succinctly when he remarked that "order is bread, disorder is hunger."[47] That the dockworkers endeavored with brutal directness to encourage the tranquillity of the city is evident in a passage from Ricci's diary: "The *facchini* and *Veneziani* pledge to break the arms and legs of those who disturb the public order, to whom they attribute, and with reason, the sluggish commercial activity."[48] The merchant community had clearly found important allies among an influential section of the working class. It would remain to be seen, however, given the sudden shifts in the political situation, whether it could maintain that alliance or, more importantly, whether it could pacify the vast residue of unskilled workers who had not formed part of a privileged company at the beginning of the revolution of 1848.

CHAPTER SEVEN

Pressure from Below

By winning the right to form closed, privileged companies, the Manovella and Sacco could not help but spark similar requests from other sectors of the city's working population. The uncertainty of the economic situation and the stiff competition of an overcrowded labor market in which the vast majority of jobs required few skills insured that workers, if given the opportunity, would band together in an attempt to guarantee themselves employment and better working conditions. The reestablishment of the guilds, Giuliano Ricci remarked, was impossible. But there existed among the working-class population at that time an inclination to establish analogous institutions as the best way to combat pauperism and to insure future security.[1] Demands were advanced from the whole spectrum of the city's manual occupations— from bakers, bricklayers, packers, pourers (grain), weighers (grain), haulers (baggage, iron, wood, and charcoal), wine carters (distinguished by container), barge and towboat captains, and fruit, lard, salt-meat, and pork vendors.

To trace the demands of all these groups would be tedious. Three examples, however, will provide a sense of their nature and their potential for social disruption. First, let us examine the bakers. On the night of 28 October, 1847, approximately fifty individuals, some of whom were reported to be bakery workers, assaulted a man named Virgilio, an independent proprietor of a bakery in the Borgo Cappuccini (the neighborhood surrounding the Capuchin church). On the night of 2 November, three or four individuals entered a bakery behind the Voltone (today the Piazza della Republica), clubbed down the old proprietor, and rushed into the adjoining workshop, where they wounded two of the workers with knives and needles.[2]

These incidents represented the climax of agitation on the part of bakery workers in Livorno and provided a dramatic introduction to a difficult period of labor unrest in the city.[3] In October, 250 bakery workers in the city had banded together into a society, and in a published manifesto they had presented a series of demands to the proprietors and the government.[4] Principally, they called for an end to night work, for a guaranteed wage for normal and overtime employment, for the maintenance of a minimum of four workers at each oven, and for the elimination of children and foreigners (*gente di montagna*) from the occupation. Until their demands were met, they pledged to refrain from all night work.

The general population of the city did not support the bakery workers' demands. To the moderates, the demands threatened the principle of free trade and competition, impinging on the right of a proprietor to exercise his profession as he saw fit. Moderates also feared the appearance of a disciplined coalition of workers, which was a new phenomenon in the city and seemed dangerously socialistic.[5] The demands of the baker workers won little support even among the masses. Many, as we have seen, disapproved of any action that threatened to disturb public order and thus the commercial prosperity of the city. Others opposed the demands because they did not seem merited—with the bread that a baker could consume on the job and take home to his family, a bakery worker's income was superior to that of most other occupations in the city.[6] Finally, any concession to the demands seemed destined to raise the price of bread, which at the time neither the masses nor the government could tolerate.[7]

The efforts of the bakery workers, though unsuccessful,[8] were only the first of a long series of attempts on the part of workers in the city to secure employment and improved working conditions. On 8 May 1848 a large crowd of masons and day laborers—far superior to the number authorized— reported for work on a public works project at the Porta a Mare. Fearing disorder and responding to a series of past abuses, government officials announced that the project was being suspended.[9] Angry, the crowd moved to another construction site and, alleging that nonresidents were working on the project, demanded that work cease until everyone could be guaranteed employment. In the course of the assembly several shots were fired from the crowd. Only the arrival of 2,000 civic guards restored order.[10]

The sailors mounted similar protests. On 28 December 1848 a group of Tuscan sailors boarded ships flying the state flag in the port and, alleging infractions of the regulations, expelled all foreign crewmen. From here they moved to the port office and demanded the publication of a fixed wage scale.[11] This incident climaxed a series of related protests by sailors and stevedores (primarily charged to handle cargo once it was actually aboard ship).[12]

In March 1848 a group of stevedores had presented a petition on behalf of both groups. Arguing that the organization of work and a fair measure of return were essential to insure public order, the stevedores proposed the formation of a company to handle the movement of cargo aboard ship and of lumber (for ship repair) on land. At the same time they demanded that captains and owners of ships flying the state flag be forced to grant two-thirds of their crew positions to Tuscans and attacked what they considered the practice of treating sailors as mere tools of production, to be picked up or laid aside at will.[13]

In July 1848 the stevedores advanced a more formal petition to raise their occupation to the privileged status enjoyed by the Manovella and Sacco, effectively closing the work to unaffiliated individuals from outside the company.[14] To government officials, the demands of the stevedores (and sailors) appeared not only to challenge the concept of a free labor

market—so instrumental in promoting the morality of the
working classes and the general prosperity of the Tuscan
economy—but also to threaten the very existence of the Tuscan merchant marine. If, it was argued, shipowners and captains were told whom to hire and how much to pay, they
would simply transfer their vessels to another flag.[15]

In all three of these examples the concept of a free labor
market was challenged, and if this fact proved disturbing to
government officials, it proved equally unsettling to the merchant community. Indeed, merchants in the city found themselves in a special quandary. On the one hand they firmly
believed in the value of a free labor market, while on the other
they were under increasing pressure to sacrifice this principle
in the interest of insuring public order.

The tension between these two perspectives was strikingly
evident in the resolution of 20 August 1847, which announced
the government's intention to abolish the old privileged company. The preface of the resolution stated clearly that the
company was being dissolved in the name of economic freedom, "that in the general interest of commerce . . . and to
favor the city's numerous population the grand duke was
abolishing the concept of privilege and restoring to free competition that extremely important branch of public service."[16]
The body of the resolution, however, indicated that in fact a
new privileged company of local dockworkers was simply
being substituted for the old company of foreigners.[17] The
incongruity between principle and provision was patent
though not difficult to explain. The resolution itself attempted
to justify it by stating that an instantaneous leap from regulation and privilege to complete freedom might jeopardize
the security of commerce. The uncertainty of the political
and social situation in the city at the same time, as we have
seen, made it incumbent on the merchants to win support
among the workers and certainly to not alienate a group that
by now was well organized and, if its demands were not met,
could prove extremely volatile.[18] Moreover, the government—
strapped for funds to finance military and social reform—was
quite willing to transfer the burden of compensating the old
company (which amounted to 460,500 lire) to the newly

sanctioned companies of local dockworkers.[19] However, while ample justification could be found for compromising the principle of free competition on this one occasion, the precedent would only serve to make further compromises inevitable.

In the revolutionary period of 1848–49, requests for privileged status were rejected energetically if the petitioning group seemed unable to pose a threat to the city's internal economic and social order. Thus, in November 1848 the chamber of commerce turned down eight petitions for privilege from small working-class groups in the city. In so doing it seized the occasion to affirm its adherence to the principles of free trade and competition (*libertà d'industria*) and to pose as the defender of the interests of all workers against attempts to limit employment to a privileged few.[20]

However, when the petitioning group performed a vital role in the city's commerce or posed a real threat to public order in the city, it seemed advisable to sacrifice principle or a sense of equity and to grant a veiled or modified form of privilege. Such, for example, occurred in the case of the grain pourers and the ballast and baggage haulers. In June 1848 the grain pourers advanced a clever petition that at once affirmed the value of free trade and competition and, based on the particular circumstances of the city and the concessions granted to the Manovella and Sacco, advanced a demand for privilege.[21] Previously the group had requested a raise in pay, boldly stating that due to its poorly remunerated labors its members had been forced to "appropriate" (*appropriarsi*) a small amount of the cereal that passed through their hands, "which was demoralizing and at the same time injurious to commerce."[22] Given the direct threat to the interests of the merchant community, it was not surprising that the chamber of commerce, "in the interests of commerce and public tranquility," recommended organizing the grain pourers into a disciplined company[23] and that the governor, "in the light of the particular and as it were exceptional conditions in the port," recommended a special, limited abrogation of the principle of free trade.[24]

A similar, though perhaps more veiled, circumvention of the principle of free trade and competition was made in the case of the ballast haulers. This group had made repeated requests for a regulation that would distribute work, set charges, and control equipment in the trade.[25] The issue had been raised with the destruction of the old walls of the city in the mid-1830s, as small coastal vessels (the *navicelli*) began transporting the rubble to ships in the port and selling it as ballast at a price below the traditional tariff.

Although this might be cited as a good example of the advantage of free competition—which was driving down the price of ballast and thereby encouraging ships to use the port—government officials were forced to take a longer view. The traditional boats (*gozzi*) engaged in this activity were specially designed to draw little water and hence were able to obtain their ballast from beaches outside the port. The supply of rubble inside the city was limited, and the silting which occurred in moving it to ships in the port was proving detrimental to the city's canals.[26] The governor noted that although it was not in harmony with the principle of free competition, some regulation appeared desirable in order to protect a group that was engaged year-round in supplying ships in the port with sand and gravel for ballast at considerable personal and economic risk. Efforts were made, however, to preserve the fiction of free competition. Ship captains could choose to obtain their own ballast, and the company of ballast haulers would have to remain open to new men adjudged suitable by the captain of the port.[27] Nevertheless, the vague notion of what was suitable—and, on occasion, more direct pressure—served to limit access to the profession and to keep the price of ballast high.[28]

Requests from baggage porters in Livorno for the right to form a privileged company generated a vibrant controversy among government officials and members of the city's moderate elite. To the auditor (the chief police official in Livorno), the requests provided an excellent opportunity to regulate an occupation that had long been a source of disorder and public lament.[29] To the chamber of commerce, however, granting the requests would serve only to narrow the sphere open to the beneficent effects of free competition and to encourage a host of similar demands from other groups in the city.[30]

In February 1848 a group of porters from the railroad station won support for their position from Giuliano Ricci. He felt that it was important to assure casual workers a regular sustenance to keep them out of trouble (*onde ritirarli dal tumulto*), and for this reason abstract principles occasionally had to give way to high political considerations.[31] Ricci worked hard to win support for the porters but, he said, found himself continually blocked by the insurmountable resistance of petty functionaries who opposed doing anything and simply pontificated about free trade.[32] Only in February 1849, when the minister of finance announced that a patent was being granted to the porters for the formation of a company, did it seem that Ricci's efforts had borne fruit. Once again the government asserted that the concession was granted without any prejudice regarding the principle of free competition.[33] A group of advisers to the governor, however, more honestly stated the situation when it expressed mournful resignation at the repeated violation of deeply felt principles and the hope that in the near future the entire situation would be rectified.[34]

The opportunity to do so did not present itself immediately. With the flight of the grand duke and his entourage to Gaeta in February 1849 and the establishment of a more democratic ministry in Florence (under the leadership of Francesco Domenico Guerrazzi), the tendency of the government to give in to the stream of demands for privileged status advanced by worker groups in Livorno was reinforced. Along with this reinforced tendency came a growing sense of resignation on the part of the merchant community and local government officials. Thus, although the secretary of finance had in December 1848 rejected in the name of free competition a request for privileges from a group of wine carters in the city, when the petition was presented again in March 1849 the governor's advisers argued that the whole issue would have to be reconsidered.

Later instances [*fatti*] have somewhat modified the rigor of the principles proclaimed [remarked the advisors] . . . permitting the establishment of porter companies . . . set up with appropriate regulations and with approved tariffs.

Given these precedents, the advisers considered that the request of the carters could not be given the virtually automatic rejection that it had received on its first presentation.[35] Similarly, in response to a petition from porters in the city market for exclusive control over hauling duties in that location, a police commissioner noted that although he personally favored free trade and competition, the city now contained privileged companies of every sort and that, therefore, the demand had the backing of clear precedents.[36]

It was ironic, perhaps, that this wave of concessions came during the ministry of Guerrazzi, who—in assuming office in January 1849—had announced that in the interest of providing jobs for as many as possible, he would resolutely oppose granting privileges to any segment of the city's working population.[37] It was evident, however, that the very workers for whom Guerrazzi wished to maintain a free labor market were just as anxious to close it in their favor and that in the turbulent political situation of the first four months of 1849 they were able to make their wishes predominate.[38]

With the growing tensions among the city's working-class population and the progressive erosion of the principle of free competition, the chamber of commerce rapidly lost interest in exercising its right to supervise and discipline the new companies of the Manovella and Sacco, the principal social gain it had received from the abolition of the old privileged company. By the middle of 1848, the chamber had already begun to regret its newly won authority. The complaints of the Sacco that its tariff and the ability of its members to work inside the customhouse were not on a par with the rights enjoyed by its sister company were shrugged off by the chamber, which clearly wanted to avoid the "embarrassment and hatred" bound to spring from any attempt to resolve the conflict.[39] Later, several members of the Manovella complained that the chamber of commerce was neglecting its supervisory role over the internal affairs of the company and requested—unsuccessfully—that this function be turned over to the municipal government.[40]

The chamber's reluctance to exercise its newly won powers continued even after the restoration of the grand ducal government and its official reaffirmation of the principle of free competition.[41] No longer, however, was the issue merely one of embarrassment and fear—the chamber now sought simply to preserve its dignity and to avoid wasting time in policing the details of the two companies.[42] Clearly, the chamber had moved a long way from its belief in the desirability of establishing effective links with important sections of the city's working-class population. As we shall see, this change in attitude would condition its policies in the period that followed.

Map of Livorno showing the tariff wall constructed in the 1830s encircling the city.

A romanticized view of the Torre del Marzocco and the city of Livorno from the north.

Late nineteenth-century view of the Via Grande facing north from the Piazza Grande to the Piazza Carlo Alberto (della Republica).

Piazza Carlo Alberto (della Republica) with statues of Ferdinand III and Leopold II, facing north-east, 1881.

Venezia Quarter facing west.

City meets port. Statue of Grand Duke Ferdinand I and the four Moors in the foreground, the Orlando shipyard in the background. Late nineteenth century.

View of the inner harbor, wharf, and port, facing west.

Ships in port.

Mouth of the inner port with its customs house.

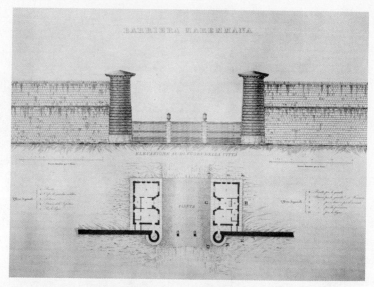

Sketch of the Barriera Maremmana, a gate in the new tariff wall of the 1830s with a design of the entrance. View from the south facing the city.

Sketch of the Dogana D'Acqua, the customs house in the 1830s tariff wall on the canal to Pisa, from the north facing the city.

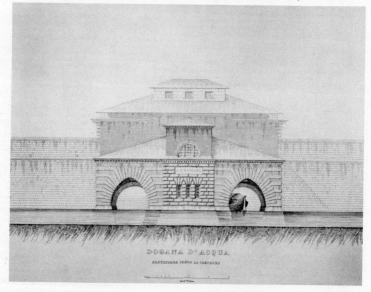

PART FIVE

Reform Stalled

CHAPTER EIGHT

1848: The Trauma of Merchant Benevolence

Underlying the discussion of merchants and dockworkers in the preceding chapters is the theme of a growing disenchantment with the possibilities of effective social reform. From this perspective, the revolution of 1848 represents a crucial experience, one that sapped the vitality of the merchant community and dealt the reform movement a shock from which it would never recover. Given the impact of this event on attitudes toward reform, it is necessary to examine the revolutionary process more systematically, fixing as we go the response of the community to the turbulent succession of events.

The general character of the revolution of 1848 is a matter of historical record.[1] From January to March, revolutionary outbreaks occurred across the European continent. The nature of these outbreaks and the demands of the revolutionaries varied from place to place. In the more advanced societies of western Europe, revolutionaries focused on stimulating liberal-democratic reform and on introducing social programs to alleviate the condition of the urban masses. In the less developed area of central Europe, revolutionaries sought to curb the tyranny of existing regimes and to establish new, independent nations. At first the revolutions seemed successful. During the first months of 1848 a republic was established in France, constitutional monarchies sprang up across Europe, and initial efforts were made to carve nation-states out of the Austrian empire.

By the summer of 1848, however, the revolutionary tide appeared to be on the wane. In June the bloody suppression of a popular uprising in Paris unmasked fundamental divisions in the revolutionary movement. In France the fracture divided the advocates of moderate and radical reform. This division was reinforced in central Europe by disputes over organizing the new nations. In most instances armies had remained loyal to the old regimes and could now be employed against the revolutionaries, whose ranks were divided. The revolutionaries had failed to win or sustain the support of the landed aristocracy, the peasantry, and even a large section of the bourgeoisie, increasingly alarmed by the threat of political anarchy and the prospects of radical social revolution.

By December 1848 revolutionaries seemed on the defensive everywhere. Louis Napoleon Bonaparte had begun to impose order in France. The Hapsburgs had initiated steps to reconstitute their regime by moving against radicals in Vienna and nationalists throughout the Austrian empire. In Prussia the reactionary turn of the court signaled the erosion of liberal concessions throughout the northern German states and exposed the utter ineffectiveness of negotiations in Frankfurt for national union. Sardinian efforts to renew the struggle against Austria and the last-ditch resistance of Livorno, Rome, and Venice to the counterrevolution could not reverse the general trend. By the fall of 1849 the flames of revolution had been extinguished virtually everywhere.

In Italy the tensions that had produced the revolutions of 1848 had been building for decades. The situation, however, became especially intense after the mid-1840s. A severe economic crisis weakened the legitimacy of the existing regimes, and the election of a liberal pope (Pius IX) in June 1846 seemed to provide at last the impetus necessary for success. The initial reforms of the papal administration—the granting of an amnesty for political prisoners and exiles, a more liberal press law, the creation of a council of state, and the formation of a civil guard—were in themselves neither radical nor totally unprecedented, but they made an enormous impact on a society ripe for change. A year before the papal election, Vincenzo Gioberti, in exile, had published a book entitled *Il Primato morale e ciuile degli Italiani,* in which he stressed the importance of an alliance between the progressive movement and the Catholic church.[2] Such an alliance, he suggested, would generate the popular support necessary for success and would provide a leadership capable of winning for the national movement the support of the conservatives and the Italian princes. The election of Cardinal Mastai-Ferretti as pope seemed to indicate that the papacy was joining the modern age and that a workable solution to the problem of Italian unity was imminent.

Three stages would mark the revolution in Italy. In the first (from January to March 1848), revolts throughout the peninsula produced civic reforms (free speech, a free press, and the right of assembly) and the granting of constitutions setting up liberal parliamentary regimes. Ironically, given the normal pattern of development in the peninsula, the movement spread from south to north—from Palermo in January to Naples, central Italy, and the kingdom of Sardinia. Finally, the revolt spread to Lombardy and Venetia, territories under direct Austrian control. In March, news of a revolt in Vienna and the flight of Metternich produced the Cinque Giornate, five days of urban revolt in Milan which forced the Austrian commander, General Radetzky, to pull his army out of Lombardy. In response a provisional government was set up in Lombardy, and a republic was organized in Venice under the leadership of a liberal lawyer, Daniele Manin.[3]

Stage two of the revolutionary process in Italy focused on the national dimension of the struggle and produced a direct conflict between the kingdom of Sardinia and Austria. Responding to the appeals of the Lombards and the pressure of liberals in his own kingdom of Sardinia, Charles Albert invaded Lombardy on March 22. As his army moved across the frontier, the king received the support of both regular forces and volunteers from the Papal States and from Tuscany, Naples, and Sicily.

The resulting euphoria, however, quickly subsided. Growing suspicion about Sardinian intentions to use the war of liberation simply to increase its own territory produced friction between the Sardinian regular army, the volunteers, and the local population. In April the papacy proved unwilling to continue pursuing armed struggle against a major Catholic power and withdrew its troops from the campaign. In May a counterrevolution in Naples tamed the liberals and enabled Ferdinand II to recall Neapolitan troops. All of this allowed General Radetzky to reinforce his army and in July 1848 to impose a crushing defeat on the Sardinian army at Custoza. In March 1849, Charles Albert reopened the campaign but suffered another decisive defeat at Novara. The Sardinians had saved face with this ultimate gesture, which would eventually enable them to assume a position of national leadership, but Austria was now free to reimpose its authority over its former territories and help snuff out the vestiges of revolution in central Italy. The third and final stage of the revolution in Italy witnessed heroic but ultimately futile efforts to maintain revolutionary centers in Livorno, Venice, and Rome against the general tide of reaction.

Livorno was an active participant at all stages of the revolution. The liberal sentiments that sparked the revolutions of 1848 were well rooted there. The city's commercial situation made the merchant elite especially supportive of the principles of economic liberalism—free trade and a free market for labor. In addition, the city's tradition of autonomy and the elite's desire to direct personally the economic and social affairs of the city made the merchant community very responsive to an extension of political liberties, which a constitutional regime could guarantee. The reforms pressed by the commercial elite put this group in touch with the aspirations and activities of liberals elsewhere, and, as the revolutionary ferment grew, Livorno found itself actively involved in agitating for freedom of the press, the formation of a civil guard, and the achievement of constitutional guarantees. In addition, as we shall see, Livorno would prove to be an active center of radical democratic revolution: it would energetically recruit volunteers for the struggle against Austria, and in May 1849 it would mount a last-ditch resistance to the counterrevolution.

In Livorno the moderate and radical elements of the revolution were for a time closely interrelated despite differences in scope and methods between the two camps. While moderates stressed law and order and progressive liberal reforms and attempted to maintain a fundamentally hierarchic and paternalistic social order, radicals emphasized the importance of a democratic and republican solution to the problem of national union and the acceptability of using conspiracy and popular violence to achieve their stated goals.[4] Differences in social background also distinguished the two groups. Moderates tended to come from the liberal aristocracy, the commercial classes, and the professions, groups that identified their future with an orderly evolution of the sociopolitical order. Radicals tended to be drawn from the popular classes—in Livorno, artisans, port workers, and sailors—and to them political change was vaguely linked with expectations of a fundamental improvement in their material existence.[5] Yet, while fundamentally different in method and social background, neither moderates nor radicals existed entirely in isolation. Several members of Livorno's commercial elite had been members of the radical, conspiratorial movement in their youth (Pietro Bastogi and Ricci being notable examples),[6] and the leading livornese radical, Guerrazzi, as we have seen, actively pushed moderate reforms as editor of the *Indicatore livornese* and would continue to do so later, in 1849, as head of the Tuscan government.

Guerrazzi provides a good introduction to the radical, democratic current in Livorno and its link to a wider world. Like many radical leaders, his family had clear ties to the people. His father was a woodcarver (*intagliatore in legno*), and his mother is described as having had a rough, nononsense character (*popolana aspra e rozza*).[7] Guerrazzi demonstrates the popular origins of the radical movement, but his training and appeal also made him more esoteric. In the 1820s he studied law at the University of Pisa, where he fell under the influence of the most progressive political currents circulating in Tuscany and was touched by the charisma of Lord Byron, who had taken up residence in Pisa in 1821. The years after Guerrazzi's graduation were taken up more with literary and political pursuits than with launching a professional legal career. In 1827 he published his first major work (*La Battaglia di Benevento*). In it were crystallized the principal elements of his style, a frenetic patriotism and a taste for unbounded passion and the macabre, which—inflated with classicisms and other linguistic mannerisms—make much of his imaginative writing unread today.[8]

Guerrazzi's other activities during these years involved, as we have seen, the founding of the *Indicatore livornese*, which was dedicated to furthering both literary and social progress, the latter necessarily expressed in a reformist language. In 1830 a commemorative discourse at the Labronica Academy in honor of General Cosimo del Fante, who had died during the Napoleonic invasion of Russia, gave Guerrazzi an outlet for his patriotic ideals and resulted in his enforced confinement in the small town of Montepulciano for six months. In 1833, Guerrazzi was forced to spend several months actually in prison for participating in a conspiracy to force the grand duke to grant a constitution. During this enforced leisure, Guerrazzi wrote a good portion of *L'Assedio di Firenze*, a novel of patriotic resistance against foreigners, which assured Guerrazzi a place at the center of the revolutionary movement in Tuscany.

Though quick to express a desire for national liberation, Guerrazzi was not by nature a party man. In the 1830s the republican leader, Giuseppe Mazzini, repeatedly praised Guerrazzi's genius and his patriotism but recognized the futility of keeping him in his conspiratorial organization, La Giovine Italia. In the course of the 1848 revolution, as we shall see, Guerrazzi was identified with the Livornese radical movement, and, at one point early in 1848, was forced to spend several more months in prison for instigating—according to the charge—a popular movement in the city against the central government. Nevertheless, though intuitively popular with the Livornese populace, Guerrazzi maintained his independence and at times was as critical of what he

called "radical utopias" as he was of "moderate hypocrisy."
What remained constant were his popularity, his vigor, and
his ability to mobilize the popular radicalism of his native city
into a coherent and disciplined movement. As such, given
the destabilizing currents of Livornese radicalism, he would
prove to be a natural choice to head the Tuscan government
after the failure of more moderate regimes. However, as we
shall see, Guerrazzi's Machiavellian diplomacy and his efforts
to steer a middle course in internal policy would eventually
lose him the support of moderates and radicals alike.

In the initial stages of the revolution, both moderates and
radicals expressed a common disenchantment with the existing regime in Tuscany. From the mid-1840s the forces of
liberalism were taking the offensive in Europe, and the Tuscan government appeared unable to keep pace. The abolition
of the Corn Laws in England (June 1846), the election of Pope
Pius IX and the first stages of liberal reform in Rome (July
1846), the visit to Tuscany of the British liberal leader Richard
Cobden (greeted by a host of welcoming speeches that al-
luded to the inexorable link between economic and political
freedom) (February 1847), and the liberals' victory over the
Sonderbund and the expulsion of the Jesuits in Switzerland
(November 1847) all indicated the spread of a new, progressive spirit in European political life.[9] A number of incidents
in Tuscany, however, suggested that the grand ducal regime
was standing against the tide. In January 1846 the government's decision to extradite a revolutionary leader (Renzi) to
Rome and to expel from Tuscany Massimo D'Azeglio, who
had written an account critical of the Roman state under
Gregory XVI, appeared to identify the grand duke with the
forces of reaction.[10] Efforts to establish a pro-Jesuit convent
in Pisa in February 1846 (seemingly with the knowledge and
approval of the government) and the regime's failure to match
in scope or energy the reform movement in Rome after the
election of Pius IX—particularly in relaxing censorship and
establishing and equipping a civil guard—reinforced this
opinion.[11] The outbreak of famine in the winter of 1846 and
the government's ineffective response to the hunger of its
own subjects further weakened its legitimacy.[12]

Clashes between the forces of repression and the people focused initial critical attention on the state's archaic police system. In October 1847—following a comparatively minor episode in which a policeman roughed up a beggar—the entire system collapsed. Police posts were assaulted, records burned, prisoners freed, and—in a symbolic gesture of scorn for the existing system—the guillotine was burned on the banks of the Arno.[13] On October 29 the existing system of police administration, with its hated network of police spies (*sbirri*), was formally abolished, and its duties were transferred provisionally to a paramilitary force of *carabinieri*. As we shall see, the *carabinieri* would prove incapable of effectively undertaking ordinary police work, and, in any event, this group had already established a reputation for brutality which would make it unpopular for the entire course of the revolution.[14] By the end of 1847 the internal administrative system had broken down at many points as magistrates refused to suppress internal disorder or abandoned their offices entirely.[15]

The foreign policies of the regime aroused even more frustration and open criticism. The occupation of the Tuscan frontier territories of Fivizzano and Pontremoli by the duke of Modena in November 1847 was sanctioned by the agreement that allowed the duchy of Luca to pass to Tuscany. However, it symbolized for public opinion the pusillanimous character of the grand duke, who was unable to prevent their occupation and was thereby forced to cede them over the wishes of the subject population to a principal agent of Austrian influence and repression in the peninsula.[16] To patriots the affair was indicative of the untrustworthiness of the grand duke—of his strong ties to Austria and his ambivalent relationship to the national movement—and of the need to take the political situation more firmly in hand.[17] Official lethargy, however, bothered even those who believed in the government's basic good faith. Moderates who previously had backed the government pressed the ministry to arm the civil guard, to reinforce the army, and to garrison the frontiers. When the government failed to back its verbal assurances with concrete action, even this group began to swing into opposition.[18]

By January 1848 disenchantment with the grand ducal regime produced a major instance of revolt in Livorno. The frustration with the slow pace of government reforms combined with a sense of imminent national peril to provoke popular demonstrations calling for an immediate arming of the civil guard and for the creation of a government of national emergency. To allay popular passion—as we have seen—a delegation was formed to transmit the public concern to the central government.[19] However, the government's decision to stand firm and resist popular pressure and the support that the central government received from communes throughout Tuscany strengthened the position of the regime and gave moderates in Livorno the resolve to distance themselves from the radical opposition and to reassert their control over the city's internal situation. The results of the whole episode seemed to indicate the strength of the moderate position and the ability of the elite to retain its influence over the popular movement. But during the next few months, economic and political strains would dissolve this spirit of cooperation, pushing the revolution into a more radical phase and ultimately forcing the merchant community to abandon its faith in the possibilities of effective social reform.

On the eve of the revolution Livorno's economic and social problems were proving intractable. From 1814 to 1850 the population of the city had grown from 50,000 to 83,000 (approximately 66%).[20] As suggested earlier, Livorno's demographic expansion in the period was not constant or excessive in comparison to the growth of other Tuscan cities or to the rate of increase in Tuscany as a whole.[21] However, it did raise a serious threat of pauperization and ultimately made it impossible for the institutions of the moderate reform movement to achieve their stated goals. As noted, the voluntary schools—while indicative of a vital strain of merchant benevolence—were capable of meeting the needs of only a small portion of the city's school-age population.[22] Saving banks, also indicative of merchant concern, ultimately attracted more funds from the cautious rich than from the industrious poor for whom they were designed.[23]

Significantly, the Livornese economy provided at best a

precarious living for the city's lower orders. For this reason, municipal authorities constantly struggled to deal with the harsh realities under Livorno's image of prosperity. During the post-Napoleonic famine in 1817, for example, hoards of migrants were attracted to the city by grain shipments arriving in the port. Stimulated by their threatening presence and by an outbreak of petechial typhoid, municipal authorities (aided by private subscriptions) set up a large relief administration designed to provide food and medical attention to the migrants before they were returned to their homes.[24] In the 1820s the government advanced large sums of money to private entrepreneurs to employ a portion of the city's indigents, "so as to lessen the inconvenience for the inhabitants which results from the swarm of beggars."[25] From all indications, however, these experiments proved unsuccessful.[26] In the 1830s the government officially attempted to meet the problem of indigence through public works. One high official noted that the expansion and beautification of the city in the period "above all were political acts designed to overcome urban discontent and incipient revolt."[27] Despite the dramatic changes in the physical aspect of the city, public works could serve the needs of only a small portion of Livorno's unemployed population.[28]

In essence, the fundamental problem was the sporadic nature of commercial operations in the city and Livorno's failure to attract large-scale enterprise. In 1841 the census record from the parish of S. S. Trinità noted that the large number of individuals classified as sailors were in fact better described as "casual indigents." This was so because sailors were unemployed for a good portion of the year, and when they went to sea they often left their families so unprovided for that the families were forced to rely on public assistance. Among the casual indigents the census record also placed boatmen (*barcaiuoli*), apprentice bakers (*garzoni di forno*), naval carpenters (*maestri d'ascia*), and caulkers (*calafati*), both because of the sporadic nature of the work in these occupations and because even when these workers were employed their incomes were often barely sufficient to provide the basic necessities.[29]

In Livorno—as in Tuscany generally—the size of firms

tended to be small, and the population of the port was too accustomed to casual labor to welcome the more sedentary occupations of industry, which, in any event, were discouraged from settling in the city due to the restricted locales and the high cost of labor.[30] Small wonder, then, that the Livornese elite linked the well-being of the city's population to the prosperity of its commerce. Ironically, though, such an attitude had produced an enlargement of the free port in 1834, which (as we have seen) further discouraged the development of large-scale industry and increased the cost of living for a large section of the urban population.[31]

The situation worsened during the 1840s. A major flooding of the Arno River in 1844 and a severe earthquake in Pisa two years later demoralized the Tuscan population.[32] A harsh winter in 1846 ruined much of the olive crop and produced a suspension of outdoor work.[33] At the same time, crop failures and a potato blight created famine conditions throughout Europe, seriously depleting Livorno's grain reserves. The city's poor were caught in an economic squeeze. From December 1844 to the summer of 1847 the price of grain increased by 71 percent. Industries in the free port experienced economic difficulties, and unemployment increased.[34] An official report indicated that from 1844 to 1847 employment in the biscuit industry had decreased by approximately three-fourths, in the clothing industry by one-half, and in the liquor industry by one-third. Declines were also noted in hides, candy, and ships. The reasons advanced for the decline included the high cost of raw materials and the general uncertainty of the market. Employment in the affected industries declined by more than half. In addition, women and children working on a piece-rate basis in hats, socks, glass, and rags saw their modest subsidiary wages disappear entirely. For those still employed, wage rates remained the same, but the significant increase in the cost of basic necessities produced a serious erosion of their standard of living.[35]

In this situation, the possibilities of maintaining harmonious relations between commercial and artisan groups in the city seriously diminished. While over the short run the European subsistence crisis of the mid-1840s stimulated commercial activity in the port and provided employment in the haulage trades for grain shipped to Livorno from the Black Sea, political uncertainty during the revolution generally depressed economic activity and produced a precipitous drop in commercial operations. Thus, as noted in table 7, the arrival of large square-rigged sailing ships in the port increased to 2,201 in 1847 and dropped to 1,587 in 1848 and 1,307 in 1849.[36]

Given the economic uncertainty and stiff competition in an overcrowded labor market where the vast majority of jobs required few skills, it was natural that workers would band together in an effort to guarantee themselves employment and better working conditions. By winning the right to form corporations and to control particular aspects of the city's haulage trades in 1847, local porter groups had set a precedent that provoked demands for similar concessions from other sectors. Under the impact of this pressure, as we have seen, the commercial elite's confidence in its ability to secure an acceptable alliance with the working-class population of the city diminished.

The chamber of commerce, motivated by a fear of the consequences if it refused and by a hope that a measure of support would stabilize economic and social relations in the city, had initially supported the formation of Livornese dockworker companies. However, the difficulty of carrying out the supervisory and administrative duties that the chamber had won under the agreement and the growing pretentiousness of other worker groups in the city soon soured it on the whole arrangement.[37] The merchants found it difficult to compromise their belief in free trade and a free market for labor. The basic appeal of the city for them, after all, lay in the absence of the tariffs, formal regulations, and other restraints which burdened commercial operations elsewhere. Under certain circumstances (e.g., to insure discipline in a crucial operation or to secure an important social or political goal) the merchants were willing to compromise. But the crescendo of demands and threats from the workers and the increasing number of concessions that they were able to extract from the government eventually served to disenchant merchants with the revolution.[38]

This disenchantment was reinforced by underlying fears of socialism. Following the February revolution in France, liberals in Tuscany anxiously watched efforts to organize work in Paris and the implicit threat that they posed to the principles of economic liberalism. When, for example, the French provisional government passed a maximum-hours bill for workers and initiated vast public-works projects to deal with the problem of pauperism, Tuscan liberals worried about a dangerous abridgement of the free relationship between employer and worker and a threatening incursion of the government into the marketplace.[39] In fact, the fears of the liberals preceded the actual reforms in France. Following the proclamation of freedom of the press in May 1847, Tuscan radical journals reported discussions on the organization of work in the French capital and illustrated their commentaries with lengthy passages drawn from the works of French socialists.[40] Not surprisingly, the commercial elite in the port city was quick to view agitation for a shortening of the working day and for the erection of privileged companies to provide security of employment as a pernicious import from France. In October 1847, Ricci remarked that in Livorno "a new, great phenomenon begins to manifest itself, that which elsewhere is expressed under the heading of an organization of work. On every side, various groups of unskilled workers agitate to obtain privileges incompatible with the well-reasoned theories that regulate our commerce."[41] A week later Ricci more openly categorized the whole phenomenon as "symptoms of socialism."[42]

In practice, categorizing social agitation in the city as a foreign import made it possible for the commercial elite to preserve at least a modicum of good feeling for the people. If, after all, the population was not inherently subversive but had simply been led astray by foreign propaganda, the benevolent relationship between the elite and the masses might, with proper nurturing, be reestablished. In fact, however, from the way in which the worker demands were formulated, it would appear that socialist agitation played at most a minor role in generating worker agitation in the port city. Far more significant were the economic and political uncertainties of the period and the specific example of traditional corporate organization in the haulage trade. For this reason, the demands of the workers drew more from local practices than from foreign propaganda, although both worker agitation and artisan discontent would provide a fertile breeding ground for radical agitation.

Notwithstanding the sources of worker agitation, the fears of the merchants were genuine, and the combination of worker discontent and a radicalization of the political situation within the city would eventually sour many merchants on the revolution and pave the way for reaction.

The situation from December 1847 to September 1848 was to prove especially traumatic for the merchants. By the end of 1847, Austrian troop movements in Lombardy and the duchies along with the continuing dispute with Modena over Fivizzano sparked demands for military reform. The Livornese, as we have seen, were particulary adamant in demanding the arming of the recently instituted civil guard. The government's plea that it lacked sources of domestic production or funds to purchase the arms abroad fell on deaf ears. To the local population, the government's hesitation was simply one more instance of official lethargy (or, it was suggested, even collusion with Austria). On December 26, 1847, a large demonstration took place outside the governor's palace. Spokesmen threatened that if arms were not forthcoming by the first of the year, the people would go to Florence en masse and demand arms from the grand duke in person.[43]

For the time being, the government was able to mollify the crowd. Arms that were in the arsenal or that could be purchased locally were distributed to the guard. To complete the armament, orders were transmitted abroad for the necessary purchases.[44] But despite the official efforts, agitation was renewed on January 6. Sparking the new demonstrations, it seems, was the circulation of an anonymous pamphlet in the city the day before, attributed because of its emphatic style to Guerrazzi. The fundamental message of this pamphlet was a call for the people to reject the existing regime and to take the defense of Tuscany and the future of Italy into their own hands.

Tuscans! You spontaneously offered life and sustenance to support your brother in Fivizzano and Pontremoli. Fivizzano was abandoned. Pontremoli is being abandoned. . . . Enemy occupation of the passes would place you like so many animals in a shooting gallery. . . . The German will come, because once Tuscany is occupied the contiguous character of the Italian league will be broken. Piedmont will be separated from Rome, Charles Albert isolated, the people terrified, and the epoch of the "Risorgimento" will be postponed for a century.[45]

The author criticized the government severely for allowing the state to be exposed to such grave peril.

Oh statesmen, oh ministers, you are traitors! What does it matter to us whether you are so for perversity or for incompetency; the consequences remain the same; you are betraying the fatherland.[46]

The criticisms were severe, but the remedies proposed were even more stringent, recalling the most frenetic days of the French Revolution.

Clear out traitors and cowards, clear out arcadians, sophists, and doctrinaires! The destiny of a people is a volume too large and heavy for the hands of eunuchs and pygmies. The fatherland is in danger! Do you know how to save it? . . . You call on men who do not fear death, and who have their hearts full of holy love for the fatherland . . . you declare the fatherland in danger, you organize public prayers to God so that He will not abandon our cause; you set up commissions in permanent session; you open public subscriptions; you send people swiftly to buy arms; you make 3,000 pikes . . . you build blast furnaces to make cannons; you take copper, lead, and bronze from the houses and the bells of the churches, leaving them one for divine services with a promise to remake the others more beautiful with the return of security to the fatherland; you write on the altars the names of the volunteers who are marching against the enemy; you ask the women to prepare bandages for the wounded . . . you take the horses of the idle rich to draw the cannons; the servile you scare with a roar the first time, the second time woe to them; with these and other similar provisions you save the fatherland, and, in any case, if you do not win, you die honored, leaving your name celebrated, to be revenged by your offspring, an example of glory to be imitated by the people.[47]

The circulation of this pamphlet increased political tensions in Livorno. On January 6 groups moved through the city denouncing traitors and demanding arms. They prevented officers from mobilizing the civil guard and forced the mayor, Francesco De Larderel, to come to the governor's palace to explain what the central government was doing to meet the external threat. Refusing to accept the official assurances, the assembled crowd supported the nomination of a deputation charged to work out a direct agreement between the people and the central government for the defense of the state.[48]

To the royal court, the situation in Livorno amounted to a virtual revolution. The wife of the grand duke wrote a hysterical note to her sister comparing the plight of the ducal family to that of Louis XVI on the eve of his arrest, trial, and execution.[49] The central government appeared to believe that the delegation selected in Livorno had taken full possession of the commune and had become the actual government of the city. To end the threat, the government, for once, organized energetic countermeasures. Troops were mobilized at Piombino, Lucca, and Pisa and placed at the disposal of the prime minister, Ridolfi, who was dispatched to Livorno as a special commissioner to ensure the return of order.[50] At the same time, the grand duke appealed to communes across the state to rally around the throne and help assure Livorno's submission.

For the first but not the last time during the revolution, Livorno found itself completely isolated from the rest of Tuscany and confronted by a hostile advancing league.[51] On this occasion, Livorno opened its gates and allowed the grand ducal regime to reassert its authority in the city without serious opposition. Later the situation would not be resolved so easily.

The radical tendencies momentarily checked in January resurfaced later in the year with the arrival in the city of the radical Bolognese priest, Father Alessandro Gavazzi. Gavazzi was already well known for his support of Italian independence. In March 1848, bestowed with the title of Captain Major of the Italian Crusade, he had announced his intention of leading 7,000 troops from Rome to expel the Austrians occupying the papal city of Ferrara. Upon learning that the Austrians had decided to leave the city voluntarily, Gavazzi had turned his attention to Florence. His arrival in the city on June 28 was designed "to stimulate the Florentines to sacrifice the gold and silver necessary to sustain the expenses of war" and to pressure the government to mobilize the men and material needed to pursue it successfully.[52] His message was delivered in nightly harangues to crowds gathered outside his lodging. His speeches included a great deal of gratuitous assault on Ridolfi, whom he castigated as a "golden boy" (*fanciullo dorato*) for his aristocratic background and as a traitor to the fatherland.[53] Such verbal abuse and the uproar that it occasioned in the streets of Florence did not endear Gavazzi to the government, and on July 5 he was expelled from the state and ordered never to return without prior authorization. This exclusion was confirmed in letters from the minister of foreign affairs to the courts of Turin, Rome, and Naples.[54]

Gavazzi's arrival in Livorno on August 23, therefore, was in itself a revolutionary act. Upon learning that the priest was aboard a ship in the port and that a police order was preventing his disembarcation, popular delegations were dispatched to the ship to verify the situation and to bring him into the city for a suitable reception.[55] In an effort to make the best of a difficult situation, the government granted Gavazzi's request for transit through Tuscany to his home in Bologna on the condition that he leave immediately. On August 25, following patriotic sermons to the local radical club and to a large crowd assembled in the Piazza Grande, Gavazzi headed toward Florence, accompanied by a twelve-member popular delegation.[56] In an effort to prevent further demonstrations, the government intercepted the party at Signa (near Florence) and with a combined detachment of *carabinieri,* cavalry, and local militia escorted Gavazzi to the Bolognese frontier.[57]

News of the party's interception unleashed a storm of protest in Livorno. A correspondent for the Florentine paper *Alba* reported on August 25 that he had never seen the city so agitated. With the spread of a rumor that Gavazzi and the delegation had been arrested at Signa, the telegraph lines linking the port and the capital were cut, arms were seized, and the governor of the city was placed under arrest.[58] A delegation was selected and approved by popular acclamation to maintain order in the city and to defend it against troops rumored to have been dispatched from Florence.[59] On August 26, efforts were made to dispel the rumors. A delegation returned to Livorno from Florence and announced that Gavazzi was on his way to Bologna, that no one had been arrested, and that the government had no intention of dispatching troops to Livorno. The return to calm, however, was interrupted when a crowd, attempting to seize arms and munitions, was repulsed by the civil guard at the cost of several lives.[60]

The central government was very concerned with reimposing order and reestablishing its sovereignty over the city. To do so it dispatched Leonetto Cipriani to Livorno with special powers. On September 1, Cipriani ordered the restitution of arms seized from state arsenals and from the barracks of the civil guard. On September 2, he ordered the following notification affixed to the city walls:

> Meetings of the political club and any other reunion are prohibited from today. Members and proprietors of halls and houses who sanction such meetings will be liable for the punishments stipulated by the laws on proscribed societies.[61]

This notice was defaced throughout the city. The *Corriere livornese* reported that a veteran from the campaign against Austria lacerated one of the notices and said to the *carabinieri* attempting to arrest him, "I have fought for Italian independence and my life was miraculously spared at Montanara. I do not mind losing it in the defense of liberty at home." By six that evening word had spread that if Cipriani closed the political club, the people would organize as many clubs as necessary in the open air.[62]

In attempting to break up these spontaneous assemblies, Cipriani provoked an armed clash between his troops and the local population. After the first skirmish, Cipriani ordered his men drawn up in the Piazza Grande to rake the area with cannon and musket shot. For the most part, however, the shots bounced harmlessly off the walls of buildings lining the streets leading into the square. At the end of three hours of fighting, the people reported only one casualty, a woman who had been accidently struck while she stood in a cafe. The fire from the other side was reportedly more effective. Using the roofs and windows facing the square and moving rapidly back and forth between the nine streets feeding into it, the people killed fifty-seven troops and wounded sixty.[63] The people took particular aim at the paramilitary companies of the *carabinieri* and *cacciatori*, that were the subject of long-standing resentment. The regular troops, many of whom were reported to have fired into the air, were generally spared. At the conclusion of the battle the local population along with the civil guard seized the city gates, disarmed the sentries, and cut Livorno's contact with the interior. Cipriani's desperate pleas for reinforcements were intercepted and, amid a hail of catcalls and stones, he was forced to retire with the remnant of his forces to the Porta Murata, a fortification overlooking the port.[64] In accord with the popular will, the chamber of commerce unanimously agreed to send four merchants to Florence to demand that the government dispatch Neri Corsini and Guerrazzi to resolve the dispute.[65]

Livorno and the central government were once more at an impasse. With the first confused news of the clash, the central government began assembling units of the Tuscan civil guard in Pisa preparatory to their march on the port city.[66] On September 10 and 13 the two houses of the Tuscan parliament declared that the sense of autonomy conveyed by the setting up of an emergency government in Livorno was contrary to the legitimate sovereign powers of the central government and the constitution.[67] Already, though, efforts had been undertaken by the two sides to settle their differences peacefully. On September 7, Livorno had been promised a general amnesty in return for its reorganization of the local civil guard and its resumption of a state of legality (*stato legale*).[68] On September 10, Livorno's local government, in conformity with requests from Florence, had dissolved three of its four commissions, established a provisional guard, and selected

Guerrazzi and Antonio Petracchi to form a provisional executive commission.[69] But efforts to resolve the situation failed
again when on September 28 the local population steadfastly
refused to permit Ferdinando Tartini—sent from Florence to
assume the post of governor—to enter the city. At this point
the central government cut off all official ties with Livorno.[70]

The situation was especially serious in that Florence informed the governments of Europe that it had broken contact
with Livorno and could no longer guarantee the personal
safety or property of foreigners in the port. This represented
a virtual declaration of anarchy, which could have a disas-
trous impact on a city so dependent on foreign trade. In
response, a general meeting of the city's population on October 1 voted to establish a commission to maintain order in
the city and to send a delegation to Florence to press the
following demands: full amnesty, the ending of the state of
emergency and return to normal constitutional government,
and the dispatch to Livorno of a governor in whom the city
could have full confidence. Should these demands be rejected, the meeting declared, Livorno would take measures
necessary to insure the city's well-being and would dispatch
information on the situation to all the courts of Europe.[71]

Ultimately a compromise was effected on the major issue
of concern to both sides, the choice of governor. For the
central government, the most important consideration was to
humiliate Guerrazzi, who had been closely identified with
the popular movement in Livorno since the inception of the
revolution. Guerrazzi was denied the governor's post and
angrily returned to Florence to resume his position as a deputy in the lower house.[72] At the same time, however, it was
clear that Livorno would not accept a governor too closely
identified with the moderate faction, as Tartini was. Happily,
a candidate acceptable to both sides had reappeared recently
on the Tuscan political scene. Giuseppe Montanelli—an ar-
dent patriot—had returned from the grave as it were, to
become once again an active participant in the political struggle. His reported death at the battle of Montanara in the first
campaign against Austria (he was actually wounded and later
repatriated) had evoked eulogies from both moderates and

radicals. His selection as governor was greeted enthusiastically by the local population. In his first public address in the
new position, Montanelli's call for the convocation of a constituent assembly in Rome to effect the first steps in the
political union of the peninsula made him wildly popular in
the city and placed Livorno even more firmly in the vanguard
of the radical national movement in Tuscany.[73]

This enthusiasm, however, was not shared by the moderates. Montanelli's speech actually had been cautious. He had
traced the pedigree of his proposal to the prime minister, the
Florentine patrician Gino Capponi. He had not identified a
date when representatives were to be chosen to form a national government, nor had he mentioned that these deputies
would be chosen by universal suffrage (features that made
later formulations of the plan so radical). Rather, he had
declared simply that "Tuscany must select its representatives
and invite the other Italian governments to do likewise" and
had stressed the importance of forming a permanent central
diet to coordinate the struggle for liberation. Still, the speech
had fired up the audience by giving the plan an aura of
popular initiative and by holding out imminent prospects of
a war of liberation, a national revolution, and the establishment of a republic.[74]

Other issues also dampened the moderates' enthusiasm.
The economic fortunes of the city clearly had suffered as a
result of the revolutionary turmoil. The growing radicalism
of the local population had weakened the traditionally deferential ties binding elite and mass society. Struggles with
Florence had enhanced the city's volatile reputation and had
weakened the confidence of foreigners, so necessary for the
port's commercial prosperity.

At the same time, Livorno's role in the Tuscan revolution
far outstripped the expectations of the moderates. Livorno
had been a leader in pushing for freedom of the press, a civil
guard, and for a wholehearted pursuit of the war for Italian
independence. The city had also actively endorsed the constitution and resisted—occasionally by force—efforts to modify or revoke the freedoms it guaranteed. Firmly standing for
the freedom, independence, and unity of the peninsula, the

popular movement in the city ended by actively contributing to the fall of the government responsible for dispatching Cipriani to Livorno. With the resignation of Capponi on October 12, the Livornese demonstrated in the port city and in Florence itself to intimidate moderates and to pressure the grand duke to appoint a ministry more responsive to the position they espoused.[75] On October 26 their efforts were crowned with success when the court, endeavoring to bring the opposition into the government to mollify the popular movement, on the advice of the British ambassador selected Montanelli and Guerrazzi to form a new ministry. The revolution in Livorno had moved to center stage. The attitude of the commercial elite toward this development would remain to be seen.

Initially, relations between the new government and Livorno's commercial elite appeared quite cordial. On December 15, the official government newspaper (the *Monitore toscano*) published statements of mutual esteem from the Livornese merchant community and from Guerrazzi, now minister of the interior, which appeared primarily designed to allay fears about the radical pedigree of the new regime. The merchants praised Guerrazzi for "the way in which you have used your talents to restore to our town order and tranquility indispensable for the security of commerce and industry, your untiring boldness, your wisdom in dissolving the heated and complicated problems of contemporary politics, and finally the self-denial for which you do not spare sleepless nights, suffering, and discomfort . . . [to work] on our behalf."[76]

Guerrazzi replied in the same spirit, thanking the merchants for their support and assuring them that "if at first I did not work enough to merit your praise, I will not slacken my efforts until I correspond to the view that you have formed of me. You entrust my city and its commerce to me. They are well entrusted."[77]

Notwithstanding official expressions of sympathy and mutual understanding, the radical image of the new regime and the nature of its programs could not help but generate anxiety in the commercial elite. In February, the grand duke, alleging that he could not subject himself and his subjects to a papal ban by approving a bill calling for the establishment of a constituent assembly in Rome, fled into exile. This act, which led to the formation of a provisional government in which Guerrazzi held effective power, enhanced the radical character of the regime. Indeed, from its inception the government appeared linked to the radical democratic movement in Tuscany, for on February 8 the Circolo del Popolo—a large democratic club in Florence—had massed its supporters in the Piazza della Signoria and pressured the Tuscan legislative assembly to select the men who would eventually hold power in the regime.[78]

The first acts of the new government, designed to relieve popular misery and establish a foundation of mass political support, also represented a radical departure from existing practice. On February 11 the government reduced the price of salt by one-third (from twelve to eight quattrini a pound) and abolished the transit tax levied on pedestrians entering the major cities of the kingdom at night.[79] A week later the government abolished the family tax, eliminated consumer taxes on certain items of public consumption, and initiated some significant works of public beneficence.[80] Most indicative of its character was the new government's policy on rents. Rents traditionally were considered private contractual agreements not subject to government supervision or control. In Florence they were customarily paid on a semiannual basis, eight months in advance. The economic difficulties and the existence of a vocal popular movement provoked opposition to the traditional practice and put pressure on the government to change the system. In response, on February 15 the government placed rents under its direct authority on a month-to-month basis and pressured landlords in Florence to accept the practice of a two-month advance.[81]

The social reforms of the government were in part an expression of its political character and in part the result of a conscious effort to win support among the lower orders, particularly in the countryside, where sympathy for the grand duke had traditionally been strong. The abolition of certain taxes, however, produced a significant loss of revenue and exacerbated an already critical financial situation. The budget of 1848 had ended with a deficit of 2.5 million lire, and already in January the minister of finance was arguing that not only did the government not have the means to satisfy its mandated commitments but it also did not even have the resources necessary to meet the daily expenses of administration.[82] All of this was occurring at a time when the government was endeavoring to provide financial aid to Venice and to prepare for a renewal of the war against Austria.[83]

In an effort to solve its fiscal problems, the government passed a bill on February 12 calling for the emission of 6 million lire in treasury notes (*Buoni del Tesoro*), which would pay 5 percent interest and would have the force of legal tender.[84] The success of the measure—and, according to government spokesmen, the avoidance of more radical solutions—depended primarily on the bill's being adopted by the business community. On February 24 the minister of finance directed a circular to private capitalists in which he praised the community for the degree of acceptance that the bills were receiving and encouraged even greater efforts to insure the availability of hard currency necessary to pay the troops.[85]

In fact, the situation was far from rosy. Moderate to conservative business interests tended to resist the effort in the name of economic freedom and, where feasible, refused to accept the bills or threatened to draw their hard currency out of circulation entirely.[86] Even those who were better disposed toward the government were reluctant to aid the effort because of the uncertainty of the economic situation and the state's poor financial prospects. In an effort to encourage acceptance of the plan, Guerrazzi turned for support to the merchant community of his native city. In an address to parliament he cited the example of the Livornese firm of Rodocanacchi and Company, which at the first hint of the legislation had sent 200,000 scudi to Genoa. Following approval of the plan, Guerrazzi noted, the loyalty of even a basically foreign merchant community came to the fore. Rodocanacchi recalled his funds from Genoa and invested them in the new bills, and his example was followed by many others.[87]

Despite this support, opposition among more conservative elements in the business community remained implacable. The theoretical roots of this opposition had already been articulated by the Livornese merchant banker Pietro Bastogi in January, when debate on the treasury bills had still been in progress. In a pamphlet, Bastogi argued that paper currency represented the worst catastrophe that could befall a people after slavery and civil war.

> It smashes every social tie, insults the sanctity of contracts, forces the goverment—even though honest—to lose the trust of the governed, violates the right of property, destroys industry and commerce, impoverishes the rich, brings hunger to the poor, and disperses both private and public wealth. In short, paper currency represents a kind of famine with the whole run of evils which accompany it.[88]

Underlying the ardor of Bastogi's polemic was his faith in Livorno's traditional economic structure and his fear that its commercial reputation would be ruined by the new provisions. In the course of his discussion, Bastogi attempted to assess the consequences should merchants be unable to pay for foreign grain with a currency that could be converted into gold. "Gradually," he concluded, "ships with their cereal cargoes would be directed toward more secure markets, and the city's deposit trade would cease." The loss to interested groups in the city, Bastogi calculated, would exceed 2 million lire, while the public treasury would suffer a loss of approximately 330,000 lire a year.

Despite the criticism, the government's commitment to issuing treasury bills sprang, in part, from its desire to avoid imposing more radical measures to meet the fiscal crisis.[89] The pressing financial needs of the government and the evolving political situation in the peninsula, however, compelled the government to resort to more forceful measures. On February 21 it imposed a small surcharge on every lira of taxable revenue.[90] With the end of the Salasco armistice and Piedmont's renewal of the war against Austria on March 15, the situation became even more critical. In response, two days later the government reversed its earlier position and issued the call for a forced loan, placing an obligation "on the wealthier members of society, on the largest capitalists, and on commercial and industrial companies of all sorts," with the obligations ranging from 14 to 50 percent, depending on the value of the capital possessed.[91]

If moderates generally opposed the government's fiscal policies, they found its internal policies even more threatening. From one perspective Guerrazzi was a consummate political realist who found himself repeatedly forced to check the ambitions of his more radical followers. It was he, for example, who initially advised the grand duke against supporting the idea of a constituent assembly, for it might result in Grand Duke Leopold's losing his crown.[92] Instead, Guerrazzi had proposed a tripartite division of the peninsula—with Charles Albert controlling the north, Leopold II controlling a central Italian kingdom, and the king of Naples controlling the south—as a way of establishing a broad consensus for unification. Later Guerrazzi steadfastly opposed transforming the provisional government into a republic and fusing Tuscany and Rome, for he felt that only a small minority supported a republic and that such a move would prove very offensive to moderate forces in the peninsula, particularly in Piedmont.[93]

From another perspective, though, the internal policies of the regime seemed to threaten the constitutional guarantees of free speech, assembly, and worship, which represented a fundamental achievement of the revolution. One could not deny that threats against the regime—and against the peace and tranquillity of Tuscan society—were serious. On February 21, for example, a series of riots coincided with an expected move on the part of General De Laugier to march on Florence and restore the grand duke. Groups of peasants moved through the hills surrounding the capital, lighting bonfires, ringing bells, and shouting slogans against the regime. An attempt by the rural population to enter Florence and assault members of the provisional government was repulsed with several casualties.[94] Efforts to mobilize a national guard on February 27 were met with renewed signs of resistance. Groups that had assembled in the Tuscan countryside to protest the new law seized conscription lists, shredded draft notices, and threatened public officials. In response to the disorder, the government ordered nobles who had fled to their country estates and were suspected of colluding with the rioters to return to the city and take up their customary residences under threat of heavy fines.[95] In addition, it endeavored to assure the loyalty of the clergy—particularly in the countryside—and moved to arrest or replace those suspected of undermining the authority of the regime.[96]

On February 22 the government promulgated an emergency decree (*legge stataria*) that established a war commission and empowered it to judge under military law those suspected of attempting to subvert the existing order. The sentences of this panel were without appeal and were to be executed within twenty-four hours.[97] Ultimately, the decree served more as a threat than as a functioning series of provisions to restore public order.[98] However, to the moderates the flavor of this legislation—and its similarity to radical measures promulgated in France during the most hectic days of the Revolution—could not but increase their apprehension about the antiliberal nature of the regime.

Despite all efforts to provide a stable, patriotic regime, then, the provisional government failed to win the support necessary for its survival. The treasury bills and the forced loan antagonized the business community and property holders without providing the necessary increase in public revenue. The emergency decree and the efforts to control the influence of the nobles and clergy alienated moderate opinion without generating support among the radicals.[99] The regime's economic reforms diminished its revenue without winning the allegiance of the masses.[100] In striving for support from the moderates, the provisional government alienated many of its radical supporters. The provisional nature of the regime marked it as indecisive. While its support for Italian independence was genuine, to radicals its adherence to the general line of conservative policy in Piedmont—including that government's suppression of a popular revolutionary movement in Genoa in April 1849—and its straining for a broad political consensus in Tuscany prevented it from undertaking the radical programs necessary for victory. The government's failure to declare a republic, to undertake truly significant political and social reforms (including, for some, a redistribution of property), and to establish a cooperative effort with radical groups throughout the peninsula made it impossible for it to generate true popular support for the unity and independence of Italy. Ultimately, even some of Guerrazzi's closest supporters accused him of abandoning his democratic origins and of being more interested in winning power for himself than in working for Italy.[101]

Notwithstanding this criticism, Guerrazzi still commanded the allegiance of his native city. The government's positions limiting the political advocacy of the clubs, rejecting a republic, forcing the radical governor of Livorno, Carlo Pigli, to resign, and refusing to aid Genoa were greeted more with disappointment than with outright hostility toward the leader of the government. Guerrazzi's popularity endured, as his final visit to the city as leader of the provisional government clearly demonstrated. On April 7, Guerrazzi appeared before an immense crowd in Livorno's cathedral to make a final appeal "to the youth that remained [*a quanta gioventù rimane*]" to organize themselves into regiments and to rush to the frontier to defend Tuscany from an imminent Austrian invasion. Following the appeal, patriotic enthusiasm reached a fever pitch, and the next day a large number rushed to join the hastily formed battalions and left the city immediately.[102]

As patriots moved toward the frontier, Guerrazzi's position in Florence became more vulnerable to a rising tide of reaction. In early April frequent dispatches were sent from the capital to Livorno calling for arms and men to beef up the garrison. The government's increasing reliance on the Livornese to support its political position in the capital, however, intensified municipal hostility and provided a ripe opportunity for the reactionaries. Quickly mobilized, armed, and sent to the capital, the Livornese troops were not models of discipline. Their rough-and-ready manner and their frequent clashes with the local population made them a ready target for popular resentment. The hostility of the Florentines was exacerbated by the Livornese resemblance to Janissaries and by a desire on the part of elements of the local population to overthrow the provisional government and welcome back the grand duke in order to escape an Austrian occupation.[103]

On April 11 one of the usual disputes between the Florentines and the Livornese led to an armed clash.[104] Those Livornese whom the government could separate from the mob were escorted to the railroad station and placed on trains for home. Many, however, were caught in side streets or found hiding in shops or houses and were murdered on the spot by Florentines or by members of the paramilitary companies, anxious to avenge the humiliation that they had suffered with Cipriani in Livorno the previous September. The popular uprising against the Livornese coincided with an irruption of peasants into the capital, which, in turn, provided an opportunity for the Florentine municipality to seize control of the government, to place Guerrazzi under arrest, and to formally invite the grand duke to reassume the reigns of government. On April 12 all of Tuscany, save Livorno (and, initially, Pisa), returned voluntarily to the rule of the grand duke. Livorno—self-styled emporium of democracy, major supporter of the provisional government, and principal spokesman for the revolution in Tuscany—responded to the situation by closing its gates and preparing a last-ditch resistance to the reaction.

This final period of radical resistance, from April 16 to May 11, provided a culminating shock to moderate opinion in the city and in the country at large. The economic situation was desperate. Livorno was increasingly isolated from the hinterland, with its commerce disrupted and normal business activity disturbed by recurrent waves of popular hysteria.[105] Though grain reserves were abundant, the city found itself short of flour because most of Livorno's mills were located in the hinterland. The people, tired of subsisting on polenta and potatoes, attacked the bakeries to seize existing stores of bread.[106]

In these difficult economic circumstances, public works provided an important source of employment, but they could meet the needs of only a small percentage of the population.

Popular disturbances occurred frequently at the sites of public works as more people appeared than could be put to work, and the drying up of public funds threatened to stop the projects altogether.[107] Realizing the importance of this activity for the maintenance of public order, the chamber of commerce and the Jewish community advanced 200,000 lire to the municipality in interest-free loans, but this funding could keep the projects going only temporarily.[108]

Following the Austrian victory at the battle of Novara on March 27 and the initial movement of its troops into Tuscany, social and political tensions in the city intensified. Radical proposals were advanced in popular assemblies for the abolition of private property and the creation of a true state of popular democracy. When Giovanni Guarducci, a member of the governing council, in a public address referred to the population of the city as composed of a variety of classes (*ceti*), he was shouted down in a storm of invective.[109] Because of their wealth and distinctiveness, foreigners and Jews felt especially vulnerable to popular reprisals. "Special contributions" were demanded constantly and seemed to be only the first step in a general *"caccia ai codini"* (a hunting down of reactionaries and the seizure of property of those defined as "enemies of the fatherland").[110] Under the circumstances, flight appeared the better part of valor, but this move was resisted by radicals and the urban poor, who saw in the emigration of the wealthy the loss of jobs and financial assistance and perhaps a mediating influence on the advancing Austrians (who had declared Livorno's resistance illegal and therefore any acts of repression not subject to the rules of war).[111]

Under these circumstances, it is noteworthy that moderates in the city fared as well as they did. Loans to the municipality and the decision of the chamber of commerce to pay stipends to the members of the governing commission undoubtedly helped the situation.[112] Despite the invectives against subversives and exiles, private property remained secure, and individuals were allowed to discreetly leave the city.[113] Nevertheless, the moderates clearly had lost control of the political situation in Livorno. In this period of final resistance, initiative passed to a small group of radical nationalists who opposed accommodation and compromise. Their heroic efforts would provide an important legacy for the Risorgimento over the long run, suggesting at least the possibility of a popular foundation for the movement. Their more immediate defeat, however, signified the failure of popular revolution in Tuscany and set the stage for its defeat in Rome and Venice as well. Lacking the support of the moderates, rejected by the peasantry (which in Livorno, as in Florence, was closely identified with the counterrevolution), and unable to achieve the active support of France, the radical movement was doomed. For those who decided to return, Livorno's situation following the Austrian assault and capture of the city on May 11 was grim. Physically, Livorno was in shambles. Its economy was stagnant, and heavy fiscal exactions were placed on the population to pay for an Austrian army of occupation and to punish the city for its rebelliousness.

PART SIX

Reform Rejected

CHAPTER NINE

The End of Reform

The revolution of 1848 sapped the vitality of the merchant community and dissipated its commitment to reform. The commercial dislocations of the revolutionary period, the heavy fiscal obligations of financing a war and, later, contributing to an Austrian army of occupation,[1] and—most of all—the shock of popular revolt destroyed the optimism of the commercial elite. The sense of growing despair was already evident in mid-1848 in the writings of Giuliano Ricci, who, as we have seen, was a principal leader in the reform movement. In March, Ricci decried the growing sense of anarchy in Livorno.[2] By August, with all hope for popular reform evaporated, Ricci declared that it was no longer possible to exercise any benevolent influence on the people (*nostro popolo*)[3] and searched for an excuse to leave the city.[4] How appealing a life of retirement in the country now seemed, for "there I would still be able to do some good, because although the ignorance is great the spirit of goodwill is not less."[5]

The old confidence of the merchant community failed to return with the restoration of the grand ducal government in May 1849. Eulogies on the spirit of association—the ideological expression of the community's desire to join together to promote projects of fundamental economic and social reform for the city—continued sporadically but rang hollow. The

247

revolution had discredited philanthropic educational associations. In September 1849 the Kindergarten Society in Livorno reported a deficit of 20,000 lire, and for the first time in its history it requested a government subsidy. The reasons cited for this first annual deficit were the city's general economic difficulties and the resignation of many of the society's supporting members, a sign that many people had lost their old enthusiasm for the possibilities of education or were simply out to punish the people for supporting the revolution.[6] In vain, Tuscan educational reformers such as Rafaello Lambruschini attempted to reassert the conservative role of popular education.[7] To the members of Livorno's chamber of commerce, though, the failings of popular education were clear and impelled a shift in priorities from philanthropy to repression.[8] In response to this attitude, control over primary education was transferred from the largely indifferent local community to a government ministry in Florence, a loss of authority that previously the city would have staunchly resisted.[9]

The decline of an autonomous reform initiative extended to other areas as well. As we have seen, the merchant community made repeated attempts to insure the security of the port. In 1839 a group of important merchant houses in Livorno sponsored an ambitious project to achieve this end.[10] In 1847 pressure from an expanding trade in grain and other comestibles stimulated renewed petitions from the merchant community.[11] In 1851 the chamber of commerce unanimously recommended an enlargement of the port, which one writer at the time described as "the most dangerous, inconvenient, and, in various categories, expensive among the major ports."[12] In each of these instances the government proved unresponsive. In May 1851, however, without informing the community of its intentions or seeking its advice, the government itself assumed the initiative.[13] Requests from the chamber of commerce to be allowed to communicate with the organizers of the project to explain the needs of commerce were rejected. Having initiated the work, the government replied, it would not do to distract the engineer in charge with accessory considerations.[14] Strategic motives linked to strengthening the Austrian military presence in central Italy may have combined with a growing distrust of speculation in public-works projects (already forcefully expressed in the Dalgas memorandum of 1847) to check the scope for private initiative.[15]

Even Livorno's discount bank, perhaps the most significant new institution established by the merchant community in the first half of the nineteenth century, was radically transformed in this period. In the 1850s the bank proved increasingly unable to maintain the extended functions that it had assumed during the revolution of 1848. Large loans to municipal governments and to the central government in Florence (which in themselves reflected the harsh fiscal situation of the period) ultimately restricted the institution's lending capacity and its ability to perform its principal function, the discounting of commercial paper to facilitate the city's commerce.

The years 1853 and 1856 represented the most active in the bank's twenty-year history.[16] In 1856 the bank's lending capacity was strained to the utmost, creating a serious currency problem in the city and generating a fear that the bank would be unable to meet its obligations. The government intervened cautiously, liquidating certain loans of its own and encouraging communities and large capitalists to do likewise.[17] In addition, the government permitted the bank to close for a month and made supplemental funds available as needed to convert into specie the bank's notes.[18] Under the impact of this crisis initial efforts were made to fuse the discount banks in Livorno and Florence into a larger, more stable institution, eventually realized in July 1857 with the opening of the Banca Nazionale Toscana.

At the time the opinion of the bank's shareholders was sharply divided between a minority of speculators "hoping to make considerable gains from trading on the shares of the amalgamated society" and a majority that "found distasteful the possibility of amalgamation and was intolerant of a policy of centralization, which in their minds signified dependency and the neglect and humiliation of the city."[19] Clearly municipal sentiments were still strong, but with the shocks of the revolution and the difficulties of the ensuing period they were yielding to newer perspectives that were at once broader and more impersonal.

The social dimension of this change is especially evident in the chamber's eagerness to divest itself of supervisory authority over the dockworkers. As noted, on the eve of the revolution of 1848 a close bond had existed between the chamber of commerce and the principal dockworker companies in the city, the Manovella, Sacco, and *Veneziani*.[20] In 1847 the chamber finally agreed to support the formation of the first two companies and the granting of special privileges to the third, and in the process it had been given extensive supervisory authority over the city's haulage trades. Initially, the situation benefited both sides. The income and job security of members of the companies improved and, in return, the companies forcefully intervened to preserve the tranquillity of the city in the early stages of the revolution.

Events during and after the revolution, though, soured the relationship. The demands of a variety of groups for exclusive control over other portions of the city's haulage trade increased social tension in the city during the revolution and provoked a reaction against all forms of worker privilege.[21] Continuing dockworker problems in the ensuing period impelled the chamber to relinquish its supervisory role.[22] It pushed for the formation of a commission to work out a new regulation for the companies which would lessen the chamber's responsibility.[23] It encouraged the appointment of an inspector to supervise the dockworkers but refused to compensate him for his duties or to involve itself in the terms of his office.[24] In moments of particular difficulty (e.g., work stoppages) it attempted to renounce its supervisory authority altogether, arguing that responsibility properly belonged to the government and the customhouse.[25]

Ultimately, the chamber showed little residual interest in the companies, believing that the best solution to problems in this sector would be to suppress the companies and to open haulage duties to the benevolent influences of free trade, more precisely to the *facchini di banco*, who were in the direct employ of the merchants. Pressured by continual disputes, then, the merchant community attempted to withdraw from its paternalistic relationship with the dockworker companies, pushed the government to assume the duties of regulation and supervision, and concentrated on its own private affairs.

Significantly, at precisely this time when institutions and reform initiatives at the local level were in decline, the central government took steps to undermine municipal governance and to gather political and administrative authority into its own hands. With the restoration of the grand ducal regime in 1849, the government solidified its control over the municipalities. Stringent measures restricted electoral participation and officeholding, granted the central government power to set aside municipal decisions and to dissolve municipal councils, and empowered the grand duke with the authority to appoint and remove *gonfalonieri* (which, in effect, made them functionaries of the central government rather than spokesmen for their communities). These provisions combined with the strict limitation of communal deliberations to administrative—as opposed to political—matters to tighten political authority and to lay the foundations for an absolutist regime.[26]

Attacks on local political initiative represented a further erosion of the liberal principles that we have traced in the course of this book, principles that had provided the very foundation of the merchant community's reform program. For the city's liberal elite, freedom signified not simply a legal guarantee against the arbitrary authority of the state but also the liberation of individual energy and initiative. As such, it represented not simply a right but—in its affirmation of human potentiality—a duty.[27] To encourage its development, as we have seen, the merchant community clearly demarcated the spheres of action appropriate to public and private authority. Government action should be directed primarily toward providing basic facilities (such as lazarettos) and insuring a modicum of public order. Voluntary economic and philanthropic associations, however, would insure the fundamental well-being of the community at large. In this spirit merchants had drafted projects for the discount bank, railroads, and an enlarged port and had actively supported primary schools and a savings bank. In this spirit they had supported the chamber of commerce in its role as the spokesman for their economic interests and, particularly in the late 1840s, they had sought to strengthen political participation and power at the local level.

These efforts were not limited to Livorno. On the eve of the revolution, liberals throughout Tuscany took advantage of the freer political atmosphere to assert more forcefully the importance of municipal politics. In a pamphlet on the foundations of the Tuscan municipal system, Ricci stressed that, like individuals, municipalities possessed certain inalienable rights and therefore wished "by themselves through their own officials to direct their internal affairs."[28] To adequately achieve this end, he argued, required a loosening of the controlling authority of the central government and a widening of political participation at the local level to include not only the landed elite but businessmen and professionals as well.[29] To Ricci, and to Tuscan liberals generally, the issue was not simply one of administrative and political reorganization; it was a moral issue as well. Self-governing local administrations would strengthen civic virtue and gradually instill in the population at large habits of responsible political participation. The underlying vision was perhaps best captured by Leopoldo Galeotti, a leading advocate of Tuscan liberal reform: "Communal institutions are to liberty as elementary schools are to science. They are destined, that is, to introduce liberty as something normal and everyday, to instill a taste for its benefits, and to insure its calm and regular exercise."[30]

The revolution of 1848 dashed these hopes, and the loss of confidence in the possibilities of autonomous economic and social reform which resulted from it made it easier for moderates to allow authority and initiative to pass to the central government. Far from decrying the change, moderate opinion on the whole welcomed it as providing a firmer guarantee of public order. The liberal consciousness that had developed up until 1848 and had informed the merchant community's reform program was clearly giving way to the bureaucratic, centralizing principles of a new age.[31]

It is ironic that it was during this period that a general

acceptance of the principle of free trade—an ideal long supported by Livorno's merchant community—would set into motion the final erosion of the city's prosperity as a free port. The famine of the late 1840s had induced most European states to begin removing their protective tariffs on grain: England replaced its Corn Laws with a fixed tax on imported grain in 1846, and this tax was abolished in 1869. Holland eliminated its sliding-scale protection of grain in 1846, and full freedom was granted (as with Belgium) in 1850. Sweden, the kingdom of Sardinia, and the Papal States followed suit in the 1850s, France in 1861, and the German Zollverein in 1865. For several decades European commerce would remain unencumbered by tariff and trade restrictions. In this situation, however, Livorno's traditional role as a port of deposit and transshipment for grain and as a principal mediator between the grain-producing areas of southern Russia and the markets of western Europe would in effect end. With the liberalized commercial policies of the European states, Tuscan authorities noted, not even Tuscan ships were putting into the port of Livorno as often as before. Many of these ships were being chartered in the grain ports of the Black Sea and were transporting their cargoes directly to markets in Europe without touching the free port.[32] In future, grain imports into the city would be increasingly restricted to serving the needs of Tuscany and its neighboring states.

The erosion of the spirit of reform in Livorno and the decline of its traditional commerce prepared the ground for the final abolition of the city's status as a free port. The political situation, in any event, was not propitious to its survival. The successful unification of the Italian peninsula in 1860 called into question traditional privileges and immunities. The legal and administrative centralism resulting from the state-building process proved especially threatening to the survival of autonomous local and regional units. The desire for uniformity and order, conditioned in part by a sense of the tenuous character of the national achievement, discouraged exceptions to standardized fiscal and economic practices. Italy's first customs regulation (29 October 1861) called for the survival of existing free ports in the peninsula.

However, growing opposition to them within the government produced a bill that decreed their abolition effective January 1866. Under this ominous threat, public opinion in Livorno mobilized for a final defense of the city's privileges. Exploring this opposition provides a clearer sense of Livorno's economic interests at the time and of the merchant community's capacity to adjust to a very different economic and political reality.

Initially, the merchant community resolutely defended Livorno's traditional privileges. In 1862 the chamber of commerce commissioned an attorney to prepare a memorial on the damage that Livorno's economy would suffer as a result of the suppression of the free port.[33] The dire predictions of this memorial reflected the more extensive considerations of the last head of the government under the grand ducal regime.[34] In a pamphlet entitled *Livorno ed il suo portofranco considerato nel passato, nel presente e nell'avvenire da un vecchio livornese, socio dell' Accademia Labronica*, Giovanni Baldasseroni stressed the intimate connection between Livorno's status as a free port, its commercial prosperity, and its ability to support an active, growing population.[35] Under the benevolent guidance of the Medicean and Lorenese dynasties, he argued, the city had grown from a malaria-infested outpost to one of the principal ports in the Mediterranean, supporting close to 100,000 inhabitants. Over the centuries, the city had suffered only when its privileges were violated, he wrote. The best example of this had occurred in 1812, when the French occupation of the city served to depress its commercial activity and to drive down its population. Following the return of the Lorenese dynasty, though, the city's privileges were first restored and then amplified, and the ensuing prosperity, in Baldasseroni's view, merited calling Leopold II the city's second founder.[36] To Baldasseroni, Livorno's privileges provided the sole basis for its prosperity and survival. No concessions could provide adequate compensation for their abolition. A free-deposit zone in a portion of the port (as in Genoa) would simply depress commerce and ruin the city's property owners, whose rents and taxes were based on Livorno's pervasive economic activity.[37] The construction of new warehouse facilities and the mechanization of the docks—while perhaps useful in the long run—would leave large numbers of the city's porters and carriers unemployed.[38] Baldasseroni's pamphlet accurately reflected the traditional climate of opinion in the port city. Livorno's privileges were good for commerce, for industry, and for the welfare of the population at large. As such, they represented the fruit of centuries of enlightened rule and, understandably, had won the sanction of all the major European powers. Any tampering with these privileges, therefore, would not only be illegal but would return the port city to a situation of absolute desolation.[39] Needless to say, Baldasseroni's message made a strong appeal to merchants (concerned for the future of their traditional activity), to porters (preoccupied with the future status of their organizations), and to consumers (who linked the city's privileges to the availability of cheap provisions).

Not surprisingly, this perspective made the merchant community initially ambivalent about Italian political unification. In January 1859, on the eve of the Italian wars, the governor of the city dispatched a fundamentally optimistic note to the minister of the interior. Sardinian propaganda, he reported, was operating in the city but would make little headway, because republican agitators there despised monarchical Piedmont and because merchants considered that an eventual union of Tuscany and Piedmont would prove harmful to the city's economy.[40] Concern about enhanced competition from the rival port of Genoa combined, it seems, with a fear of commercial disruption and popular disorder to dampen enthusiasm for the national movement.[41]

The flight into exile of the grand duke and the establishment of a provisional government in April 1859 (the transition to eventual formal unification) was officially ignored by the chamber of commerce, whose only formal proposal in the matter was to recommend against arming a national guard, which it saw as more of a peril than an aid to public order.[42] Small wonder, then, that nationalists attacked the deputies in the press as foreigners extraneous to Italy's national aspirations.[43] Francesco Malenchini, representing the chamber, eloquently protested the charges by demonstrating the patriotic sentiments and sacrifices of several members and the body's long-standing reform initiatives.[44] Baldasseroni's pamphlet, however, could only strengthen the impression that the merchants were rooted in the past and that the community possessed a deep-seated nostalgia for the Old Regime.[45]

From Livorno itself, though, began to emerge opinions more favorable to an acceptance of the new economic and political order. In October 1862, Guerrazzi, often caustic and critical toward the merchant community, introduced a different perspective on the free-port issue in a local radical journal, *Lo Zenzero.* He began by acknowledging the importance of the city's privileges in the initial stages of its development as an aid in stimulating commerce, establishing a market, constructing a navy, securing business contacts, and the like.[46] But he argued that what was useful in a state of infancy did not necessarily serve a positive function when economic relations became more developed. Indeed, in the case of Livorno, the spread of civilization and the growing facility of communications made the free port more noxious than useful, for "[it] inhibits local industries and promotes foreign ones, foments contraband, and with contraband, laziness, thievery, and fraud, the plagues of civic life."[47]

Five years later an anonymous pamphlet provided extensive support for Guerrazzi's position. At the same time, it attacked point by point the assertions of Baldasseroni, an indication of the continuing rancor of the debate.[48] To the anonymous author, the public's first task was to accept that deposit commerce was dead and that Livorno's economic future depended on its ability to establish closer ties with the hinterland and with industries appropriate to a new age. In future, the author stated, the basic wealth of a country—that which enabled the population to work and the poor to survive—was industry: "The country that lacks industry dies of hunger."[49] Livorno's industrial development, however, could only follow the abolition of its traditional privileges, for the current fiscal situation represented an insurmountable obstacle to the city's economic growth. It forced businessmen to pay tariffs on goods introduced into the hinterland because these were considered foreign, and at the same time it forced them to pay tariffs on goods shipped abroad because these were considered Italian. In addition, Livorno was the only city forced to pay an additional commercial tax on goods introduced into the city, which placed it at a particular disadvantage in competing with other ports to service the needs of the internal market. In effect, under the current regime, the author noted polemically, "Free city means *slave city*, freedom suggests *servitude*, and what seems to be free is [in fact] fetters."[50] In the long run, then, the abolition of the free port would benefit merchants and manufacturers. It would also profit consumers, who drew most of their basic necessities from the hinterland, and landlords, who would benefit from the city's renewed economic activity.[51]

Ultimately, the merchant community was not intractably opposed to abandoning the free port. In 1859, at the climax of Italy's national unification, the community's defense of its privileged status had been understandably prudent and restrained. Later, the dire predictions contained in the memorial that the chamber commissioned in 1862 were softened as the deputies worked to correct the record and to provide a less exaggerated picture.[52] Merchants themselves began to pressure for an abandonment of the city's privileges. In April 1865 a substantial number of them presented a memorial to the chamber calling for the abolition of the city's commercial tax (*tassa di commercio*), arguing that "it had brought so much harm to import commerce that it would be preferable, rather than maintaining it, that the privileges fall even before the stipulated date."[53] The chamber refused to support the request, less from an inherent belief in the economic advantages of the free port per se than from a desire to win substantial concessions from the government. This was openly admitted by the deputy Bondì, who noted "that to obtain compensation one must sustain the great importance for Livorno of deposit commerce and the scarce importance of transit commerce even if this no longer corresponds to the actual situation."[54]

In reality, commercial interests in the city were also attracted by the economic prospects of an expanded hinterland and renewed commercial activity between northern Europe and the eastern Mediterranean. They resented not only the liability of the commercial tax but also the special concession granted to the free ports of Ancona and Messina, which could introduce their indigenous manufactured goods into Italy without charge—a favor that had been denied to Livorno.[55] With the unification of the peninsula, Livorno's hinterland had been vastly expanded and offered the promise of raw materials, markets, and commercial profits far exceeding those of the former Tuscan state. This posed a painful dilemma, for the relatively free access to other states of the peninsula which Livorno had enjoyed when these states were technically foreign no longer applied now that they were Italian.

Each phase of the unification process, therefore, threatened to cut the city off from more of its traditional commercial contacts.[56] In response, the merchant community suggested a variety of temporary remedies, from piecemeal tariff concessions to transforming the city's Fortezza Nuova into a free-deposit area for Italian imports, which would enable Livorno in a modest way to establish the same relationship with Italy that it enjoyed with foreign states.[57] Transit commerce appeared even more promising, for the completion of the Suez Canal and a central Italian railway system could make Livorno a nodal point in a commercial network linking northern Europe and the Orient.[58] Ultimately, as things turned out, the optimism was excessive, but it did enable the merchant community to accept more easily the imminent abolition of the free port.[59]

Despite the predictions, the postunification period represented a difficult time of transition and readjustment. The decline of Livorno's traditional commerce of deposit and transshipment appeared irreversible, but new commercial relations, new industry, and a new set of attitudes were slow to take its place. Predictions of the imminent dawn of a new industrial era were especially inflated. In 1856, Francesco Bonaini, discussing Livorno's economy at the Georgofili Academy in Florence, concluded that "one does not doubt the ability to establish there a new and second Manchester."[60] The anonymous 1867 pamphlet discussed earlier noted forty-eight industries that could benefit from free access to the internal market.[61] In addition, the author suggested new industries (textiles, metallurgy, and sugar) for which conditions in the city appeared especially propitious.[62] Developments in these sectors, he argued, would allow the city to pass securely into a new industrial age.

The reality, however, at least in the short term, appeared to be quite different. Discussions of the city's industrial activity in the 1850s and 1860s indicated that principal sectors were still closely related to the city's traditional economic activity. Bonaini, for instance, indicated the growth of naval construction but also stressed the importance of furniture, soap, and hides, which were based on easy access to foreign raw materials and markets.[63] In 1867 a memorial on behalf of various manufacturers in the city stressed the importance of men's ready-to-wear clothing. Ten large firms and eighteen smaller establishments invested a total averaging 4.6 million lire a year in raw materials, employed roughly 5,500 workers, and paid total annual salaries of 800,000 Tuscan lire. Finished products were sent to the eastern Mediterranean and the Levant.[64] Sixty additional firms handled the marketing of another 240 industries that also utilized foreign raw materials and were principally geared to supplying foreign markets.[65] Even Mario Baruchello, a staunch advocate of new industrial activity, was forced to admit the importance of this sector. He noted that "clothing warehouses are enormous" and that the products found a large market due to their reasonable prices, "owed to the moderate value of the materials and low labor costs for their confection."[66]

The strength of traditional economic activities in the city inhibited the formation of a consensus on Livorno's economic future and weakened the pressure that the merchant community could bring to bear on the central government. This was evident in the protracted struggle to construct general warehouse facilities and a dock in the city. In May 1865 the law that fixed the date for the abolition of free ports in the peninsula opened, in compensation, a credit of 6 million lire to serve in part for the construction of general warehouses. These facilities were warmly supported in study commissions and in meetings of the chamber of commerce by Giuseppe

Ferrigni, who argued that they would modernize procedures for handling merchandise, cut turnaround time for the city's shipping, and smooth Livorno's transition from a commercial to an industrial center.[67] Ferrigni's arguments, however, appeared to make little impression on the community at large. Critics saw the new facilities as a poor substitute for a free port and capable of merely raising false hopes in a city whose commerce had by now been reduced mainly to consumption and simple transit.[68]

A concrete project on the matter, which Gino Pachò presented to the chamber in March 1866, met with general indifference.[69] Two years later the issue was reopened and subjected to an intensive scrutiny, but it remained unresolved.[70] In February 1869 the government reduced its projected contribution to 2.7 million lire.[71] In 1870, following the lead of Ancona, Livorno abandoned the project entirely and settled for a small *punto franco* (free-deposit zone), ultimately constructed and administered by the municipality.[72] In this way, the city retained the semantic allure of a free commercial zone without the modernization of its facilities, which warehouse facilities and a dock would have stimulated.

Just as indicative of the harmful effects of a lack of consensus in the community was the city's failure to secure a place on the central Italian rail network. In January 1860, Bettino Ricasoli, chief spokesman for the government in Tuscany, spoke in Livorno and promised that the city would be included on any such line.[73] Despite repeated complaints from the chamber of commerce to the central government in the years following unification, however, specific initiatives won little support in the port city.[74] A projected line from Livorno to Grosetto in 1860, for example, met with general indifference.[75] In 1871, when Pisa obtained the concession for a line linking it to Collesalvetti, efforts in Livorno were rekindled, and a project was drafted for a line from Viareggio to Cecina via Livorno. Once again, however, overall support for the line was lukewarm, and the project failed.[76] Strong divisions of opinion in the port city, provincial rivalries, and the opposition of one of the city's former leading capitalists insured the failure of the rail projects.[77] As a result, Livorno found itself cut off from the major north-south coastal rail artery, which passed only a few kilometers from its walls. This situation would be rectified only in 1907 with governmental approval of a birail project linking Livorno and Cecina. Until that time, however, Livorno's commerce with the interior would be handled primarily with facilities constructed before unification.[78]

Although the difficulties faced by the city in the late nineteenth century resulted in large part from the disorientation of its commercial elite, some responsibility must also be borne by the central government. Despite Livorno's strategic position in central Italy and its commercial importance in the period before unification, government expenditures for improving its facilities were comparatively insignificant. Shortly after unification, for example, Naples received 50 million lire from the government to construct the facilities necessary to attract modern shipping.[79] In the 1870s work was initiated in Genoa to double the size of the city's commercial port.[80] These initiatives were merely the first stage of a long, continuous effort. In contrast, in the early years of the present century the port of Livorno retained essentially the same character that it had possessed under the Medici.[81] Large parts of the docking area remained exposed to dangerous currents, and its 6.5-meter depth was inadequate for modern shipping. Of all the Italian ports, Livorno had the poorest ratio of total tonnage to meters of dock capable of accommodating modern liners.[82] New facilities for expediting the handling of bulk products such as grain, cotton, and coal were nonexistent.[83] The backward state of the port's facilities was reflected in Livorno's inability to keep pace with its commercial rivals: from tenth position among European ports in 1832, Livorno slipped to thirty-first in 1887 and to forty-seventh in 1898.[84]

Livorno's history in the postunification period, though, did possess some positive features. From 1879 to 1898 the Orlando shipyard in Livorno won government contracts of approximately 56 million lire, which stimulated employment in the city and helped to encourage the development of heavy industry.[85] Changes in the general economic character of the peninsula were reflected in the changing character of

Livorno's imports. Despite the structural deficiencies of the port and the inadequate nature of its ties to the hinterland, Livorno increasingly served as a supplier of coal for the expanding industrial activity of Tuscany and central Italy. From 1894 to 1913 coal represented approximately one-half the total volume of the city's imports, and its place in the commercial life of the port was as important as grain had been earlier in the century. The constant increment of Livorno's coal imports enabled commercial tonnage in the port to surpass a half million tons by 1897 and 1 million tons by 1906.[86] The impact of this rapid growth stimulated renewed pressure to improve the port's facilities. In response, the government-sponsored Cozza plan drafted in 1906, supplemented by the Coen-Cagli plan in 1922, finally endowed Livorno with the facilities of a modern industrial port.[87]

With the changing nature of its commercial activity and the completion of its new facilities, Livorno was definitely transformed from an isolated commercial emporium into a city serving the needs of an industrial hinterland. In the process, the locus of the city's commercial activity shifted from the old Medicean port to a new zone developed north of the city (the site of the ancient Porto Pisano). However, even today, after the bombardment of World War II, the herringbone pattern of the old city, its sleepy canals, and its dilapidated fortifications and warehouses remain as reminders of Livorno's former unique role as a free port. At present, the city's burgeoning commerce and its leadership in the container trade suggest that its location and physical situation and the energy of its merchants and workers may yet again restore Livorno to its prosperity and position of a former age.[88]

Yet the city's relationship to the past is tenuous, at best. The port's unique international role and the vitality of its reform program in the first half of the nineteenth century would not survive the shocks of the revolution of 1848 and the political and economic changes of the postrevolutionary period. The reforms that followed would be initiated and administered by the central government. In contrast to previously accepted interpretation, this study has demonstrated that the economic and social life of Livorno in the first half of the nineteenth century was not one of irremediable decline but of imaginative and energetic efforts at reform.

While merchants endeavored to strengthen the bonds of community in the city, however, they demonstrated little interest in working systematically for the political unification of the peninsula. Their tangible concerns lay in working for a well-functioning liberal order and in preserving Livorno's international commercial position. Their interests, which were at once local and cosmopolitan, mitigated against any consistent effort to achieve Italian national union. Despite the patriotic sentiments expressed by members of the merchant community, then, the impetus for political unification would have to come from other sectors of the social order and from regions more impelled to work for a modern unified state. This study thus reinforces the picture of complex aspirations among a middle-class elite. It demonstrates the efforts of a group working energetically for reform but at the same time endeavoring to retain the foundations of a fundamentally traditional order.

CHAPTER TEN

Conclusion: Livorno and the Risorgimento

This study has examined the reform program of Livorno's merchant community within the context of a rich historical setting, stressing the complexity of Massimo D'Azeglio's "revolution in open daylight" by focusing on a specific local area. In concluding, however, it is important to reemphasize how this perspective can enrich our understanding of the broader concerns of Risorgimento historiography. Specifically, what does Livorno tell us about the overall nature of reform movements in the period, about the role of the business community in the Risorgimento, and about the achievements and limitations of the Italian unitary process? What clarification can it offer to the theoretical controversies and historiographic debates on post-Risorgimento Italian politics and on the role of liberalism and nationalism in nineteenth-century Europe?

This study documents first of all the existence of a practical reform program early in the Restoration period. It indicates a series of reforms grounded in specific economic and social realities and designed and implemented by a local elite. Though lacking any overt political content, these reforms were cast within a liberal framework and, like liberalism generally, had both a progressive and conservative dimension.

They were progressive in that the reformers sought to implement economic and social changes to ameliorate the living situation of the masses, and they were conservative because at the root of these efforts was the belief that only in this way could they counter the threat of social revolt generated by the demographic pressure, economic uncertainties, and ideological ferment of the age.

From today's perspective, these reforms may seem to have been unexceptionable. Primarily practical and economic, they offered little theorizing or overt challenge to existing institutions. Moreover, they failed ultimately to resolve the specific economic and social problems for which they were intended. Livorno did not become a major port as a result of the lowering of charges and the improvement of commercial practices; indeed, its relative position declined after Italian unification. Livorno's discount bank fell on difficulties in the 1850s and was absorbed by its sister institution in Florence. Its rail line brought some profits to speculators but failed to make Florence "a second Manchester" (for which, incidentally, we can all be grateful). In the area of social reform, the voluntary schools reached only a small minority of the school-age population, and the savings bank proved more attractive to the middling ranks of society than to the working poor, for whom it was designed. What began as an effort to open up the labor market to benefit Livornese workers in their efforts to secure jobs held by a "foreign" privileged company led during the revolution of 1848 to a stronger reassertion of labor privilege, this time by companies of local workers. As perhaps the final irony, the achievement of free trade—a policy long advocated by the merchant community—ultimately eroded the very foundations of Livorno's prosperity.

In this regard, what Livorno demonstrates best is the tentative nature of the reform program and the reasons for its failure. Though the reformers believed in the possibilities of a gradual transformation of society, their efforts were highly tentative, excessively paternalistic, and on occasion even hypocritical. Their fixation on the concrete—while a useful antidote to the rhetorical exaggerations of the democratic movement—seemed at times almost pathologically conditioned by a fear of repression from above and revolutionary excess from below. In Livorno, as we have seen, there were particular reasons to eschew nationalism and fear social rebellion. The port, after all, stood to gain little economically from Italian unification. Moreover, long before 1848 the city had developed an unsavory reputation for social turbulence. Elsewhere as well, though, reformers tended to embrace liberalism more warmly than nationalism and to stick with piecemeal economic reforms almost as a defense against the dangers of the political.[1] From this perspective, 1848 merely confirmed the worst fears of the reformers. With the intensification of political activity in the mid-1840s, the old reform movements disappeared, and reformers and masses alike were drawn into a chain of events over which they could exercise little effective control.

Livorno, then, provides concrete evidence of the importance of the midcentury revolutions in transforming the reform movement. In Livorno, the events of 1848 demonstrated the impossibility of achieving a liberal consensus that would draw into one camp elites and masses. With the uncertainty of the economic situation the masses expressed little interest in a free labor market. They wanted security. The pretensions of the workers, coupled with the ominous threat of the revolutionary process itself, destroyed a shaky paternalism and transformed the liberals' social dream into a nightmare. From this point the reform impetus would come not from the local community but from the central government, which was first in Florence and then, following the unification of the peninsula, in Piedmont. In Gramscian terms, with the collapse of hegemony the local elite turned to coercion to protect its position and looked to the central state government to apply it.

What all this meant for Italian liberalism and for the political life of post-Risorgimento Italy has been a subject of much debate. During the Fascist era, Benedetto Croce—a liberal senator and unquestionably the most influential intellectual in Italy at the time—wrote two long historical essays in which he depicted the Risorgimento as the heroic chapter in modern Europe's epic "story of liberty."[2] To Croce, the importance of the Risorgimento and of the policies of leaders such as Camillo Cavour and Giovanni Giolitti lay in a fundamental dedication to the principles of liberalism. Profoundly committed himself to these ideals, Croce believed that despite the dangers and occasional setbacks the issue really was never in doubt. To him liberty stirred and breathed almost as a transcendent spirit, a secular faith, an idea larger than the men who were its instruments.[3] From this perspective, Fascism had nothing to do with the Risorgimento: it represented merely a historical accident, "a venomous growth sprung from the evil of the postwar Italian and European crisis."[4]

In contrast to this largely hagiographic vision, critics of the Risorgimento—often of democratic or Marxist persuasion—have stressed the incompleteness of the process, its failure to involve the active participation of the masses or to respond to their needs. They have tended to see Fascism as the product of fundamental flaws in the Italian unitary experience.

The fervor of this evolving historiographical debate has been well summarized elsewhere.[5] Though the general interpretive polarities are well marked, however, much can still be discovered by focusing on a particular area and exploring in detail the relationship of economic and social change to an emerging political consciousness. This study of Livorno has demonstrated that in the most unlikely of places—in a city known for its detachment from the political hinterland and among a commercial elite that by reputation cared little for the local environment—there existed a concern not only for private profit but also for solidifying the foundations of the city's economic and social order and for building a society founded on liberal principles. The shock of 1848 and the ensuing decline of the reform program do not negate the effort and have enabled us to present a full picture of this practical liberal undertaking.

Livorno's particular nature makes it difficult to generalize automatically from its experience, but it does demonstrate in concrete terms the nature of one practical liberal middle-class reform effort and the reasons for its failure. Furthermore, it demonstrates that at least in the case of Livorno the collapse of the reform movement occurred long before the final achievement of Italian independence and unity. It suggests that the so-called decade of preparation witnessed not only a weakening of the democratic movement (which most historians acknowledge) but also evidence of a fundamental realignment of power among the moderates, which would provide a more centralized, disciplined, administrative quality to the final achievement. All this is not to negate the importance of the final result but rather to suggest that the nature of the outcome had already been prefigured a decade earlier.

Although Livorno had its own special characteristics, evidence suggests that its situation was not wholly unique. As noted in the introduction to this work, Milan, Venice, and Genoa all provide evidence of middle-class lethargy. Though all three cities ultimately experienced more prosperity than Livorno, their business elites required constant cajoling from liberal publicists and government officials interested in economic development. Cavour's view of the Genoese commercial elite as lacking in talent and vision and his general condemnation of that city for having produced "not even any merchants above the common run" is unique only for its acute sense of exasperation.[6] Only in Livorno, it would appear, did the articulation of a cohesive reform program spring directly from the merchant community, and even here the movement ultimately could not be sustained. Though working for reform, the Livornese merchants demonstrated little interest in transforming the peninsula's economic and political life. They remained content with their traditional commercial enterprises and with the special advantages offered by the city's privileges. As a group they demonstrated little interest in new forms of production, and their enthusiasm for transportation facilities seldom extended beyond the short-term speculative promise of such facilities. To this group Italian unification possessed little inherent appeal, for it threatened the unique advantages of the city's free port.

In bringing Livorno forward as an example of the shock of 1848 and suggesting the revolution's impact on the decline of a liberal reform movement, I have no intention of imposing a German model on the Italian peninsula. It would be far too easy to move from the unhappy experience of the twentieth century to a search for parallels going back to the nineteenth to a suggestion that totalitarianism was simply the product of liberalism's 1848 collapse.

Recently, two thoughtful essays have demonstrated the shortcomings of using a German model of failed liberalism even in Germany.[7] The presence of a strong state regardless of the social composition of its central administration does not preclude the existence of a vital civil society in which bourgeois aspirations and interests can contribute to the shaping of national policy. The rule of law, the free development of capitalist property relations, a rich associational life, and progressive cultural norms can occur and even flourish without the achievement of a fully liberal parliamentary regime. A "silent bourgeois revolution" can take place in civil society without the necessity of capturing the state. An authoritarian regime sympathetic to bourgeois aspirations and interests can be an acceptable, even a desirable, alternative. Regardless, the breakdown of a political regime cannot be pinned rigidly to a single turning point but must be examined in the context of a society's total historical experience.

This study has demonstrated the gradual maturation and precipitous decline of Livorno's reform program. Despite its loss of initiative, however, there is no inherent reason why Livornese interests could not have been adequately served by the central state administration. Certainly, though occasionally sluggish, Florence had established the foundations of the port's special status and the basis of its particular appeal. In addition, as noted in the preceding chapter, the contribution of the new Italian state was not entirely negative. Obviously, for one reason or another, the city proved incapable of articulating its needs and gaining acceptance for them in the new halls of power.

The reason was partly sectoral. Central Italy was crucial neither for the new nation's political consolidation nor for its economic development. More importantly, the ingrained mentality of the free port and the traditional privileges of the city prevented Livorno from responding as quickly and flexibly to new opportunities as did its rivals. Livorno's liberal outlook was too closely bound up with its traditional autonomy and its historic privileges. Ironically, the creation of a liberal Italian state, rather than establishing a basis for the city's renewed prosperity, merely enhanced Livorno's relative decline.

With regard to theory, this study has emphasized the importance of focusing on a particular local setting. Croce's generalizations about nineteenth-century liberalism do little to demonstrate the actual sources of liberal action and aspiration. Antonio Gramsci's concepts work better because they are more concretely rooted. In the introduction to this work, I suggested the importance of Gramsci's concepts of hegemony and passive revolution for this study. The local, autonomous reform program designed and implemented by the merchant community in Livorno, though ultimately unsuccessful, represented an exercise in hegemony. The shock of 1848 and the political realignments that followed produced a full expression of Gramsci's concept of passive revolution. The failure of the Action Party to effect a radical revolution and the co-option of its leaders helped to render the masses passive. The collapse of a locally based reform program and the withdrawal of the reformers indicated the passivity of the moderates. Effective political power passed from a locally based civil society to a central, bureaucratic state. That both definitions of passive revolution are present in Gramsci's work is one of the central points made in the introduction to this study.

In a third sense as well, I believe, Gramsci's concept of passive revolution helps to clarify the situation in Livorno. From his theoretical investigations and from his experience in Italy, Gramsci noted cases of slow, molecular change in which traditional economic forces demonstrated enormous resilience and more advanced productive relationships appeared only late, when the conditions for their preservation were fully mature. Gramsci saw in the survival of traditional economic and social institutions a basic characteristic of Italian history. Livorno has demonstrated concretely the nature of that survival. Contrary to previous interpretation, the traditional commercial activity of the port—the commerce of deposit and transshipment—did not collapse early in the Restoration period but continued to play a dominant role in the city's economy in the period under study. The grain trade, in particular, remained crucial for the city's commercial prosperity into the 1850s, and a manufacturing sector geared to transforming imported raw materials for external markets remained important into the 1860s.

In all three cases, then—in the absence of the masses from the political stage, in the withdrawal of the local elite from positions of leadership, and in the long-term durability of traditional economic structures—Gramsci's concept of passive revolution works well for Livorno.

Gramsci is sensitive also to the importance of 1848 to the transformation of the political situation in the peninsula, and, not surprisingly, he draws some important examples from Livorno. In a brief passage in *The Prison Notebooks*, Gramsci suggests that the radical 1848 revolution in Livorno frightened moderates throughout the peninsula and retarded the democratic process in the ensuing period.[8] In another passage he notes the particularist loyalties of the moderates—especially in Tuscany—their attachment to the Old Regime, and their unwillingness to take an active part in the struggle for Italian unification.[9] Obviously, as in any generalization of this sort, the author was exaggerating. However, this study has demonstrated that with regard to Livorno, Gramsci's insights were quite perceptive.

Unquestionably, certain aspects of Gramsci's theory have little relevance to Livorno. The Livornese elite had little interest in Tuscan agricultural policy and in the situation of the kingdom's peasantry. For the most part, as we have seen, the Livornese elite's relationship to the surrounding countryside was limited to the ownership of a villa or to an interest in a public-works project or an extracting industry. Its social policy, like its political vision, seldom extended beyond the limits of the city's walls. The Livornese reformers would have taken Gramsci's Jacobin prescriptions more as a threat than as an opportunity. The elite was serious in its efforts to reach the masses, but its efforts were primarily paternalistic and defensive. The reformers wanted community, but only on their own terms. They wished to neutralize the masses, much as Cavour later neutralized the leadership of the Action Party and co-opted much of the political initiative of local moderate groups. Once the events of 1848 had demonstrated the impossibility of a deferential relationship, Livornese moderates showed little interest in continuing the reform effort.

In this respect the Livornese were as important for what they did not do as for what they did. To them, liberalism remained largely a defensive creed, detached both from the dangers of democracy and from the blandishments of nationalism. Locked into a localistic perspective, the Livornese were able to retain a critical attitude toward some of the more unsavory aspects of Italian politics in the nineteenth and twentieth centuries, but in the process they failed to move effectively between civil society and the state, doing battle within the political arena and assuring in the process that the state would remain responsive to their needs. A noted Risorgimento historian, H. Stuart Hughes, has suggested in analyzing postunification Italy that the country got the regime it deserved.[10] If this is so, it was not the Livornese alone who failed to make an effective contribution. Still, an understanding of that city's experience during the nineteenth century suggests in ample measure both the promise and the defects that shaped the character of modern Italian history.

Biographical Sketches of Some Individuals Mentioned in the Text

ADAMI, Pietro Augusto (born 11 July 1812 in Livorno; died 17 December 1898 in Pisa). From a commercial family A. received a practical education and eventually opened his own firm, which prospered. In 1848, though virtually unknown, A. was selected by Guerrazzi to serve as minister of finance. He proved to be a person of integrity, energy, and capacity, managing to construct and administer an imaginative set of policies at a time of fiscal emergency and political crisis. Following the collapse of the provisional government and the return of the grand duke, A. suffered a brief imprisonment and witnessed the collapse of his financial affairs (he was eventually forced into bankruptcy). He ended his career working for the state's tobacco monopoly.

BALDASSERONI, Giovanni (born 27 November 1795 in Livorno; died 19 October 1876 in Florence). Although his father wanted B. to become a lawyer, he abandoned his legal studies in 1812 and went into public administration. In 1824, B. entered the ministry of finance; in 1838 he was named administrator of the Royal Revenues; and in 1845 he became a minister without portfolio. B. believed in enlightened, responsible administration, principles that were rooted in the political tradition of the eighteenth century. He defined himself as a moderate conservative and as such remained somewhat detached from the more progressive ideological currents of his time. Largely self-taught, B. was not a participant in the vibrant university culture at Pisa, and his religiosity and moral rigorism tended to distance him from the liberals. B. believed, though, that the dynasty would survive only if it could win the support of the moderate liberals. Following the return of the grand duke in 1849, B. became the head of the government. He sought to preserve the autonomy of the state and its constitution and argued for the establishment of an Italian league to stabilize the political situation in the peninsula. The refusal of the regime to support any of this program eroded its political support and eventually produced the collapse of the dynasty in 1859.

BASTOGI, Pietro (born 15 March 1808 in Livorno; died 21 February 1899 in Florence). B. came from a commercial family, originally from Civitavecchia, which enriched itself by engaging in the spice and colonial trades during the continental blockade. Like many of his peers, B. was educated at the Istituto dei Padri Barnabiti in Livorno. As a young man B. was active in the Mazzinian movement: during the early 1830s he was treasurer of the Livorno branch of the society and, with Enrico Mayer, traveled abroad to alleviate the economic difficulties of the exiles. In the late 1830s he withdrew from the movement and concentrated primarily on his business affairs. Gradually the focus of his affairs moved from commercial and maritime activities to the realm of public and private finance. In 1847, B. advanced 12 million lire to the grand ducal regime and, as a pledge on the return, was granted the revenues from the Azienda delle Miniere e Fonderie, which controlled the mining of iron ore on the island of Elba and the manufacture of iron at Follonica. During the revolution of 1848, B. was a deputy in the Tuscan parliament and openly opposed the financial policies of the Guerrazzi government. In the 1850s, B. continued his close financial association with the grand ducal regime, was president of Livorno's chamber of commerce, and played an important role in the fusion of the discount banks in Livorno and Florence into the Banca

Nazionale Toscana. Following unification B. was a deputy and minister of finance under Cavour and Ricasoli and was actively involved in organizing the new nation's fiscal structure. In 1862, B. set up the Società Italiana per le Strade Ferrate Meridionali to construct a rail network in southern Italy, winning the concession over the Rothschilds. In 1862, B. was condemned by a parliamentary commission for bribery and questionable profit-taking associated with the company, and he withdrew from active political life. At the end of his career B. devoted himself to his business affairs and to encouraging the study of economics by helping to found the Associazione Adamo Smith and the weekly journal *L'Economista*. In 1890 he was named a senator of the realm, with the title of count.

BINI, *Carlo* (born 1 December 1806 in Livorno; died 12 November 1842 at Carrara). Bini's father was a merchant in victuals originally from Fivizzano (a small town in Tuscany). He attended the College of S. Sebastiano in Livorno, where he associated with the sons of the local elite. Forced by his father to work in the family business (which he hated), B. nevertheless spent as much time as he could on his literary pursuits. B. also tended to divide his time between mixing with progressive members of the city's elite and with members of the working classes. His deep sympathy for the sufferings of this group remains an important source of his continuing appeal. Knife wounds received while returning home from an inn contributed to his early death. In the late 1820s, B. collaborated on the *Indicatore livornese* and helped diffuse radical ideas among the city's masses. In 1832, B. was arrested along with Guerrazzi and placed in mild confinement at Portoferraio.

BONAINI, *Francesco* (born 20 July 1806 in Livorno; died 28 August 1874 near Pistoia). B. came from a family of converted Jewish descent. His father, Domenico, was a *mezzano di cambi* (an agent dealing in currency exchanges) and his mother was the daughter of the captain of the port. Following his father's suicide, B. was able to obtain scholarships to study theology and civic and canon law at the University of Pisa. After graduation he obtained a chair at the Collegio Teologico Fiorentino. Later B. left the clergy and devoted much of his time to historical studies, particularly those involving medieval Pisa. In 1848 he was a captain in the university battalion and went to Lombardy with the Tuscan volunteers. Struck by a mental affliction, he was sent to recover at a hospital in Perugia, where he was able to continue his historical investigations and publications. In 1852 he guided the official commission that established the state archive in Florence, which opened in 1855 with B. as its first superintendent. From 1851 to 1868, B. was secretary and a director (*arciconsolo*) of the Academy of the Crusca. He labored unsuccessfully at the end of his career to assure the establishment of a solid archival administration in central Italy under the new regime.

CAPPONI, Gino (born 1792 in Florence; died 1876 in Florence). C. sprang from an ancient and noble Florentine family. In 1799 while his father followed the court into exile, C. remained with his mother in Florence. C. studied Latin and Greek and was a consummate historian; his work on the history of the Florentine Republic is still consulted. C. was married at nineteen to the daughter of another Florentine noble, but his wife died several years later in childbirth. From then on C. concentrated on his travels, his intellectual pursuits, and his political activities. He journeyed throughout Europe, studying the customs and institutions of the places he visited. He worked with Vieusseux to establish the *Antologia* (a liberal cultural and political journal modeled on the *Edinburgh Review*) and endeavored to further the work of liberal reform in Tuscany. He opposed violence and believed that a truly liberal society must be based on custom and tradition. From this came his belief in the importance of education and in a gradual process of improvement. In 1848, though he was by then totally blind, C. agreed to serve as prime minister following the resignation of Ridolfi. His ministry lasted for only seventy days and, in initiating discussion on a customs union and a constituent assembly, demonstrated more success in pushing the Italian cause abroad than in maintaining order at home. Upon his resignation C. recommended as a practical necessity the formation of a democratic ministry. Following the collapse of the provisional government, he served on the governing commission that welcomed back the grand duke but was extremely saddened when the Austrians entered Florence in May 1849. In 1859 he participated in the vote that deposed the Lorenese dynasty. He was later named senator of the realm.

CIPRIANI, *Leonetto* (born 16 May 1812 in Corsica; died 1888 in Corsica). C. came from an old Tuscan family. His father, Matteo, was a staunch Bonapartist who, with the fall of Napoleon, settled in Livorno, where he owned property. C. attended the Collegio di S. Caterina in Pisa for four years and then was placed in charge of the family's Tuscan properties. In 1830, C. participated in the French expedition to Algiers; in 1834 he spent time both sorting out the family's affairs in Trinidad after the abolition of slavery in the British possessions and traveling in America and Europe. C. became increasingly attached to the economic and political fortunes of the Bonapartes, while at the same time he began breaking his earlier ties to the Mazzinian movement, particularly after the failed insurrection of 1843 and the subsequent death of his brother Alexander. With the outbreak of the first war for Italian independence in 1848, C. convinced the Tuscan prime minister, Ridolfi, to dispatch Livornese volunteers into the Lunigiana. He also participated at the battle of Curtatone under General De Laugier and was decorated for valor. With the Piedmontese defeat at Custoza and the declaration of an armistice, C. returned to Tuscany. Capponi, following his failure to restore order in Livorno, dispatched C. to Turin to seek the intervention of Piedmontese troops and then to Paris to buy arms. With the installation of a democratic regime under Guerrazzi and Montanelli, C. renounced his mission and stayed in Paris. He returned to Italy to participate in the second campaign against Austria as an officer in the Sardinian army. With the defeat and the restoration of the grand ducal regime in Tuscany, C. left for the western United States, where he served as the Sardinian consul in San Francisco and engaged in the livestock trade. In 1855 he returned to Italy and helped facilitate negotiations between Napoleon III and Victor Emanuele (particularly regarding the proposed marriage between Gerolamo Napoleon and the Princess Clotilde of Savoy). In 1859 he served as a colonel in the Sardinian army and later was named governor of the Romagna. His suspected ties with Napoleon III and his hatred of the democrats and the papacy complicated his mission, and with the vote for annexation to Piedmont he was forced to leave office. In 1864 he was named at once senator, count, and general.

CORSINI, Neri (born 13 July 1805 in Florence; died 1 December 1859 in London). From a distinguished Tuscan family, C. showed early a special aptitude for public affairs, and in 1840 he obtained the post of governor of Livorno. In 1847 he was removed from his post for his willingness to cooperate with the liberal movement in the city. Shortly thereafter he had a frank conversation with the grand duke in which he indicated that to assure order and maintain control over the political situation it was necessary to grant a constitution and to initiate a truly national policy. With the granting of a constitution, C. agreed to serve both as minister of foreign affairs and minister of war. He fell into disgrace under the provisional government and was accused of high treason for advocating the armed intervention of Piedmontese troops to restore the grand ducal regime. In 1859 he attempted to save the dynasty by getting it to support a national liberal policy and also by getting the grand duke to abdicate in favor of the hereditary prince. In the period between the fall of the Lorenese and the annexation of the region to Piedmont, C. represented Tuscan interests at the courts of France and England.

DOVERI, Giuseppe (born 14 July 1792 in Siena; died 1858 in Livorno). Though not born in Livorno, for his many contributions to the city D. was awarded Livornese nobility. He received his early education in Florence and a degree in mathematics from the University of Pisa. At the end of the Napoleonic regime he held a chair in mathematics and nautical science at a college in Livorno. In addition to his educational pursuits D. administered a glassworks and a pharmacy. D. possessed a lifelong commitment to philanthropy and education. He helped to promote a savings bank and kindergartens in the city and for seven years ran an Istituto dei Padri di Famiglia.

GIOBERTI, Vincenzo (born 5 April 1801 in Turin; died 25 October 1852). With the death of his father and the family's ensuing financial straits, G., with the encouragement of his religious mother, decided to enter the clergy. In 1816 he became court chaplain, and in 1823 he received a doctorate in theology from the University of Turin. Despite his delicate health, G. traveled widely in Italy and studied history, philosophy, and literature in addition to theology. From an early age G. was suspect for his liberal sympathies and was an implacable opponent of the Jesuits. With the death of the archbishop of Turin, G. found himself deprived of his principal protector precisely at the time when the court was becoming more reactionary. In 1833, G. was charged with conspiring with a Mazzinian element in the army and nourishing liberal, republican, and Saint-Simonian sentiments. As a result he was dismissed from the court, expelled from the theological college, and thrown into prison. Before the completion of his trial G. was allowed to go into exile. In France, G.'s initial attraction to the Mazzinian movement ended as he saw the futility of Mazzini's policy of insurrection, and he came to believe that the regeneration of Italy could come only through a general European crisis. In 1834, he accepted a teaching position at a secondary school in Brussels, where he remained until 1845. In 1843, G. published his most famous work, *Del primato morale e civile degl'Italiani*, which condemned conspiracy and violence and predicted the eventual regeneration of the Italians. His view that the papacy represented the principal unitary element in the peninsula attracted a large part of the clergy to the Italian cause. In 1847, G. published *Il Gesuita moderno*, a documented exposé of the company, its pedagogy, and its politics. In 1848 he returned to Italy and assumed the post of deputy in the Piedmontese chamber. In December he became prime minister. His proposal to invade

Tuscany and restore the grand ducal regime met staunch opposition within the government and led to his resignation. In 1849 he returned to private life and to voluntary exile in Paris. In 1851 he wrote *Il Rinnovamento civile d'Italia*, in which he definitively embraced a Piedmontese solution to the problem of Italian unification.

GUERRAZZI, Francesco Domenico (born 12 August 1804 in Livorno; died 23 September 1873 near Cecina [Tuscany]). G. was born in a family with strong ties to the people. His father was a wood-carver and his mother had a rough, no-nonsense character. By training and inclination, though, G. was more elitist. G. studied law at the University of Pisa, where he fell under the influence of the most progressive political currents circulating in Tuscany during the Restoration and was touched by the charisma of Lord Byron, who had taken up residence in Pisa in 1821. Following graduation, G. seemed more interested in his literary and political enterprises than in launching a professional legal career. In 1827 he published his first major work, *La Battaglia di Benevento*, and initiated work that resulted in the *Indicatore livornese*, a journal dedicated to fostering progress in literature, society, and politics. In 1830 a commemorative discourse at the Labronica Academy for General Cosimo del Fante gave Guerrazzi a natural outlet for his patriotic revolutionary sentiments and resulted in his enforced confinement in the small town of Montepulciano for six months. In 1833, G. was forced to spend several months actually in prison for participating in a conspiracy to force the grand duke to grant a constitution. During this time of enforced leisure G. wrote a good portion of *L'Assedio di Firenze*, a novel of patriotic resistance against the foreigner, which placed Guerrazzi at the very center of the patriotic movement in Tuscany. Though quick to express popular, patriotic fervor, G. was not a party man. In the 1830s, Mazzini recognized G.'s abilities but saw the futility of trying to keep him within a disciplined party organization. By 1848, G. was closely identified with the radical movement in the city. In January he was forced to spend more time in prison for allegedly having sparked a popular movement against the authority of the central government. Under enormous popular pressure G. was eventually brought into the government, first as minister of the interior and a member of the ruling triumvirate and finally as virtual dictator. His effort to steer a moderate political course while in power failed to win him the support of the moderates and eroded his support among the radicals. With the collapse of the provisional government, G. was arrested and tried for lèse majesté, and after spending four years in prison he was allowed to go into exile. In the postunification period, G. sat among the opposition in the Italian chamber of deputies.

LAMBRUSCHINI, Raffaello (born 14 August 1788 at Genoa; died 8 March 1873 at S. Cerbone di Figline [Tuscany]). L. came from a wealthy family with close ties to the church: one uncle was a cardinal; the other, bishop of Orvieto. L. studied the ecclesiastical disciplines and classical languages. The family opposed Napoleon, and L. was forced to spend two years in confinement in Corsica. Following the Restoration, L. appeared destined for an ecclesiastical career, but ultimately he preferred evangelical simplicity to the worldliness of the Roman church. He retired to a family farm at S. Cerbone and devoted himself to the education and economic and moral improvement of the peasantry. He studied botany in Florence and helped found the *Giornale agrario toscano* and (himself) organized the journal *Guida dell'educatore* (1836–1845), which presented to a wider public the educational insights of himself and others. A moderate-liberal, L., along with others of a similar persuasion, promoted the founding of the political journal *La Patria* in 1848 and disapproved of the Montanelli Guerrazzi ministry and likewise of the reimposition of absolutism in 1849. L. spent much of the 1850s at S. Cerbone. In 1859, though, he was a deputy in the Tuscan assembly that voted to depose the grand duke. In 1860, L. was made a senator of the realm.

LARDEREL, Francesco [De] (born in France [date unknown]; died 15 June 1853 in Florence). L.'s family migrated to Livorno at the end of the eighteenth century to escape the revolutionary turmoil in France. In 1818, L. recognized the economic potential of the sulfuric fumaroles in the Maremma plain and developed a boric acid industry that brought him enormous profits. During the revolution of 1848, L. was mayor of the city and a member of an emergency governing commission designed to restore order. For his achievements L. was made a senator of the realm.

MALENCHINI, Vincenzo (born 8 August 1813; died 21 February 1881 at Collesalvetti [near Livorno]). M.'s family came originally from Lombardy, where his father exercised a merchandising trade. The father was awarded Livornese nobility for numerous acts of philanthropy. M. received his secondary education at the Ducal College in Lucca and a law degree from the University of Pisa. Due to the family's patrimony, however, he never had to practice a profession. In 1848, M. served as a captain in the infantry and was elected to the Tuscan parliament from Livorno. During the democratic regime he commanded a battalion of volunteers but came to oppose government policies, renounced his commission, and served as a simple soldier at the battle of Novara. In 1859 he organized a new battalion of volunteers, served as a member of the provisional government, and was elected to the constituent assembly, where he favored the annexation of Tuscany to Piedmont. A member of the Italian parliament until 1876, M. vigorously represented the interests of his Livornese constituency.

MAYER, Enrico (born 3 May 1802 in Livorno; died 29 May 1877 in Livorno). Son of a German father and a French mother, M. studied languages, literature, and mathematics at the College of San Sebastiano in Livorno. He was actively involved in the reform efforts of moderate liberals in Florence and wrote numerous articles on educational and philanthropic institutions for the *Guida dell'educatore*. M. traveled widely and had important contacts with the exile community living abroad, including Mazzini. In 1840, M. was arrested in Rome for sedition and held in prison for two months. M. supported the reform efforts of Pius IX as well as his opposition to the Austrian occupation of Ferrara, but he never considered himself a neo-Guelf ("We are all supporters of the Pope and will continue to be so as long as the Pope remains Italian.") M. enrolled as a volunteer in the first campaign against Austria and served as secretary to General De Laugier. As a foreigner, M. was not able to run for public office but was offered the post of minister of public instruction in the Tuscan government. In 1860, when M. was granted Italian citizenship, he refused to stand for public office so as, he said, to make way for the younger generation.

MICHON, *Carlo* (born 19 September 1771; died 14 November 1839). Son of a lawyer and a noblewoman, M. studied at the Cicognini College in Prato. He received a law degree and after the death of his father was admitted to the bar in Florence, but he never practiced. Instead, he devoted himself to agrarian studies and to administering his patrimony. His acts of public charity and his arrest and exile during the French occupation enhanced his reputation. In 1825, M. completed what he considered to be his principal civic achievement, the founding of a school of architecture and design. M. was known for his openhanded public charity. Perhaps the most dramatic case of this was his wish to adopt all the children in his parish who had been orphaned in a cholera outbreak in the 1830s.

MONTANELLI, *Giuseppe* (born 21 January 1813 at Fucecchio [in Tuscany]; died 17 June 1862 in Fucecchio). M. graduated in law from the University of Pisa and wrote philosophical articles for the *Antologia*, along with some sentimental poems of a vaguely Christian flavor. At twenty-seven years of age, M. was named professor of civil and commercial law at the University of Pisa. In 1844 he founded the secret society Fratelli Italiani [Italian brotherhood]. He considered himself part of the general movement for reform, but at the same time he prepared clandestine writings to stimulate nationalist agitation. In 1845 he participated in a protest against the establishment in Pisa of the Sisters of the Sacred Heart, which reputedly was attached to the Jesuits. M. was initially an important proselytizer of the Saint-Simonian movement in Tuscany but later transferred his support to the neo-Guelfs. In 1848, M. enrolled as a volunteer and was wounded at the battle of Montanara and taken captive by the Austrians. He was repatriated after the Salasco armistice and was elected a deputy in the Tuscan parliament. He advocated a conciliatory policy towards Livorno and was named governor of the city. With the fall of the Capponi ministry, M. was asked to head a new government, which he did on the condition that Guerrazzi be named minister of the interior. A member of the provisional government, M. broke with Guerrazzi over the issues of the constituent assembly and M.'s wish to fuse Tuscany and Rome. To resolve a difficult situation, M. was sent as Tuscany's representative to London and France in an effort to build diplomatic support against an Austrian invasion. Following the return of the Lorenese dynasty, M. remained in France, and in 1859 he enrolled in a voluntary brigade led by Garibaldi. He was elected to the Italian parliament shortly before his death.

ORLANDINI, *Francesco Silvio* (born 11 May 1805; died 25 December 1865 in Florence). O. studied law at the University of Siena but was forced for personal reasons to leave the university before graduation. He spent the rest of his life as a teacher. In 1836 he moved to Livorno. He was active in educational and philanthropic institutions and served as secretary to the Labronica Academy. In addition, he collaborated on educational journals, especially the *Guida dell'educatore* and the *Letture di famiglia*. In 1848, a delicate constitution kept O. from enrolling as a volunteer, but he established a journal, *Il Cittadino italiano*, which advocated a moderate political program. In 1859 he was named to the municipal council in Livorno; later he was called to direct the Liceo Fiorentino and was active in promoting a subscription for the erection of a monument to Dante in Florence.

ORLANDO, *Giuseppe* (born 14 March 1820; died 23 September 1893 in Livorno).
   Luigi (born 2 March 1814; died 14 June 1896 in Livorno).

Paolo (born 8 July 1824; died 1 July 1891).

Salvatore (born 29 July 1818; died 10 October 1881). The four brothers were sons of Giuseppe Orlando, a landowner from Syracuse (Sicily) who settled in Palermo and established a machine shop. The father died in 1825, and the company was then directed by Luigi, later aided by Salvatore. Luigi, who was political, enrolled in Mazzini's Giovine Italia and, under cover of his business affairs, helped prepare the insurrection of 1837. Following the failure of that revolt, the firm diversified its operations, manufactured steam engines for mills, extended its operations to Rome, and helped prepare for the initial insurrections of 1848. After the failure of the revolution the family transferred its operations to Genoa, building ships for the Rubbatino Company, founding a navigation society, and running the Ansaldo Company, which manufactured cannons and projectiles. The family was staunchly republican but was willing to support the Savoiard dynasty, provided that it worked for Italian unity and independence. The family supported the Mazzinian uprising of 1857, and Giuseppe supported Garibaldi's invasion of Sicily. Giuseppe was the engineer on Garibaldi's ship, the *Lombardo,* and after the landing Giuseppe sank the ship to prevent its falling into the hands of the Bourbons. Meanwhile, Paolo went to England to elicit support; Salvatore went to France to find ships; and Luigi stayed in Genoa gathering arms and other materials. In 1865 the family leased the government shipyard of S. Rocco in Livorno, which became the center of its renewed activity, especially for the construction of steamships.

PIGLI, Carlo (born 9 July 1802 in Arezzo; died 3 November 1860 in Florence). P. was a doctor, an eloquent speaker, and a radical. As a young man he was active in the secret societies. In 1831 he was named professor of physiology at the University of Pisa, where he was enormously popular with students for his eloquence and his patriotism. Suspected of liberalism and materialism, P. was suspended from his post briefly in 1832. In 1840 he was named professor of the history of medicine (considered a subject less inflammatory than physiology). In 1846 he retired from the university altogether.

In June 1848 he was elected to the Tuscan parliament and sat with the opposition. In November he was appointed governor of Livorno. His inflamed oratory and his refusal to tame the popular movement in the city made him unpopular with Guerrazzi (then minister of the interior), and P. was forced to resign. Though he opposed the provisional government, he was excluded from the amnesty of November 1849. Condemned in absentia to fifteen years in prison, P. spent the 1850s in exile in southern France and Corsica. In 1859 he returned to Tuscany, but because of poor health he was unable to take part in politics.

RICCI, *Giuliano* (born 1803 in Livorno; died 24 September 1848). R. distinguished himself intellectually at an early age. He attended secondary school in Volterra and later went to the University of Pisa, where he studied law, languages, history, and philosophy. In the course of his studies he was expelled from the university for insubordination but was later readmitted on a pardon from the grand duke. He published works on philosophy, economics, and history. He was particularly known for his work on the Tuscan economy and on municipal traditions in Italy. Of particular importance are his *Saggio del municipio considerato come unità elementare della città e della nazione italiana*, in which he argued that the basis for Italian resurgence lay in the tradition of freedom and public well-being provided by the country's municipal traditions, and his *Cenni sopra le basi del sistema municipale toscano*, which served as a basis for discussion on a proposed bill in the Tuscan chamber. Of staunch moderate-liberal principles, R. was active in pushing institutional reforms. Tragically, he drowned while returning home after being sworn in as a member of the Tuscan parliament.

UZIELLI, *Sansone* (born 30 October 1797 in Livorno; date and cause of death unknown). Though he was a member of a Livornese Jewish banking family, U. spent most of his career in literary and pedagogical pursuits. At twenty-four he traveled to England and Scotland, including New Lanark, to study architecture and educational institutions. For the *Indica-*

tore livornese, U. wrote a series of three articles discussing the importance of Benjamin Franklin's writings for social improvement. U. was also active in promoting suitable texts for popular education. With the death of his father in a cholera epidemic in 1835, U. was forced to direct the family firm. At the same time, though, he and his wife actively promoted the kindergarten school movement in Livorno, Pisa, and Florence and were the principal founders of the society in Livorno. U. was also active in administering the discount bank and engaged in a bitter legal dispute with Guerrazzi over the competence of the bank's administrators.

VIVOLI, Giuseppe (born 1786; died 11 February 1853). V. was initially destined for a commercial career like that of his father, but he demonstrated little inclination for this field and instead studied literature and science and became a Florentine notary. In 1815 he was named vice secretary of the sanitary office (*Ufficio di sanità*) in Livorno. Within a year he was named secretary of that office. V. made regular study tours through the Italian peninsula, and in 1842 he published his *Annali di Livorno*, which traced the history of Livorno until the end of the Medici regime. Later, V. published guides and biographies of the city and its important residents. In 1849 V. published a proposal to enlarge the port. In 1850 he was made a member of the noble order of Santo Stefano.

Notes

The following abbreviations have been used in the notes:

Archival Deposits

ACCL	Archivio della Camera di Commercio, Livorno
AME	Archives du Ministère des Affaires Étrangeres, Paris
ANF	Archivio Notarile Distrettuale di Firenze
ASF	Archivio di Stato, Florence
ASG	Archivio di Stato, Genoa
ASL	Archivio di Stato, Livorno
AST	Archivio di Stato, Turin
BLL	Biblioteca Labronica, Livorno
BNF	Biblioteca Nazionale, Florence
GCM	Museo del Risorgimento, Casa di Giuseppe Mazzini, Genoa
PRO	Public Records Office, London

Journals

AGA	*R. Accademia dei Georgofili di Firenze, Atti*
ASI	*Archivio Storico Italiano*
BBL	*Bullettino Storico Livornese*
BSP	*Bullettino Storico Pisano*

EHR   *Economic History Review*
GAT   *Giornale Agrario Toscano*
RHES   *Revue d'Histoire Économique et Sociale*
RSI   *Rivista Storica Italiana*
RSR   *Rassegna Storica del Risorgimento*
RST   *Rassegna Storica Toscana*

Introduction

1. Massimo D'Azeglio, *Programma per l'opinione nazionale italiana* (Florence, 1847). For the general historiography of the Risorgimento, I have drawn heavily on the insights provided by Walter Maturi in *Interpretazioni del Risorgimento*, 5th ed. (Turin, 1962).

2. *Biblioteca storica del Risorgimento italiano*, serie 8, no. 3 (Milan-Rome-Naples, 1916).

3. *Biblioteca di storia italiana recente, 1800–1870*, 10: 133–484 (Turin, 1921).

4. See in particular the work of Arnaldo Agnelli, "Il Fattore economico nella formazione dell'unità italiana," *Il Risorgimento italiano* 6 (1913): 253–278, 471–488; "Il Materialismo storico e il Risorgimento italiano. Posizione del problema," *Rendiconti del R. Istituto Lombardo di Scienze e Lettere* 46 (1913): 183–196. For the impact of Marxism on Livornese studies, see in particular the discussion of the work of Giorgio Mori and Nicola Badaloni in chapter 2.

5. Gino Luzzatto, "La Vigilia e l'indomani dell'unità," *Orientamenti per la storia d'Italia nel Risorgimento* (Bari, 1952).

6. Ibid.

7. Rosario Romeo's introductory essay to the revised edition of the work (Baltimore, 1965) provides valuable insights on the genesis of the work and its place in the historiography of the Risorgimento.

8. Ibid., p. xxii.

9. Ibid., p. l.

10. Ibid., p. 2.

11. Ibid., p. 3.

12. Ibid., p. 4.

13. Ibid.

14. Ibid., p. 263.

15. Ibid., pp. 80, 143.

16. Arturo Codignola, *Dagli albori della libertà al proclama di Moncalieri (Lettere del Conte Ilarione Petiti di Roreto a Michele Erede dal marzo 1846 all'aprile del 1850)*, *Biblioteca italiana di storia recente* (Turin, 1930), 13: 97, 161, 172, 229–232, 277, 286, 288, 375.

17. Paul Ginsborg, *Daniele Manin and the Venetian Revolution of 1848–49* (New York, 1979).

18. Ibid., p. 36.

19. Ibid.

20. Ibid., p. 14.

21. Ibid., p. 51.

22. Ibid., p. 158.

23. Ibid., pp. 236–237.

24. Ibid., p. 378.

25. For an analysis of the importance of these two concepts I have benefited especially from the following: Joseph V. Femia, *Gramsci's Political Thought: Hegemony, Consciousness, and the Revolutionary Process* (Oxford, 1981), pp. 23–60; Walter L. Adamson, *Hegemony and Revolution: A Study of Antonio Gramsci's Political and Cultural Theory* (Berkeley, Los Angeles, London, 1980), pp. 169–201; Anne Showstack Sassoon, ed., *Approaches to Gramsci* (London, 1982), pp. 94–148; Raymond Williams, *Marxism and Literature* (Oxford, 1977), pp. 108–114; Christine Buci-Glucksmann, *Gramsci and the State* (London, 1980); John A. Davis, ed., *Gramsci and Italy's Passive Revolution* (New York, 1979), pp. 11–66; Geoff Eley, "Reading Gramsci in English: Some Observations on the Reception of Antonio Gramsci in the English-Speaking World, 1957–1982," Working Paper no. 314 (Ann Arbor: Center for Research on Social Organization, University of Michigan, 1984), pp. 31–49; Perry Anderson, "The Antinomies of Antonio Gramsci," *New Left Review* 100 (Nov. 1976–Jan. 1977): 5–78; Gwen A. Williams, "The Concept of 'Egemonia' in the Thought of Antonio Gramsci: Some Notes on Interpretation," *Journal of the History of Ideas* 21 (1960): 586–599; Thomas R. Bates, "Gramsci and the Theory of Hegemony," *Journal of the History of Ideas* 36 (1975): 351–366; and the editors' introductory sections in *Selections from the Prison Notebooks of Antonio Gramsci* (hereafter, *SPN*), ed. Quintin Hoare and Geoffrey Nowell-Smith (New York, 1971). References to Gramsci's work will be made to the critical edition of the *Prison Notebooks*: Antonio Gramsci, *Quaderni del Carcere* (hereafter, *QC*), vols. 1–4 (Turin, 1975), and, where appropriate, to the English edition (*SPN*). I have used the excellent translations provided in the English edition when available; the others are my own.

26. Femia, p. 24. See also *QC*, pp. 751–752.

27. See, in particular, Anderson.

28. *QC*, p. 866; *SPN*, p. 238.

29. *QC*, p. 41; *SPN*, p. 59.

30. Vincenzo Cuoco, *Saggio storico sulla rivoluzione napoletana del 1799*, ed. N. Cortese (Florence, 1926), p. 83.

31. Ibid., p. 90.

32. *QC*, p. 51; *SPN*, p. 79. Ginsborg provides an excellent discussion of Gramsci's view of France and the Jacobin experience in Davis, pp. 31–66.

33. *QC*, pp. 1774–1775; *SPN*, pp. 106–109.

34. Karl Marx, *A Contribution to the Critique of Political Economy* (Chicago, 1904), p. 12.

35. *QC*, pp. 481–482; *SPN*, pp. 53–54 (nn.); Antonio Gramsci, *Lettere dal carcere*, ed. Sergio Caprioglio and Elsa Fubini (Turin, 1972), pp. 481–482.

36. *QC*, pp. 37–38; *SPN*, pp. 97–98.

37. *QC*, p. 2011; *SPN*, p. 58.

38. *QC*, pp. 800, 1228–1229; Walter L. Adamson, "Gramsci's Interpretation of Fascism," *Journal of the History of Ideas* 41 (1980): 615–633.

39. *QC*, pp. 1228–1229, 2139–2147; *SPN*, pp. 279–287.

40. *QC*, p. 1775; *SPN*, p. 107 (and n.).

41. *QC*, p. 1822; *SPN*, pp. 104–105.

42. See: Ginsborg's discussion in Davis, pp. 50–52; Femia, p. 47; and Adamson, *Hegemony and Revolution*, pp. 177, 189–190, 192.

43. *QC*, pp. 1823–1824; *SPN*, pp. 105–106.

44. *QC*, p. 1634.

45. Ibid., p. 1633; *SPN*, p. 190.

46. *QC*, pp. 2053–2054.

47. Ernest Labrousse, "Une Histoire de la bourgeoisie occidentale (1700–1850)," in *Relazioni del X Congresso Internazionale di Scienze Storiche*, vol. 4 (Florence, n.d.).

1: Patterns in Livorno's Commerce

1. These provisions are most conveniently summarized in Mario Baruchello, *Livorno e il suo porto. Origini, caratteristiche e vicende dei traffici livornesi* (Livorno, 1932), pp. 185–200.

2. The promise of houses, shops, and warehouses was made in a decree of 18 October 1590; the other provisions were contained in a decree of 13 February 1591. These decrees are summarized in Baruchello, pp. 185–186. The latter decree is reproduced in Giuseppe Gino Guarnieri, *Origine e sviluppo del porto di Livorno durante il governo di Ferdinando I dei Medici* (Livorno, 1911), pp. 94–96.

3. The provisions of the *Livornina* are summarized in Baruchello, p. 200.

4. For a copy of the final decree see Guarnieri, *Livorno marinara* (Livorno, 1962), pp. 602–603. A full text of the legislation is provided in Baruchello, pp. 294–300.

5. For the development of Livorno's status as a neutral port see ibid., pp. 323–333 and 342. In 1652, during the war between Great Britain and Holland, the Venetian ambassador in Florence wrote: "Livorno is greatly benefiting from the gold that both nations are spending there to provide for their every need" (quoted in Ettore Di Pietro, *La Funzione economica del porto di Livorno alla fine dell'600* [Livorno, 1931], p. 24).

6. Gino Luzzatto, *Per una storia economica d'Italia* (Bari, 1967), pp. 162–163.

7. Di Pietro, p. 27. A report dated 1765 and entitled "Porto di Livorno, suo commercio, privilegi, vantaggi e neutralità" concretely demonstrated the advantageous position enjoyed by foreign merchants (and Jews) in the city. "This is the fundamental reason why there have not been and are not at present a large number of Tuscan commercial houses. To be a successful merchant in Livorno you need good correspondents outside the city. Three or four London houses, for example, will direct so much merchandise, will recommend so many ships, and will give so many orders to an English merchant [in Livorno] that these transactions in themselves will produce at the end of the year a considerable profit without his [the English merchant's] having risked anything of his own. It is difficult for Tuscans to have contacts and correspondents of this sort. As a result it is necessary for them to force themselves and to get involved in deals the outcome of which many times is not happy. From this it follows that it is more easy for them to fail and that if a Tuscan house has had the luck to get rich, if it continues to do business for a long period of time, rarely will it preserve the wealth acquired." The author made an exception for Jews, who "although they can be considered Tuscan are not in this regard at the same disadvantage. Not only do they have an infinite number of correspondents but they also have branch offices in many foreign countries." This document is reproduced in Guarnieri, *Livorno marinara*, pp. 664–665.

8. Ibid., p. 661.

9. See the report entitled "Caratteristiche del governo e del commercio, in generale, di Livorno, con particolare riguardo a quello marittimo, alla fine del granducato di Pietro Leopoldo I." It is reproduced in Ibid., p. 679.

10. In his annual report in 1826 the *gonfaloniere* of Livorno noted that the city's neutrality had been the principal cause of the port's

brilliant commercial prosperity during the early years of the wars of the French Revolution, when, with the English blockade of Genoa and the coast of Provence, speculators had been forced to conduct their affairs in Livorno. The establishment of political equilibrium in Europe after the Restoration, he argued, had enabled other ports to enjoy similar rights and advantages and was the principal reason for the city's commercial decline. (ASL, *Comunità*, f. 636. Livorno, 20 February 1826: *gonfaloniere*, "Prospetto.")

11. In 1832 it was reported to the minister of foreign affairs in Florence that few merchant ships under 150 tons were undertaking voyages for the Archipelago, Constantinople, and the Black Sea. (ASF, *Affari Esteri*, f. 2472. 11 June 1832: Quaglia to V. Fossombroni.) Patricia Herlihy reports that a direct shipment from Odessa to England required from sixty to seventy days in a sailing ship and only twenty days if shipment was by steam. (Patricia Herlihy, "Russian Trade and Mediterranean Markets 1774–1861" [Ph.D. diss., University of Pennsylvania, 1963], p. 20.) In the decades immediately following its introduction, however, steam navigation was used primarily for the movement of goods of low bulk and high value and especially for passenger traffic. Bulk items such as cereals continued to be transported in sailing ships. Ibid.; Luigi Serristori, *Livorno ed i suoi traffici* (Florence, 1839), p. 9.

12. *Annali universali di statistica, economia pubblica, geografia, storia e viaggi* 54 (1837): 350–355. The author was noted only by the initials "B. C." and was later identified by Nicola Badaloni as Barone Corvaja (*Democratici e socialisti livornesi nell'Ottocento* [Rome, 1966], p. 27). On Corvaja, see Delio Cantimori, *Utopisti e riformatori italiani, 1794–1847* (Florence, 1943), pp. 203–229.

13. *Annali universali di statistica* 54 (1837): 353–354.

14. Ibid., 351–352.

15. ASF, *Fin. Seg.*, f. 799.

16. BNF, MS *Fondi Capponi* CLVI. (Pierallini), "Osservazioni sulla pace cogli Ottomani e sulla marina e commercio di Livorno," 1764.

17. ASF, *Seg. Gab.*, f. 165. 10 January 1820.

18. See, for example, the series of reports made by the *gonfaloniere* of the city to the central government (ASL, *Comunità*, f. 636–644), in which the notion that Livorno's role as a port of deposit had ended was repeatedly stated. An article in *Hunt's Merchants' Magazine* of July 1846 (translated from *Giornale Lloyd Austriaco*) informed the American public that "the last thirty to forty years have entirely changed the nature of Tuscan commerce. . . . Livorno used to be one perpetual fair for the interchange of oriental and Western

products. This has now altogether ceased" ("Present State of Commerce and Industry in Italy," *Hunt's Merchants' Magazine* 15 [July 1846]: 24).

19. ASF, *Seg. Gab.*, f. 165. 10 January 1820; Luigi Serristori, *Livorno ed i suoi traffici*, p. 6. On the struggle with Genoa for the control of sources of supply and markets in the hinterland, see Enrico Guglielmino, *Genova dal 1814 al 1849; gli sviluppi economici e l'opinione pubblica* (Genoa, 1940), pp. 75, 197–200. On the free port of Ancona, see Alberto Caracciolo, *Le Port franc d'Ancone croissance et impasse d'un milieu marchand au XVIIIe siècle* (Paris, 1965).

20. ASF, *Fin. Seg.*, f. 799.

21. "That these same products developed and perfected in so many styles for several years have nourished our relations with other areas, and have compensated for the loss of traffic with them which previously was carried out with those foreign products of which the deposit here has been lost" (ASL, *Comunità*, f. 644. Livorno, 4 Aug. 1830: *gonfaloniere*, "Prospetto"). This differed sharply from the *gonfaloniere's* view four years earlier that Livorno lacked the elements of an active national commerce and that with the exception of oil, silk, marble, alabaster, and straw "very few and insignificant are the objects of export" (ibid., f. 636. Livorno, 20 February 1826: *gonfaloniere*, "Prospetto").

22. *Giornale di commercio* 20 (20 May 1829).

23. Piero Innocenti, *Il Porto di Livorno* (Milan, 1968); Lando Bortolotti, *Livorno dal 1748 al 1958. Profilo storico-urbanistico* (Florence, 1970).

24. Giorgio Mori, "Linee e momenti dello sviluppo della città, del porto e dei traffici di Livorno," *La Regione: Rivista dell'unione regionale delle provincie toscane* 3 (1956): 3–44.

25. Giovanni Bowring, *Statistica della Toscana, di Lucca, degli Stati Pontifici e Lombardo-Veneto e specialmente delle loro relazioni commerciali* (London, 1838), pp. 21–24.

26. Mori, p. 21. To Mori these considerations "went right to the heart of the question and . . . no polemicist, however able, could reject them." On the basis of them he concluded that "the twenty years which had passed since the return of the Lorenese dynasty, if reconsidered from the perspective of Livorno and its economic life, could not but support the conclusions of B. C. [in the *Annali di statistica*]."

27. Bowring, p. 24.

28. Ibid., p. 21.

29. Edoardo Mayer's report dated 13 March 1838 is an un-

cataloged ms. in the Biblioteca Labronica, Livorno. I would like to thank Mr. Piero Brizzi of the library for making it available to me. It supplied much of the information on Livorno's commerce presented by E. Repetti in his *Dizionario geografico, fisico, storico della Toscana contenente la descrizione di tutti i luoghi del Granducato,* vol. 2 (Florence, 1832–1845).

30. H. Ferguson, an English merchant in Livorno, remarked to E. Mayer that the amount of manufactured items sold for export "I should estimate at two-thirds at *least* [and] perhaps three-fourths. Indeed, the latter is fully *less* than the proportion of our own sales for export—other houses, however, are more in the house-trade—and I should think three-fourths pretty near the mark" (ibid.). In his annual report in 1830 the *gonfaloniere* of Livorno remarked that of goods deposited in Livorno the principal item was English cottons, which found a prodigious sale in the Levant (ASL, *Comunità,* f. 644. Livorno, 4 August 1830: *gonfaloniere,* "Prospetto"). Livorno possessed special advantages as a deposit port for British manufactured goods: "Imported English cottons found in the port of Livorno an immense sale because they paid nothing entering, nothing remaining, and nothing for the goods consumed in Livorno. They paid only a tariff of 15 percent on the value of the goods introduced into the Tuscan hinterland for consumption, and it was the merchant who fixed the value" (I. Imerciadori, *Economia toscana nel primo '800 dalla restaurazione al regno, 1815–1861* [Florence, 1961], p. 197).

31. ASF, *Seg. Gab.,* f. 669, MS, Giuseppi Vivoli, "Accrescimento progressivo di Livorno," 2 vols.

32. ASL, *Gov.,* f. 1000. *Copialettere governatore,* Livorno, 5 September 1817: to the secretary of finance, ASL, *Gov.,* f. 108. Florence, 6–8 September 1817, for the reply of the secretary of finance discussing possible locales in the city for temporary grain storage.

33. A request from the chamber of commerce for additional storage facilities was transmitted by the governor to the secretary of finance in 1826 (ASL, *Gov.,* f. 1010, *Copialettere governatore,* Livorno, 6 September 1826). It appears from the letter of the governor that no request for additional storage facilities had been made between 1817 and 1826.

34. The deputies of the chamber recognized the justice of the request of the officials and resolved that their memorial be given greater weight by having it signed by all interested members of the merchant community before it was sent to the governor, "accompanied by the strongest recommendations" of the president of the

chamber (ACCL, *Delib.*, 7 September 1839). In transmitting this memorial to Florence, the governor remarked that the central government had not previously responded to the need because projects had been advanced "by several individual speculators to undertake these constructions at their own expense [*per proprio conto*]." Since then, however, due to the pulling out of one of the members of the project as well as to "other circumstances," there remained little hope that the pits would be constructed by private capitalists, and the governor recommended that the government once again begin working on the projects to meet the needs of the city (ASL, *Gov.*, f. 190, Livorno, 16 October 1841: governor to the secretary of finance).

35. ASF, *Misc. Fin. 1.*, f. 41. Livorno, 18 October 1843: A. G. Mochi: Report 25 (July–Sept. 1843) of the discount bank.

36. Carlo Bargagli to the governor of Livorno: "Today the deposit trade in grain is the principal branch of commerce in this city" (ASL, *Gov.*, f. 205, n. 7. Livorno, 25 Jan. 1844).

37. "There is no doubt that commerce in cereals constitutes in fact the principal and most profitable branch of the commerce of our city" (ASL, *Gov.*, f. 235, n. 135).

38. ASL *Gov.*, f. 342, n. 1037. Livorno, 22 July 1850: chamber of commerce to the Delagato Straordinario.

39. The sources of these figures in chronological order are the following: ASF, *Misc. Fin. I.*, f. 41; ASL, *Gov.*, f. 173, n. 176; ASF, *Misc. Fin. I.*, f. 41; Ibid.; ASL, *Gov.*, f. 205, n. 8; ASF, *Min. Fin. I.*, f. 41; Ibid.

40. "With regard to particulars, the statistical data of the journal in question are highly imperfect particularly with respect to the category of 'diverse articles'" (ASF, *Min. Fin. I.*, f. 41. Livorno, 10 April 1844).

41. "From which one can deduce that it is not true that our commerce can be reduced only to cereals as some discouragingly suppose" (ASL, *Gov.*, f. 173, n. 176. Livorno, 7 October 1840).

42. ASF, *Misc. Fin. II.*, f. 530, b. 59.

43. Leone Levi, *The History of British Commerce and of the Economic Progress of the British Nation, 1763–1878*, 2d ed. (London, 1880), p. 213.

44. Ibid., p. 215.

45. ASF, *Misc. Fin. II.*, f. 505. Director of the customhouse in Livorno. See also Herlihy, pp. 114–115.

46. ASF, *Fin. C.R.*, f. 20. R. R. Dogana [customhouse], "Dimostrazione dei cereali forestieri introdotti nel porto franco di Livorno ed estratti dal medesimo e travasati nel molo l'anno 1815."

47. Ibid.

48. ASF, *Fin. C.R.*, f. 17. Livorno, 4 June 1840: "Nuovo parere di Forni."

49. Serristori, *Livorno ed i suoi traffici,* p. 13. The consumption of Livorno itself is excluded from the estimate.

50. ASF, *Fin. C.R.*, f. 17. 13 June 1840: administrative office of the Royal Revenues, "Sulla sostituzione."

51. In 1782–83, Tuscany consumed an average of 184,301 sacks more than it produced. During the span of good harvest years from 1787 to 1791 it was able to sell a little grain on the foreign market. Herlihy, p. 194 (from material in ASF, *R. R. Rendite,* 1842, no. 541, 18 March 1842). This source is not available at present for public consultation, and I have therefore relied totally on Herlihy.

52. In answer to a query from the French consul concerning the wheat situation, the minister of foreign affairs remarked that "for the future, prices could be expected to reflect the facility with which wheat could be brought from Egypt and the Black Sea . . . from whence Tuscany draws the greater part of its wheat for its consumption needs." The minister closed with the statement that "who then . . . does not know that Tuscan production even in the years of greatest abundance is never enough to suffice for the needs of the country" (ASF, *Affari Esteri,* Protocollo 476.84, 24 July 1854).

53. This and the following paragraph rely heavily on the material presented in Herlihy, pp. 191–194. Mrs. Herlihy has drawn her material from the archives of *R. R. Rendite* and the *Affari Doganali* in the ASF. At present neither is open for public consultation.

54. PRO, *Foreign Office,* 79/115, 7 December 1845, Consul Macbean.

55. In a memorial dated 30 November 1818, the minister remarked: "For the Livornese merchants the evils of famine in the Tuscan interior provide an occasion of genuine delight" (ASF, *Seg. Gab.,* f. 160, n. 8). In a memorial dated 26 June of that year the president of the chamber of commerce, G. Saunders, had lamented charges on grain entering the port of Livorno which, he said, in view of the current price, amounted to 2.5 to 3 percent of the value of the product. He concluded pessimistically that "the decline of prices and the general abundance of the harvests in Tuscany and the neighboring provinces does not certainly provide an object of grain speculation for our merchants, and consequently we cannot delude ourselves into expecting that they [grain cargoes] will arrive here in the number that they did previously" (ibid., 26 June 1818).

56. In 1839, O. Forni, head of the customhouse in Livorno, re-

marked to the secretary of finance, Cempini, that the chamber of commerce sought to alleviate the annual tax of 300,000 lire to which the merchant community was liable. It proposed that the tax be cut in half and that the balance be raised from a .50 to a .75 percent charge on merchandise entering the Tuscan state (ASF, *Fin. C.R.*, f. 17. Livorno, 13 September 1839: Forni to Cempini). In 1841, Cempini remarked to the governor of Livorno that no proposed revision of the commercial tax would be sanctioned "that aims in substance to transfer a portion of the debt owed by the commerce of Livorno to consumers in the hinterland, who justly for this end must not be subject to any burden" (ASL, *Gov.*, f. 186, n. 328. Florence, 26 June 1841: secretary of finance to the governor).

57. Antonio Zobi, *Manuale storico delle massime e degli ordinamenti economici vigenti in Toscana* (Florence, 1847), p. 367.

58. Major statements of this group on the question are the following: Gino Capponi, "Discorso intorno ad alcune particolarità della presente economia toscana," *Antologia* 14 (April 1824): 114–124; Cosimo Ridolfi, "Memoria sulla libertà del commercio frumentario," *Antologia* 14 (June 1824): 97–109; Rafaello Lambruschini, "Sul cambiamento di prezzi de'grani," *GAT* (1829): 278–297; and L. Landucci, "Sulla libera importazione delle granaglie," *GAT* (1837): 161–187. The following is a useful, more recent article on the economic attitudes of this group: Carla Ronchi, "Liberalismo e protezionismo in Toscana prima del 1848," *Studi storici* 1 (1960): 244–284.

59. For the number of large sailing ships arriving at the port of Livorno from 1815 to 1852, see table 7.

60. For the clearest presentation of Livorno's population growth in this period see Pierfrancesco Bandettini, *La Popolazione della Toscana dal 1810 al 1959* (Florence, 1961), p. 181.

61. "Who does not recognize in fact in Livorno's population many of the external characteristics of prosperity and even of wealth? Houses [*casamenti*] in large number are being erected which are larger and more pleasant than the old; furniture is increasing in quantity, value, and elegance; there exist a considerable number of carriages of which not a few are *de luxe*; private foundations have been set up to impart instruction, charity, and credit. And is all this, perhaps, a situation which has existed for many years? No. Without losing ourselves in figures, are these facts not enough to convince us that the actual condition of the inhabitants of this city is more prosperous than in the past?" (Serristori, *Livorno ed i suoi traffici*, p. 5).

62. Guido Sonnino, *Saggio sulle industrie, marina, e commercio in Livorno sotto i primi due Lorenesi (1737–1790)* (Cortona, 1909), p. 131.

Giuliano Ricci asserted that "the constant increment of the population did not fail to show the prosperity of Livorno" (Ricci, "Livorno,
origine e ingrandimento," *GAT* 11 [1837]: 111).

63. E. Repetti, *Dizionario*, 2: 752.

64. Giovanni Baldasseroni, *Leopoldo II, Granduca di Toscana e i suo
tempi; Memorie* (Florence, 1871), pp. 111–112.

65. Mori, "Linee e momenti," p. 21.

66. Ibid. Mori's figures are drawn from Cesare Caporali, *Sulla
popolazione di Livorno. Ricerche statistiche ed economiche* (Livorno, 1855),
p. 82. It should be pointed out, however, that elsewhere in his study
Professor Mori was quite willing to use demographic and commercial
statistics as literal indicators of the recovery or decline of Livorno's
economy in a given period (see G. Mori, "Linee e momenti," pp.
18–19).

67. Baruchello, p. 573.

68. Caporali, p. 62.

69. Ricci, "Livorno, origine e ingrandimento," pp. 111–112.

70. Bandettini, *La Popolazione della Toscana dal 1810 al 1959*, p. 181.
See also table 11.

71. Attilio Zuccagni-Orlandini, *Ricerche statistiche sul Granducato
di Toscana* (Florence, 1848), 1: 10–14.

72. These memorials were a regular occurrence up until the time
that the stallage and 1 percent duties were abolished in 1834. They
were especially frequent in the period of adjustment after the restoration of the grand ducal government in 1814. Among the most
interesting are those signed by the president of the chamber of
commerce, Panajotti Palli, dated 16 August 1816 (ACCL, *De-
liberazione*, 16 August 1816) and by President G. G. Saunders, dated
26 June 1818 (ASF, *Seg. Gab.*, f. 160). The stir created by this latter
memorial is discussed in the notes to chapter 3.

73. ACCL, *Delib.*, 6 May 1815.

74. For what follows I have relied primarily on Gino Luzzatto,
*L'Età contemporanea. Storia economica dell'età moderna e contem-
poranea*, Parte seconda (Padua, 1960), pp. 224–225; Giorgio Candeloro, *Dalla restaurazione alla rivoluzione nazionale 1815–1846. Storia
dell'Italia moderna*, 3d ed. (Milan, 1962), 2: 242; and Elie Halévy,
England in 1815 (London, 1964), p. 311.

75. PRO, *Board of Trade*, 6/51. Livorno, 25 July 1817: John Falconar, British consul.

76. John Falconar remarked that in the past "when the market
here was found to be overstocked with British manufacturers, the
merchants frequently transferred considerable quantities to Trieste,

from whence they found their way into the Austrian and neighboring territories, but as that cannot be resorted to, I fear that the sales of the current year will be found to fall even short of the last" (ibid., 6/61. Livorno, 31 January 1818: John Falconar, British consul). In 1817, Austria established a tariff law that, among other provisions, prohibited the introduction into Lombardy of cotton weaves and knits from abroad or from the other territories of the empire (save Hungary, upon the payment of a high tariff) (Candeloro, 2: 252). An anonymous report in 1820 cited earlier remarked on this point: "The protective system recently adopted by the Austrian Emperor has taken away from Livorno the extensive commerce which it carried out with the kingdom of Lombardy-Venetia and with Trieste" (ASF, *Seg. Gab.*, f. 165. Livorno, 10 January 1820).

77. Luigi Torelli, *Dell'Avvenire del commercio europeo e in modo speciale quello degli stati italiani, Ricerche* (Florence, 1858), 2: 47.

78. Luzzatto, *Storia economica contemporanea*, p. 223.

79. The series begins only in 1823 and contains notable lacunae, particularly in 1825 and in the extremely important period from 1844 to 1847. In addition, frequent complaints were voiced by Tuscan and foreign merchants about inaccuracies in the journal (see ASL, *Gov.*, f. 202. *Affari Diversi*, 1842. Livorno, 23 Nov. 1842: Giovanni Chelli, president of the chamber of commerce, to the governor, and ibid., f. 216, n. 570. For the compilation see table 12).

80. ASF, *Affari Esteri*, f. 2621. *Carteggio Governatore Livorno*, 1814–1819.

81. Zobi, *Manuale storico delle massime e degli ordinamenti economici vigenti in Toscana* (Florence, 1847), p. 362.

82. Pierfrancesco Bandettini, *I Prezzi sul mercato di Firenze dal 1800 al 1890* (Rome, 1957). Bandettini's figures are based on the summaries of government market officials which are collected in the Florentine communal archive. His figures are reproduced in table 13.

83. The prices through 1835 are expressed in pezze; from 1837, in lire toscane per one hundred pounds. One pezza equals 5.68 Tuscan lire. For the reform of weights and measures which brought the change in the manner of declaration see chapter 4.

2: The Merchant Community

1. Francesco Pera, *Ricordi e biografie livornesi* (Livorno, 1867), p. 124.

2. ASF, *Seg. di Gabinetto*, f. 609; MS, Vivoli, "L'Accrescimento progressivo di Livorno," vol. 2, n. 291.

3. James Fenimore Cooper, *Excursions in Italy*, cited in Lando Bortolotti, *Livorno dal 1748 al 1958* (Florence, 1970), pp. 107–108.

4. ASL, *Gov.*, f. 23. Livorno, 5 July 1781: governor of Livorno to the grand duke, cited in Bortolotti, p. 105.

5. Henry James, *All'estero*, cited in Bortolotti, p. 108.

6. Giuseppe Mery, *Scene della vita italiana*, cited in Pera, p. 86.

7. A useful reference are the social definitions provided by Elinor G. Barber, *The Bourgeoisie in 18th-Century France* (Princeton, 1955), pp. 14–33.

8. The auditor of the government noted that the system for conceding credit status in the customhouse "does not admit to that benefit merchants who resell the merchandise in retail shops" (ASL, *Gov.*, f. 198, n. 254. *Aff. Div.*, 1848. Livorno, 25 June 1842: auditor to the governor of Livorno).

9. F. D. Guerrazzi noted that the English merchant Giovanni Grant had refused admission to a party to a young man engaged in retail commerce (BLL, *Carte Vivoli*, f. 25, note of 15 June 1829).

10. For the eighteenth-century regulations (drawn up in 1758 and 1759), see ASF, *Fin. C.R.*, f. 65.

11. Ibid., *Misc. di Fin.*, f. 533. Livorno, 10 May 1823: Livorno customhouse.

12. Perhaps more significant were instances of merchants stepping down into the position of *mezzano*. For an instance of this, see ASL, *Gov.*, f. 163. *Aff. Div.*, 1837. Livorno, 8 January 1837: David Ferdinandes Leiba to the governor of Livorno.

13. See n. 11.

14. G. Mori, "Linee," pp. 21–22; Nicola Badaloni, *Democratici e socialisti livornesi nell'Ottocento* (Rome, 1966), p. 86. The interpretation of these two Marxist historians is adopted *in toto* by the non-Marxist Bortolotti (*Livorno*, p. 75).

15. G. Mori, "Linee," p. 22.

16. Narrative descriptions of manufacturing in Livorno abound. For more accessible published accounts see Gino Guarnieri, *Livorno marinara*, pp. 392–397 (summarizing an account of F. Bartoletti in 1829); Repetti, *Dizionario*, 2: 765; Bowring, *Statistica*, pp. 29–30; Torelli, *Dell'avvenire del commercio Europeo e in modo speciale quello degli stati italiani* (Florence, 1858), 3: 57; Gino Galletti, "Le Industrie del passato," *La Rivista di Livorno* I (Nov.–Dec., 1926): 3–12; and Serristori, *Livorno ed i suoi traffici*. Manuscript accounts include ASL, *Comunità*, f. 636. Livorno, 20 February 1826: *gonfaloniere*, "Prospetto";

ASF, *Fin. C.R.*, f. 20; and BLL, *Carte Vivoli* (1817). Livorno, 20 September 1817: Labronica Academy to the Academy of the Georgofili. For a specific discussion of the relationship of the privileges of the city to the development of manufacturing see Temistocle Pergola, *Sulla franchigia commerciale di Livorno* (Livorno, 1862).

17. Badaloni, *Democratici e socialisti*, p. 79. For a description of a steam mill and a list of the principal partners see ASL, *Catasto*, f. 280, n. 184.

18. Both memorials are in ASF, *Fin. Seg.*, f. 799.

19. Baruchello, pp. 361, 557.

20. Torelli, 3: 59.

21. The regulation reproduced in ACCL, *Delib.*, 7 October 1815.

22. See chapter 1, n. 7.

23. *La Settimana* 4, no. 9 (26 February 1899). Pietro Bastogi dictated these notes on the early history of the firm in 1888.

24. G. Mori, "Linee," pp. 20–22.

25. ASF, *Seg. di Fin.*, f. 149. 12 July 1834: report of the council.

26. ACCL, *Delib.*, 14 January 1839 indicates that a letter was received from the governor with requests from three noble families (Malenchini, Bevilacqua, and Bertolacci) for exemption from the commercial tax, "[their] not being merchants." The chamber denied the request on the grounds that although the three could not be considered merchants, they were nevertheless heavily engaged in commercial activity.

27. ASL *Gov.*, f. 186, no. 328. *Aff. Div.*, 1841. Livorno, 6 July: governor to the secretary of finance.

28. ASL, *Comunità*, f. 636. Livorno, 20 February 1826, *gonfaloniere*, "Prospetto."

29. Ibid. See also E. Repetti, *Dizionario*, 2: 773–774.

30. See n. 31.

31. This series is to be found in the archive of the *catasto* in the ASL. The series runs from f. 276 (1821) to f. 288 (1833) and contains a detailed list of all property that changes in value (generally due to new construction) or in which there is a change in the person (or persons) liable for the taxes. As such this series notes all property bought and sold in the community and provides detailed descriptions of the real property holdings of a family when title passes from the defunct to the heirs.

32. See, for example, the villa property sold by Carlo Sansoni, an attorney and important dabbler in real-estate speculation, to the English merchant Giovanni Grant. The house is described as palatial, and the vines are "of select quality" (ASL, *Catasto*, f. 278, n. 32).

33. "An elegant little palace" constructed south of the city for Jacob Attias (ibid., f. 280, n. 225).

34. The exception was a villa (or "former palace") sold by Carlo Sansoni, to Giovanni Grant (ibid., f. 278, n. 32). See n. 32.

35. Bortolotti, *Livorno*, p. 29. The maps are in ASF, *Regie Fabbriche*, A. 3, n. 1, cartone 5 ("Porto di Livorno e suoi annessi").

36. Bortolotti, pp. 29–30. Discusses the controversy over the measure and the equalization of the assessments in 1803.

37. The following Jewish families possessed villa holdings: Attias, Arbib, Bacri, Busnach, Della Longa, Rignano, Sajegh, Sacuto. Jewish families can be identified from the records of the archive of the Jewish community of the city and from members of the community chosen to represent it in the chamber of commerce.

38. See, for example, the announcement of the leasing of three shops (*botteghe*) in the center of town by Salamone Tedeschi in 1820 (ASL, *Catasto*, f. 275, n. 103) and that of the purchase of two shops and a warehouse by Tommaso Appleton, the American consul general in 1831 (Ibid., f. 286, n. 60).

39. Important purchases of palaces in the central city were made by Domenico Castelli in 1826 (ibid., f. 279, n. 118) and Giorgio Gower in 1828 (ibid., f. 283, n. 208); similar edifices in the quarter of Venezia Nuova were purchased by Marco Regini and Giovanni Chelli in 1824 (ibid., f. 279, n. 129) and Carlo Grabau in 1831 (ibid., f. 286, n. 133). Other important contracts were registered by Giovanni Grant in 1828 (ibid., f. 283, n. 250 and f. 280, n. 63). Significant acquisitions of similar properties were made in the older suburbs to the north of the city (on the road to Pisa) by the Pachò family in 1828 (ibid., f. 283, n. 221) and Gherardo Stub (1829) (ibid., f. 284, n. 83).

40. Ibid., f. 278, n. 99.

41. Ibid., f. 279, n. 1.

42. ASF, *Stato Civile*, f. 12308. *Cenna statistica della univ. israelitica livornese, 1837.* Notes the traditional nature of Jewish investment and also notes that with regard to new construction and speculation, the Jews were falling behind other sectors of the population.

43. Bortolotti, pp. 103–104, 112.

44. The most important relaxation of the restrictions occurred in 1776 when a government provision allowed proprietors to build within one mile of the city walls, previously prohibited for reasons of military defense. See G. Vivoli, Ms, "L'Accrescimento progressivo," 1: 139, 228–230; and 2: n. 296 and 412; Bortolotti, pp. 69, 117.

45. Bortolotti, p. 116. Due to the different ways of calculating

revenue, Bortolotti used the top four classes for the assessment of 1830 and the top three for 1850.

46. Ibid., pp. 114–115.

47. The description of the purchases is in ASL, *Catasto,* f. 286, n. 277; f. 286, n. 192; f. 287, n. 242; f. 285, n. 15; f. 287, n. 417; f. 287, n. 163.

48. For a description of the construction, see ibid., f. 287, n. 366.

49. Bortolotti, p. 138.

50. ASL, *Catasto,* f. 285, n. 146.

51. Ibid., f. 286, n. 284; f. 287, n. 417; f. 287, n. 163; f. 288, n. 225.

52. Ibid., f. 287, nos. 34, 176, 282 for Malenchini. For Michon, see chap. 2, n. 56.

53. Ibid., pp. 140–141.

54. Baldasseroni, *Leopoldo II,* p. 83. The author notes that approximately 2.5 million lire in private capital had been invested in these projects and that an important source of it came from Livorno: "Having need, the capital was not lacking. Wealthy Livorno was near, and the two colonies drew from it powerful assistance."

55. Ibid., pp. 462–463. An excellent discussion of the iron industry can be found in G. Mori, *L'industria del ferro in Toscana dalla restaurazione alla fine del granducato (1815–1869)* (Turin, 1966). ASL, *Gov.,* f. 219, n. 751 bis., provides a concrete illustration of merchant capital invested in a mining venture for the excavation of mercury.

56. The manifesto of the society is in BLL, *Carte Vivoli,* f. 35. The organizers of the project were Giovanni Pietro Ulrich, Gino Pachò, Luigi Fauguet, and Salvatore Carreras. For a description of the project see Bortolotti, p. 144.

57. Carla Ronchi, *I Democratici fiorentini nella rivoluzione del '48–'49* (Florence, n.d.), p. 40, indicates that of the more than twenty societies established in the approximately ten-year period after 1835, only a few had prospered. *Hunt's Merchants' Magazine* (15 [1846]: 26) noted the importance of investments in the Maremma and the long-term nature of the returns: "Investments in these undertakings can be rendered profitable to sons and grandsons only; and whoever seek to realize immediate profits, must betake themselves to other objects of investment."

58. ASF, *Nobiltà Toscana. Repertorio dei Libri d'Oro.*

59. Ibid., f. 125. *Copialettere Nobiltà e Cittadinanza:* 24 November 1814.

60. ASL, *Comunità.* f. 53. *Deliberazioni Magistrali per la Comunità:* Livorno, 30 July 1818.

61. The following are some of the more summary justifications:

Bartolomei—"one of Livorno's richest families in terms of real property"; Cipriani—"a rich patrimony in real property"; Coppi—"a large patrimony in real property . . . joins to his wealth extensive cognition"; Danti—"united in matrimony to a noble Pisan, and he is the wealthiest landowner in Livorno"; Papanti—"his wife is the daughter of a Cavaliere di Santo Stefano. He possesses a wealthy patrimony in real property, as a Livornese citizen he has filled diverse civic offices in a praiseworthy manner, and he has a great deal of talent"; Rodriguez—"he has a reasonable patrimony . . . Livornese citizenship . . . and several of his forefathers who died without descendants were justly accorded noble status."

62. See n. 61.

63. ASL, *Gov.*, f. 1001. *Copialettere governatore*, 1818: 28 August to the Avvocato Regio.

64. Ibid.

65. ASF, *Nobiltà Toscana*, f. 203.

66. Ibid.

67. Ibid., f. 96. *Processi di Nobiltà*, 1838. Livorno, 25 January 1838: A. Martellini, *gonfaloniere*, to the Deputazione sulla Nobiltà.

68. Ibid.

69. ASL. *Gov.*, f. 1017. *Copialettere governatore*, 1833: 13 March to the Avvocato Regio.

70. Ibid., f. 249, n. 199. *Aff. Div.*, 1846. Livorno, 28 March: Auditor to the governor.

71. Ibid., f. 1015. *Copialettere governatore*, 1831: 31 October to the governor of Siena.

72. Florence, 1833–1846.

73. This correspondence between Mayer and Repetti is uncataloged in the ms. collection of the Biblioteca Labronica. Mayer's communication is dated 13 March 1838.

74. Serristori, *Livorno ed i suoi traffici;* Giuliano Ricci, "Livorno," *GAT* 11 (1837): 101–116.

75. Serristori, pp. 3–4.

76. Giuliano Ricci, "Livorno," p. 113.

77. *Benjamin Franklin écrites par lui-même: traduction nouvelle* (Paris, 1828). *La strada di far fortuna o la scienza del buon'uomo Riccardo*, trans. G. Fantoni (Bologna, 1801). The definitive study of this material remains Antonio Pace, *Benjamin Franklin and Italy* (Philadelphia, 1958). Pp. 222–224, from which I have drawn heavily, deal specifically with the propagation of Franklin's writings in Livorno.

78. *Indicatore livornese* 1, nos. 8, 9, 10, 14.

79. See L. Cambini, *L'Indicatore livornese* (Milan-Rome-Naples,

1925) and Raffaella Abenicar, "La Formazione Politico-Culturale di F. D. Guerrazzi" (Tesi di Laurea, Università degli Studi di Firenze, Facoltà di Magistero, 1972), pp. 4–6.

80. The articles were signed only with a "Z." The author was identified by Cambini, p. 79. See also C. Carocci, *Prose e poesie di Sansone Uzielli* (Florence, 1899).

81. Temistocle Pergola, *Memoria ai miei amici* (Livorno, 1861), pp. 4–6.

82. Renato Treves, *La Dottrina sansimonisma nel pensiero italiano del Risorgimento* (Turin, 1931), pp. 7, 25.

83. Abenicar, p. 10. On the diffusion of the doctrines see D. Levi, "Prima fase del socialismo in Italia. Il Sansimonismo," *Nuova Antologia* 11 (June 1897): 434. On G. P. Vieusseux and the Corresponding Society see Raffaele Ciampini, *Gian Pietro Vieusseux, i suoi viaggi, i suoi giornali, i suoi amici* (Turin, 1953); Paolo Prunas, *L'Antologia di Gian Pietro Vieusseux: Storia di una rivista italiana* (Rome, 1906); Lambruschini, *Elogi e biografie* (Florence, 1872); and Ettore Passerin, "G. P. Vieusseux, lo spirito ginevrino e i moderati toscani," *Nuova Rivista storica* 30 (1954): 389–401.

84. Treves, pp. 25, 27.

85. Ibid., p. 30.

86. Ibid., and Giuseppe Montanelli, *Memorie sull'Italia e specialmente sulla Toscana dal 1814 al 1850* (Florence, 1963), p. 44.

87. Among the direct adherents to the new sect, Treves (p. 30) noted Enrico Mayer and Vincenzo Malenchini.

88. Cosimo Ridolfi, "Dell'influenza dello spirito d'associazione negli stabilimenti di pubblica beneficenza," *AGA* 3 (1828): 378–389.

89. Giuliano Ricci, "Sui caratteri generali dell'industria in Toscana," *GAT* 12 (1838): 283–297; idem, "Delle condizioni generali dell'agricoltura toscana," ibid., 365–381.

90. B. Levantini-Pieroni, ed., *Scritti editi e postumi di Carlo Bini reintegrati sui manoscritti originali e notevolmente accresciuti* (Florence, 1869), cited by Badaloni, *Democratici e socialisti*, p. 31.

91. Rosolino Guastalla, ed., *Note autobiografiche e poema di F. D. Guerrazzi* (Florence, 1899), cited in Badaloni, p. 33.

92. G. Vivoli, Ms, "L'Accrescimento progressivo," 1: 218, 222, and 2: n. 387; Carlo Giorgio Ciappei, "Intorno alle origini ed agli statuti dell'Accademia Labronica," *La Rivista di Livorno* 1 (April 1926): 216–221.

93. BLL, *Carte Ricci*, no. 10: "Pagine Sparse—Associazioni di vario genere esistenti." On the suspension of activity, Giuliamo Ricci remarked: "[It] suspends its meetings in 1829 for a variety of reasons,

of which the principal is the antipathy between the old and young members . . . and the opposition of the old members to the admission of new ones" (the recommendation of the governor for the reopening of the academy is in ASL, *Gov.*, f. 1021. *Copialettere governatore*, 1837: 6 May to the president of the Buon Governo).

94. The address was delivered on 6 May 1838 and is contained in the acts of the academy. BLL, uncataloged ms. collection. See also "Estratto dal diario delle adunanze scientifiche dell'Accademia Labronica, Livorno, 6 Maggio 1838," *GAT* 12 (1838): 279–293.

95. F. S. Orlandini, "Accademia Labronica. Adunanza solenne del 6 Maggio 1838," *GAT* 12 (1838): 272–283.

96. A discussion of the session in BNF, *Carteggio Vieusseux*, A76/20, 15 June 1838: Orlandini to Vieusseux. The paper of Ricci is published in the *GAT* (see n. 93), the presentation of Lattini is in the Acts of the academy, and that of Bastogi has not been traced.

97. Ibid., A76/35, 22 April 1839: Orlandini to Vieusseux. Remarked on a session of the academy "to bang your head on the wall!" and closed: "dear Vieusseux, believe me, this academy is irretrievably juvenile, and not only I am saying it but so is the sanest part of the city."

98. Ibid., A76/99, 1 February 1843: Orlandini to Vieusseux.

99. On this theme see in particular Ezio Barsanti, "Il Consiglio del Commercio di Livorno," *Liburni civitas* 9 (1931): 179–192, and Rodolfo Misul, *Le Arti fiorentine decadenza e soppressione: Le Camere di Commercio origine-modificazioni* (Florence, 1904).

100. Barsanti, 182. The author also reports that when Gian Gastone, the last Medici grand duke, asked whether the merchant community would welcome the reestablishment of a council of commerce, he received a negative response that was overwhelming, "above all for the suspicions and jealousies that divide the merchants of the various nations, including the Jewish."

101. See in particular the comments of Francesco Maria Gianni, one of the principal eighteenth-century Tuscan reformers, in *Scritti di pubblica economia, storico-economici e storico-politici* (Florence, 1848–1849), 2: 298, 313.

102. Barsanti, 184–187.

103. The provisions of the *Regolamento* are reproduced in ACCL, *Delib.*, 7 Oct. 1815.

104. Ibid., article 27, pts. 103.

105. Ibid., articles 30, 32, 34–36.

106. See the remarks of the secretary of finance, Frullani, in his memorial of 30 November 1818 in ASF, *Seg. Gab.*, f. 160, b. 8.

107. See chapter 4.

108. The role of the chamber of commerce as the legal representative of the merchant community was a controversial subject. In response to a report of the administrative office of the Royal Revenues (13 June 1840) which had labeled the chamber of commerce of Livorno "a purely consultative body without representative capacity or a mandate to contract obligations in the name of commerce itself," the governor of Livorno, Neri Corsini, remarked (4 August 1840) that "this chamber had always been the organ of the votes [*voti*] and requests of the merchants, and this for very long custom," and for that reason, "the *tassa di commercio* must be regarded as the offering of the legal representatives of the merchant community [*corpo dei negozianti*] in Livorno." Both reports are in ASF, *Fin. C.R.*, f. 17. For the specific functions of the chamber of commerce in the administration of the *tassa*, see articles 6 and 8 of the notification of 24 July 1834 (*Bandi e Ordini*, 1834, n. 43).

109. See the *Regolamento pei facchini di manovella e pei facchini di sacco*, approved 7 October 1847. Article 27 stated: "The company will be wholly dependent on the chamber of commerce and must observe all the provisions and regulations that it promulgates, pending, as needed, the approval of the central government."

110. For the *tassa di commercio* see chapter 4; for the dockworkers, chapter 7.

111. ACCL, *Delib.*, 7 Oct. 1815. *Regolamento*, 8 September 1815, article 2.

112. Ibid., articles 14, 15.

113. Ibid., articles 16, 18.

114. Ibid., article 17. With regard to the residency requirement, exception was made for those merchants who took up residence in the city in the period immediately following the signing of the Treaty of Paris in 1814. The government permitted merchants enjoying the "*fido* in dogana" to pay their customs charges in a lump sum every two months. This concession was granted only on petition and was awarded to merchants of proven repute. Only bona fide wholesale merchants were eligible for the *fido*, which meant in effect that retailers or other social groups whose primary function was not wholesale commerce were excluded from direct representation in the chamber.

115. ASL, *Gov.*, f. 111. *Aff. Div.*, 1819. Florence, 6 January: Frullani to the governor of Livorno.

116. Ibid., and article 11 of the *Regolamento* of 8 September 1815.

117. These important lists of merchants enjoying the *fido* may be found in ASF, *Fin. C.R.*, f. 20.

118. *Regolamento*, articles 9, 10.

119. See, for example, ASL. *Gov.*, f. 111. *Aff. Div.*, 1919. Florence, 6 January 1819: Frullani to the governor of Livorno for the way in which the selection passes through the various stages and results in the selection of the top candidates proposed by the chamber of commerce. A comparison of the annual lists of candidates recommended by the chamber with the deputies finally selected will confirm the practice.

3. Tariffs and Port Charges

1. Luigi Dal Pane, *La Finanza toscana dagli inizi del secolo XVIII alla caduta del granducato* (Milan, 1965), p. 111.

2. Ibid., p. 278; Bowring, *Statistica*, pp. 16–18.

3. Corrado Barbagallo, *Le Origini della grande industria contemporanea 1750–1850* (Venice, 1930), 2: 293–297.

4. ACCL. *Delib.*, 5 August 1816. Reports that the notification was published by the administrative office of the Royal Revenues on 27 July 1816.

5. Ibid., *Delib.*, 26 September 1816; ASF, *Misc. Fin. II*, f. 539, n. 93. Livorno, 30 Sept. 1816: chamber of commerce. Panajotti Palli, president. "Memoria."

6. Edict of 15 May 1825.

7. Edict of 30 December 1831.

8. Edict of 6 April 1833; ASF, *Fin. C.R.*, f. 17. Contains the protests of many manufacturers of *panni di lana ordinarie* and strong support for the measure from Domenico Cappelli, head of the customhouse in Livorno.

9. ASF, *Seg. Gab.*, f. 391. A notification of 12 March 1822 increased the gabelle on foreign wine destined for the consumption of the inhabitants of Livorno and the hinterland and diminished the excise tax on Tuscan wine introduced into Livorno. On 5 December 1823, Cappelli outlined the positive results of the measure in a note to the secretary of finance.

10. ACCL, *Delib.*, 16 April 1814. The chamber agreed to continuing the prohibition on the extraction of Tuscan rags but refused to support any restrictions on the reexport of foreign rags.

11. Ibid., *Delib.*, 17 May 1814. Argued that restrictions on the extraction of oil should apply only to Tuscan cooking oil. Commerce in machine oil was primarily one of deposit and transshipment, and the absence of machinery in Tuscany made the internal demand virtually nil.

12. Carlo Di Nola, *Politica economica e agricoltura in Toscana nei secoli XV–XIX* (Rome, 1948), p. 51.

13. Notification of 17 May 1817. In 1823, Cappelli defended the measure for favoring Tuscan agriculture and commerce without damaging the wool industry. In the past six years, he said, the sheep population in the region had grown considerably. Wool manufacturers, who were engaged primarily in the production of ordinary cloth, used only a small proportion of the indigenous product, which they found too fine for their needs. The majority of their raw material came from the Barbary Coast and the Levant, and an efficient commercial network insured that this product was always available at a reasonable price (ASF, *Misc. Fin. II*, f. 500. Livorno, 5 December 1823: Cappelli, "Memoria").

14. Notification, 6 July 1819.

15. Edict of 21 July 1825. The governor of Livorno, Garzoni Venturi, enumerated the positive results that merchants in Livorno said would result from the measure: a larger number of English ships would be attracted to the port, which, in addition to silk, would export other products, "to the secure advantage of commerce and the state treasury" (ASL, *Gov.*, f. 1008. *Copialettere governatore*, 1825: 29 June to the secretary of finance); ibid., letter of 1 August to the department of finance transmitted the gratification of the chamber of commerce. See also BLL, *Carte Vivoli*, f. 23. 21 July 1825.

16. Edict of 11 November 1830.

17. Edict of 10 July 1832.

18. Edict of 15 November 1840. G. Baldasseroni saw this measure as important evidence of the government's desire to return to a general system of free trade (Baldasseroni, *Leopoldo II*, p. 123).

19. Baruchello, p. 547.

20. Dal Pane, *La Finanza toscana*, p. 322.

21. The memorial of the chamber to the central government is transcribed in ACCL, *Delib.*, 16 August 1816.

22. Notwithstanding the follow-up letter of the president of the chamber, Panajotti Palli (ASF, *Misc. Fin. II*, f. 539, n. 93. Livorno, 30 September 1816).

23. Ibid., Livorno, 23 October 1816: customhouse to the secretary of finance, which concluded that the laments of the chamber of commerce were "lacking in any foundation."

24. ASF, *Seg. Gab.*, f. 160, n. 8. Livorno, 26 June 1818: G. G. Saunders, president of the chamber, to the governor.

25. ASF, *Seg. Gab.*, f. 160, n. 8. 30 November 1818, "Memoria." "For the Livornese merchants the evils of famine in the Tuscan

interior provide an occasion of genuine delight."

26. In 1818 the governor of Livorno, for example, clearly felt that the decline in prices was only temporary. He opposed the imposition of a flexible tax for the current fixed charge on grain imports, arguing that merchants would suffer when the price rose: "In fact, diminishing the tax at this time . . . and in consequence ending the fixed rate, it seems to me, raises the danger of seeing it increase with the price of grain, eventually returning to 30 or 40 lire." Instead, he urged the abolition of the tax of 1 percent. (ASL, *Gov.*, f. 1001. *Copialettere governatore*, 1818: 1 June to the president of the chamber of commerce.)

27. On the complaints of the harsh sanitary practices of the port see also BLL, *Carte Vivoli*, 1816. Livorno, 8 July 1816: M. Appleton, the American consul in Livorno, to the governor. In 1817, Giovanni F. Manjony, the Tuscan consul in Boston, reported that American ships were being diverted to Trieste, "the only motive [being] that there they are exposed only to a simple quarantine of five days" (ibid., 1817. Boston, 25 November 1817: Manjony to the governor of Livorno).

28. The papers relative to the response of the central government are in ASF, *Seg. Gab.*, f. 160, no. 8. They consist principally of observations from I. Pistolesi to the secretary of finance (15 July 1818), a series of memoranda from Frullani to the governor of Livorno (2 and 7 July and 15 August 1818), and a long, unsigned memorial dated 30 November 1818.

29. The governor of Livorno supported the petition of the chamber for extending the deferment of customs payments (ASL, *Gov.*, f. 1001. *Copialettere governatore*, 1818: January 28 to the secretary of finance). Frullani opposed the proposed extension and criticized merchants for not paying the charges when due and then holding up the government for loans at 15 to 20 percent interest (ASF, *Seg. Gab.*, f. 160, n. 8, 2 July 1818, Frullani to the governor of Livorno). The memorial of November 30 (ibid.) indicated that the government had successfully cracked down on merchants not making their customs payments.

30. The memorial of 30 November 1818 reported that "Consul Frullani has suggested that he does not know whether the grand duke, informed of the insidious maneuvres of the chamber, will not resolve to take some determination on the suppression of the same."

31. See the letters of Frullani to Spannocchi cited in n. 28.

32. The relatively subtle hint of possible removal expressed by Frullani in August ("Hence one can easily combine a man endowed with all the administrative virtues without their being well informed

of the causes that produce certain predetermined effects in both political and financial legislation and therefore do not allow him to meet effectively the true object of his mission") was expressed even more forcefully in the memorial in November: "It is necessary, therefore, to place at the head of the Livornese government a governor who knows commerce and understands the greed of the Livornese merchants who are for the most part foreign." In his reply to Frullani, Spannocchi did not hesitate to reaffirm his respect for the foreign consuls resident in Livorno and for the position of the *Livornesi*: "From the tone of your memorial, which I will keep private, it would appear, and I am sorry for it, that you are not at all a friend of the Livornese; in truth, I am, because I have always found them good, obedient to the laws, and attached and respectable to the government" (ibid., 12 August 1818).

33. A published copy of this notification is in BLL, *Carte Vivoli*, f. 22.

34. See the introduction to the published tariffs of the tax of 1 percent in ASF, *Misc. Fin.*, f. 2820 and ASL, *Gov.*, f. 119. Florence, 8 March 1822: secretary of finance to the governor of Livorno.

35. Ibid.

36. ASL, *Gov.*, f. 144.

37. Ibid., Livorno, 26 April 1830: Bell, De Young and Company to the chamber of commerce. This sentiment was repeated in the company's petition to the central government of the same date and to the governor, 28 April 1830.

38. Ibid., Florence, 25 November 1830: Neri Corsini, secretary of state to the governor of Livorno. Notification that the official value of certain types of coffee was lowered from 80 to 35 lire per hundred pounds.

39. From the information supplied by Bell, De Young and Company, the chamber of commerce called for a complete revision of Livorno's stallage duties (ACCL, *Delib.*, 15 and 22 March 1831).

40. Bowring, *Statistica*, p. 28.

41. ACCL, *Delib.*, 13 January 1834.

42. ASL, *Gov.*, f. 154. Florence, 22 February 1834: Cempini to the governor of Livorno.

43. ASL. *Gov.*, f. 1018. *Copialettere governatore,* 1834: 26 February to the president of the Buon Governo.

44. Ibid.

45. Ibid., 28 February 1834 to Cempini.

46. G. Vivoli, Ms, "L'Accrescimento progressivo," vol. 2, note 14.

47. ACCL, *Delib.*, 8 March 1834.

48. ASF, *Seg. Fin.*, f. 1149. I have surmised that the conclusions of the commission are contained in a paper entitled, "Conclusioni della commissione." It is undated and unsigned.

49. Ibid., "Rapporto del consiglio." The contents of a missing *filza* in this series (ibid., f. 1148) would undoubtedly throw light on the working out of the provisions of the new system.

50. Repetti, *Dizionario*, 2: 753.

51. ASF, *Seg. Fin.*, f. 1149. "Rapporto del consiglio."

52. Ibid.

53. Notification of 24 July 1834, paragraph 6. *Bandi e Ordini*, 1834, n. 31.

54. Ibid., paragraph 7.

55. Notification of 24 July 1834.

56. ACCL, *Delib.*, 11 March 1834.

57. ASL, *Gov.*, f. 1018. *Copialettere governatore*, 1834: 26 July to Cempini for the response of the merchant community; ibid., f. 155. Florence, 29 July 1834: Cempini to the governor for the permission to send a delegation.

58. ACCL, *Delib.*, 8 August 1834. The social attitudes and philanthropic activities of the merchant community are presented in chapter 5.

59. Enrico Guglielmino, *Genoa dal 1814 al 1849: Gli Sviluppi economici e l'opinione pubblica* (Genoa, 1940), p. 104.

60. ASF, *Seg. Fin.*, f. 1149. Livorno, 17 Sept. 1834: Niccola Manteri, president of the board of assessment to the chamber of commerce.

61. ACCL, *Delib.*, 7 October 1834.

62. On the problem see ASF, *Fin. C.R.*, f. 17. administrative office of the Royal Revenues, 13 June 1840, "Memoria sulla sostituzione"; also ibid., Livorno, 4 August 1840: report of the board of assessment to the chamber of commerce. "The elements which provide the basis of the tax, that is business, capital, and profit, are mysteries hidden in the ledgers of the respective taxpayers."

63. ASF, *Seg. Fin.*, f. 1149. Livorno, 27 October 1834: A subject [*un suddito*] to Cempini.

64. Thus, the administrative office of the Royal Revenues argued that the notification of July had called for the exemption of all retail merchants and that the extension of the tax to wine and coffeehouses, etc., was illegal. (ASF, *Fin. C.R.*, f. 17. 13 June 1840, "Sulla sostituzione" [memorial].) But a letter to the department of finance (signature illegible) remarked that "the decree declares subject to the tax persons exercising any kind of trade, even retail, provided that

it is not considered truly slight and insignificant" (ibid., *Seg. Fin.*, f. 1149. Livorno, 13 August 1834: to Cempini).

65. Reported in ACCL, *Delib.*, 20 November 1834. In the previous deliberation (11 November) the chamber, while stressing that it had no power to intervene in an affair that concerned the board of appeal, put itself on record as opposing the automatic extension of a revision to an entire class of taxpayer. Revisions, it argued, should be granted only to specific, individual claims.

66. ASF, *Fin. C.R.*, f. 17. Livorno, 4 August 1840: report of the board of assessment to the chamber of commerce.

67. C. A. Dalgas, vice president of the chamber, remarked to the secretary of finance that to prevent general malcontent the tax had to fall largely on the wealthy. But, he remarked, the number of large speculators in Livorno was limited, and if the tax continued to fall primarily on them, as it had in the past two years, the consequences could be distasteful (ibid., Livorno, 30 May 1840: Dalgas to the secretary of finance).

68. ACCL, *Delib.*, 2 July 1838. Fortunato Regini, president of the chamber of commerce, "Memoria."

69. A glance at the deliberations of the chamber in this period will give some sense of the scramble. ACCL, *Delib.*, 30 November 1837: The deputies voted to send the tax rolls back to the board of appeal for further revision. *Delib.*, 16 July 1838: The chamber voted to revise the tax roll itself before having it published and considered adding to it groups that in the past had been excluded. *Delib.*, 18 July 1838: The deputies agreed to meet continuously and to examine every name on the list of contributors and to vote on each proposed assessment. *Delib.*, 11 December 1838: In a heated discussion the chamber criticized the board of appeal, which had rejected many of its recommendations. *Delib.*, 13 December 1838: The announcement of a compromise between the chamber and the board.

70. ASF, *Fin. C.R.*, f. 17. Livorno, 4 August 1840: report of the board of assessment to the chamber of commerce.

71. ACCL, *Delib.*, 2 July 1838.

72. ASF, *Fin. C.R.*, f. 12. Livorno, 9 August 1839: O. Forni to R. Cempini. Those rumored to be doing this were Chelli, Rodocanacchi, and Lloyd.

73. ACCL, *Delib.*, 2 July 1838.

74. ASL, *Gov.*, f. 1023. *Copialettere governatore*, 1839: 23 January to the chamber of commerce. The governor informed the chamber that two memorials, one from the board of assessment and the other from a group of merchants—in line with government resolutions of

17 February and 10 July 1838—were not being transmitted to Florence because they were "conceived in vague and generic terms." The governor remarked that if the chamber could come up with a concrete proposal that would guarantee the treasury an equal annual compensation, it would receive serious consideration.

75. ASF, *Fin. C.R.*, f. 17. Livorno, 14 February 1839: Rodocanacchi to the chamber of commerce. The author was probably either Michele or Giorgio Rodocanacchi, both wealthy Greek merchants and active in the chamber in this period.

76. A summary of this plan is found in ibid., Livorno, 13 September 1839: O. Forni to Cempini.

77. ASF, *Fin. C.R.*, f. 17. Livorno, 30 Nov. 1839: chamber of commerce to the auditor of the governor. Also ibid., Livorno, 30 May 1840: chamber of commerce (Dalgas, vice president) to the secretary of finance.

78. Ibid., Livorno, November 1838: twelve signatories to the chamber of commerce. The memorial was originally signed by twenty, but eight of the signatures were crossed off.

79. Ibid., administrative office of the Royal Revenues. The two memorials are dated 17 July 1839 and 13 June 1840.

80. Ibid., Livorno, 4 August 1840: Neri Corsini, "Osservazioni."

81. ASL, Gov., f. 1023. *Copialettere governatore*, 1839: 23 January to the chamber of commerce.

82. ASL, *Gov.*, f. 186, n. 328. Florence, 26 June 1841: secretary of finance, Cempini, to the governor of Livorno. The chamber remarked that with this stipulation it would not be possible for them to propose a way of compensating the government for the loss of 300,000 lire (ASL, *Gov.*, f. 186, n. 328. Livorno, 9 June 1841: governor of Livorno to the secretary of finance).

83. "The principal aim for Livorno . . . [is to] eliminate with the suppression of minute contraband a deplorable corruptive influence on the people" (Giuliano Ricci, "Livorno," *GAT* 11 (1837): 106. See also Serristori, *Livorno ed i suoi traffici*, p. 7).

84. For the protest of the butchers see the long memorial of Francesco Grazzini, a butcher in the old city, in ASL, *Gov.*, f. 146. Livorno, 24 July 1831. For the bakers see ASL, *Gov.*, f. 1017. *Copialettere governatore*, 1833: 4 September to the administrative office of the Royal Revenues.

85. ASF, *Misc. di Fin. II*, f. 505. Undated report of the customhouse explaining the decline in the gabelles on animals, flour, and wine in 1825.

86. ASL, *Gov.*, f. 1017. *Copialettere governatore*, 1833: 4 September

to the administrative office of the Royal Revenues. The comparison would be more convincing if some indication were given of the size of the shops in the two areas.

87. ASL, *Gov.*, f. 146. Livorno, 24 July 1831: F. Grazzini to the grand duke.

88. Ibid.

89. Ibid., f. 1015. *Copialettere governatore*, 1831: 16 May to Cempini.

90. Ibid., f. 1017. *Copialettere governatore*, 1833: 4 Sept. to the administrative office of the Royal Revenues.

91. Ibid. Also ASL, *Gov.*, f. 1015. *Copialettere governatore*, 1831: 16 May to Cempini.

92. The new wall and customhouses cost 3,984,365 lire; the cost of demolishing the old wall came to 635,140 lire. These expenses were a major cause of the deficit budget of 1835. See Dal Pane, *La Finanza toscana*, pp. 331, 347.

93. Lando Bortolotti, *Livorno dal 1748 al 1958*, p. 115.

94. ASF, *Seg. di Fin.*, f. 1149. 12 July 1834, report of the administrative council: "If the government wishes to recover its lost revenue by subjecting the inhabitants of the suburbs to the consumer taxes or other charges, the Livornese population, rather than seeing the suppression of the tax of 1 percent as a favor, would see this partial measure only as a financial speculation at its expense."

95. Some sense of the care with which business locations were chosen is provided by Baldasseroni, *Leopoldo II*, pp. 104–105: "And not a few industrial workshops were established in the old city as well as in the suburbs, and more in the latter than in the former, depending on the return to the speculators."

96. ASF, *Seg. Fin.*, f. 1149. 12 July 1834: report of the administrative council.

97. See, for example, the letter of Girolamo Novella to Vittorio Fossombroni, the head of the government administration (ibid., Livorno, 14 July 1834). Novella, a merchant and manufacturer of combs and other luxury items in ivory and horn in the suburbs outside the Pisan gate, complained that if the rumored extension of the free port took place and his establishment were cut off from the hinterland, he would face certain ruin.

98. Notification of 24 July 1834, article 5.

99. A list of manufacturers in the city in 1847 notes three manufacturers of wax candles, three of tallow candles, three of munitions, three of soap, and three of hides (ASF, *Fin. C.R.*, f. 20, report of the customhouse).

100. Ibid., Livorno, 7 July 1848. See also Bortolotti, p. 77.
101. G. Mori, "Linee," p. 22.

4. Elimination of Abuses

1. See, for example, Serristori, *Livorno ed i suoi traffici,* p. 7. See also Giuliano Ricci, "Livorno," *GAT* 11 (1837): 114.
2. *Bandi e Ordini Toscani,* 1836. Notification of 12 August 1836. A copy of the original concession dated 8 October 1590 is printed in Guarnieri, *Livorno marinara,* p. 511.
3. Ricci, "Livorno," p. 114. See also Serristori, *Livorno ed i suoi traffici,* p. 6.
4. For example, the Parisian merchant Auguste Degas in a letter to the merchant firm of Morre, Ulrich, and Company in Livorno called the use of a *sotto-sconto* in the sale of a cargo of Degas's tobacco in Tuscany "oppressive and abominable." The transaction, it was noted, conformed to local practice but was obviously not calculated or understood by the seller (ASL, *Gov.,* f. 1020. *Copialettere governatore,* 1836: 8 October to the secretary of finance, Cempini).
5. ACCL, *Delib.,* 18 June 1822.
6. Ibid., 27 June 1822. This meeting was attended by important members of the merchant community who were not currently serving as deputies in the chamber. The final vote in favor of the proposal was thirty-five to eight.
7. The concerns of small retail merchants were clearly outlined in a general proposal of reform made by the chamber of commerce to the merchant community in 1835 (ASL, *Gov.,* f. 158. *Aff. Div.* 1835, 9 June 1835) and in a letter of the governor to the secretary of finance (ASL, *Gov.,* f. 1020. *Copialettere governatore,* 1836: 8 October 1836 to Cempini).
8. The tactic was described in a letter of the governor to the secretary of finance (ibid., f. 1019. *Copialettere governatore,* 1835: 27 March 1835 to Cempini).
9. ASL, *Gov.,* f. 1007. *Copialettere governatore,* 1823: 24 November to the secretary of finance.
10. Ibid., f. 1008. *Copialettere governatore,* 1825: 14 March to the secretary of finance.
11. Ibid.
12. ASL, *Gov.,* f. 131. *Aff. Div.,* 1826: 24 August, secretary of finance to the governor of Livorno.
13. ASL, *Gov., Aff. Div.,* 1835: 9 June, memorial of the chamber of commerce.

14. ASL, *Gov.*, f. 899, *busta:* camera di commercio 1835. Livorno, 3 July 1835: Panajotti Palli, president of the chamber, to the governor of Livorno, forwarding the letters of important merchant firms in Livorno, all in support of the proposed reforms.

15. Ibid., f. 1020. *Copialettere governatore,* 1836: 8 October 1836 to Cempini.

16. Ibid., "the eye principally turned to large foreign commerce."

17. Ibid.

18. Ibid., f. 162. *Aff. Div.* 1836: Florence, 26 December 1836: secretary of finance to the governor of Livorno. For a published summary of the abuses and the provisions of the new law see Bowring, *Statistica,* pp. 30–31.

19. In 1818 the secretary of finance, Frullani, remarked polemically that the chamber of commerce should concern itself primarily with the business practices of the *mezzani* which, he said, were alienating foreigners far more than the tax of 1 percent. ASF, *Seg. Gab.,* f. 160, b. 8. Florence, 7 July 1818: Frullani to the governor of Livorno.

20. Ibid., *Misc. di Fin.,* f. 533. Livorno, 10 May 1823: customhouse of Livorno, Moretti. Typical was the expression of an anonymous writer who remarked that "in our city the profession of *mezzano* is the refuge of all those people who for their social position are unwilling to practice the mechanical trades, or other unfortunates, otherwise honorable, who did not succeed in commerce" (ibid., *Fin. C.R.,* f. 63). For the case of a merchant falling on hard times and becoming a *mezzano,* see ASL, *Gov.,* f. 163. *Aff. Div.,* 1837. Livorno, 3 January 1837: David Ferdinandes Leiba to the governor of Livorno. One of the memorials of the "nations" in Livorno to the Tuscan government in 1757 remarked that "notwithstanding long-standing regulations forbidding them to exercise commerce on their own behalf, they [*mezzani*] have adopted the custom of keeping the best deals to themselves, either openly or through utilizing a fictitious name" (Baruchello, p. 494).

21. The most important summary sets of regulations governing the profession were promulgated 21 November 1758 and 24 January 1769.

22. See articles 34 and 35 of the 1815 regulation governing the chamber's activities.

23. The French "nation," for example, reported in 1757 that "in Livorno all wish to leave the occupation of laborer or artisan to become a *mezzano* such that there is a lack of skilled and even unskilled labor" (Baruchello, p. 494).

24. For the above see the reports from the Livorno customhouse

in ASF, *Misc. di Fin.*, f. 533. 10 May 1823: Livorno customhouse, Moretti. 5 September 1823: A. D. Cappelli, director of the customhouse to the administrative office of the Royal Revenues, Florence. See also the complaint of Carlo and Luigi Vecchi, Luigi Costa, and Leone Coen, freight *mezzani*, against the unauthorized handling of freight contracts by clerks in commercial firms (ibid., *Fin. C.R.*, f. 63. Livorno, 2 August 1834).

25. See ACCL, *Delib.*, 11 December 1815. In the meeting of 23 December 1816 (ibid.), "it was decided to represent to the government that the chamber believes it neither advantageous to commerce nor useful to the royal treasury to limit the number of *mezzani*." The chamber opposed especially limiting the *mezzani di cambio* to ten: "The instances of exchange that are exercised in this city annually reach very large numbers so that the actual number of *mezzani*—ten—authorized to handle this activity by law is insufficient," especially since "some of those who have the authorization do little or nothing in this branch of commerce."

26. Ibid., 11 December 1815.

27. ASF, *Fin. C.R.*, f. 65. Livorno, 20 November 1850: Agostino Kotzian, Francesco Cartoni, Cesare Papanti, Giovanni Formigli, Pietro Bastogi, *Rapporto della commissione istituita con la resoluzione ministeriale del 3 Feb. 1850 intorno al progetto di regolamento sopra i mezzani della piazza di Livorno.*

28. See n. 24.

29. See especially the observations of G. Baldasseroni (22 April 1846), those of a commission of merchants and bankers in the city (20 November 1850), and those of the Consulta di Stato (12 January 1853), all in ASF, *Fin. C.R.*, f. 65.

30. Contents of the letter reported in ACCL, *Delib.*, 31 October 1815. In reply, however, the chamber stressed the detriment that any restriction on the extraction of specie would have on the principle of free trade.

31. ASL, *Gov.*, f. 1001. *Copialettere governatore*, 1818: 19 January to the secretary of finance.

32. Ibid., f. 1002. *Copialettere governatore*, 1819: 18 September to the secretary of finance.

33. ASF, *Fin. C.R.*, f. 16. Livorno, 12 June 1829: Walser, Senn, Bacry to the secretary of finance, Cempini.

34. Ibid., Livorno, 5 March 1829: Walser, Senn, Bacry to the I. and R. Governo [the Imperial and Royal Government]. See also ASL, *Gov.*, f. 1020. *Copialettere governatore*, 1836: 14 September to the director of the department of finance.

35. *Gazzetta di Firenze,* 14 July 1829.

36. *Indicatore livornese,* 3 August 1829.

37. Ibid.

38. Ibid.

39. ASF, *Fin. C.R.,* f. 16. Livorno, 20 May 1829: memorial of Walser, Senn, and Bacry to the governor of Livorno. Ellipsis in original.

40. For the discussion of the difference between useful and useless employment of capital and the role that the discount bank would play in encouraging the former see ibid., the memorial cited, and a second memorial from the same authors to the secretary of finance, Cempini, 21 June 1829.

41. Guido Sonnino, *Saggio sulle industrie, marina, e commercio in Livorno sotto i primi due Lorenesi (1737–1790)* (Cortona, 1909), p. 49.

42. ACCL, *Delib.,* 25 November 1815. For a general summary of the proposal see Baruchello, p. 564.

43. Ibid., 28 November 1815.

44. Ibid., 30 November 1815.

45. ASF, *Seg. Gab.,* f. 160, no. 8. Livorno, 22 July 1818: B. Bartoletti to the secretary of finance, Frullani. Bartoletti was the secretary of the chamber of commerce. See also ASF, *Fin. C.R.,* f. 16, Livorno, 20 May 1829: Walser, Senn, Bacry to the Throne.

46. ASL, *Gov.,* f. 1001. *Copialettere governatore,* 1818. Livorno, 19 January: governor to the secretary of finance.

47. ASF, *Seg. Gab.,* f. 160, no. 8.

48. The proposals are in ASF. *Fin. C.R.,* f. 16. March 1829: Walser, Senn, Bacry to the I. and R. Governo; 20 May 1829: Walser, Senn, Bacry to the governor of Livorno; 12 June 1829 to Cempini, the secretary of finance. The last contains a summary project for the bank.

49. ACCL, *Delib.,* 15 March 1831.

50. Ibid., 22 March 1831.

51. Baruchello, pp. 584–585.

52. This paragraph is based in large part on material drawn from Commissioner Mochi's first two reports, 7 October 1837 and 9 January 1838. Both are in ASL, *Gov.,* f. 899, b: Banca di Sconto, 1837.

53. ASF, *Misc. Fin. I,* f. 41. Report 13: Mochi, Livorno, 7 October 1840. "And in truth if in the past bankers had been the greatest users, today they are for the most part surpassed by the other merchants."

54. ASL, *Gov.,* f. 194, n. 7. *Aff. Div.,* 1842. Livorno, 28 May 1842: Mochi to the governor of Livorno; ibid.: Mochi's letter of 21

June 1842 announced that the discount rate had been lowered to 4 percent.

55. ASF, *Misc. Fin. I*, f. 41. Livorno, 24 September 1842: Mochi, report 21.

56. Ibid., report 25: 18 October 1843.

57. ASL, *Gov.*, f. 279. *Aff. Div.*, 1848. Livorno, 29 February 1848: Mochi, special report.

58. The issue of the *baratto* illustrates the support that the discount bank enjoyed in the merchant community. Early in 1849, the president of the bank remarked that the excessive redemption of notes issued by the organization was threatening to exhaust the bank's entire cash reserve (ASL, *Gov.*, f. 325, no. 17. *Aff. Div.*, 1850. Livorno, 13 May 1851: discount bank, published annual report). In response, the most wealthy members of the merchant community promised in writing to abstain from this activity and, insofar as it was possible, to use their specie to buy bank notes. The action, however, was considered merely palliative and temporary. Pressure for some form of government relief was made not directly by the bank—a private corporation—but by the chamber of commerce. In response the government declared a moratorium on the redemption of bank notes with a face value above 200 lire from February 9 to July 10. On February 12, merchants and bankers in the city pledged to continue employing bank notes in their commercial operations. As a result they were held in high esteem throughout the period—higher, indeed, than the treasury notes issued by the government (ASL, *Gov.*, f. 300, no. 15. *Aff. Div.*, 1849. Livorno, 9 July 1849: Mochi, report 48).

59. Mochi declared that were it not for the extraordinary factors described in n. 58 the profit for 1849 would not have exceeded that of 1848 (ibid., Livorno, 20 January 1850: Mochi, report 50).

60. The police commissioner for the San Marco quarter reported to the governor that a memorial was circulating in the merchant community demonstrating the damage that would result to commerce from the emission of paper money. The commissioner reported that public opinion was generally opposed to paper money and that this view was shared by the majority of deputies in the chamber of commerce (ASL, *Gov.*, f. 300, no. 20. *Aff. Div.*, 1849. Livorno, 10 January 1849: delegazione di San Marco to the governor of Livorno).

61. The only significant instance occurred during the first year of the bank's operation (Enrico Mayer, "Banca di Livorno. Primo Bilancio presentato dal direttore della medesima il dì 11 Maggio

1839," *GAT* 13 (1839): 141–149. Debts that remained uncollected for one year were often collected the following year and were reflected in the subsequent budget (ASL, *Gov.*, f. 300, n. 15. *Aff. Div.*, 1847. Livorno, 28 May 1849: Mayer, published report).

62. See the bank's first balance sheet published in *GAT* (see n. 61). See also ASL, *Gov.*, f. 181, n. 14. *Aff. Div.*, 1841. Livorno, n.d.: Mochi, report 14.

63. Information drawn from the published annual reports of the bank in ASL, *Gov.*, f. 194, 205, 233.

64. Ibid., f. 261, n. 11. *Aff. Div.*, 1847. Livorno, 5 October 1847: Mochi, report 42.

65. Ibid., f. 279, n. 12. *Aff. Div.*, 1848. Livorno, 13 May 1848: Mayer, published report.

66. Serristori, "Delle banche toscane di sconto e di circolazione," *AGA*, nuova seria 3 (1857): 194–203. "Moreover, it should be noted that the bank of Florence today prefers to entrust its çapital to landed proprietors rather than business men, which is contrary to its initial scope" (ibid., p. 195).

67. Kent Roberts Greenfield, *Economics and Liberalism in the Risorgimento*, pp. 142–143.

68. The system consisted of setting up individual revolving accounts in twenty-one classes varying from 1,000 to 150,000 lire. The lowest class was added to insure the participation of tradesmen and retailers. Credit was granted to a member of this class, however, only if the request was cosigned by someone enjoying a credit limit of 10,000 lire or above (ASL, *Gov.*, f. 8–9, b. Banca di Sconto, 1837. Livorno, 7 October 1837: Mochi, report 1).

69. In 1844, Mochi estimated that of the 1,313 shares in the bank held by people residing in Livorno, 504 shares were held by nonmerchants. He attributed this to the fact that many found shares in the bank to be a more attractive and secure investment than land (Ibid., f. 222. *Aff. Div.* 1844, no. 11. Livorno, 27 May 1844: Mochi, report 22).

70. ASF, *Misc. Fin. I*, f. 41. Livorno, 18 October 1843: Mochi, report 25.

71. Ibid.

72. Torelli wrongly asserted that it was the only example of the spirit of association (Torelli, *Dell'avvenire del commercio europeo*, 3: 59).

73. Pierallini, Ms, "Osservazioni sulla pace cogli Ottomani e sulla marina e commercio di Livorno," 1764.

74. The petition was signed by Alessandro Patrinò, Moise Fernandez, Domenico Castelli, Stefano Bielietz, Mospignotti, Iallia, and Despotti, G. O. Tossizza, and Giorgio Reggio. All styled themselves

as "public traders in this city who own ships" (ASL, *Gov.*, f. 124. Livorno, 24 July 1823 to the governor of Livorno).

75. Ibid., f. 1007. *Copialettere governatore*, 1823: 25 July to the secretary of state, Florence.

76. ASL, *Gov.*, f. 124. Florence, 25 Nov. 1823: secretary of state to the governor of Livorno.

77. Ibid., f. 1008. *Copialettere governatore*, 1825: 14 March to the I. and R. Governo.

78. Ibid.

79. ASF, *Estero*, f. 2623, b. *Carteggio Governatore Livorno*, 1828. Livorno, 2 January 1828: Francesco Janer to Garzoni-Venturi, governor of Livorno. The urging of the deputies of the chamber of commerce on the issue in ACCL, *Delib.*, 29 December 1827.

80. Article II of the treaty stipulated: "Passage through the Dardanelles and the canal of the Bosphorus from now on will be entirely open to merchant ships under the Tuscan flag with or without cargo whether coming from the Mediterranean to pass into the Black Sea or vice-versa. The above-named Tuscan ships cannot be arrested nor held under any pretext, with the result that true merchant ships flying the Tuscan flag will enjoy free navigation in the Black Sea under the same conditions and with the same privileges accorded to the subjects and ships of Austria."

81. ASL, *Gov.*, f. 153. *Aff. Div.*, 1833. 22 October 1833: chamber of commerce (Niccolo Pezzer, vice president) to the governor of Livorno.

82. Ibid. Both requests were warmly supported by the governor. Ibid., f. 1017. *Copialettere governatore*, 1833. 25 October: governor to the secretary of state.

83. ASL, *Gov.*, f. 1007. *Copialettere governatore*, 1823: 24 September to the I. and R. Governo.

84. Ibid., 26 September 1823 to the I. and R. Governo. That the *Aristide* was engaged in the commerce of Russian grain seems evident from a letter of the captain of the port reporting that in order to receive permission to pass into the Black Sea the ship was forced to raise the Austrian flag (ASF, *Estero*, f. 2624, b. *Carteggio Governatore Livorno*. Livorno, 21 July 1830: D'Angiolo, captain of the port to G. Vivoli, secretary of the *ufficio di sanità*.

85. ASL, *Gov.*, f. 1009. *Copialettere governatore*, 1824: 14 May to the I. and R. Governo.

86. Ibid.

87. ASL, *Gov.*, f. 180.

88. By the 1850s, though, the hauling of grain from the Mediter-

ranean to the ports of Western Europe appears to have been extremely lucrative (ASF, *Fin. C.R.*, f. 67. Livorno, 6 May 1853: I.R. Uffizio Principale di Marina Mercantile to the R. Delegato Straordinario di Livorno); ibid., f. 101. Livorno, 23 October 1857: captain of the port to the governor of Livorno; ibid., *Misc. di Fin.*, Series II, f. 464. Livorno, n.d.: captain of the port.

89. Serristori, *Livorno ed i suoi traffici*, p. 12.

90. ASL, *Gov.*, f. 153. *Aff. Div.*, 1833. 22 October: Niccolo Pezzer to the governor of Livorno.

91. ASF, *Fin. C.R.*, f. 67, b. *Marina Mercantile Toscana*. Livorno, 3 December 1849: captain of the port to the R. Delegato Straordinario.

92. In 1827, Cappelli, head of the customhouse in Livorno, remarked that although in September and October of that year a few more ships entered Livorno than Genoa, "it was not without interest to note that the proportion of foreign to national ships arriving in the two ports was one to two in Genoa and thirteen to one in Livorno" (ASF, *Seg. Gab.*, f. 391. Livorno, 5 November 1827: Cappelli to Giuseppe Parer, Seg. Intimo., Florence). A comparative prospectus of the arrivals in Genoa and Livorno in 1831 noted that the excess of 149 arrivals in Genoa was due in large part to the exclusive commerce of the former with the ports of Spain, Portugal, and Sicily, commerce handled with the ships of its own nation, "the number of which is far superior to that of Tuscany" (ibid., *Misc. di Finanza*, series I, f. 13).

93. See note 80. See also Baldasseroni, *Leopoldo II*, p. 123.

94. ASF, *Misc. di Fin.*, Series II, f. 481, b. *Carteggio Governatore di Livorno*. Livorno, 10 October 1836: governor to the secretary of finance.

95. ASL, *Gov.*, f. 218. *Aff. Div.*, 1843. 7 May 1843: unsigned memorial.

96. ASF, *Fin. C.R.*, f. 67, b. *Marina Mercantile Toscana*. Livorno, 31 December 1849: captain of the port to the R. Delegato Straordinario.

97. Baldasseroni, *Leopoldo II*, p. 195.

98. In this matter the government moved with extreme caution. To protect its revenue it refused to lower charges levied on ships from states enjoying favored status but instead simply doubled anchorage charges on those that did not enjoy such status. For the moment the government refused to tamper with its customs charges. Special exemptions continued in force for the ships of all nations carrying cereals, then in critically short supply. For a good sense of the prevailing caution, see ASL, *Gov.*, f. 250. *Aff. Div.*, 1846, n. 271.

Livorno, 3 October 1846: governor of Livorno to the secretary of state.

99. Negotiation dated 23 February 1847. MS in the BLL.

100. For a copy of these agreements see ASF, *Fin. C.R.*, f. 67.

101. In 1819 the Tuscan government, through its consuls in Genoa, Marseilles, and Naples, supported the efforts of the monastery of Montenero (roughly five miles southeast of Livorno) to sell timber from its excellent stands ("the resource and commerce of that monastery") to foreign states for ship construction (ASL, *Gov.*, f. 1002. *Copialettere governatore*, 1819. Livorno, 13 February to Tuscan consuls in Genoa, Marseilles, and Naples).

102. Guido Sonnino, *Saggio sulle industrie, marina, e commercio in Livorno*, p. 60.

103. Rope manufacturers in Genoa and Marseilles used the poorer quality hemp produced in Piedmont (ASL, *Comunità*, f. 644. Livorno, 4 August 1830: *gonfaloniere*, "Prospetto."

104. Ibid. The rope industry in 1830 was one of the largest in Livorno. Rope was produced in four large and four small factories; in time of full production it employed from 200 to 300 workers (Francesco Bonaini, *Livorno, considerato nelle sue presenti condizioni e nel suo avvenire, principalmente in ragione del taglio dell'Istmo di Suez e della Centrale Italiana* (Florence, 1856), pp. 49–50.

105. Filippo Mariotti, "Delle esposizioni industriali e delle industrie toscane nel 1854," *AGA*, 2 (1855): 504.

106. ASL, *Gov.*, f. 1003. *Copialettere governatore*, 1820. Livorno, 26 June 1820: to the department of state.

107. Ibid.

108. ASF, *Estero*, f. 2623, b. *Carteggio Governatore di Livorno*, 1828. Livorno, 6 June: governor to the secretary of state.

109. ASL, *Comunità*, f. 638. Livorno, 29 June 1827: *gonfaloniere*, "Prospetto." Also ibid., f. 640. Livorno, 12 July 1828: *gonfaloniere*, "Prospetto."

110. ASF, *Estero*, f. 2622, b. *Carteggio Governatore di Livorno*, 1825–1826. Livorno, 10 November 1826: report of the governor. Also G. Vivoli, Ms, "Accrescimento progressivo," 1: p. 228. And G. Baldasseroni, *Leopoldo II*, pp. 102–103.

111. ASL, *Comunità*, f. 644. Livorno, 4 August 1830: *gonfaloniere*, "Prospetto."

112. ASF, *Misc. di Fin.*, Series II. f. 464, b. Marina. *Prospetto numerico dei bastimenti quadri di bandiera toscana addetti al porto di Livorno e all'Isola dell'Elba dell'anno 1820 all'anno 1850 inclusive.*

113. ASL, *Gov.*, f. 145. *Aff. Div.*, 1831. Livorno, 26 March 1831:

R. D'Angiolo, captain of the port, to the governor of Livorno. An extensive report on the state of the Tuscan merchant marine in 1829–30.

114. ASF, *Misc. di Fin.*, Series II. f. 464, b. Marina. "Prospetto."

115. ASL, *Gov.*, f. 145. *Aff. Div.*, 1831. Livorno, 26 March 1831: captain of the port to the governor of Livorno.

116. In 1842, Carlo Bargagli, the captain of the port, remarked on the difficulty of recruiting skilled captains who met the residence requirements and "who correspond ably and faithfully to the proprietors both in keeping down expenses and in executing shrewdly their commercial speculations." He attributed to this fact the slow rate of growth [*poco incremento*] of the merchant marine in Livorno after 1823 (ASL, *Gov.*, f. 199. *Aff. Div.*, 1842, no. 356. Livorno, 3 June 1842: Bargagli, captain of the port).

117. The poor quality of crewmen serving on Tuscan ships was a cause of general lament. Carlo Chigi remarked that as governor of Portoferraio (Elba), he had tried to maintain the Elban flag distinct from that of Tuscany, "because of the disagreeable practices [*cattive operazioni*] which were committed under the latter" (ASF, *Misc. di Fin.*, Series II. f. 464, b. Marina. Livorno, 9 January 1851: Chigi to the R. Delegato Straordinario, Livorno).

118. The situation, however, was not uniform throughout the entire duchy. On the island of Elba, which possessed poor soil and a numerous population, there existed a strong incentive for the development of an indigenous marine. Faced with the necessity of drawing their livelihood from the sea, the Elbans developed a fleet and in addition to fishing entered into commercial relations with the ports of Spain and southern France (Serristori, *Livorno ed i suoi traffici*, p. 10).

119. Ibid., pp. 10–11.

120. ASF, *Misc. di Fin.*, Series II. f. 464, b. Marina. Florence, 28 July 1852: Adriano Piccolommi to the minister of the interior.

121. Ibid., *Fin. C.R.*, f. 67. Livorno, 21 June 1850: Uffizio Principale di Marina Mercantile, "Nota dei bastimenti mercantili toscani che hanno lasciato la bandiera toscana e preso qualla gerosolimitana."

122. Ibid., *Misc. di Fin.*, Series II. f. 394 and 464.

123. Ibid., *Fin. C.R.*, f. 67. Livorno, 22 June 1850: Carlo Bargagli, captain of the port, to the R. Delegato Straordinario. Ibid., *Misc. di Fin.*, Series II. f. 394, b. 101. Alexandria: Tuscan consul, duke of Casigliano, to the minister of finance.

124. See chap. 7.

125. The number of large merchant ships based in Livorno was

73 in 1847, 76 in 1848, 70 in 1849, and 73 in 1850 (ASF, *Misc. di Fin.*, Series II, f. 464, b. Marina).

126. Bonaini, *Livorno*, pp. 10–11.

127. From 1846 to 1855 the number of middle-range ships in Livorno and Elba (*bastimenti di gran cabotaggio*) grew from 54 to 71 and the long-range ships (*lungo corso*) from 30 to 100 (ibid., p. 272). A good portion of the coastal trade was now being handled by steamships.

128. See the attacks made on the recommendation of the consul of Alexandria that the Tuscan merchant marine strive to win as many ships to its banner as possible (ASF, *Misc. di Fin.*, Series II, f. 464, b. Marina. Livorno, 9 January 1851: Carlo Chigi to the R. Delegato Straordinario; ASL *Gov.*, f. 319, n. 1347. *Aff. Div.*, 1849. Livorno, 19 January 1851: R. Delegato Straordinario to the minister of finance).

129. The governor estimated that the entire job would cost about 100,000 scudi and that over the long run it would pay for itself, since more commerce would be attracted to the port and ships using the new facilities could be assessed a small charge, which they would gladly pay for the added protection (ASL, *Gov.*, f. 1004. *Copialettere governatore*, 1827. 26 June: to the secretary of finance).

130. BLL, *Carte Vivoli*, f. 35 (1840). Livorno, 30 September 1840: A. Mighi to the captain of the port.

131. Ibid.

132. Ibid., f. 34 (1839). Florence, 8 May 1839: secretary of finance to the governor of Livorno.

133. Primarily in the *Annali di Livorno dalla sua origine sino all'anno di Gesù Cristo 1840* (Livorno, 1842–46), in four volumes. Despite its title, the *Annali* terminated at the time that the city fell under the domination of Francis II of Lorraine. Vivoli continued his chronicle of Livorno's history in the "Accrescimento progressivo," a two-volume manuscript in the ASF, *Seg. Gab.*, f. 670.

134. Ibid., map 13: "Livorno quale probabilmente dovrà addivenire allorquando farà d'uopo aprire il nuovo porto al fanale."

135. Ibid.

136. BLL, *Carte Vivoli*, f. 34 (1840). Livorno, 25 May 1840: Vivoli to the *segretario intimo del gran duca*.

137. Ibid., f. 35. Livorno, 1 August 1840: G. Vivoli to Fratelli Valaperta, Galli, and Brambilla, Natt. di P. Cajrati, Gug. Ulrich, C. E. Pasteur, and Gaddi di Angiolo. Given the secret nature of the negotiations, no official announcement was made when they were broken off. Vivoli remarked later that the project simply had "an

unhappy outcome." (Vivoli, *Progetto per ampliare il porto di Livorno grandemente, in tre anni e con lieve spesa* [Livorno, 1849], p. 12). Semiani E. Borgheri, one of the project's backers, remarked in 1847 that capital that had been pledged for the enterprise (largely by Milanese firms) was allowed simply to disperse (*Corriere livornese* 1, no. 12 [3 August 1847]).

138. ASL, *Gov.*, f. 284, n. 255. *Aff. Div.*, 1848. Livorno, 3 March 1848: captain of the port to the governor of Livorno.

139. *Corriere livornese* 1, no. 10 (27 July 1847).

140. ASL, *Gov.*, f. 266, n. 281. *Aff. Div.*, 1847. Livorno, 13 April 1848: Carlo Bargagli, captain of the port, to the governor.

141. This pressure took the form of petitions from individual merchants to the central government (many collected in ASL, *Gov.*, f. 266, n. 281. *Aff. Div.*, 1847), articles in the *Corriere livornese* (see especially the issues of July 27 and 30 and August 3 and 10, 1847), and the formal resolutions of the chamber of commerce (see ACCL, *Delib.*, 9 March, 12 April, 9 July, and 12 August 1847).

142. ACCL, *Delib.*, 12 April 1847.

143. G. Mori, "Linee e momenti," pp. 22–23.

144. Dalgas, "Ancora del porto di Livorno," *Corriere livornese* 1, no. 14 (10 August 1847).

145. ASF, *Fin. C.R.*, f. 52. Florence, 23 February 1836: R. Cempini to O. Forni, director of the customhouse, Livorno. Cempini urged Forni to solicit specifically the opinions of the merchants Filicchi, Dalgas, Ulrich, Grant, and Moor.

146. Ibid., Livorno, 27 Feb. 1836: Filicchi to Forni.

147. Ibid., Livorno, 7 March 1836: Ignazio Torricelli to Forni.

148. Ibid., Livorno, 11 March 1836: Dalgas to Forni.

149. Ibid., Livorno, 7 March 1836: Torricelli to Forni.

150. Ibid., Livorno, 8 May 1836: Forni to Cempini.

151. ASF, *Fin. C.R.*, f. 52. Florence, 10 April 1838: A. Kotzian to the grand duke.

152. Ibid. The announcement was dated 12 April 1838.

153. For the protests of Dini-Castelli that he had been despoiled by his principal financial intermediaries and his demands for compensation see ibid., Florence, 23 July 1838: Dini-Castelli to the secretary of finance. Also ibid., f. 53. Florence, 22 December 1840: Dini-Castelli to the secretary of finance.

154. Carlo Corsini, "La Prima ferrovia in Toscana: La Strada Ferrata Leopolda. Da Firenze a Livorno" (Tesi di Laurea in Storia Economica: Facoltà di Economia e Commercio, 1960–61), p. 424. I would like to take this opportunity to extend my thanks to Professor

Corsini for making his dissertation available to me and for facilitating my research in other ways.

155. Seven people signed a cover letter that accompanied a formal request for approval of the project from the chamber of commerce. The list was headed by Niccola Manteri and included Giorgio Pietro Ulrich and Fortunato Regini, who had condemned the project in 1836 (ASF, *Fin. C.R.*, f. 52. Livorno, 4 April 1838: Commissione provissoria per la strada ferrata to the chamber of commerce).

156. Ibid., Livorno, 5 April 1838: chamber of commerce to the governor of Livorno. See also ACCL, *Delib.*, 5 April 1838.

157. A position indicated in an unsigned note (probably from the secretary of finance) to the governor, dated 16 April 1838 (ASF, *Fin. C.R.*, f. 52).

158. Ibid., Florence, 24 April 1838: Fenzi-Senn, *Manifesto*.

159. Ibid.

160. Ibid., Florence, 5 June 1839: Fenzi-Senn to the grand duke. The number represented one-sixth of the total shares. The author of an article in *Hunt's Merchants' Magazine* (15 [July 1846]: 27) was mistaken when he remarked that "the Leopold railway had not a single shareholder in Tuscany."

161. ASF, *Fin. C.R.*, f. 52. Florence, 5 June 1839: Fenzi-Senn to the grand duke.

162. Ibid., Livorno, 20 December 1839: A. Kotzian to the secretary of finance, Cempini.

163. "As long as the doubt remains of whether or not the government will grant the requested concession one cannot hope for any new shareholder." (Ibid.)

164. Ibid. Though unsigned, a document in the same file entitled "Osservazioni sulle dimande [*sic*] qui appresso notate dei Signori Fenzi e Senn, e concernenti il privilegio per la costruzione della strada ferrata da Livorno a Firenze," provided, it seems, an official response to the demands. It opposed letting the promoters arbitrarily set freight and passenger rates and argued that they should be set to insure a maximum return of 6 percent to the investors. Also, it opposed absolutely any notion of partial construction, arguing that the line had to be built as a single unit.

165. ASF, *Fin. C.R.*, f. 52. Florence, 15 June 1840: Fenzi-Senn to A. Manetti, direttore R. Consiglio degl'Ingegneri: "We have the pleasure of informing [the government] that the entire capital of 30 million stipulated in our proclamation of 24 April 1838 has already been accumulated and assured."

166. Baldasseroni, *Leopoldo II*, p. 150.

167. Baruchello, p. 596.

168. *Hunt's Merchants' Magazine* 15 (July, 1846): 27.

169. "This first concession [the *Leopoldina*] stimulated also among us a speculative mentality geared to request the favor of other concessions of this sort" (Baldasseroni, *Leopoldo II*, p. 152).

170. Carlo Ilarione Petiti, *Delle strade ferrate italiane e del migliore ordinamento di esse. Cinque discorsi* (Capolago, 1845), p. 227.

171. *Hunt's Merchants' Magazine* 15 (July 1846): 27.

172. Baldasseroni, *Leopoldo II*, p. 152.

173. The preliminary concession for the line was awarded to Teodoro F. Mastiani Brunacci, Giorgio G. Zust, Michel'Angelo Barlugi and Son, Leone Arbib and Company, Enrico Rodolfo Ghebard, Angiolo Bartoli, and Bonaiuto Paris Sanguinetti (Petiti, *Delle strade ferrate*, p. 221).

174. Ibid.

175. Ibid., p. 242.

176. Ibid.

177. Ibid.

178. Ibid., pp. 221–222, 243.

179. See pp. 161–164.

180. Baldasseroni, *Leopoldo II*, p. 153.

181. C. De Biase, *Il Problema delle ferrovie nel Risorgimento italiano* (Modena, 1940), p. 16.

182. "Still [despite the abuses of speculation]—in the end, Tuscany found itself endowed with a more extensive rail network than normally, with its own efforts, it would have been able to construct" (ibid., p. 145).

183. See pp. 158–159.

184. Guerrazzi, "Osservazioni intorno al discorso della corona," in *Corriere livornese* 2, no. 138 (25 July 1848).

185. See pp. 217–218.

5: Social Attitudes and Voluntary Associations

1. Giuliano Ricci, "Sui caratteri generali dell'industria in Toscana," *GAT* 12 (1838): 283–297; idem, "Delle condizioni generali dell'agricoltura toscana," ibid., 365–381. Both articles were originally presented orally at the Labronica Academy.

2. Ricci, "Sui caratteri generali dell'industria," p. 291.

3. Ibid., p. 293; idem, "Delle condizioni generali dell'agricol-

tura," pp. 373–374. Obviously, the very self-sufficient character of the Tuscan economy was a sign of its relative backwardness. It was also, to Ricci, as we shall see, one of its relative strengths.

4. Ibid., pp. 379–380.

5. In addition to the published acts of the academy see Carlo Pazzagli, *L'Agricoltura toscana nella prima metà dell'800* (Florence, 1973).

6. The best introduction to this material is Carla Ronchi, "Liberismo e protezionismo in Toscana prima del 1848," *Studi storici* 1 (January–March 1960): 244–284.

7. BLL, *Carte Ricci*. Ms, "Educazione in Livorno," September–October 1838, pp. 4–5.

8. Ibid., pp. 8–9.

9. Ibid.

10. See Enrico Mayer, "Istituto dei Padri di Famiglia in Livorno," *Guida dell'educatore* 2 (September–October 1837): 331–335; *Regalamento della società* (dei Padri di Famiglia] (Livorno, 1840).

11. Ibid. A list of emeritus members of the school, which includes such important families as the Doveri, Dalgas, Grabau, Chelli, Fernandes, De Larderel, Binard, Pachò, D'Angiolo, Sansoni, and Macbean, shows that the institution made a definite appeal to the local elite.

12. "If many similar schools should be opened in Livorno, nothing better would I desire of my native city" (Ricci, Ms, "Educazione in Livorno," p. 11).

13. Ibid.

14. Antonio Benci, in his "Intorno all'educazione italiana per rispetto al popolo" (*Antologia* 32 [May 1826]: 113), indicated that the schools hoped to get the child through the entire course of study in two years. An inspector from the school in Pisa, however, reported that although the course in that city had been pared down to eighteen months it was still too long to allow many to complete it (Inspector Raimondo Merconi to the society in Pisa, ibid. 46 [June 1832]: 87).

15. Luigi Ridolfi, *Cosimo Ridolfi e gli istituti del suo tempo* (Florence, 1901), pp. 41–42. Francesco Baldasseroni, *Il Rinnovamento civile in Toscana* (Florence, 1931), pp. 104–105.

16. Società per la Diffusione del Metodo di Reciproco Insegnamento, "Adunanza 27 February 1826," *Antologia* 24 (November–December 1826): 89.

17. Ibid. 10 (May 1823): 80–81.

18. Scuole di reciproco insegnamento, "Rapporto," ibid., 33

(March 1829): 172.

19. Segretario della Società pel Mutuo Insegnamento di Livorno, "Terzo Rapporto," ibid., 43 (August 1831): 117.

20. Ibid.

21. Enrico Mayer, "Frammenti d'un viaggio pedagogico, no. 11. Friburgo—Il Padre Girad," *Guida dell'educatore* 2 (1837): 43–44.

22. Lambruschini, "Sull'Istruzione del popolo" (Memoria letta ai Georgofili 4 December 1831), *Antologia* 45 (January 1832): 76.

23. ASL, *Gov.*, f. 183, n. 146. Livorno, 5 February 1848: Governor Corsini to the Soprintendenza agli Studi.

24. Ibid., Florence, 8 February 1841: I. e R. Soprintendeza agli Studi to the governor of Livorno.

25. Francesco Pera, *Ricordi e biografie livornesi* (Livorno, 1867), p. 87.

26. This announcement, dated 25 August 1828, can be found in BLL, *Carte Vivoli*, f. 25 (1825).

27. Augusto Dussauge, secretary of the society in 1845, estimated the average annual cost of maintaining a child in the school at 28 lire. *Duodecimo Rapporto della Società del Mutuo Insegnamento* (Livorno, 1845), p. 21.

28. Carlo Sansoni, *Secondo Rapporto della Società del Mutuo Insegnamento* (Livorno, 1842), p. 6.

29. Giuseppe Doveri, "Terzo Rapporto della Società del Mutuo Insegnamento," *Antologia* 43 (August 1831): 110.

30. Doveri, *Quarto Rapporto della Società del Mutuo Insegnamento* (Livorno, 1833), p. 12.

31. Doveri, *Sesto Rapporto della Società del Mutuo Insegnamento* (Livorno, 1835), p. 5.

32. Membership in the society was restricted to Christians. In 1832 a society was formed in the Jewish community, and the philanthropic energies of the Jewish commercial elite were tapped for the support of its efforts to diffuse instruction among the Jewish population of the city.

33. ACCL, *Delib.*, 8 August 1834.

34. Augusto Dussauge, *Rapporto Asili Infantili* (Livorno, 1844), p. 8.

35. Dussauge, *Rapporto e regolamenti degli Asili Infantili* (Livorno, 1836), p. 7.

36. Ibid., p. 9.

37. Dussauge, *Rapporto sugli Asili Infantili* (Livorno, 1837), p. 19.

38. Dussauge, *Rapporto sugli Asili Infantili* (Livorno, 1846), pp. 4, 15. From a method devised by Ferrante Apporti, the original founder

of the kindergartens in Italy, it was estimated that there were roughly 6,000 children of both sexes of kindergarten age in Livorno.

39. Enrico Mayer, *Una Scuola elementare per le fanciulle povere da far seguito agli Asili Infantili: Pensieri diretti alle signore componenti la Società per gli Asili in Livorno* (Livorno, 1837).

40. Dussauge, *Rapporto sugli Asili Infantili di carità per le femmine in Livorno per gli anni 1840 e 1841* (Livorno, 1842).

41. As indicated from a perusal of Livornese marriage contracts in ANF.

42. The most cogent statement of this position is provided by Enrico Mayer in *Una Scuola elementare:* "Let us educate, therefore, our pupils in a way which is consonant with their future; let us not cut them out of their condition but improve this condition by studying the life of the people to learn the way to decrease the vices and increase the virtues. . . . Let instruction [technical training] continue to be graded according to the various social categories. Education, however, does not admit grades. It is the same for everyone, because morality and religion, which form its basis, still speak to the true equality of men. Good mother, good daughter, virtuous woman, these are titles that apply to all social categories. Nor are they vain titles. And woe to him who prevents the most abject among the daughters of the poor by practicing these virtues to carry her head high among those that the world styles more fortunate and grand."

43. The list included such families as the Bastogi, Cipriani, Dalgas, Doveri, Dussauge, Giera, Gordini, Grabau, Lardarel, Macbean, Manteri, Mayer, Pate, Sansoni, Senn, and Ulrich (report dated 2 July 1833 in the *Carte Vivoli,* f. 27). From 1833 to 1836, as membership in the society expanded from 56 to 113, it included many more important local families, among them the Bartolomei, Borgheri, Castelli, Grant, Malenchini, Ricci, Rodocanacchi, and Stub (ibid., f. 30).

44. For detailed breakdowns of the extraordinary income of the society see the reports of the secretary, Dussauge, dated 15 February 1840, 12 March 1842, and 22 March 1844, and found respectively in the *Carte Vivoli,* f. 35, 37, and 38.

45. "E cosa non può cotesto spirito? Nel mentre che educa, ed ingentilisce gli animi, crea dei prodigi. Dal Vosto piccolo Istituto alle più vaste imprese di pubblica e privata beneficenza, di cui van liete le prime capitali d'Europa, tutto è dovuto alla legge di associazione" (Dussauge, *Rapporto e regolamenti degli Asili Infantili* [Livorno, 1836], p. 7).

46. *Indicatore livornese* 1, no. 29 (14 September 1829). The opening of the savings bank in Florence was described in greater detail in a letter dated 5 July 1829 from the president of the new institution,

Cosimo Ridolfi, to the secretary of the administrative council, Ferdinando Tartini Salvatici (*GAT* 3 [1829]: 481–483).

47. "Manifesto per l'istituzione di una Cassa di Risparmio in Livorno," in *Documenti relativi alla Cassa di Risparmio di Livorno* (Livorno, 1836).

48. Livorno, 30 December 1837. Bali Ferdinando Sproni, *Rapporto annuale Cassa di Risparmio*, pp. 10–11.

49. "Manifesto," in *Documenti relativi alla Cassa di Risparmio di Livorno.*

50. G. Pachò, *Rapporto e prospetto della Cassa di Risparmio, Livorno 1840* (Livorno, 1841), p. 19.

51. Ibid. The adventitious character of the working-class population in Livorno, however, made the task especially difficult: "A great part of them live independent and nomadic existences in the very bosom of society and therefore do not experience the direct influence of the other more civilized and moral classes." In 1836 the administration of the bank had attempted to break down the popular prejudice by sending three savings books to each of the sponsors and urging them to distribute the books to those members of the lowest classes over whom they had the greatest influence, "exhorting them to profit from this praiseworthy institution which will bring them those benefits and advantages for which it is exclusively destined" (Livorno, 28 November 1836. Bali Ferdinando Sproni to the sponsors in BLL, *Carte Vivoli*, f. 30). From the subsequent appeals it appears that the plan proved successful.

52. "Manifesto," article 3, in *Documenti relativi alla Cassa di Risparmio.*

53. Ibid., articles 4, 8, and 9.

54. Ibid., article 20.

55. Pachò, *Rapporto Cassa di Risparmio, 1840*, p. 18.

56. Ibid., p. 10.

57. Ibid., pp. 22–23.

58. Pachò, Rapporto e prospetto della Cassa di Risparmio, Livorno, 1839 (Livorno, 1841), p. 21. While Pachò urged granting loans to private individuals, he suggested that they be secured by dependable cosigners rather than mortgages, which would require too much time to liquefy if the loans were forfeited.

59. Ibid.

60. Ibid., p. 6.

61. Ibid., p. 11.

62. Ibid.

63. Ibid., p. 18.

64. Ibid., pp. 18–19.

6. Merchants and Porters

1. Baruchello, p. 219.

2. On the lack of assimilation and the cultural roots of the resentment, see in particular F. D. Guerrazzi, *Raccolta di documenti relativi ai facchini forestieri detti di dogana* (Livorno, 1847).

3. Baruchello, p. 521.

4. ASF, *Fin. C.R.*, f. 17. Also Bortolotti, p. 85.

5. Ibid.

6. ACCL, *Delib.*, 22 March 1831.

7. "The Chamber limits itself for the moment to implore . . . that the government deign to order that the loading functions be left open to favor the local dockworkers [*facchini del paese*]. Without it, these miserable individuals would be forced to take bread bathed in the sweat of their labor out of the mouths of their innocent children and turn it over to those few individuals (already rich) who make up the privileged company of foreigners and who have not even participated in the work for which the fee has been paid." Ibid.

8. An anonymous opinion dated 21 April 1834 (Livorno) noted that the proposal would open the occupation to the blessings of free trade and free competition and would result in lower costs to the benefit of commerce in general and the individual merchants in particular: "portage charges no longer determined by the tariff which regulates the work of the *facchini di dogana* would visibly decline to the advantage of commerce and the class of merchants who would now be free to entrust the work to whomsoever would prove most advantageous to them." In Guerrazzi, *Raccolta di documenti relativi ai facchini*, p. 11.

9. ASL, *Gov.*, f. 155. *Aff. Div.*, 1834. 30 July: president of the Buon Governo to the governor of Livorno.

10. Ibid., f. 156. *Aff. Div.*, 1834: 22 September: Deputati Michel Angiolo Lanfranchi and Pietro Bassi.

11. Ibid., 9 October: president of the Buon Governo to the governor of Livorno.

12. Ibid., f. 1019. *Copialettere governatore*, 1835: 6 February to the president of the Buon Governo.

13. The sovereign dispatch reconfirming the rights of the privileged company was reported dated 27 March 1837. I have been unable to trace it in the archives or in the published collection of *leggi e bande*. I have discovered a notification of the administrative office of the Royal Revenues dated 28 May 1837 which declared that

"the company of dockworkers attached to the customhouse will continue to exercise the monopoly of which it is in possession in all of the city and free port in the cases and modes established by the orders in force. The obligations that it [the company] has contracted with the customhouse, commerce, and the [local] dockworkers who aid the company in the diverse tasks will remain in force. ASL., *Gov.*, f. 163. *Aff. Div.*, 1837. Court cases in which the privileges of the company were upheld against the merchants reported in ASF, *Fin. C.R.*, f. 17. 7 December 1837: *facchini* to Cempini.

14. ASL, *Gov.*, f. 187. *Aff. Div.*, 1841, n. 400. Livorno, 2 July 1841: governor to the secretary of finance.

15. Ibid., f. 186, n. 340. Livorno, 2 June 1841: Francesco Benigni and Giovanni Favilli to the governor of Livorno.

16. Ibid., nos. 240, 328. Livorno, 22 June 1841: Niccola Manteri, president of the chamber of commerce, to the governor of Livorno. The chamber of commerce in particular considered that the assertion would not be advantageous to commerce and would further oppress a large number of porters already suffering under the current system of privilege.

17. Ibid., f. 179, n. 713. Livorno, 6 November 1840: F. Rodocanacchi, president of the chamber of commerce, to the governor of Livorno.

18. Ibid., f. 185, n. 270. Livorno, 6 May/15 June 1841: governor of Livorno to the auditor.

19. Ibid., f. 272, n. 604. *Aff. Div.*, 1847. Livorno, 11 June 1847: auditor to the governor of Livorno.

20. ASF, *Seg. Gab. Append.*, f. 21. Report to the grand duke dated 23 July 1847. An unsigned report asserted that the deputies who really opposed the resolution were in the majority and that merchants were more apt to express support for the privileged company in private than in public. ASF, *Fin. Seg.*, f. 1149, "Conclusioni della commissione."

21. ASF, *Seg. Gab. Append.*, f. 21. Report to the grand ducal government, 27 July 1847.

22. Ibid., 4 September 1847.

23. ASL, *Gov.*, f. 272. Livorno, 9 August 1847: governor to the secretary of finance. Recommends that the privileged company be dissolved and that a commission be set up to work out a new regulation on the whole matter. Ibid., Florence, 20 August 1847: secretary of finance to the governor of Livorno. Announces the sovereign intention to abolish the privileged company and to appoint a commission to study the whole matter. Ibid., Livorno, 27

August 1847: governor to the secretary of finance. Reports the gratitude of the chamber of commerce for the above resolution in which it sees "great advantages and benefit for a large portion of the numerous population of this city."

24. ASF, *Seg. Gab. Append.*, f. 21. Report to the grand ducal government 27 August 1847. Reports an impromptu violin concert given on the steps of the house of Francesco Domenico Guerrazzi, who had written a work favorable to the cause of the local dockworkers. See n. 2, chapter 6.

25. Reported in the *Corriere livornese* 1, no. 15 (13 August 1847).

26. Both the governor and the *gonfaloniere* of the city reported on 28 September that the local dockworkers believed that they would be enjoying the rights of the dissolved privileged company by October 1 and that if they were disappointed there could be trouble. ASF, *Misc. di Fin. II*, f. 481, b: *Carteggio Governatore di Livorno*. Livorno, 28 September 1847: G. Sproni to the secretary of finance. ASL, *Gov.*, f. 272. *Aff. Div.*, 1847. 28 September: governor to the secretary of finance. The secretary of finance replied to the governor that time was needed to work out a regulation to take the place of one that had functioned for centuries, but assured him that the principle of abolition had already been established and was not under discussion. This fact, he said, circulated among the dockworkers should serve to eliminate any diffidence. Ibid., secretary of finance to the governor of Livorno. The report of the final negotiations between the government and the spokesman for the dockworkers, Luigi Fabbri, is in ibid. The final regulation dated 7 October is in ASF, *Fin. C.R.*, f. 19.

27. "The Company will be wholly dependent on the chamber of commerce and must observe all the provisions and regulations that it promulgates, pending, as needed, the approval of the superior government." Ibid., article 27.

28. Ibid., *Seg. Gab. Append.*, f. 21, Ins. 1. Report to the grand ducal government: 8 August 1847. "Some would propose a commercial police force made up of Livornese dockworkers excluding those from Bergamo."

29. For the January uprising see in particular Vittorio Marchi, *Memorie e rimembranze nella vita politica di Agostino Micheli* (Livorno, 1969). The events are also described in Enrico Mayer, "Una Parola al popolo Livornese," *Corriere livornese* 2, no. 62 (25 January 1848), and Giuliano Ricci, "I Fatti di Livorno," ibid., no. 63 (28 January 1848). See also BLL. *Carte Ricci.* "Copialettere," 13 January 1848: to Aglebert, Bologna.

30. Ibid.

31. Reported in the *Corriere livornese* 2, no. 59 (14 January 1848).

32. Ibid.

33. Ibid.

34. ASF, *Seg. Gab. Append.*, f. 23, b. 2. Florence, 15 January 1848: G. Baldasseroni, secretary of finance, to De Larderel, *gonfaloniere* of the city of Livorno.

35. ASL, *Gov.*, f. 280, n. 67. *Aff. Div.*, 1848. Livorno, 24 January: governor to the secretary of finance. Ibid., Florence, 26 January 1848: secretary of state to the governor of Livorno indicated that the requests had been granted.

36. *Corriere livornese* 2, no. 64 (1 February 1848).

37. BLL, *Carte Ricci.* "Memorie," 17 March 1848.

38. Ibid., 1 May 1848. "I have reason to believe that they [the *facchini*] along with the people of the *Venezia* quarter are the linchpins of internal order."

39. Ibid., 8 May 1848.

40. Ibid., 27 May 1848.

41. Ibid., 4 June 1848.

42. Ibid., 13 June 1848. In response to threats on Ricci's life. "I am receiving advice from all sides that my life is in danger: the *Veneziani* tell me not to fear, but I know that in secret they are watching over me. Oh! If all my friends were like them."

43. Ibid., 30 May 1848. Referring to Bartelloni and Guerrazzi.

44. BLL, *Carte Ricci.* "Copialettere." 11 June: to Gino Capponi.

45. ASL, *Gov.*, f. 279. *Aff. Div.*, 1848, n. 12. Livorno, 16 April 1848: A. Mochi, Report 44 on the discount bank.

46. Proclamation published in the *Corriere livornese* 12, no. 64 (1 January 1848).

47. Ibid., 12, no. 62 (25 January 1848).

48. BLL, *Carte Ricci.* "Memorie," 20 May 1848. "I facchini e i Veneziani dal conto loro si dispongono a troncar le braccia e le gambe ai perturbatori cui attribuiscono e con ragione lo stagnar dei commerci."

7: Pressure from Below

1. BLL, *Carte Ricci.* "Memorie," 27 January 1848.

2. Both incidents were reported in the *Corriere livornese* 1, no. 39 (5 November 1847).

3. The best summary of this whole affair is in Palmira Jona, *I*

Moti politici di Livorno, 1848–49 (Milan, 1909), pp. 20–22. For the murder of Roberti, one of the leaders of the society, and the lynching of an assistant accused of attacking a baker see ibid., p. 45.

4. A copy of the manifesto may be found in BLL, *Carte Vivoli,* f. 40. It was dated 23 October 1847 (Livorno) and signed by the leaders of the organization: Gustavo Lauri, Giorgio Roberti, Giorgio Malanima, Fran. Colombo, Giuseppe Bartolini, and Francesco Cambiaso.

5. Giuliano Ricci was struck by the novelty of the phenomenon in Livorno and thought it worthy of study. He described the incident in some detail, he said, "Because the phenomenon of a true coalition of workers is new for us, and merits study." Talking to the bakery workers, Ricci sensed the influence of foreign ideas: "Their words indicate ideas poorly digested and not theirs, ideas which clash sharply with the uncultivated way in which they are formulated and delivered." But he did not consider the phenomenon inherently threatening: "The outcome has convinced me ever more that among us popular indifference, if not antipathy, makes serious agitation of this sort impossible" (BLL, *Carte Ricci.* "Copialettere," 28 October 1847: to Cosimo Ridolfi).

6. The average wage of the baker's apprentice was five paoli. In addition, he could eat all the bread he wanted at work and take a pound of it home. Ricci considered the income of the baker's apprentice "much above the other monthly wage earners in the city" (ibid.).

7. ASL, *Gov.,* f. 294, n. 1015. *Aff. Div.,* 1848.

8. Ibid., n. 1010. Florence, 15 December 1848: minister of the interior to the governor of Livorno, announcing the final rejection of the bakery workers' petition.

9. Ricci reported that "the abuses of a mob which doesn't work and wishes to be paid have forced a suspension of the work" (BLL, *Carte Ricci.* "Memoria," 8 May 1848).

10. The incident reported in the *Corriere livornese* 2, no. 97 (9 May 1848). See also ASL, *Gov.,* f. 287, no. 462. *Aff. Div.,* 1848: "Popolare tumulto di muratori e manuali per asserta mancanza di lavori di loro professione in Livorno."

11. ASL, *Gov.,* f. 297, n. 1202. *Aff. Div.,* 1848. Livorno, 28 December 1848.

12. The protests of the two groups were linked because traditionally stevedores were drawn exclusively from the oldest active sailors (*"agli individui addetti alla marina più anziani"*); ibid., f. 315, n. 1093. *Aff. Div.,* 1849. Livorno, 27 September 1849: captain of the port, Bargagli, to the Delegato Straordinario.

13. "The captains and owners of coastal vessels in Livorno, not obligated by a fixed tariff, fix the terms for the sailors they enroll as they please in such a way that all losses are borne by them. In this way they become an object of speculation for the ship owners . . . and in their hands the sailors become material objects, much as the tools of production are in the hands of the artisan" (ibid., f. 285, n. 343. *Aff. Div.*, 1848. Livorno, March 1848).

14. Ibid., f. 290. *Aff. Div.*, 1848, n. 694. Livorno, 1 July 1848: *facchini* to the *gonfaloniere*.

15. Ibid., Livorno, 3 July 1848: *gonfaloniere* to the governor of Livorno. Ibid., f. 297. *Aff. Div.*, 1848, n. 1202. Florence, 4 January 1849: minister of finance, Adami, to the governor of Livorno. Ibid., f. 315. *Aff. Div.*, 1849, n. 1093. Livorno, 27 Sept. 1849: captain of the port, Bargagli, to the Delegato Straordinario.

16. The resolution is quoted in the BLL, *Carte Sproni*. Lucca, 22 September 1876: P. Pieri, G. Chica, Corte Appello, *Comparsa Conclusionale Facchini Livornesi Manovella vs. Real Governo*.

17. Ibid.

18. See chapter 6, n. 18.

19. BLL, *Carte Sproni*. Livorno, 6 July 1870: Luigi Fabbri, "Parere per la verità a favore della carovana dei facchini di manovella di Livorno."

20. ACCL, *Delib.*, 28 Nov. 1848.

21. ASL, *Gov.*, f. 277. *Aff. Div.*, 1847, n. 972. Livorno, 3 June 1848: *facchini di travaso* to the governor of Livorno.

22. In a letter of December 1847 in ibid.

23. Ibid., Livorno, 12 May 1848, chamber of commerce (T. Borgheri, president) to the governor of Livorno.

24. Ibid., Livorno, 24 June 1848: governor to the secretary of finance, Florence.

25. Ibid., f. 273, n. 760. *Aff. Div.*, 1847. Zavoranti Livornesi, "Reclami a carico dei navicellai; Regolamento disciplinare," notes that a proposed regulation had been transmitted to the governor on 27 August 1841.

26. Ibid., Livorno, 7 November 1847. C. Bargagli, Uffizio di Sanità to the governor of Livorno.

27. Ibid., f. 295., n. 1074. *Aff. Div.*, 1848. Livorno, 3 January 1849: governor to the minister of finance, Florence.

28. Ibid., f. 310, n. 764. *Aff. Div.*, 1849. Livorno, 26 July: Vincenzo Paolini to the Delegato Straordinario on efforts to block boats without suitable equipment from carrying ballast. Ibid., Livorno, 27 July 1849: captain of the port to the Delegato Straordinario. Notes complaints of captains in the port on the excessive price of ballast. Ibid.,

f. 311, n. 805. Livorno, 9 July 1849: Lori and Company to the Delegato Straordinario. Complaints about threats made by the "traditional company" on the life of Pietro Damerini, whom Flori had commissioned to haul ballast.

29. Ibid., f. 275. *Aff. Div.*, 1847. Livorno, 9 November: auditor to the governor.

30. Ibid., Livorno, 4 November 1847: chamber of commerce (Elia L. Panà, president) to the governor.

31. BLL, *Carte Ricci.* "Memorie," 28 February 1848.

32. Ibid., 6 July 1848.

33. ASL, *Gov.*, f. 295, n. 1070. *Aff. Div.*, 1848. Florence, 1 February 1849: proclamation of the minister of finance, Adami.

34. Ibid., f. 303, n. 280. *Aff. Div.*, 1849. Livorno, 28 March: *consiglieri del governo.* "Pending the return of our economic principles . . . which we hope to assist in the near future by revoking completely the privileges inauspiciously conceded to the different portage services in this city, we feel obliged to recommend granting the requests given the clearly established precedents and our extraordinary circumstances."

35. Ibid., f. 302, n. 267. *Aff. Div,* 1849. Livorno, n.d.: *consiglieri del governo* to the governor of Livorno.

36. Ibid., f. 304, n. 282. Livorno, 23 March 1849: Delegato Governatore di San Leopoldo to the governor of Livorno.

37. See Guerrazzi's strong public pronouncement on this theme in the *Corriere livornese* 3, no. 273 (5 January 1849).

38. ASL, *Gov.*, f. 304. No. 282. *Aff. Div.*, 1849. Livorno, 5 April 1849: Commissione Governativa to the Segreteria di Stato, Florence: "Despite the open violation of economic principles, the commission proposes for political necessity that it be conceded."

39. Ibid., f. 290, n. 750. *Aff. Div.*, 1848. Livorno, 20 July: chamber of commerce (Torello Borghieri, president) to the governor of Livorno.

40. Ibid., f. 295, n. 1060. Livorno, 20 December 1848: governor of Livorno to the ministry of finance.

41. The decree—dated 18 May 1849—abolished all privileges accorded to "consortia or companies of porters, and other Livornese laborers" authorized between 1 November 1848 and 11 April 1849. Ibid., f. 305, n. 392. *Aff. Div.*, 1849. Florence, 18 May 1849.

42. ACCL, *Delib.*, 16 July 1850. The chamber complained "how impossible it was for the chamber of commerce, both for its dignity and for the loss of time, to involve itself in the details of the dockworker company and to police its affairs."

8: Trauma of Merchant Benevolence

1. Peter N. Stearns, *1848: The Revolutionary Tide in Europe* (New York, 1974), provides the best recent synthesis. Priscilla Robertson, *Revolutions of 1848: A Social History* (New York, 1952), is still useful, particularly for the bibliography on Italy. Giorgio Candeloro, *La Rivoluzione nazionale 1846–1849.* Storia dell'Italia moderna, vol. 3 (Milan, 1960), provides the best synthesis and bibliography for the revolutions in Italy. Delio Cantimori's article "Italy in 1848" (in *The Opening of an Era: 1848*, edited by Francois Fejtö [New York, 1966], pp. 114–142) provides an intelligent outline of the Italian situation in English. Charles Breunig's *The Age of Revolution and Reaction* (2d ed. [New York, 1977]) provides a good general introduction to the period.

2. Giorgio Candeloro, *Dalla restaurazione alla rivoluzione nazionale 1815–1846.* Storia dell'Italia moderna, 3d ed. (Milan, 1958), 2: 353–364.

3. For Venetian events I am heavily indebted to Paul Ginsborg, *Daniele Manin and the Venetian Revolution of 1848–49* (New York, 1979). Ginsborg also does an excellent job of setting Venetian events within a general Italian and European context.

4. Candeloro, 2: 275–310.

5. Carlo Francovich, *Albori socialisti nel Risorgimento* (Florence, 1962), pp. 139–173.

6. On the importance of the University of Pisa for the formation of a radical culture among Tuscan youth see Ersilio Michel, *Maestri e scolari dell'università di Pisa nel Risorgimento nazionale (1815–1870)* (Florence, 1949).

7. Aside from the useful biographical information found in the *Enciclopedia italiana* and the *Dizionario del Risorgimento nazionale*, I have found to be particularly illuminating Guerrazzi's *Note autobiografiche e poema* (Florence, 1899) and his *Apologia della vita politica scritta da lui medesimo* (Florence, 1851).

8. Benedetto Croce, *La Letteratura della Nuova Italia: Saggi critici* (Bari, 1914), 1: 27–44.

9. Cesare Spellanzon, *Storia del Risorgimento e dell'unità d'Italia* (Milan, 1936), 3: 119–120.

10. Agostino Gori, *Storia della rivoluzione italiana durante il periodo delle riforme* (Florence, 1897), p. 77; Antonio Zobi, *Storia civile della Toscana* (Florence, 1852), 5: 27.

11. Gori, p. 81; Spellanzon, pp. 117–118, 180.

12. Zobi, p. 41.

13. Gori, p. 47.
14. Ibid., p. 348.
15. Ibid., p. 349.
16. Zobi, pp. 307–322; Giovanni La Cecilia, *Memorie storico-politiche dal 1820–1876* (Rome, 1877), 4: 105, 114–115.
17. Ibid., p. 108; ibid., 5: 143; Gori, p. 467.
18. La Cecilia, 4: 116.
19. See pp. 196–197.
20. See table 11.
21. See p. 51.
22. See pp. 183, 333–334 n. 38.
23. See pp. 187–188.
24. The best description of this whole incident and of the official and private relief efforts can be found in ASF, *Seg. di Gab.*, f. 670. G. Vivoli, Ms, "L'Accrescimento progressivo di Livorno," vol. 1, entry for 1817. See also the random materials in BLL, *Carte Vivoli*, f. 21.
25. ASL, *Comunità*, f. 633. Livorno: 26 January 1824. F. Sproni, "Prospetto."
26. Ibid.; ibid., f. 635. Livorno, 19 February 1825: *gonfaloniere*, "Prospetto."
27. Baldasseroni, *Il Rinnovamento civile*, p. 372.
28. *Corriere livornese* II, no. 79 (24 March 1848).
29. ASF, *Stato Civile*, 12130. "Comunità di Livorno. Stato delle Anime, Parrocchia Santissima Trinità, 1841."
30. ASL, *Comunità*, f. 636. Livorno, 20 February 1826: *gonfaloniere*, "Prospetto." R. Busacca, "Sulle condizioni economiche delle Toscana relativamente al commercio delle manifatture," *AGA* 2 (1855): 399.
31. See above pp. 125–127.
32. Guido Quazza, *La Lotta sociale nel Risorgimento. Classi e governi dalla Restaurazione all'unità (1815–1861)* (Turin, 1951), p. 106; Gori, pp. 175–176.
33. Ibid.
34. Nicola Badaloni, *Democratici e socialisti livornesi nell'Ottocento* (Rome, 1966), p. 80.
35. Ibid.
36. ASL, *Governatore*, f. 266, n. 281 supplies the figures for large square-rigged ships arriving in the port from 1827 to 1846. ASF, Fin. C. R., f. 101 supplies the figures for 1847–1852. On the general relationship of subsistence crisis and depression in 1848 see Ernest Labrousse, "Panoramas de la crise," in *Aspects de la crise et de la depression de l'économie française au milieu du XIXe siècle, 1846–1851*

(Bibliothèque de la Révolution de 1848, *Études* XIX) (La Roche–Sur–Yon, 1956), pp. iii–xiv.

37. See pp. 208–209.

38. See pp. 204–209.

39. Badaloni, pp. 90–91.

40. Quazza, p. 180.

41. Giuliano Ricci, "Copialettere," 20 October 1847.

42. Ibid., 28 October 1847.

43. Spellanzon, p. 460.

44. Ibid.

45. Zobi, 5: 291–292. Zobi argues that Guerrazzi was not the author of the anonymous pamphlet.

46. Ibid., p. 292.

47. Ibid., p. 293.

48. Spellanzon, p. 460.

49. Ibid., p. 416.

50. Ibid.

51. Ibid., pp. 461–462.

52. Pietro Martini, ed., *Il Quarantotto in Toscana. Diario inedito del Conte Luigi Passerini de'Rilli* (Milan, n.d.), p. 61.

53. Ibid., p. 63.

54. Ibid., p. 64.

55. Ibid., p. 96.

56. Ibid.

57. Ibid., p. 98.

58. Ibid.

59. Ibid., pp. 99–100.

60. Ibid., p. 100.

61. Ibid.

62. Ibid., p. 111.

63. Ibid., p. 112.

64. Ibid., pp. 112–114. This source presents three accounts of the affair which, despite their different biases, generally agree on the sequence of events. These include the *Corriere livornese*, the official *Gazzetta di Firenze*, and the memoirs of the radical leader Giovanni La Cecilia.

65. Ibid., p. 113.

66. Ibid., pp. 114–116 reproduces proclamations of the central government dated 3 and 4 September 1848.

67. Ibid., pp. 126–127 reproduces material from the *Gazzetta di Firenze* and the *Verbali dell'Assemblea*.

68. Ibid., p. 123.

69. Ibid., pp. 128–129 reproduces the minutes of the meeting drawn from an *Estratto dal registro della communità di Livorno.*
70. Ibid., pp. 136–137 reproduces the official report from F. Tartini, G. Bondi, and A. Duchoque to the minister of the interior.
71. Ibid., pp. 138–139.
72. Ibid., p. 141.
73. On Montanelli's political career see Giuseppe Montanelli, *Memorie sull'Italia e specialmente sulla Toscana dal 1814 al 1850* (Florence, 1963).
74. Vittorio Marchi, *Memorie e rimembranze nella vita di Agostino Micheli* (Livorno, 1969), p. 85.
75. On October 13 a large delegation arrived at the railroad station in Florence from Livorno and marched to the Pitti Palace (the royal residence) shouting for the creation of a Montanelli-Guerrazzi ministry (P. Martini, ed., *Diario Passerini,* p. 148). On October 20 a large demonstration was held in Livorno to protest efforts to select moderate candidates for a new ministry (ibid., pp. 150–151). At the same time, La Cecilia received a short note from Guerrazzi: "La Cecilia! Tomorrow I need a loud popular demonstration. The *Corriere* [*livornese*] must provide it. The intrigues and plots of the moderates are incredible; they need to be silenced by fear" (ibid., p. 151; La Cecilia, 4: 231).
76. *Monitore toscano,* 15 December 1848, cited in Badaloni, *Democratici e socialisti Livornesi,* p. 128.
77. Ibid.
78. Ada Foà, "La Politica interna del governo provisorio toscano," *Archivio Storico Italiano* 77 (1919): 233.
79. Announcement in the *Corriere livornese* 3, no. 308 (12 February 1849).
80. Ibid., 17 February 1849.
81. Ibid.; Foà, p. 241.
82. Ibid.
83. Ibid., pp. 242–243.
84. Ibid., p. 243.
85. Ibid., p. 244.
86. Marchi, pp. 125–126.
87. Ibid., pp. 272–273.
88. Pietro Bastogi, *Della carta monetata e dei suoi effetti in Toscana. Discorso di Pietro Bastogi scritto in Pisa il 10 Gennaio 1849* (Pisa, 1849), cited in V. Marchi, *Memorie e rimembranze,* p. 273. I have been unable to find a copy of the original pamphlet.
89. Foà, p. 244. In a speech before parliament on January 25,

Guerrazzi rejected a forced loan as difficult to assign, perilous to collect, and impossible to execute quickly. (*Assemblee del Risorgimento,* vol. 5; Tuscany, no. 2, *Seduta* 25 January 1849, p. 374.)

90. Foà, p. 245.

91. Ibid., p. 246.

92. Guerrazzi, *Apologia della vita politica,* pp. 145–153.

93. For Guerrazzi's views on the viability of a republican form of government see *Corriere livornese* 2 (8, 11, and 15 April 1848).

94. P. Martini, ed., *Diario Passerini,* p. 277.

95. Ibid., pp. 249–250.

96. Ibid., pp. 256–261.

97. Ibid., p. 250.

98. Ibid., pp. 253, 255.

99. Foa, p. 261.

100. Ibid. notes that despite the reforms, sympathy for the grand duke remained strong. With the collapse, virtually all the economic provisions of the provisional government were abolished without visible protest.

101. La Cecilia, 5: 233.

102. P. Martini, *Diario livornese: Ultimo Periodo della rivoluzione del 1849* (Livorno, 1961), pp. 50–55.

103. Ibid., p. 62.

104. Ibid., pp. 68–74.

105. The fate, first, of the local companies of volunteers isolated in the Tuscan countryside and then of the city as it faced an advancing Austrian army kept the state of opinion at a fever pitch. P. Martini's report for April 16 is typical. "Early, the central plaza and the surrounding roads were crowded with armed men, menacing in their appearance and their language. Merchants and industrialists—seeing that it would be a day of strikes and of general disorder [*gran bailamme*]—did not even attempt to put their hands on their keys (ibid., p. 113).

106. Attacks on the bakeries occurred on the mornings of April 16 and 17. These attacks possessed a class character, because at a time of scarcity only the rich could afford bread and thus avoid the less palatable substitutes. In response to the riots, the government sought to obtain the necessary flour by permitting bakers to send grain to mills in the hinterland—at Pisa and Calci—to be ground into flour, "with the responsibility that they bring back as many sacks of flour as sacks of grain exported" (*Corriere livornese* 3 [17 April 1849]). This provision, however, could work only as long as these areas were not under the full control of the forces of reaction.

107. For the inability of public works to meet more than the needs of a small percentage of the population see *Corriere livornese* 2, no. 79 (24 March 1848). For clashes at the sites in April 1849 see P. Martini, *Diario livornese,* p. 105. For the sad state of public finance see ibid., p. 283.

108. The loans were announced April 25 (ibid., pp. 211–212).

109. Ibid., pp. 184–185. For the importance of a Jacobin legacy in the resistance see also Badaloni, *Democratici e socialisti livornesi,* p. 146 and F. Catalano, "Socialismo e comunismo in Italia dal 1846 al 1849," *RSR* 38 (1951): 314. In response to Guarducci, a member of the crowd shouted that "democracy cannot recognize or admit class distinctions" and concluded that "to resolve our cause, the sole competent sovereign is the offended party—that is, the sovereign people [*il popolo re*]!"

110. P. Martini, *Diario livornese,* p. 164.

111. Ibid., pp. 207, 241, 279, 287.

112. The stipend was initiated on April 23. In announcing his decision to accept it, Guarducci said that he was turning over his officer's pay in the civil guard to the families of those who had helped to defend the fatherland and of those who had been killed or wounded in the Florentine reaction (ibid., p. 201).

113. Moderates on the governing commission (such as Dr. Gaetano Salvi) consistently sought to restrain the radicals and permit free emigration from the city, on occasion even carrying families past armed vigilantes waiting at the gates of the city to detain them (ASF, *Seg. di Gab., Append.* f. 28, b. 12: "Rapporto del Dottor Gaetano Salvi concernente la di lui condotto nel disimpegano delle proprie ingerenze come Deputato al Governo di Livorno dal 19 Aprile a tutto il 6 Maggio 1849."

9: The End of Reform

1. Livorno's position in the state marked it for special fiscal exactions. In March 1848 the government imposed an extraordinary 700,000 lire tax on Tuscan commerce and indicated that over half (360,000 lire) would be imposed on Livorno (ACCL, *Delib.,* 1 April 1848). The move was especially resented by the merchant community, as the burden placed on the port city was more than three times that placed on the capital (ibid., 4 May 1848; 28 July 1848). A year later the exaction was transformed into a 140,000 lire tax and a 220,000 lire interest-bearing loan (ibid., 29 May 1849). In April 1849,

as the city prepared to defend itself against an Austrian army, the chamber of commerce consented to grant an immediate loan of 100,000 lire to the commune (ibid., 22 and 23 April 1849). Following the city's defeat, the Austrian general D'Aspre imposed on the city a war tax of 1.2 million lire, to be paid in twenty-four hours (ibid., 17 May 1849). Finally, to meet the grave financial situation in the postrevolutionary period, the government doubled the commercial tax on Livorno's imports and levied a forced loan on the state of 30 million lire. (On the commercial tax see Luigi Dal Pane, *La Finanza toscana dagli inizi del secolo XVIII alla caduta del Granducato* [Milan, 1965], p. 364; on the forced loan and other exactions of the period see Baruchello, *Livorno,* pp. 599–602.)

The immediate effect of these measures was to aggravate bitterness toward Florence, to enhance the separateness of foreign merchant houses in the city, and to stimulate several families to formally renounce commerce. (For the resentment toward the relatively light burdens placed on the commerce of Florence see ACCL, *Delib.,* 28 July 1848.) Efforts of foreign merchant houses in the city to avoid paying the charges imposed on Livornese commerce were repeatedly rejected, even when these efforts were backed by the representatives of their native states (ibid., 22 April and 28 August 1849). The government, however, was willing to exempt those who could prove that they had ceased to engage in commercial activity (ibid., 12 August 1849).

2. BLL, *Carte Ricci.* "Copialettere." Livorno, 22 March 1848: to Landucci.

3. Ibid., "Memorie," 24 August 1848.

4. Ibid., 29 August 1848.

5. Ibid., 12 September 1848.

6. ASL, *Gov.,* f. 313. *Aff. Div.,* 1849, n. 917. Livorno, 11 September 1849: Delegato Straordinario to the minister of public instruction, Florence. Ibid., Florence, 9 January 1850: minister of public instruction to the Delegato Straordinario reported the government's rejection of the petition. See also ASF, *Fin. C.R.,* b. 1849: 25 August to 11 September, *Asili Infantili di Livorno.*

7. Raffaello Lambruschini, "Considerazioni sull'insegnamento del popolo," *Il Pensiero pedagogico del Risorgimento,* edited by Lamberto Borghi (Florence, 1958), pp. 229–230.

8. ACCL, *Delib.,* 16 June 1849.

9. A law on public and private instruction in June 1852 placed primary education under the control of a new ministry of public instruction and charity.

10. See pp. 155–157.

11. See pp. 157–158.

12. On the chamber's recommendation see ACCL, *Delib.*, 10 and 18 February 1851. On the description of the port see Alessandro Cialdi, *Studi idrodinamici nautici e commerciali sul porto di Livorno e sul miglioramento ed ingrandimento del medesimo* (Florence, 1853), p. 68.

13. A decree of 13 May 1851 entrusted to a French engineer, Poirel, "the task of systematizing the port of Livorno" (Baruchello, *Livorno*, p. 603).

14. ACCL, *Delib.*, 14 April 1852 and 29 March 1853.

15. On the military argument see G. Mori, "Linee," p. 22. On the Dalgas memorandum see pp. 158–159.

16. The value of discounted paper in 1853 was 35,736,322 lire, and in 1856, 35,785,788 lire. This surpassed the previous high of 23,446,144 lire in 1840 (ASL, *Gov.*, f. 641, n. 530).

17. Ibid., f. 531, n. 693. Florence, 5 May 1856: minister of finance to the governor of Livorno.

18. Ibid., 30 August 1856: minister of finance to the governor of Livorno.

19. ASF, *Fin. C.R.*, Livorno, 9 July 1856: A. Mochi, commissioner of the discount bank.

20. See pp. 196–200.

21. See pp. 208–209.

22. From the deliberations of the chamber of commerce, problems occurred in the following areas: First, conflicts over jurisdictional rights: these included jurisdictional disputes between the companies of the Manovella and Sacco and claims by them and other groups for exclusive rights in handling new sectors of the city's trade. Second, internal disputes in the companies: these included grievances about work assignments, worker insubordination and supervisor arbitrariness, and efforts by retiring workers to handpick their successors. Third, worker dishonesty, which consisted principally of thefts of merchandise passing through the city and of fraud in measuring. Fourth, disputes over existing tariffs, which produced two major work stoppages.

23. ACCL, *Delib.*, 6 May 1851 and 29 January 1857.

24. Ibid., 21 September 1853 and 24 November 1853.

25. Ibid., 25, 28 April 1860 and 16 July 1860 contains information and responses for the first strike of the dockworkers; 5, 6 April 1865 contains information and responses for the second strike.

26. This process culminated in the abolition of the constitution in 1852 and in a further weakening of municipal authority in 1853.

A clear, perceptive analysis of this process can be found in the following works of Giuseppe Pansini: "Gli ordinamenti comunali in Toscana dal 1849 al 1853," *RST* 2 (1956): 33–75, and "I Liberali moderati toscani e la crisi amministrativa del granducato," ibid., 5 (1959): 29–154.

27. J. Luchaire, *Essai sur l'évolution intellectuelle de l'Italie de 1815 à 1830* (Paris, 1906), pp. 230–231.

28. Giuliano Ricci, *Cenni sopra le basi del sistema municipale toscano per occasione della legge del 30 maggio 1847* (Livorno, 1847), p. 4.

29. Ibid.

30. Leopoldo Galeotti, *Della riforma municipale. Pensieri e proposte* (Florence, 1847), p. 26.

31. It is only fair to note that this interpretation of the evolution of liberal opinion clashes in one or more respects with other views of the liberal phenomenon in Tuscany. It is in fundamental disagreement with the interpretation of Raffaelo Cempini that in the first half of the nineteenth century, "Tuscan moderates 'did not shake themselves much from a paternalism little more enlightened and far ranging than of old," and that in them "there did not seem yet mature a true liberal consciousness" (R. Cempini, *Contributo alla storia del 1848 in Toscana*, in *Il 1848 nella storia italiana ed Europa*, edited by Ettore Rota, vol. 2 (Milan, 1948). It also disagrees with his view that "such a consciousness would be born later, during the decade of foreign domination, along with the belief in national unification [*coscienza unitaria*]" (ibid.).

While disagreeing with Paolo Alatri's implicitly negative view of Tuscan liberalism in the first half of the nineteenth century, this interpretation generally supports his assertion that during the 1850s, after the restoration of the grand ducal regime, "there was not progress of a liberal consciousness . . . [but instead] a general retreat that touched all spheres" (P. Alatri, "I Moderati toscani, il richiamo del granduca e il decennio di preparazione." *RSR* 39 no. 4 [1952]: 354). While agreeing with Giuseppe Pansini's assessment of the centralizing tendencies of the grand ducal government after 1849, my evidence does not support his view of the continued strength of municipal sentiments in the 1850s. Rather, it follows the views of Ernesto Ragionieri ("Politica e amministrazione nello stato unitario," *Studi storici* 1 [1960]: 472–512), Carlo Pischedda ("Appunti ricasoliani (1853–1859)," *RSI* 68 [1956]: 37–79), and Arnoldo Salvestrini (*I Moderati toscani e la classe dirigente italiana* [Florence, 1965]) that after 1850, moderate-liberals in Tuscany were more concerned with order and good administration than with freedom. Having supported Louis

Napoleon's coup d'état in France, they transferred their support from the grand ducal regime in Tuscany to Victor Emmanuel in Piedmont when it appeared that the grand duke's connection with Austria and his refusal to actively support the drive for national liberation might provoke a renewed outbreak of popular disorder.

32. ASF, *Fin. C.R.*, f. 101. Livorno, 23 October 1857: Cav. Martellini, captain of the port, to L. Bargagli, governor of Livorno. The situation was well summarized by the captain of the port (Cantini) in 1854: "If the movement of cereals in this city has been extraordinary, this must be attributed to the unlimited freedom that has been given to speculators of this and similar goods for which this port has become a center of activity. One can predict that insofar as the principle of free trade spreads, Livorno will lose its extraordinary advantage, given the tendency of things left to their natural course to balance themselves out" (ASF, *Misc. di Fin. II*, f. 464. Livorno, 1854: comments of Cantini, captain of the port). For an understanding of Livorno's decline as a free port of deposit I am indebted to Patricia Herlihy ("Russian Trade and the Mediterranean Markets, 1774–1861," p. 204; and "Russian Wheat and the Port of Livorno, 1794–1865," *Journal of European Economic History* 5 [1976]: 45–68).

33. ACCL, *Delib.*, 25 July 1862.

34. The memorial commissioned by the chamber was presented at its meeting of 27 December. Its dire predictions are summarized in Baruchello, *Livorno*, p. 621.

35. Giovanni Baldasseroni, *Livorno ed il suo portofranco considerato nel passato, nel presente e nell'avvenire da un vecchio livornese, socio dell'Accademica Labronica* (Florence, 1863). Wrongly attributed by G. Mori in "Linee" (p. 41) to T. Pergola.

36. Ibid., p. 39.

37. Ibid., pp. 13–14.

38. Ibid., pp. 508, 511.

39. Ibid., pp. 41–42, 48.

40. Sergio Camerani, "Lo Spirito pubblico in Toscana nel 1859," *RST* 2 (1957): 103.

41. Ibid., p. 114. See also Marion Miller, "Communes, Commerce and Coloni: Internal Divisions in Tuscany 1830–1860," *Historical Journal* 21 (1978): 844.

42. ACCL, *Delib.*, 7 May 1849; Baruchello, *Livorno*, pp. 613–614.

43. *Il Romito* I (15 October 1859). Another attack appeared in *l'Indipendenza italiana* (n. 62). A moderate reply to this article appeared in *La Nazione* 1 (9 October 1859).

44. *La Nazione* 1 (24 October 1859).

45. More immediate evidence for this position was presented in 1859. In December the British ambassador to the court at Turin, Sir James Hudson, asserted that "the Livornese would be content to lose the free port in return for the political improvements achieved with the annexation to Piedmont" (reported in ACCL, *Delib.*, 23 February 1860). The chamber formally protested Hudson's opinion, which was reported in all the newspapers, and empowered Pietro Bastogi—then in Florence—to deny the statement "and thus tranquilize the city" (ibid.). Bastogi, though, refused to intervene on the grounds that Tuscany had not yet voted for annexation to Piedmont and that the chamber, therefore, should not admit that its rights were in question (ibid., 1 March 1860).

46. *Lo Zenzero* (20 October 1862).

47. Ibid.

48. *Sull'abolizione delle franchigie della città di Livorno. Poche Parole d'un Livornese* (Livorno, 1867). Though the writer of this pamphlet is anonymous, its contents closely reflect the views of Giuseppe Ferrigni, a local manufacturer of rope and sail and a member of the chamber of commerce.

49. Ibid., p. 25.

50. Ibid., p. 21.

51. Ibid., pp. 13–14, 57. The author argued that the elimination of the city's privileges would increase the prices of sugar, coffee, and pepper but would lower the prices of such basic articles of mass consumption as wine, oil, meat, cheese, flour, pasta, and bread.

52. ACCL, *Delib.*, 2 and 23 January 1863 indicates that this had been partially accomplished with the preparation of a memorial by the president of the chamber, Francesco Malenchini: Camera di Commercio e Arti di Livorno, *Memoria sulle franchigie commerciali della città. Al Governo e al parlamento* (Livorno, 1863). Ibid., 9 and 22 December 1863 indicates that another memorial on the issue had been prepared by Tomaso Corsi. Both, officially sanctioned by the chamber, modified the tone of strident protest and more or less openly acknowledged the diminished role that the city's privileges continued to play in its commercial life and the necessity of government help in enabling the city to adjust to a very different economic future. These concerns were also expressed in the memorial of a group generally quite partial to preserving the city's traditional privileges. (See *Memoria dei negozianti di manifatture, chincaglierie e ferrareccie della città di Livorno a S.E. il presidente del consiglio dei ministri del Regno d'Italia* [Livorno, 1867].)

53. Reported in Baruchello, *Livorno*, p. 627. The merchant com-

munity of the city found the tax particularly aggravating after its rate was doubled in 1850. In that year income from the tax climbed to 824.731.16 lire from the 340.658 lire of the previous year (Dal Pane, *La Finanza toscana*, p. 364).

54. Baruchello, *Livorno*, p. 627.

55. ACCL, *Delib.*, 3 and 24 June 1865; Baruchello, *Livorno*, pp. 624–627.

56. The statistics on Livorno's navigational and commercial contacts with other states of the Italian peninsula are fragmentary. Drawing on a report of the Russian government, Giovanni Bowring suggested that 18 percent of Livorno's imports in 1823 were drawn from other parts of the Italian peninsula; by 1834 the figure had climbed to 28.6 percent (Bowring, *Statistica*, p. 21). By 1881 commercial movements between Livorno and other national ports constituted 38.7 percent of the city's navigation. (Camera di Commercio ed Arti di Livorno, *Movimento del commercio e della navigazione di Livorno nell'anno 1880* [Livorno, 1881].)

57. ACCL, *Delib.*, 15 May, 27 October, and 6 December 1860; 19 April, 14 June, 11 July, and 6 August 1861; 5 and 12 June 1862. Ultimately, after extensive negotiations, the government agreed to turn over the Fortezza Nuova to the merchant community, but the community could not raise the necessary capital to mount the project.

58. These prospects were suggested in interviews between representatives of the merchant community and the king (ACCL, *Delib.*, 25 April 1860 and 12 June 1862. An optimistic assessment of Livorno's future was especially prevalent in Francesco Bonaini, *Livorno considerato nelle sue presenti condizioni e nel suo avvenire principalmente in ragione del taglio dell'Istmo di Suez e della Centrale Italiana* (Florence, 1856), pp. 12–22.

59. Bortolotti, *Livorno*, p. 170.

60. Bonaini, *Livorno considerato*, p. 30.

61. *Sull'abolizione delle franchigie*, pp. 31–32.

62. Ibid., pp. 58–60.

63. Bonaini, *Livorno considerato*, pp. 25–29.

64. *Memoria dei negozianti di manifatture, chincaglierie e ferrareccie*, pp. 15–16.

65. Ibid., pp. 16–17.

66. Baruchello, *Livorno*, p. 619.

67. Municipio di Livorno. *Atti della commissione per l'istituzione di magazzini generali o docks* (Livorno, 1867), pp. 29–30.

68. Ibid., pp. 111–115.

69. ACCL, *Delib.*, 14 March 1866; Baruchello, *Livorno*, p. 628.
70. Ibid., 21 May 1868.
71. Baruchello, *Livorno*, p. 632.
72. G. Mori, "Linee," p. 25. The project was completed in 1878.
73. Baruchello, *Livorno*, p. 656.
74. Formal requests for linking the city to a central Italian rail network were expressed in sessions of the chamber of commerce on 21, 25 April and 15 May 1860 and on 12 June 1862. On two occasions (in 1860 and 1862) the requests were made directly to the king. (See ACCL, *Delib.*)
75. Baruchello, *Livorno*, p. 656.
76. Ibid.
77. Nicola Badaloni reports that Livorno's inclusion in a central Italian rail network was opposed by Pietro Bastogi. Bastogi and his associates, it seems, controlled the major newspaper in Livorno, *La Gazzetta di Livorno*, and thus were able to influence public opinion in the city. On the occasion of parliamentary elections in 1865, Vincenzo Malenchini—one of the city's representatives in parliament—made explicit references to Bastogi's position: "If Livorno reelects Bastogi it would mean that it was wrong to request a station on the Alta Italia. It would also mean that Livorno must not even request something that would be clearly useful to the city if it should go against the personal interests of the large banker" (BLL, Ms, "Lettere di Vincenzo Malenchini ad Ugo Federighi," 15 March 1875. Cited in Nicola Badaloni, "La Vita politica a Livorno fra il '60 e l'80," *Movimento operaio* 4 [1952]: 419). Municipal rivalry with Pisa was especially intense. In 1871, Pisa's successful request for a line to Collesalvetti in effect isolated Livorno. Livorno's response—a request for a line from Viareggio to Livorno and Cecina—would have isolated Pisa. The project was resurrected in 1903, but the stretch from Viareggio to Livorno was ultimately not considered because "it was not other than the response to an act of hostility completed by Pisa in 1871" (Baruchello, *Livorno*, p. 659).
78. Salvatore Orlando estimates that of the 706,892 tons of merchandise introduced into the port in 1904, approximately 500,000 were shipped into the interior, 137,000 of these via the canal (*fosso dei navicelli*) constructed at the time of Cosimo I (1530) (Salvatore Orlando, *Il Porto di Livorno. Qual'é e quale dovrebbe essere* [Livorno, 1906], pp. 7, 11).
79. Baruchello, *Livorno*, p. 634.
80. Ibid., p. 635.
81. Orlando, *Il Porto di Livorno*, p. 13.

82. Orlando (ibid., p. 15) provides the following comparative statistics:

Port	Tonnage	Dock (meters)
Genoa	5,700,000	8,300
Venice	1,987,000	2,300
Naples	1,205,366	2,100
Livorno	1,125,000	150
Palermo	700,000	780
Messina	497,000	480
Savona	1,089,891	1,400
Spezia	400,000	500

83. Ibid.

84. Gustavo Uzielli, *Genova e Livorno: Porti europei* (Florence, 1906), cited in Baruchello, *Livorno,* p. 661.

85. If true, this would represent a significant portion of the 99,477,627 lire reportedly spent by the government on naval construction in the period. Francesco Saverio Nitti, *Il Bilancio dello Stato dal 1862 al 1896–97* (Naples, 1900), p. 242, cited in G. Mori, "Linee," p. 42.

86. Ibid., p. 30. The figures on coal imports are drawn from Giorgio Ricci, *I Porti e la loro funzione nella economia nazionale* (Livorno, 1926), p. 102.

87. The best introduction to the history of these plans (with illustrations) can be found in Baruchello, *Livorno,* pp. 647–656, 663–682.

88. On recent developments in the container trade see *Livorno produce* (Livorno, 1979).

10: Conclusions

1. Denis Mack Smith remarks that "far more influential in the Risorgimento than national feeling was the diffuse sense of rebellion against governmental oppression. In retrospect people too easily assumed a necessary connection between nationalism and liberalism." He notes "that the pivotal rebellions of the Risorgimento were local risings against oppressive government, in fact that the key motives at first were more liberal than national" (Denis Mack Smith,

"A Prehistory of Fascism," in *Italy from the Risorgimento to Fascism: An Inquiry into the Origins of the Totalitarian State,* edited by A. William Salomone [Garden City, N.Y., 1970], pp. 109–111).

2. *Storia d'Italia dal 1871 al 1915* (Bari, 1928; English translation Oxford, 1929), and *Storia d'Europa nel secolo decimonono* (Bari, 1932; English translation London, 1934).

3. Salomone, ed., *Italy from the Risorgimento to Fascism,* pp. 16–17.

4. Ibid., p. xxxi.

5. Ibid. See also Giuseppe Galasso, *Croce, Gramsci e altri storici* (Milan, 1969), and Ruggiero Romano, *La Storiografia italiana oggi* (n.p., 1978).

6. Letter to Salvatore Pres di Villamarina, Sardinian minister in Paris, 9 July 1857, cited in F. Ridella, *La Vita e i tempi di C. Cabella* (Genoa, 1923), p. 209.

7. David Blackbourn and Geoff Eley, *The Peculiarities of German History. Bourgeois Society and Politics in Nineteenth-Century Germany* (New York, 1984).

8. *QC,* p. 1, 997.

9. Ibid., pp. 784–785.

10. H. Stuart Hughes, "The Aftermath of the Risorgimento in Four Successive Interpretations," *The American Historical Review* 61 (1955): 76.

Bibliography

Manuscript and Archival Sources

Livorno

A. *Archivio di Stato*

1) Archivio del governatore

a) Affari generali e carteggio della segreteria civile e militare.

Papers grouped chronologically and by material. Includes petitions to the governor of the city and correspondence between the governor and various public officials. The series covers the entire period of the study and is well indexed.

b) Affari governativi staccati.

One filza containing miscellaneous papers on the chamber of commerce and the discount bank.

c) Auditore di governo (Buon Governo e Rota Criminale).

Reports and papers of the principal police official in the city from 1814 to 1844. Organized chronologically. No index.

2) Archivio della comunità

    a) Series 2: Deliberazioni degli anziani e del consiglio generale.

    b) Series 3: Elenco dei possidenti per servire alla tratta dei priori. An invaluable listing of assessed real property evaluations for the approximately 1,000 wealthiest residents of the city.

    c) Series 4: Copialettere del gonfaloniere.

3) Archivio del Catasto

    a) Contains descriptions and assessed valuations for all property in the community in which there is a change either in the value of the property or the person liable for the payment of the tax (from 1821–1833).

4) Archivio della Sanità Maritima

    a) Series 13: Registri di arrivi. Lists the port of origin, route, length of voyage, type of ship, captain, and cargo of all ships arriving in the lazarettos of the city.

B. *Biblioteca Labronica:* Extremely valuable both for its manuscript materials and for its collection of books and pamphlets pertaining to the history of the city.

1) Primary manuscript sources utilized in this study:

    a) Accademia Labronica, *Atti*

    Contains several valuable memorials presented to the academy and conserved in its archive.

    b) Carte Vivoli

    Miscellaneous documents on the history of the city between 1814 and 1860.

c) Carte Ricci

The papers of a leading moderate-liberal. Heavily utilized in this study.

d) Carte Sproni

Letters and documents pertaining largely to the revolution of 1848 and its aftermath.

e) Carte Bastogi

Not the papers of the merchant banker family but an autograph collection purchased by the family and deposited in the library. Contains an inventory only of names.

2) Newspapers

a) Complete collections of the *Indicatore livornese* and the *Corriere livornese* and a significant portion of the city's *Giornale di commercio*.

C. *Archivio della Comunità Israelitica:* Contains much less material for the nineteenth century than for earlier centuries. My major find in this collection was a rough (and incomplete) manuscript census of the Jewish population taken in 1840.

Florence

A. *Archivio di Stato*

1) The following *fondi* have provided material for the study:

a) Depositeria Generale—Parte Moderna
b) Segreteria Ministero Esteri
c) Finanze Capirotti
d) Finanza Segreteria
e) Finanza Miscellanea, parts 1 and 2
f) Segreteria di Gabinetto
g) Segreteria Gabinetto Appendice
h) Carte Gianni

    i)   Ministero dell'Interno
    j)   Nobiltà Toscana
    k)   Segreteria di Stato
    l)   Stato Civile

2)   Unavailable for consultation were the archives of the Reali Rendite and the Dogana.

B. *Archivio Notarile Distrettuale*

1)   Contains the papers of forty-six Livornese notaries working during the period under study.

C. *Biblioteca Nazionale*

1)   Of prime consideration were the manuscript of Pierallini, "Osservazioni sulla pace cogli Ottomani e sulla marina e commercio di Livorno" (in the Fondi Capponi) and the library's extensive collection of correspondence between the major figures in the Tuscan reform movement (particularly the Fondi Vieusseux).

D. *Istituto del Risorgimento Italiano*

1)   In addition to the periodical collection of the institute of special importance was the Carte Fenzi, which contains papers and correspondence pertaining to the rail project linking Livorno and Florence.

Genoa

A. *Archivio di Stato*

1)   R. Prefettura Sarda, 1815–1859.

    Notes on the chamber of commerce, *facchini*, marine, railroads, and various items related to commerce and industry.

2)   R. Prefettura Italiana.

    Actually includes items from the mid-1840s. Especially useful were files on industrial, commercial, and banking societies, imports and exports, and port construction, and claims which resulted from the siege of Genoa.

3) Archivio della Camera di Commercio di Genoa.

Especially valuable for the deliberations and memorials of the chamber from 1818 to 1858. Useful also for commercial and statistical materials, for business papers, and for the correspondence of the organization.

B. *Archivio Storico del Comune di Genoa:* Principally useful for administrative and tax records and for institutions geared to public instruction and beneficence.

C. *Istituto Economia Commercio*

1) Archivio d'Oria.

Records and papers of an important Genoese family.

D. *Istituto del Risorgimento Italiano, Casa Mazzini:* In addition to an excellent library, the institute contains an important newspaper collection and a collection of autographs.

Turin

A. *Archivio di Stato*

The following *fondi* of the Archivio Sistemato have proved especially useful:

a) Amministrazione territoriale
b) Commercio
c) Daziario
d) Dogana e Gabelle
e) Privative
f) Strade

London

A. *Public Records Office*

1) Records of the Foreign Office: correspondence of the British consuls in Florence and Livorno.

2) Records of the Board of Trade: some commercial statistics.

Paris

A. *Archives du Ministère des Affaires Etrangères*

1) Livourne. État Numerique de la Correspondance Consulaire et Commerciale. Vols. 67–84 (1808–1862).

2) Gênes. État Numerique de la Correspondance Consulaire et Commerciale. Vols. 94–113 (1803–1860).

Washington, D.C.

A. *National Archives*

1) Record Group 84. Livorno. Consular reports 1798–1857.

Published Sources

Abenicar, Raffaella. "La Formazione politico-culturale di F. D. Guerrazzi." Tesi di Laurea, Università degli Studi di Firenze, Facoltà di Magistero, 1972.

Sull'abolizione delle franchigie della città di Livorno. Poche parole d'un Livornese. Livorno, 1867.

Acerbo, Giacomo. *La Economia dei cereali nell'Italia e nel mondo. Evoluzione storica e consistenza attuale della produzione del consumo e del commercio politica agraria e commerciale.* Milan, 1934.

Adamson, Walter L. "Gramsci's Interpretation of Fascism." *Journal of the History of Ideas* 41 (1980): 615–633.

———. *Hegemony and Revolution: A Study of Antonio Gramsci's Political and Cultural Theory.* Berkeley, Los Angeles, London, 1980.

Adriani, G. *Socialismo e comunismo in Toscana tra il 1846 e il 1849.* Rome, 1921.

Agnelli, Arnaldo. "Il Fattore economico nella formazione dell'unità italiana." *Il Risorgimento italiano* 6 (1913): 253–278, 471–488.

———. "Il Materialismo storico e il Risorgimento italiano. Posizione del problema." *Rendiconti del R. Istituto Lombardo di Scienze e Lettere* 46 (1913): 183–196.

Agulhon, Maurice. *Une Ville ouvrière au temps du socialisme utopique. Toulon de 1815 à 1851.* Paris, 1970.

Aiano [D'], Broglio. "La Politica doganale del Piemonte dal 1815 al 1834." *Giornale degli economisti e rivista di statistica.* Nos. 4, 5 (1912): 440–461.

Alatri, Paolo. "I Moderati toscani, il richiamo del granduca e il decennio di preparazione." *RSR* 39, no. 4 (1952): 354–363.

Anderson, Perry. "The Antinomies of Antonio Gramsci." *New Left Review* 100 (Nov. 1976–Jan. 1977): 5–78.

Anzilotti, Antonio. *La Costituzione interna dello stato fiorentino sotto il duca Cosimo l de'Medici.* Florence, 1910.

———. *Decentramento amministrattivo e riforma municipale in Toscana sotto Pietro Leopoldo.* Florence, 1910.

———. "L'Economia toscana e l'origine del movimento riformatore del secolo XVIII." *ASI* 73 (1915): 82–118, 308–352.

Le Assemblee del Risorgimento. Vol. 5, no. 2. Rome, 1911.

Azeglio [D'], Massimo. *Programma per l'opinione nazionale italiana.* Turin, 1847.

Badaloni, Nicola. *Democratici e socialisti livornesi nell'Ottocento.* Rome, 1966.

———. *La Difesa di Livorno nelle ripercussioni nazionali.* Livorno, 1969.

———. "La Vita politica a Livorno fra il '60 e l'80." *Movimento operaio* 4 (1952): 405–424.

Baldasseroni, Giovanni. *Livorno ed il suo portofranco considerato nel passato, nel presente e nell'avvenire da un vecchio livorneso, socio dell'Accademica Labronica.* Florence, 1863.

———. *Memorie, 1833–1859.* Florence, 1959.

———. *Il Rinnovamento civile in Toscana.* Florence, 1931.

Bandettini, Pierfrancesco. *L'Evoluzione demografica della Toscana dal 1810 al 1889.* Turin, 1960.

———. *La Popolazione della Toscana alla metà dell'Ottocento.* Rome, 1956.

———. *La Popolazione della Toscana dal 1810 al 1959.* Florence, 1961.

———. *I Prezzi sul mercato di Firenze dal 1800 al 1890.* Rome, 1957.

Barbagallo, Corrado. *Le Origini della grande industria contemporanea 1750–1850.* Venice, 1929.

Barber, Elinor G. *The Bourgeoisie in 18th-Century France.* Princeton, 1955.

Barsanti, Ezio. "Il Consiglio del Commercio di Livorno." *Liburni civitas* 9 (1931): 179–192.

Baruchello, Mario. *Livorno e il suo porto. Origini, caratteristiche e vicende dei traffici livornesi.* Livorno, 1932.

Bastogi, Pietro. *Della carta monetata e dei suoi effetti in Toscana. Discorso di Pietro Bastogi scritto in Pisa il 10 gennaio 1849.* Pisa, 1849.

Bastogi, Ugo. *Considerazioni sul commercio a Livorno.* Livorno, 1956.

Bates, Thomas R. "Gramsci and the Theory of Hegemony." *Journal of the History of Ideas* 36 (1975): 351–366.

Bedarida, Guido. *Ebrei d'Italia.* Livorno, 1950.

Benedetto, E. "La Toscana nel 1831 e gli ultimi giorni di Pietro Colletta." *RSR* 22 (1935): 453–494.

Bertelli, Daniela. "Giuliano Ricci: L'Evoluzione del pensiero e la partecipazione alla rivoluzione quarantottesca." Tesi di Laurea, Università degli Studi di Pisa, n.d.

Berti, Giuseppe. *Russia e stati italiani nel Risorgimento.* Turin, 1957.

Biase [De], Corrado. *Il Problema delle ferrovie nel Risorgimento italiano.* Modena, 1940.

Bini, Carlo. *Manoscritto di un prigioniero.* Turin, 1944.

———. *Scritti, preceduti da un discorso di Giuseppe Mazzini.* Milan, 1926.

Blackbourn, David, and Eley, Geoff. *The Peculiarities of German History. Bourgeois Society and Politics in Nineteenth-Century Germany.* New York, 1984.

Böhme, Helmut. *Frankfurt und Hamburg: Des Deutschen Reiches Silber- und Goldloch und die allerenglischste Stadt des Kontinents.* Frankfurt am Main, 1968.

Bonaini, Francesco. *Livorno considerato nelle sue presenti condizioni e nel suo avvenire principalmente in ragione del taglio dell'Istmo di Suez e della Centrale Italiana.* Florence, 1856.

Boralevi, Guido. *L'Importanza commerciale del porto di Livorno e le vie di comunicazione con i paesi interni.* Livorno, 1911.

Bortolotti, Lando. *Livorno dal 1748 al 1958. Profilo storico-urbanistico.* Florence, 1970.

Bottini, Luigi. *Cenno storico su la R. Accademia dei Georgofili di Firenze dal 1753 al 1920.* Florence, 1931.

Bowring, Giovanni. *Statistica della Toscana, di Lucca, degli Stati Pontifici e Lombardo-Veneto e specialmente della loro relazioni commerciali.* London, 1838.

Braudel, Fernand, and Romano, Ruggiero. *Navires et marchandises à l'entrée du port de Livourne (1547–1611)*. Paris, 1951.

Breunig, Charles. *The Age of Revolution and Reaction*. 2d ed. New York, 1977.

Bruscaglioni, Emilio. *L'Ampliamento del castello di Livorno durante il tempo di Ferdinando I de Medici, Granduca di Toscana: Cenno storico*. Florence, 1901.

Buci-Glucksmann, Christine. *Gramsci and the State*. London, 1980.

———. "State, Transition, and Passive Revolution." In *Gramsci and Marxist Theory*, edited by C. Mouffe. London, 1979.

Bulferetti, Luigi and Costantini, Caludio. *Industria e commercio in Liguria nell'età del Risorgimento*. Milan, 1966.

Bulferetti, Luigi. *Socialismo risorgimentale*. Turin, 1949.

Burdese, Antonio. *La Mercuriale storica del commercio dei grani ed affini: sue vicende dal 1700 al 1898; Tariffe e statistiche, agricoltura sociale*. Bologna, 1898.

Busacca, R. "Sulle condizioni economiche della Toscana relativamente al commercio delle manifatture." *AGA* 2 (1855): 251–305.

———. "Sulle condizioni economiche della Toscana, considerate in rapporto alle industrie estrattive diverse dall'agraria, e specialmente in rapporto all'industria delle miniere." *AGA* 2 (1855): 355–406.

Calisse, Carlo. *Storia di Civitavecchia*. Florence, 1898.

Cambini, C. *L'Indicatore livornese*. Milan-Rome-Naples, 1925.

Camerani, Sergio. "I Moderati toscani e il decennio di preparazione." *Il Risorgimento* 2 (1953): 90–99.

———. "Recenti Publicazioni di storia toscana." *RST* 10 (1964): 231–250.

———. *Lo Spirito pubblico a Livorno dal 1849 al 1859*. Livorno, 1942.

———. "Lo Spirito pubblico in Toscana nel 1859." *RST* 2 (1957).

Cammett, John M. *Antonio Gramsci and the Origins of Italian Communism*. Stanford, Calif., 1967.

Cantimori, Delio. "Italy in 1848." In *The Opening of an Era: 1848*, edited by Francois Fejtö. New York, 1966.

———. *Utopisti e riformatori italiani, 1794–1847*. Ricerche storiche. Florence, 1943.

Candeloro, Giorgio. *Dalla restaurazione alla rivoluzione nazionale 1815–1846*. Storia dell'Italia moderna. 3d ed. Vol. 2. Milan, 1962.

———. *La Rivoluzione nazionale 1846–1849*. Storia dell'Italia moderna, vol. 3. Milan, 1960.

Caporali, Cesare. *Sulla popolazione di Livorno. Ricerche statistiche ed economiche*. Livorno, 1855.

Caracciolo, Alberto. "Il dibattito sui "porti franchi' nel settecento: Genesi della franchigia di Ancona." *RSI* 75 (1963): 538–558.

———. *Le Port franc d'Ancone croissance et impasse d'un milieu marchand au XVIIIe siècle*. Paris, 1965.

Carocci, C. *Prose e poesie di Sansone Uzielli*. Florence, 1899.

Carranze, Niccola. "La Crisi del porto di Livorno nel periodo del dipartimento del Mediterraneo." *BSP* 39 (1970): 173–188.

Carriere, Charles, *Négociants marseillais au XVIIIe siècle*. 2 vols. Marseilles, 1973.

Catalano, F. "Socialismo e comunismo in Italia dal 1846 al 1849." *RSR* 38 (1951): 306–316.

Cavour, Camillo Benso, conte di. *Nouvelles lettres inédites recueillies et pub avec notes historiques par Amédée Bert*. Rome, 1889.

Cecilia [La], Giovanni. *Cenno storico sull'ultima rivoluzione Toscana con note e documenti inediti*. Capolago, 1851.

———. *Memorie storico-politiche dal 1820–1876*. 4 vols. Rome, 1876–1877.

Cempini, Raffaello. *Contributo alla storia del 1848 in Toscana*. In *Il 1848 nella storia italiana ed Europa*. Edited by Ettore Rota, vol. 2. Milan, 1948.

Cerro [Del], Emilio [pseud.]. *Misteri di polizia; Storia italiana degli ultimi tempi Ricavata dalle carte d'un archivio segreto di stato*. Florence, 1890.

Cevasco, N. *Statistique de la ville de Gênes*. Genoa, 1840.

Chiappini, Guido. *L'Arte della stampa in Livorno*. Livorno, 1904.

Cialdi, Alessandro. *Studi idrodinamici nautici e commerciali sul porto di Livorno e sul miglioramento ed ingrandimento del medesimo*. Florence, 1853.

Ciampini, Raffaele. *Due Campagnoli dell'800, Lambruschini e Ridolfi*. Florence, 1947.

———. *Gian Pietro Vieusseux, i suoi viaggi, i suoi giornali, i suoi amici*. Turin, 1953.

Ciano, Cesare. "Le 'Nazioni' mercantili a Livorno nel 1799 e il Sismondi." *BSP* 36–38 (1967–1969): 149–167.

Ciappei, Carlo Giorgio. "Intorno alle origini ed agli statuti dell'Accademia Labronica." *La Rivista di Livorno* 1 (1926): 216–221.

Ciasca, Raffaele. *L'Origine del "Programma per l'opinione nazionale italiana," del 1847–1848*. Milan, 1916.

Clapp, Edwin J. *The Port of Hamburg*. New Haven, 1911.

Codice di commercio colle note tratte dalle disposizioni legislative e dalle massime della giurisprudenza francese dal 1791 al 1842. Florence, 1844.

Codignola, Arturo. *Dagli albori della libertà al proclama di Moncallieri*.

Lettere del Conte Ilarione Petiti di Roreto a Michele Erede dal marzo 1846 all'aprile del 1850. Biblioteca italiana di storia recente, vol. 13. Turin, 1931.

Conti, Elio. *I Catasti agrari della Republica Fiorentina e il catasto particellare toscano. Secoli XIV–XIX.* Rome, 1966.

Corsini, Carlo. "La Prima Ferrovia in Toscana: La Strada Ferrata Leopolda. Da Firenze a Livorno." Tesi di Laurea in Storia Economica: Facoltà di Economia e Commercio, 1960–61.

[Corvaja, Barone.] "Del commercio di Livorno." *Annali universali di statistica economia pubblica, geografica, storia e viaggi* 54 (1837): 350–355.

Croce, Benedetto, *La Letteratura della Nuova Italia; Saggi critici,* vol. 1. Bari, 1914.

———. *Storia d'Europa nel secolo decimonono.* Bari, 1932.

———. *Storia d'Italia dal 1871 al 1915.* Bari, 1928.

Cuoco, Vincenzo. *Saggio storico sulla rivoluzione napoletana del 1799.* Florence, 1926.

Daumard, Adeline. *La Bourgeoisie parisienne de 1815 à 1848.* Paris, 1963.

Davis, John A., ed. *Gramsci and Italy's Passive Revolution.* New York, 1979.

Davis, Ralph. "England and the Mediterranean 1570–1670." In *Essays in the Economic and Social History of Tudor and Stuart England in Honour of R. H. Tawney,* edited by E. J. Fisher. Cambridge, 1961.

———. "English Foreign Trade 1700–1774." *EHR* 15 (1962): 285–303.

———. "Influences de l'Angleterre sur le déclin de Venise au XVIIe siècle." In *Aspetti e cause della decadenza economica veneziana nel secolo XVII.* Venice, 1961.

———. *The Rise of the Atlantic Economies.* Ithaca, N.Y., 1973.

Diefendorf, Jeffry M. *Businessmen and Politics in the Rhineland, 1789–1834.* Princeton, N.J., 1980.

La Difesa di Livorno 10 e 11 maggio 1849. A cura del Comitato Comunale per le celebrazioni del Risorgimento nel centinario della difesa cittadina. Livorno, 1949.

Dizionario biografico degli italiani. 28 vols. Rome, 1960–1983.

Dizionario del Risorgimento nazionale. 4 vols. Milan, 1930–1937.

Doria, Giorgio. *Le Premesse (1815–1882).* Investimenti e sviluppo economico a Genova alle vigilia della Prima Guerra Mondiale, vol. 1. Milan, 1969.

Dyos, H. J. *The Study of Urban History.* London, 1968.

Eley, Geoff. "Reading Gramsci in English: Some Observations on the Reception of Antonio Gramsci in the English-Speaking World,

1957–1962." Working Paper no. 314, Center for Research on Social Organization, University of Michigan, Ann Arbor, 1984.

L'Enciclopedia italiana di scienze lettere ed arti. 36 vols. Rome, 1929–1939.

Erede, Michele. "Di alcuni dei più considerevoli vantaggi apportati al traffico genovese dal governo della Real Casa di Savoia." *Antologia italiana* 1, no. 2 (1847): 620–631.

Femia, Joseph V. *Gramsci's Political Thought: Hegemony, Consciousness, and the Revolutionary Process*. Oxford, 1981.

Filippini, J. P. "Le Commerce du blé à Livourne au XVIIIe siècle." In *Studi in Memoria di Federigo Melis*, 4: 517–570. N.p., 1978.

———. "Grandeur et difficultés d'un port franc: Livourne (1676–1737)." Mimeographed. Bulletin no. 12 (March 1979), Association Française des Historiens Économistes.

———. "I Livornesi e l'occupazione napoleonica." Unpublished ms.

———. "Il Porto di Livorno ed il Regno di Francia dall'editto del porto franco alla fine della dominazione medicea." *Atti* del Convegno "Livorno e il Mediterraneo nell'età medicea." Livorno, 1978.

Foà, Ada. "La Politica interna del governo provisorio toscano." *ASI* 77, no. 1 (1919): 232–262.

Fortini, Arturo. *Sopra alcuni progetti per il risorgimento commerciale di Livorno*. Livorno, 1871.

Fossati, Antonio. *Origini e sviluppi della carestia del 1816–17 negli Stati Sardi di terraferma*. Turin, 1929.

———. *Saggi di politica economica Carlo Albertina*. Turin, 1930.

Francovich, Carlo. *Albori socialisti nel Risorgimento*. Florence, 1962.

Galasso, Giuseppe. *Croce, Gramsci e altri storici*. Milan, 1969.

Galeotti, Leopoldo. *L'Assemblea toscana, considerazioni*. 2d ed. Florence, 1859.

———. *Delle leggi e dell'amministrazione della Toscana*. Florence, 1847.

———. *Della riforma municipale. Pensieri e proposte*. Florence, 1847.

Galletti, Gino. "Le Industrie del passato." *La Rivista di Livorno* 1 (1926): 3–12.

Galluzzi, Jacopo Riguccio. *Istoria del granducato di Toscana sotto il governo della casa Medici*. 5 vols. Florence, 1781.

Gazzo, Emanuele. *I Cento Anni dell'Ansaldo, 1853–1953*. Genoa, 1953.

Gentile, Giovanni. *Gino Capponi e la cultura toscana nel secolo decimono*. 3d ed. Florence, 1973.

Gianfrancesco [Di], Mario. "La Politica commerciale degli Stati Sardi del 1814 al 1859." *RSR* 61 (1974): 3–36.

Giani, M. "La Guerra dei corsari barbareschi nelle acque toscane (1765–1790)." *BSL* 6 (1942): 83–115.

Gianni, Francesco Maria. "Discorso sopra Livorno." In *Scritti di pubblica economia, storico-economici e storico-politici*, vol. 2. Florence,

1848–1849.

Ginsborg, Paul. *Daniele Manin and the Venetian Revolution of 1848–49.* New York, 1979.

Gioja, Melchiorre. *Nuovo Prospetto delle scienze economiche.* 6 vols. Milan, 1815–1817.

———. *Problema: quali sono i mezzi più spediti, più efficaci, più economici per alleviare l'attuale miseria del popolo in Europa.* 2d ed. Milan, 1817.

Giusti, Giuseppe. *Cronaca dei fatti di Toscana (1845–1849).* Florence, 1948.

Giusti, V. "Il Progresso in Russia e l'agricoltura in Italia." *Il Commercio* (Florence), 10 November 1858.

Gori, Agostino. *Gli Albori del socialismo (1755–1848).* Florence, 1909.

———. *Storia della rivoluzione italiana durante il periodo delle riforme, 1846–14 marzo 1848.* Florence, 1897.

Gramsci, Antonio. *Lettere dal carcere.* Edited by Sergio Cadrioglio e Elsa Fubini. 3d ed. Turin, 1972.

———. *Quaderni del Carcere.* Edited by Valentino Gerratana. 4 vols. Turin, 1975.

Gray, R. "Bourgeois Hegemony in Victorian Britain," In *Class, Hegemony and Party,* edited by J. Bloomfield. London, 1977.

Greenfield, Kent Roberts. *Economics and Liberalism in the Risorgimento. A Study of Nationalism in Lombardy, 1814–1848.* 2d ed. Rev. Baltimore, 1965 (orig. ed. Baltimore, 1934).

Grendi, Edoardo. "Genova nel quarantotto. Saggio di storia sociale." *Nuova Rivista storica* 48 (1964): 307–350.

Grew, Raymond. "How Success Spoiled the Risorgimento." *Journal of Modern History* 34 (1962): 239–253.

Guarnieri, Giuseppe Gino. *Cavalieri di Santo Stefano. Contributo alla storia della marina militare italiana 1562–1859.* Pisa, 1928.

———. *Livorno marinara.* Livorno, 1962.

———. *Origine e sviluppo del porto di Livorno durante il governo di Ferdinando I dei Medici.* Livorno, 1911.

———. *Il Porto di Livorno e la sua funzione economica dalle origini ai tempi nostri.* Pisa, 1931.

———. *Da Porto pisano a Livorno città, attraverso le tappe della storia e della evoluzione geografica.* Pisa, 1967.

Guastalla, Rosolino. *La Vita e le opere di F. D. Guerrazzi.* Rocca San Casciano, 1903.

Guerrazzi, Francesco Domenico. *XIVe Anniversario delle battaglie di Curtatone e di Montanara.* N.p., 1862.

———. *Apologia della vita politica di F. D. Guerrazzi scritta da lui medesimo.* Florence, 1851.

———. *Appendice all'apologia della vita politica.* Florence, 1852.

————. *L'Assedio di Firenze.* 2 vols. Milan, 1874.

————. *La Battaglia di Benevento; Storia del secolo XIII.* 4 vols. Livorno, 1827.

————. *Il Buco del muro.* Milan, 1862.

————. *Commemorazione di Carlo Bini morto il 12 novembre 1842.* Livorno, 1862.

————. *Discorsi di F. D. Guerrazzi davanti la Corte Regia di Firenze.* Florence, 1853.

————. *Leopoldo II descritto.* Florence, 1859.

————. *Note autobiografiche e poema.* Florence, 1899.

————. *Al principe e al popolo; intorno allo stato delle cose in Toscana.* Livorno, 1847.

————. *Raccolta di documenti relativi ai facchini livornesi ed ai facchini forestieri detti di dogana.* Livorno, 1847.

————. *Scritti politici.* Turin, 1862.

————. *Storia del processo politico, ed altri imputati di perduellione.* Florence, 1851–1852.

Guglielmino, Enrico. *Genoa dal 1814 al 1849; Gli Sviluppi economici e l'opinione pubblica.* Genoa, 1939.

Halévy, Elie. *England in 1815.* London, 1964.

Harris, H. R., ed. *Liverpool and Merseyside. Essays in the economic and social history of the port and its hinterland.* London, 1969.

Herlihy, Patricia. "Russian Trade and the Mediterranean Markets, 1774–1861." Ph.D. dissertation, University of Pennsylvania, 1963.

————. "Russian Wheat and the Port of Livorno, 1794–1865." *Journal of European Economic History* 5 (1976): 45–68.

Henderson, William O. *The Rise of German Industrial Power, 1834–1917.* Berkeley, Los Angeles, London, 1976.

Hoare, Quintin, and Nowell-Smith, Geoffrey, eds. *Selections from the Prison Notebooks of Antonio Gramsci.* New York, 1971.

Hoskins, H. L. *British Routes to India.* London, 1966.

Hughes, H. Stuart. "The Aftermath of the Risorgimento in Four Successive Interpretations." *American Historical Review* 61 (1955): 70–76.

————. *Consciousness and Society: The Reorientation of European Social Thought 1890–1930.* Rev. ed. New York, 1977.

Hunt's Merchants' Magazine 15 (1846): 19–28.

Imerciadori, I. *Economia toscana nel primo '800 dalla restaurazione al regno, 1815–1861.* Florence, 1961.

Innocenti, Piero. *Il Porto di Livorno.* Milan, 1968.

Jona, Palmira. *I Moti politici di Livorno, 1848–1849.* Milan, 1909.

Keonigsberger, H. "English merchants in Naples and Sicily in the

17th century." *EHR* 62 (1947): 304–326.

Labrousse, Ernest. "Une histoire de la bourgeoisie occidentale (1700–1850)." In *Relazioni del X Congresso Internazionale di Scienze Storiche.* Vol. 4. Florence, n.d.

———. "Panoramas de la crise." In *Aspects de la crise et de la dépression de l'économie française au milieu du xixe siècle, 1846–1851.* (Bibliotheque de la Révolution de 1848, *Études* XIX). La Roche–Sur–Yon, 1956, pp. iii–xiv.

Lavasseur, Émile. *De 1789 à nos jours.* Histoire du commerce de la France, part 2. Paris, 1912.

Lambruschini, Raffaello. "Considerazioni sull'insegnamento del popolo." In *Il Pensiero pedagogico del Risorgimento,* edited by Lamberto Borghi. Florence, 1958.

———. *Elogi e biografie.* Florence, 1872.

———. *Sull'utilità della cooperazione delle donne bennate al buon rendimento delle scuole infantili per il popolo.* Milan, 1834.

Levi, Leone. *The History of British Commerce and of the Economic Progress of the British Nation, 1763–1878.* 2d ed. London, 1880.

Litchfield, R. Burr. *Emergence of a Bureaucracy: The Florentine Patricians 1530–1790.* Princeton, 1986.

Linaker, Arturo. "G. P. Vieusseux e la stampa cooperatrice del Risorgimento." In *La Toscana alla fine del Granducato.* Florence, 1909.

———. *La Vita e i tempi di Enrico Mayer con documenti inediti della storia della educazione e del Risorgimento italiano (1802–1877),* 2 vols. Florence, 1898.

Livorno produce. Livorno, 1979.

Loevinson, E. "Le basi giuridiche della comunità israelitica a Livorno, 1593–1787." *BSL* 1 (1937): 202–208.

Luchaire, Julien. *Essai sur l'évolution intellectuelle de l'Italie de 1815 à 1830.* Paris, 1906.

Luzzatto, Gino. *Per una storia economica d'Italia.* Bari, 1967.

———. "La Vigilia e l'indomani dell'unità." In *Orientamenti per la storia d'Italia nel Risorgimento.* Bari, 1952.

———. *L'Età moderna.* Storia economica dell'età moderna e contemporanea, Parte Prima. 4th ed. Padua, 1955.

———. *L'Età contemporanea.* Storia economica dell'età moderna e contemporanea, Parte Seconda. 4th ed. Padua, 1960.

Magri, Nicola. *Stato antico e moderno, ovvero origine di Livorno in Toscana dalla sua fondazione fino all'anno 1646, già dato in luce da Nicola Magri, al presente fornito da Agostino Santelli.* Florence, 1769.

Manetti, Alessandro. *Delle opere eseguite per l'ingrandimento della città e portofranco di Livorno dal anno 1835 al anno 1842.* Florence, 1842.

Mangini, Adolfo. *I Carabinieri livornesi a Mentana*. Milan, 1908.

———. *Carlo Bini*. Rome, 1907.

———. *Compendio della storia di Livorno, 1100–1870*. Florence, 1912.

———. *La Difesa di Livorno contro gli Austriaci*. Milan, 1909.

———. "F. D. Guerrazzi e la democrazia Toscana." In *La Toscana alla fine del granducato*. Florence, 1909.

Marchi, Vittorio. *Memorie e rimembranze nella vita di Agostino Micheli*. Livorno, 1969.

Marcotti, G. *Cronache segrete della polizia Toscana*. Florence, 1898.

Mariotti, Filippo. "Delle esposizioni industriali e delle industrie toscane nel 1854." *AGA* 2 (1855): 502–510.

———. *L'Industria del cotone in Toscana*. Rocca San Casciano, 1857.

———. *Notizie storiche economiche e statistiche intorno all'arte della paglia in Toscana*. Florence, 1858.

———. *Storia del lanificio toscano antico e moderno*. Turin, 1864.

Marks, L. F. *Rapporti di consolati e legazioni inglesi in Italia dal 1830 al 1870 sulle condizioni economiche e sociali*. Rome, 1959.

Marseille sous le Second Empire: Exposition, confèrences, colloque organisée à l'occasion du centenaire du Palais de la Bourse. Paris, 1961.

Martini, Ferdinando. *Confessioni e ricordi (Firenze Granducale)*. 3d ed. Florence, 1922.

Martini, Pietro. *Diario livornese: Ultimo Periodo della rivoluzione del 1849*. Livorno, 1961.

Martini, Pietro, ed. *Il Quarantotto in Toscana. Diario inedito del Conte Luigi Passerini de'Rilli*. Milan, n.d.

Marx, Karl. *A Contribution to the Critique of Political Economy*. Chicago, 1904.

Masi, Manlio. *Il Porto di Livorno. Saggio di geografia commerciale*. Livorno, 1910.

Masson, Paul. *Histoire du commerce français dans le Levant au XVIIIe siècle*. Paris, 1911.

———. *Ports francs d'autrefois et d'aujourd'hui*. Paris, 1904.

Matteucci, Carlo. "Ravenna e Cesenatico, communicazione da Livorno all'Adriatico." *GAT* 10 (1836): 235–253.

Maturi, Walter. *Interpretazioni del Risorgimento*. 5th ed. Turin, 1962.

Mayer, Enrico. "Dell'educazione del popolo ne'suoi rapporti colla società." *Antologia* 32 (1828): 73–82.

———. "Istituto de'Padri di Famiglia in Livorno." *Guida dell'educatore* 2 (1837): 331–335.

———. *Una Scuola elementare per le fanciulle povere da far seguito agli asili infantili: Pensieri diretti alle signore componenti la società per gli asili in Livorno*. Livorno, 1837.

Memoria dei negozianti di manifatture, chincaglierie e ferrareccie della città di Livorno a S. E. il Presidente del Consiglio dei Ministeri del Regno d'Italia. Livorno, 1867.

Memoria sulle franchigie commerciali della città. Al governo e al parlamento. Livorno, 1863.

Merli, Gianfranco. "Giuliano Ricci collaboratore dell'Antologia." *Rivista di Livorno* 1 (1951): 67–72.

Michel, Ersilio. "Il Governo francese e la restaurazione granducale in Toscana (1849)." *RSR* 25 (1938): 1213–1220.

————. *Maestri e scolari dell'università di Pisa nel Risorgimento nazionale (1815–1870)*. Florence, 1949.

————. "Nel primo centenario della nascità di F. D. Guerrazzi." *ASI* 35 (1905): 498–511.

————. *L'Ultimo Moto mazziniano (1857)*. Livorno, 1903.

Milano, Attilio. *Storia degli ebrei in Italia*. Turin, 1963.

Miller, Marion. "Communes, Commerce and Coloni: Internal Divisions in Tuscany 1830–1860." *Historical Journal* 21 (1978): 837–861.

Milone, Ferdinando. *L'Italia nell'economia delle sue regioni*. Turin, 1955.

Minoletti, Bruno. *I Porti franchi*. Turin, 1939.

Misul, Rodolfo. *Le Arti fiorentine, decadenza e soppressione. Le Camere di commercio, origine, modificazioni*. Florence, 1904.

Montanelli, Giuseppe. *Introduzione ad appunti storici sulla rivoluzione d'Italia*. Turin, 1945.

————. *Memorie sull'Italia e specialmente sulla Toscana dal 1814–1850*. Florence, 1963.

————. *Nel processo politico contro il ministro democratico Toscano; Schiarimenti*. Florence, 1852.

Mori, Giorgio. *L'Industria del ferro in Toscana dalla restaurazione alla fine del granducato (1815–1859)*. Turin, 1966.

————. "Linee e momenti dello sviluppo della città, del porto e dei traffici di Livorno." *La Regione: Rivista dell'unione regionale delle provincie toscane* 3 (1956): 3–44.

————. *Studi di storia dell'industria*. Rome, 1967.

Mori, Ranato. "I Moderati toscani e la restaurazione." *Trentasettesimo congresso di storia del Risorgimento. Atti*, pp. 160–189. Rome, 1961.

Municipio di Livorno. *Atti della commissione per l'istituzione di magazzini generali o docks*. Livorno, 1867.

Nguyen, Victor. "Les portefaix marseillais: crise et déclin, survivances." *Provence historique* 12 (1962): 363–397.

Nitti, Francesco Saverio. *Il Bilancio dello Stato dal 1862 al 1896–97*. Naples, 1900.

Nobili, N. "I Moti toscani dal 1847 al 1848." In *Vita italiana nel*

Risorgimento. Florence, 1900.

Nola [Di], Carlo. *Politica economica e agricoltura in Toscana nei secoli XV–XIX*. Rome, 1948.

————. *La Situazione economica della Toscana prima e dopo il 1849*. Siena, 1953.

Novacco, Domenico. "L'Abolizione del porto franco di Livorno." In *La Toscana nell'Italia unita. Aspetti e momenti di storia toscana, 1861–1945*, edited by Giuliano Bianchi. Florence, 1962.

Nudi, Giacinto. *Storia urbanistica di Livorno*. Venice, 1959.

Orlando, Salvatore. *Il Porto di Livorno. Qual'é e quale dovrebbe essere*. Livorno, 1906.

Pace, Antonio. *Benjamin Franklin and Italy*. Philadelphia, 1958.

Pane [Dal], Luigi. *La Finanza toscana dagli inizi del secolo XVIII alla caduta del granducato*. Milan, 1965.

————. *Il Settecento*. Industria e commercio nel granducato di Toscana nell'età del Risorgimento, vol. 1. Bologna, 1971.

————. *L'Ottocento*. Industria e commercio nel granducato di Toscana nell'età del Risorgimento, vol. 2. Bologna, 1973.

Pansini, Giuseppe. "L'Inserimento della Toscana nello stato unitario." In *La Toscana nell'Italia unita. Aspetti e momenti di storia toscana*. Florence, 1962.

————. "I Liberali moderati toscani e la crisi amministrativa del granducato." *RST* 5 (1959): 29–154.

————. "Gli Ordinamenti comunali in Toscana dal 1849 al 1853." *RST* 2 (1956): 33–75.

Pardi, G. "Disegno dalla storia demografica di Livorno." *ASI* 76 (1918): 1–96.

Parenti, G. *Il Commercio estero del granducato di Toscana dal 1815 al 1859*. Turin, n.d.

————. *Le Entrate del granducato di Toscana dal 1825 al 1859*. Turin, n.d.

————. *Monete e cambi nel granducato di Toscana dal 1825 al 1859*. Turin, n.d.

Pariset, F. G., ed. *Bordeaux au XIXe siècle*. Bordeaux, 1968.

Passerin, Ettore. "L'anticapitalismo del Sismondi e i 'campagnoli' toscani del Risorgimento." *Belfagor* 4 (1949): 283–299.

————. "G. P. Vieusseux, lo spirito ginevrino e i liberali moderati Toscani." *Nuova Rivista storica* 30 (1954): 389–401.

————. "Pietro Bastogi e la fondazione della Società Italiana per le Strade Ferrate Meridionale." *BSL* 1 (1951): 6–17.

Pazzagli, Carlo. *L'Agricoltura toscana nella prima metà dell'800. Tecniche di produzione e rapporti mezzadrili*. Florence, 1973.

Pelissier, Leon B. "Livorno nel 1846." *RSR* 3 (1909): 193–213.

Pera, Francesco. *Appendice ai riccordi e alle biografie livornesi.* Livorno, 1877.

———. *Nuove Biografie livornesi.* Livorno, 1895.

———. *Nuove Curiosità inedite o rare.* Florence, 1899.

———. *Quarta Serie di nuove biografie livornesi.* Siena, 1906.

———. *Ricordi e biografie livornesi.* Livorno, 1867.

Pergola, Temistocle. *Sulla franchigia commerciale di Livorno.* Livorno, 1862.

———. *Memoria ai miei amici.* Livorno, 1861.

Petiti, Carlo Ilarione. *Delle più probabili future condizioni del commercio ligure, tre lettere a Michele Erede.* Genoa, 1847.

———. *Delle strade ferrate italiane e del migliore ordinamento di esse. Cinque Discorsi.* Capolago, 1845.

Pietro [Di], Ettore. *La Funzione economica del porto di Livorno e la sua importanza alla fine del '600.* Livorno, 1931.

Pigli, Carlo. *Cenni sul mio governo di Livorno.* Arezzo, 1852.

Piombanti, Giuseppe. *Compendio storico popolare della città di Livorno con un'appendice sugli uomini illustri livornesi.* Livorno, 1881.

———. *Guida della città e dei dintorni di Livorno.* 2d ed. Livorno, 1903.

Pischedda, Carlo. "Appunti ricasoliani (1853–1859)." *RSI* 68 (1956): 37–79.

Prato, Giuseppe. *Fatti e dottrine economiche alla vigilia del 1848. L'Associazione Agraria Subalpina e Camillo Cavour.* Turin, 1907.

Popolazione delle provincie toscane del 1860 confrontata con quella del 1859 e movimento della medesima dal 1818 al 1860. Florence, 1860.

Prunas, Paolo. *L'Antologia di Gian Pietro Vieusseux: Storia di una rivista italiana.* Rome, 1906.

Pullan, Brian, ed. *Crisis and Change in the Venetian Economy.* London, 1968.

Quazza, Guido. *La Lotta sociale nel Risorgimento. Classi e governi dalla Restaurazione all'unità (1815–1861).* Turin, 1951.

Ragionieri, Ernesto. *Politica e amministrazione nella storia dell'Italia unita.* Bari, 1967.

Ragionieri, Ernesto. "Politica e amministrazione nello stato unitario." *Studi storici* 1 (1960): 472–512.

Redford, Arthur. *Manchester Merchants and Foreign Trade 1794–1858.* London, 1934.

Repetti, Emanuele. *Dizionario geografico fisico storico della Toscana, contenente la descrizione di tutti i luoghi del Granducato, Ducato di Lucca, Gartagnana e Lunigiana.* 6 vols. Florence, 1833–1846.

Ricasoli, Bettino. "L'Assedio di Livorno nel 1849. Diario a cura di Sergio Camerani e Mario Nobili." *Nuova Antologia* 946 (1949): 113–127.

Ricci, Giorgio. *I Porti e la loro funzione nella economia nazionale.* Livorno, 1926.

Ricci, Giuliano. "Sui caratteri generali dell'industria in Toscana." *GAT* 12 (1838): 283–297.

———. *Cenni sopra le basi del sistema municipale toscano per occasione della legge del 30 maggio 1847.* Livorno, 1847.

———. "Delle condizioni generali dell'agricoltura toscana." *GAT* 12 (1838): 365–381.

———. "Livorno: origine e ingrandimento; suo porto-franco; nuove mure; commercio; industria." *GAT* 11 (1837): 101–116.

———. *Saggio del municipio considerato come unitá elementare della città e della nazione italiana.* Livorno, 1847.

———. *Toscana costituzionale 1848. Riflessioni dell'avvocato G. R. da Livorno.* Livorno, 1848.

Ricci [De], Lapo. "Delle cause dell'incremento della manifattura della paglia in Toscana." *Antologia* 20 (1825): 27–35.

———. "Progetto di società enologica in Livorno." *GAT* 11 (1837): 140–145.

Ridella, Franco. *La Vita e i tempi di Cesare Cabella.* Genoa, 1923.

Ridolfi, Cosimo. "Dell'influenza dello spirito d'associazione negli stabilimenti di pubblica beneficenza." *AGA* 3 (1828): 378–389.

Ridolfi, Luigi. *Cosimo Ridolfi e gli istituti del suo tempo.* Florence, 1901.

Riflessioni sull'opuscolo che ha per titolo "Sull'Abolizione delle franchigie della città di Livorno. Poche parole di un Livornese." 2d ed. Livorno, 1867–1868.

Robertson, Priscilla. *Revolutions of 1848: A Social History.* New York, 1952.

Romano, Ruggiero. *La Storiografia italiana oggi.* N.p., 1978.

Ronchi, Carla. *I Democratici fiorentini nella rivoluzione del '48–'49.* Florence, n.d.

———. "Liberismo e protezionismo in Toscana prima del 1848." *Studi storici* 1 (1960): 244–284.

Roth, Cecil. *The History of the Jews of Italy.* Philadelphia, 1946.

Ruggiero [De] Guido. *The History of European Liberalism.* Translated by R. G. Collingwood. London, 1927.

Salomone, A. William, ed. *Italy from the Risorgimento to Fascism: An Inquiry into the Origins of the Totalitarian State.* Garden City, N.Y., 1970.

———. "The Risorgimento between Ideology and History: The Political Myth of the rivoluzione mancata." *American Historical Review* 68 (1962): 38–56.

Salvestrini, Arnoldo. *I Moderati toscani e la classe dirigente italiana.* Florence, 1965.

Sassoon, Anne Showstack, ed. *Approaches to Gramsci.* London, 1982.

Savelli, Agostino. *Leonardo Romanelli e la Toscana del suo tempo.* Florence, 1941.

Scaramella, Gino. *Spirito pubblico, società segrete, e polizia in Livorno dal 1815 al 1821.* Rome, 1901.

Seed, John. "Unitarianism, political economy and the antinomies of liberal culture in Manchester, 1830–50." *Social History* 7 (1982): 1–25.

Segre, Arturo. *Dalla rivoluzione francese ai giorni nostri, 1789–1913. Manuale di storia di commercio,* vol. 2. Turin, 1915.

Sereni, Emilio. *Capitalismo e mercato nazionale in Italia.* Rome, 1966.

———. "Mercato nazionale e accumulazione capitalistica nell'unità italiana." *Studi storici* 1 (1959–60): 513–563.

Serristori, Luigi. *Livorno ed i suoi traffici.* Florence, 1839.

———. *Memoria sull'istruzione primaria.* Pistoia, 1818.

———. *Saggio statistico della Italia.* Vienna, 1833.

———. *Statistica dell'Italia.* 2d ed. Florence, 1842.

Sheehan, James J. *German Liberalism in the Nineteenth Century.* Chicago, 1978.

Siegelbaum, Lewis. "The Odessa Grain Trade: A Case Study in Urban Growth and Development in Tsarist Russia." *Journal of European Economic History* 9 (1980): 113–151.

Silva, Pietro. *Il Mediterraneo dall'unità di Roma all'unità d'Italia.* Milan, 1927.

Sonnino, Guido. *Saggio sulle industrie, marina, e commercio in Livorno sotto i primi due Lorenesi (1737–1790).* Cortona, 1909.

———. *Storia della tipografia ebraica in Livorno.* Turin, 1912.

Spellanzon, Cesare. *Storia del Risorgimento e dell'unità d'Italia.* Vol. 3. Milan, 1936.

Stearns, Peter N. *1848: The Revolutionary Tide in Europe.* New York, 1974.

Stuart, James Montgomery. *The History of Free Trade in Tuscany with Remarks on its Progress in the Rest of Italy.* London, 1876.

Tarlé, Eugeni. *La vita economica nell'età napoleonica.* Turin, 1950.

Tesi, Carlo. *Livorno dalla sua origine sino ai nostri tempi.* 2 vols. Livorno, 1865–1868.

Torelli, Luigi. *Dell'avvenire del commercio europeo e in modo speciale di quello degli stati italiani; Ricerche.* 3 vols. Florence, 1859.

Treitschke [von], Enrico. *Cavour*. Trans. by Giovanni Cecchini. Florence, 1925.

Treves, Renato. *La Dottrina sansimonisma nel pensiero italiano del Risorgimento*. Turin, 1931.

Tudesq, Andre-Jean. *Les Grandes Notables en France (1840–1849): Étude historique d'une psychologie sociale*. 2 vols. Paris, 1964.

Turi, G. "Viva Maria," La Reazione alle riforme leopoldine (1790–1799). Florence, 1969.

Uzielli, Gustavo. *Genova e Livorno: Porti europei*. Florence, 1906.

Vanni, G. C. "Cenni sui commercio della seta in Toscana e sui mezzi di aumentarlo." *AGA* 9 (1831): 7–21.

———. "Dei progressi dell'industria in Toscana e di quello che essa può fare per mezzo dello spirito di associazione." *AGA* 13 (1835): 232–242.

Vigo, Pietro. *Le Demolizioni e miglioramenti del quartiere di Venezia Nuova*. Livorno, 1906.

———. *Episodii della dominazione austriaca in Livorno (1849–1853)*. Città di Castello, 1914.

Vivoli, Giuseppe. *Annali di Livorno della sua origine sino all'anno di Gesù Cristo 1840*. Livorno, 1842–1846.

———. *Guida di Livorno antico e moderno*. Florence, 1956.

———. *Progetto per ampliare il porto di Livorno grandemente, in tre anni e con lieve spesa*. Livorno, 1849.

Venturi, Franco. *Settecento riformatore*. Turin, 1969.

Wallerstein, Immanuel. *The Modern World-System. Capitalist Agriculture and the Origins of the European World-Economy in the Sixteenth Century*. New York, 1974.

———. *The Modern World-System II: Mercantilism and the Consolidation of the European World-Economy 1600–1750*. New York, 1980.

Wandruska, Adam. *Pietro Leopoldo: Un Grande Riformatore*. Florence, 1968.

Wilson, R. G. *Gentlemen Merchants. The Merchant Community in Leeds, 1700–1830*. Manchester, 1971.

Williams, Gwyn A. "The Concept of 'Egemonia' in the Thought of Antonio Gramsci: Some Notes on Interpretation." *Journal of the History of Ideas* 21 (1960): 586–599.

Williams, Raymond. *Marxism and Literature*. Oxford, 1977.

Woolf, Stuart. *A History of Italy 1700–1860: The Social Constraints of Political Change*. London, 1979.

Zang, Gert, ed. *Provinzialisierung einer Region. Regionale Unterentwicklung und liberale Politik in der Stadt und im Kreis Konstanz im 19. Jahrhundert. Untersuchungen zur Entstehung der Burgerlichen Gesellschaft in der Provinz.* Frankfurt am Main, 1978.

Zobi, Antonio. "Considerazioni sullo stato della piazza e del porto di Livorno, dedotte dal discorso del senator Gianni e dalla Memoria del cav. Bonaini sullo stesso argomento." *AGA* (1857): 73–96.

————. *Manuale storico delle massime e degli ordinamenti economici vigenti in Toscana.* Florence, 1847.

————. *Storia civile della Toscana dal 1737 al 1848.* 5 vols. Florence, 1850–1852.

Zuccagni-Orlandini, Attilio. *Ricerche statistiche sul granducato di Toscana.* Vol. 1. Florence, 1848.

Index

ment with, 150. *See also* Britain; Manufactured goods

Facchini di banco. See Dockworker companies, local

Facchini di manovella. See Dockworker companies, local

Facchini saccajoli (Sacco). See Dockworker companies, local

Famine, commercial impact of, 33–35, 42–43, 56–57, 72, 107, 157–158, 222–224, 253, 298 n. 55, 311–312 n. 25

Fascism, Italian, 10–11, 266–267

Ferdinand I de'Medici (grand duke of Tuscany), 20

Ferdinand II de'Medici (grand duke of Tuscany), 21

Fernandez, Dionisio, 152

Ferrigni, Giuseppe, 259–260

Fiscal exactions, impact of on Livorno in 1848–1849, 237–239, 348–349 n. 1

Florence, hostility of Livornese toward, 348–349 n. 1

Fortezza Nuova, 258

France, Livornese shipping agreement with, 150

Franklin, Benjamin, 88–90, 287

Fratelli Italiani, 283

Free port (Livorno), 1, 7, 14–15, 19–22, 68, 253–254, 269–270

Free ports, 19

Free trade and competition, importance of in Livornese reforms, 2, 46, 68, 103–104, 134, 164, 194, 202–208, 253, 265, 352 n. 32

French Revolution, 3, 8

Frullani, Leonardo, 108–110

Galeotti, Leopoldo, 252

Garibaldi, Giuseppe, 284–285

Gavazzi, Alessandro, 228–230

Grabau, Carlo, 183

Genoa: comparison of with Livorno, 5, 7, 149, 239–240, 254, 261, 268; competition of with Livorno, 1, 54, 113, 116, 255, 295 n. 19

Georgofili, Academy of the, 46–47

Ginsborg, Paul, 6–7

Gioberti, Vincenzo, 215, 279–280

Giolitti, Giovanni, 267

Grain: Egyptian, 44–45; prices of, 55–61; Russian, 42, 44–45, 56; speculation in, 45, 47; storage of, 20, 22, 31, 296 nn. 32–33; trade in, 30–33, 35, 39–47, 71–72, 271, 297 n. 37

Gramsci, Antonio, 7–14, 292 n. 32; concepts of civil society, 8, 13; domination, 8, 12–13; hegemony, 7–9, 11, 13; leadership, 12–13; passive revolution, 7–9, 11; Piedmontization, 12–13; relevance of theory for Livorno, 266, 270–272, 291 n. 25; "war of manoeuvre," 8; war of position, 8

Greenfield, Kent Roberts, 4–6

Guarducci, Giovanni, 242

Guerrazzi, Francesco Domenico: biography of, 280–281; critic of Livornese economic and social practices, 92, 166, 208, 274, 280, 287; in 1848–49, 217–219, 226–228, 231–232, 234, 236, 238, 240–241, 275, 284, 286

Hemp, 326 n. 103

Hinterland, Livorno's relationship to, 15, 21–22, 71, 80–81, 258–259, 295 n. 21, 305 n. 57, 347 n. 106

Historiography, 2–15, 265–272, 351–352 n. 31. *See also* Liberalism; Marxism

Holland, Livorno's commerce with, 23

Hughes, H. Stewart, 272

Designer: U.C. Press Staff
Compositor: Prestige Typography
Text: 10/12 Palatino
Display: Palatino
Printer: Thomson-Shore, Inc.
Binder: John H. Dekker & Sons